KV-372-737

CASS SERIES ON SOVIET MILITARY EXPERIENCE

THE INITIAL PERIOD OF WAR
ON THE EASTERN FRONT

THE INITIAL
PERIOD OF WAR
ON THE
EASTERN FRONT

22 June – August 1941

Proceedings of the Fourth
Art of War Symposium
Garmisch, October 1987

EDITED BY
Colonel David M. Glantz

CASS SERIES ON SOVIET MILITARY EXPERIENCE, VOL. 2.

FRANK CASS
LONDON • PORTLAND, OR.

First Published in 1993 in Great Britain by
FRANK CASS & CO. LTD
Newbury House, 900 Eastern Avenue
London, IG2 7HH

and in the United States of America by
FRANK CASS
c/o ISBS, 5804 N.E. Hassalo Street
Portland, Oregon, 97213-3644

Reprinted 1997

Copyright © 1993 Frank Cass & Co. Ltd.

British Library Cataloguing in Publication Data

Initial Period of War on the Eastern
Front, 22 June–August 1941 : Proceedings of
the Fourth Art of War Symposium, Garmisch,
FRG, October 1987. — (Cass Series on Soviet Military Experience)
I. Glantz, David M. II. Series
940.54
ISBN 0 7146 3375 5 (cloth)
ISBN 0 7146 4298 3 (paper)

Library of Congress Cataloging-in-Publication Data

Art of War Symposium (4th: 1987 : Garmisch-Partenkirchen, Germany)
    The initial period of war on the Eastern Front, 22 June–August
1941 : proceedings of the Fourth Art of War Symposium, Garmisch,
FRG, October 1987 / edited by David M. Glantz.
        p.   cm.—(Cass series on Soviet military experience; 2)
    The symposium was organized by the Soviet Army Studies Office, US
Army Combined Arms Center, Fort Leavenworth, Kan., and hosted by the
US Army Institute for Soviet and Eastern European Studies in
Garmisch.
    Includes index.
    1. World War, 1939–1945—Campaigns—Eastern—Congresses.
I. Glantz, David M.   II. Title.   III. Series.
D764.A78   1987
940.54'21—dc20   92-28672

*All rights reserved. No part of this publication may be reproduced in
any form or by any means, electronic, mechanical, photocopying,
recording or otherwise, without the prior permission of Frank Cass
and Company Limited.*

Typeset by Regent Typesetting, London
Printed in Great Britain by Bookcraft (Bath) Ltd
Midsomer Norton, Avon

Contents

List of Figures

vii

Preface

This volume contains the edited version of the transcript of proceedings of the 1987 Art of War Symposium, which was held in the fall of 1987 at Garmisch, in what was then the Federal Republic of Germany. This symposium was the fourth and last in a series of symposia which had been held at the US Army War College beginning in 1984. The four symposia focused new attention on the Soviet conduct of offensive operations on the Eastern Front during the Second World War by exploiting existing and new Soviet and German archival materials and the personal reminiscences of participants in the operations.

The first three symposia, sponsored by the Center for Land Warfare of the US Army War College, were held at Carlisle Barracks, Pennsylvania, in 1984, 1985 and 1986. These symposia investigated in detail the nature of twelve Soviet offensive operations conducted between December 1942 and March 1945. Partially edited transcripts of proceedings from these symposia were published in limited quantities by the US Army War College. Depending upon the appeal of this volume, in the future those volumes may also be issued in more refined book form.

The 1987 symposium was organized by the Soviet Army Studies Office, US Army Combined Arms Center, Fort Leavenworth, Kansas, and hosted by the US Army Institute for Soviet and Eastern European Studies in Garmisch. Under the overall rubric of studying military operations during the initial period of war, it focused on the Soviet response to German operations in the initial phases of Operation Barbarossa. More specifically, it examined in detail the nature of the border battles (22–30 June 1941) across the entire span of the front and the events associated with the battle for Smolensk in July and early August 1941.

The transcript volume is organized in the same fashion as the symposium, and virtually all materials presented in the four days of symposium sessions are included in the edited volume. All symposium participants reviewed their presentations for accuracy and amended their comments, where required, to ensure they were as complete as possible. Whenever possible and appropriate, the editor has corrected the Soviet portion of the volume (in particular the numbers and the maps) to ensure that they correspond with recently released, formerly classified Soviet materials on the respective operations.

The 1987 symposium and this companion volume endeavored to present a balanced view of each operation covered by presenting both a

German and a Soviet perspective. Coverage of each operation began with an overview prepared from both German and Soviet sources, which focused on operational details from a Soviet perspective. This overview was prepared from extensive use of Soviet open and formerly classified archival sources and verified by close examination of German archival materials. Subsequently, German participants in each operation offered their detailed personal perspectives. Most of these German participants consulted their unit's war diary [*Tagebuch*] or unit history when preparing their presentations. All of the German participants prepared a short oral presentation for use in the symposium session and a longer, more complete, written version for inclusion in this volume. The day-by-day maps for each studied operation have also been corrected to match new Soviet archival materials.

Since this volume contains no formal notes or bibliography regarding the source materials used in its preparation, a few words are needed about source materials and the location of additional information about the operations. The German participants' portions of the volume are derived from the individuals' personal recollections refreshed by frequent reference and study of the participants' unit diary (located in the German military archives in Freiberg) and to his unit's official or commercially published history, whenever one existed. Some of the Germans consulted their unpublished personal diaries and wartime notes. In a sense, the accounts of the participants themselves could be considered as primary sources.

The map sets for each operation and the overviews prepared by the editor were constructed from a variety of primary and secondary sources. The editor studied each operation by researching how each operation developed "on the map", that is, by the use of annotations on daily large-scale maps of the operational region. Each daily map (of 1:400,00 scale – the same scale as used by German planners) provided the vehicle for plotting the order of battle, unit locations and daily actions of each side as determined from German archival materials and Soviet sources. Use of the German materials permitted verification of Soviet sources.

German source materials included the operational records of German Army Groups North, Center, and South and all German armies and corps which participated in the operations. These were obtained from the appropriate microfilm rolls in the National Archives Records series NAM T-311, T-312, T-313 and T-314. In addition, German intelligence appreciations were gleaned from the same series pertaining to the operations of *Fremde Heere Ost*, the appropriate rolls of series NAM T-78.

Soviet sources used were too extensive to recount in detail. They included the extensive memoir literature published since the early 1960s, including accounts of the action by Generals Bagramian, Moskalenko,

Boldin, Sandalov, Kuznetsov, Zhukov, Vasilevsky, and a host of lesser figures. Also used were the appropriate military district histories (Baltic, Belorussian, and Kiev), army, corps, division, and brigade histories (e.g. 13th Army, 4th Airborne Corps, 100th Rifle Division, and 214th Airborne Brigade), and a multitude of articles, principally from the Soviet *Military-historical Journal* [*Voenno-istoricheskii zhurnal*].

Since the conclusion of the symposium, the Soviet government has released formerly classified archival materials relating to operations during the period. For the purposes of this volume, the most significant of these materials are four volumes of the series *Collection of Combat Documents of the Great Patriotic War* [*Sbornik boevykh dokumentov Velikoi Otechestvennoi voiny*].

These volumes, classified secret and top secret, were compiled and published by the Historical Directorate of the General Staff between 1959 and 1964. They contain the records (orders, operational and intelligence reports, and after-action reports) of the Northwestern, Western and Southwestern Fronts and subordinate corps, and sometimes even divisions, for the period studied. As far as possible, this material has been incorporated into the overviews presented in this volume.

Finally, the editor must give special thanks to those who participated in the preparation of this volume. Colonel Paul Adair (British Army retired) and Dr Dieter Ose played a critical role in identifying and arranging for the orderly participation of German veterans in the symposium. Of particular significance was the work of Mrs Alice Mink, who devoted herculean efforts to the typing, formating, and correction of the volume. As editor, I am, of course, responsible for all errors of omission and commission associated with this work.

David M. Glantz

1

Introduction: Prelude to Barbarossa

The Red Army in 1941

DAVID M. GLANTZ

Over the course of three symposia, we have investigated how the Red Army eventually solved its basic offensive problems during the Russo-German war, problems which became readily apparent during the first two years. Central among those many problems was that of developing a capability for achieving operational success in offensive operations. That meant, in essence, Soviet creation of a mobile armored and mechanized force, new combat techniques to govern the operations of that force, and command and control systems which would enable that force to develop tactical success into operational and, hence, strategic success. This process progressed from its first tentative steps in late 1942 into a major Soviet capability in 1945. Now we shall look at the problems the Soviets encountered when they attempted to develop the capability for conducting deep operational maneuver, problems which, as we shall see, were woefully apparent to all parties in 1941.

We shall investigate in detail the problems of the Red Army in the initial period of the Russo-German War or, as the Soviets refer to it, the Great Patriotic War. We shall do so by surveying the expectations of the Soviets on the eve of war: in particular, how the Red Army was to function in theory. We shall examine its strategic plans, its operational and tactical techniques, and its organizational structure. We shall then view the Red Army as it attempted to practice war during the first critical months after the Germans launched Operation Barbarossa. What interests us most are the answers to three questions. First, what was the gap between theory, in terms of Soviet expectations, and practice, the reality of combat? Second, what did the Soviets do to close that gap? And third, what fundamental lessons have the Soviets derived from their close examination of the initial period of war, a topic which itself has become a major area of contemporary concern to the Soviets, both from the standpoint of German offensive operations and from the standpoint of Soviet defensive measures? Today, the Soviets articulate that issue by asking the question: in the initial period of war, what must a nation do to achieve quick victory or, conversely, avoid rapid defeat? The events of June and July 1941 remain a critical element of military experience which the Soviets continue to exploit when attempting to answer that momentous question.

The Red Army of the 1920s was essentially a foot-and-hoof army: an infantry and cavalry force with very limited capability for developing tactical success into operational or certainly strategic success. The Soviets identified this problem very early. In the 1920s, they pondered a whole series of problems and major questions, many of which the Western powers pondered too. The most important questions were: "How does one escape the crushing weight of firepower which produced the linear warfare experienced in the First World War? And how does one restore maneuver to the modern battlefield?" To answer these questions, the Soviets drew upon some Western experiences in the First World War, for example German operations in 1918, and they drew upon their own experiences in the Russian Civil War, a war of maneuver conducted across vast expanses. The Soviets, in essence, focused their attention on how to restore mobility and maneuver to warfare.

FIGURE 1
RED ARMY FORCE STRUCTURE IN THE 1920s

```
O   RIFLE ARMIES
        O RIFLE CORPS
            O RIFLE DIVISIONS (12,800)

O   CAVALRY CORPS
        O CAVALRY DIVISIONS (7,000)
```

The Soviet force structure in the 1920s was very large, but it lacked the ability to conduct deep sustained maneuver (see Figure 1). Large rifle armies were subdivided into rifle corps, which in turn were subdivided into rifle divisions. The traditional mobile arm consisted of cavalry corps, which were subdivided into cavalry divisions. The experiences of the First World War, and to some extent those of the Civil War, evidenced the inability of cavalry to function effectively given the crushing weight of firepower characterizing twentieth-century warfare.

2

FIGURE 2
FRONT OPERATIONAL FORMATION (OFFENSE), 1930

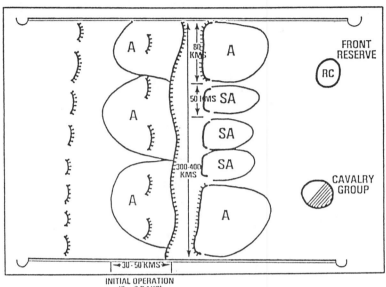

INITIAL OPERATION
(5 - 6 DAYS)

The Soviets employed this foot-and-hoof force structure in a rather conventional way. In 1930 Soviet forces at *front* (army group) level operated in the following general pattern (see Figure 2). Heavy shock armies were to conduct the penetration operation in order to smash through the enemy's tactical defenses, and thereafter, cavalry groups consisting of single cavalry corps or multiple cavalry corps were designated to exploit the tactical success of rifle forces into the operational depths. It was not an adequate system by any means. At the army level the same general pattern existed. Soviet Army commanders relied upon heavy infantry formations and lacked mobile units possessing resilience and hence, sustainability (see Figure 3). Rifle corps blasted through enemy tactical defenses and their success was exploited by rifle corps lined up behind, in virtual second echelon. At the division level, the same pattern held true. The Soviets relied on infantry shock groups, as the Soviets called them, to achieve the tactical penetration and covering groups to hold along secondary axes (see Figure 4).

In the late 1920s the Soviets began to perceive the solution to their problem. The solution seemed to rest in the creation of motor-mechanized armored forces. It is, however, one thing to theorize about

3

FIGURE 3
ARMY OPERATIONAL FORMATION (OFFENSE), 1930

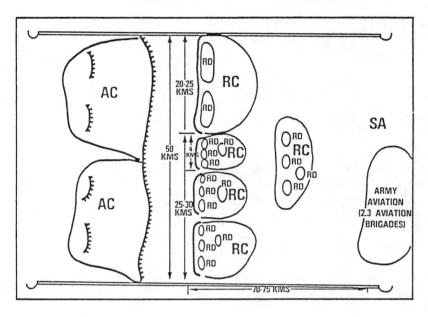

change and altogether another to actually effect change in practice. By 1929 the Soviets had incorporated into their Field Service Regulations the promise of conducting deep battle in the future, the Russian term *glubokii boi*. Deep battle meant battle conducted by mechanized and armored units designed both to support infantry and to penetrate tactical defenses, thus it was a tactical concept. Shortly after, the Soviets began creating mechanized and armored forces; first tank battalions, then mechanized and tank brigades, and finally even larger forces as the Soviet Union progressed in the 1930s. Figure 4 shows some of the earliest Soviet concepts for the use of those infantry support tanks. Various tank groupings were formed to support the initial assault and to assist advancing troops as they penetrated into the tactical depths. The 1929 Field Service Regulation (USTAV) gave direction to Soviet efforts and, of course, it was the Five Year Plans, beginning in the late 1920s, that provided the wherewithal, the weaponry necessary to implement this concept. It was a very short step indeed from producing tractors to producing tanks and the Soviets made that step quickly.

By the mid-1930s the Soviets had fully developed and implemented the concept of deep battle (*glubokii boi*). They had also constructed a force

4

FIGURE 4
RIFLE DIVISION COMBAT FORMATION (OFFENSE), 1930

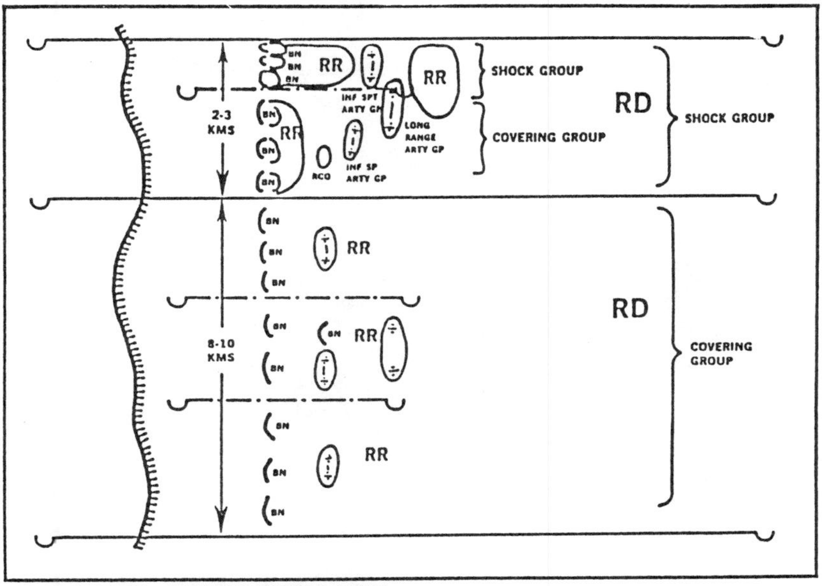

ARMOR SUPPORT — INFANTRY SUPPORT GROUP
LONG RANGE SUPPORT GROUP
LONG RANGE ACTION GROUP

structure that could actually translate those theories into practice. Figure 5 shows the force structure that had emerged by 1936. The structure included the traditional rifle and shock armies, which were in turn subdivided into rifle corps and divisions. The significant point here was the fact that armor forces were included in each level of command. Within

FIGURE 5
RED ARMY FORCE STRUCTURE IN THE 1930s

```
O  RIFLE & SHOCK ARMIES
    O RIFLE CORPS
        O RIFLE DIVISIONS (13,000-57)

O  MECHANIZED (TANK) CORPS (12,700-560)

O  CAVALRY CORPS
    O CAVALRY DIVISIONS (6,000)

O  AIRBORNE BRIGADES (3,000)
```

5

SOVIET TANKS 1941

Танк T-26

T-26

BT-5

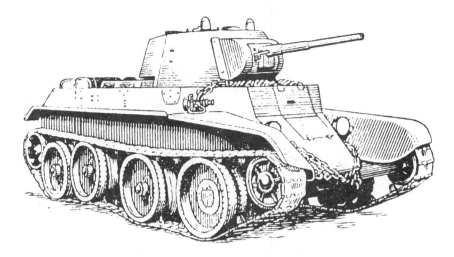

BT-7

T-28

T-35

T-34

KV-1

SOVIET TANK CHARACTERISTICS

MODEL	WEIGHT (TONS)	CREW	GUNS	ARMOR	SPEED
T-26	10.3	3	1-45mm	16mm	30 km/hr
BT-7	13.8	3	1-45mm	20mm	53.4 kms/hr (tracks) 73 kms/hr (wheels)
BT-7M	14.65	3	1-45mm	20mm	62 kms/hr (tracks) 86 kms/hr (wheels)
T-28	28	6	1-76mm	30mm	37 kms/hr
T-35	50	10	1-76mm 2-45mm	30mm	30 kms/hr
T-34	30.9	4	1-76mm	45-52mm	55 kms/hr
KV-1	47.5	5	1-76mm	75-100mm	35 kms/hr

FIGURE 6
TANK FORCES, 1938

1938 Tank Corps

```
2 tank brigades (BT)
  4 tank battalions
  1 reconnaissance battalion
  1 motorized rifle battalion
1 rifle/machine gun brigade
1 reconnaissance battalion
1 signal battalion

strength:  12,710 men
              560 tanks
              118 guns
```

- -

1938 Light Tank Brigade
```
4 tank battalions
  (54-BT, T-26;
   6-76mm arty tanks)
1 motorized rifle battalion
1 reconnaissance battalion

strength:  216 tanks
```

- - - - - - - - - - - - - - - - - - - -

1938 Heavy Tank Brigade
```
4 tank battalions
  (31-T-28, T-35;
   6-76mm arty tanks)
1 motorized rifle battalion
1 reconnaissance battalion

strength:  124 tanks
```

the lower-level rifle forces this armor was designed essentially to provide infantry support. The numbers shown are personnel and armor strengths according to the TOE or establishment of each force. Incidentally, shock armies were nothing more than heavy rifle armies designated with the task of conducting the main attack.

The most important development, however, occurred in the realm of mechanized forces. In 1930 the Soviets created an experimental mechanized (tank) brigade and by 1932 had four of these brigades. By 1936 they had increased the size of these forces to corps and by then they possessed four mechanized corps and a host of mechanized brigades, tank regiments and tank battalions. In other words, they had created armored and mechanized forces that would function at every level of command, to provide both infantry support and a maneuver capability to the Red Army. The mechanized corps of 1936, which we will look at more closely in a moment, had 560 tanks and a personnel strength of roughly a division

10

FIGURE 7
FRONT OPERATIONAL FORMATION, 1936–41

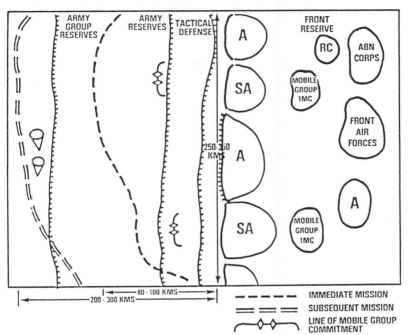

equivalent. The Soviets still maintained cavalry corps and cavalry divisions, but added to them heavy armor contingents to fight side by side with the horse units. There was a vertical dimension to these maneuver forces as well. The Soviets created airborne brigades in the 1930s and slowly expanded the number and the size of these forces by 1941. The concept from the very start was to foster close cooperation between the ground mobile arm and the vertical dimension, the airborne arm. The new Soviet tank corps (the mechanized corps of 1936 was renamed tank in 1938) consisted of two tank brigades, a rifle machine-gun brigade, and various support units totalling roughly a division's personnel strength and 560 medium and light tanks (see Figure 6). In addition, the Soviets had light tank brigades and heavy tank brigades, which were principally used for support of rifle units.

The 1936 Field Service Regulation set out how this new mechanized force was supposed to operate. This is the scheme the Soviets projected at *front* level (see Figure 7). Shock armies, which were heavy combined arms armies, were designated to conduct the penetration operation to achieve the tactical breakthrough. Thereafter a mobile group (*podvizhnaya gruppa*)

11

would exploit through the enemy tactical defenses into the operational depths. Figure 7 shows the lines denoting depth of mission (intermediate mission and subsequent mission). It also shows the airborne corps, in existence by 1941, created to cooperate with ground mobile groups in the depths of the enemy's defenses. Normally a *front* would contain one or two mechanized corps to function as its mobile group.

At the army level there were also mechanized forces integrated throughout by virtue of the 1936 Regulation. This is a shock army configurated to conduct offensive operations (see Figure 8). Tank brigades provided infantry support and a mobile group in the form of a mechanized corps conducted the exploitation operation. Again, an airborne force operated at shallower depths to cooperate with the mobile group. The basic concept shown by this simple diagram, in theory and in practice, would not change for 50 years. The only problem for the Soviets involved converting complex theory into effective practice.

Now just a word about Soviet defensive concepts, since the Soviets were most concerned about defense just before, and especially after, June 1941. According to the 1936 Regulation a Soviet army was supposed to defend in a single echelon of rifle corps, while the corps themselves organized in

FIGURE 8
SHOCK ARMY OPERATIONAL FORMATION, 1936–41

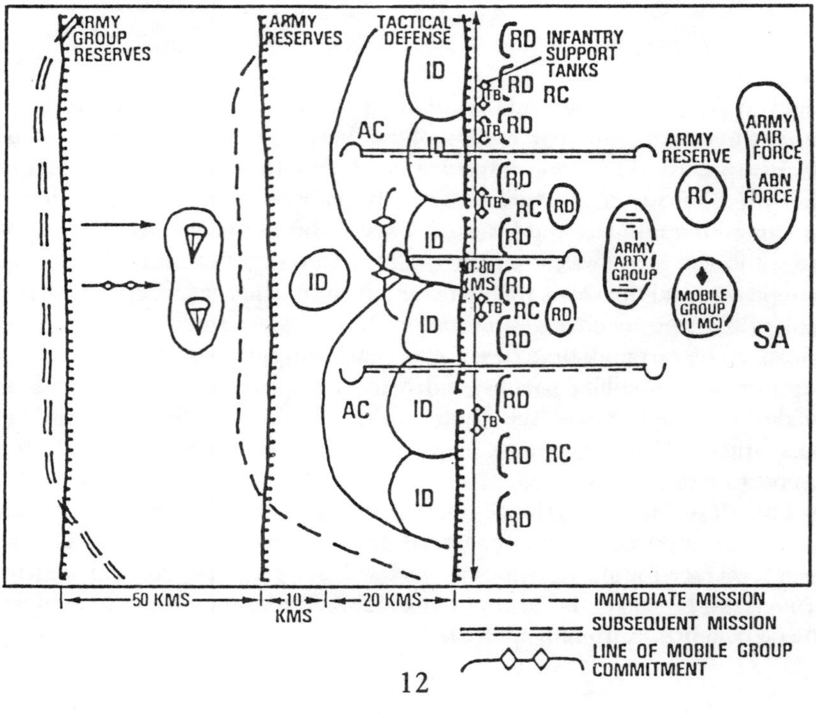

FIGURE 9
ARMY OPERATIONAL FORMATION (DEFENSE), 1936–41

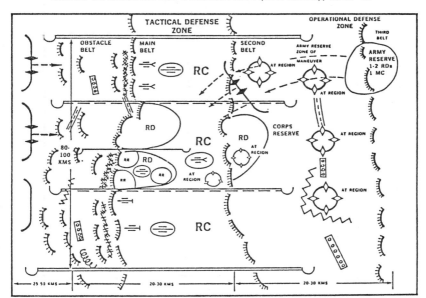

multiple echelons (See Figure 9). By this time the Soviets had developed the concept of the antitank region as the principal barrier to enemy armored attack. Antitank regions were supposed to be laced throughout the depths of the rifle corps' defense. The Soviets also planned to use their mechanized corps on the defensive, as a counterattack force to strike against enemy penetrations into the army defensive sector. At corps level the same general pattern pertained, with Soviet use of deeply echeloned defenses and increasingly strong antitank defenses. At least in theory, antitank defense involved the integration of antitank guns down to regimental level and the integration of tanks and antitank regions into the tactical defense of a corps (see Figure 10).

The Soviets experienced a considerable number of problems in the late 1930s. The purges that literally lopped the head off the Red Army by liquidating half of the officer corps certainly had an adverse impact on Soviet combat performance after 1937 and 1938. But Soviet problems went well beyond the purges. There were some very real experiences that caused the Soviets to question the utility of having a large mechanized force. In Spain for example, the Soviets sent a large armored contingent to support the Loyalist side in the Spanish Civil War. A considerable number of prominent Soviet military figures participated in that experiment. The

13

FIGURE 10
CORPS COMBAT FORMATION (DEFENSE), 1936–41

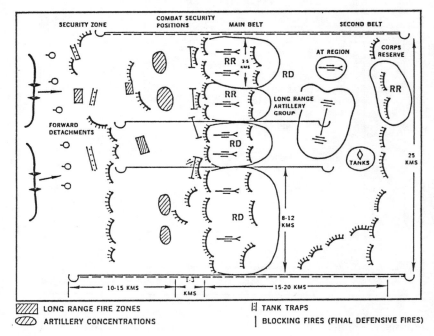

| | LONG RANGE FIRE ZONES | | TANK TRAPS |
| | ARTILLERY CONCENTRATIONS | | BLOCKING FIRES (FINAL DEFENSIVE FIRES) |

Soviets generally concluded, as a result of combat in Spain, that armored forces were indeed fragile on the battlefield unless they were fully integrated into a well articulated combined arms force. Tanks proved very vulnerable to artillery fire, and when their supporting infantry was stripped away they were very vulnerable to destruction by enemy infantry as well. When they returned from Spain, many Soviet military leaders recommended the creation of smaller armored units of more balanced combined armed nature.

The Soviets also had rather poor experience using armor in the Finnish War of 1939–40. The one mechanized corps they used accomplished virtually nothing and ended up providing just infantry support. Also in 1939, when Soviet forces rolled into eastern Poland two tank corps took part in the operation. Marshal Eremenko, who was associated with one of those tank corps, commented that the Soviet cavalry corps performed far better than the tank corps, since the tank corps moved at a snail's pace and were constantly hindered by mechanical and logistical problems.

In fact, the entire Red Army's logistical state in 1939, in terms of

14

FIGURE 11
MECHANIZED AND TANK FORCES, 1939–1940

1940 Motorized Division

   2 motorized rifle regiments
   1 tank regiment
   1 artillery regiment
   1 antiaircraft battalion
   1 antitank battalion
   1 reconnaissance battalion
   1 signal battalion
   1 light engineer battalion
     supply units

strength: 11,650 men
            275 tanks
             98 guns/mortars
             49 armored cars

1939 Motorized Rifle Division

   3 motorized rifle regiments
   1 tank battalion
   1 artillery regiment
   1 antiaircraft battalion
   1 antitank battalion
   1 reconnaissance battalion
     support units

strength: 10,000 men
             37 tanks
          209 guns/mortars
           58 armored cars

FIGURE 12
TANK BRIGADES, 1940

1940 Light Tank Brigade

   4 tank battalions
   1 motorized rifle battalion
   1 reconnaissance battalion

   strength: 258 tanks (BT, T-26)

1940 Heavy Tank Brigade

   4 tank battalions
   1 motorized rifle battalion
   1 reconnaissance battalion

   strength: 156 tanks
              (T-28, T-35)

communications equipment, weaponry, maintenance, and fuel and ammunition supply was poor. Support was insufficient to sustain those large mobile groups as well as the Red Army in combat. Consequently, in late 1939 the Soviets abolished their tank corps, and in their place created a number of smaller entities, one of which was the 1939 motorized rifle division (see Figure 11). This was supposed to be a more balanced

15

combined arms force, and it had a small tank complement of 37 tanks. Shortly after, the Soviets created a second type of mobile division, the motorized division, which consisted of two motorized rifle regiments and a tank regiment with a total strength of 275 tanks. These divisions were supposed to replace the larger and more cumbersome tank corps that had performed so badly in the preceding months. The Soviets maintained in their force structure a variety of tank brigades (see Figure 12). The 1940 light and heavy tank brigades were tailored to provide basic infantry support and were fairly heavy with 258 and 156 tanks respectively. Most of these tanks were older heavy, medium, and light varieties.

The subsequent events of 1939 and 1940 shattered Soviet confidence that they had made the right decision in abolishing their tank corps. They looked upon German operations in Poland with wonderment and awe. They later looked at German operations in France, and in several superb articles published in late 1940 and 1941, the general Soviet comment was, "My God, they picked up on our ideas and are effectively implementing them while we have gone in the opposite direction". These were excellent analytical articles. Consequently, the Soviets very hastily began an attempt to recreate a large armored force structure in late 1940 and in 1941.

Figure 13 shows the Soviet force structure which would emerge partially complete in June 1941. It was a large force structure formed around a nucleus of rifle armies of traditional shape and form, which were made up of rifle corps and divisions. These forces were supposed to have tank representation down to division level. These units will be examined

FIGURE 13
RED ARMY FORCE STRUCTURE, JUNE–DECEMBER 1941

```
JUNE 1941                                    DECEMBER 1941
o RIFLE ARMIES                               o RIFLE ARMIES
   o RIFLE CORPS                                 o RIFLE DIVISIONS (11,600)
      o RIFLE DIVISIONS (14,500-16)              o RIFLE BRIGADES (4,400)

o MECHANIZED CORPS (36,000-1,031)            o TANK BRIGADES (1,470-46)
   o TANK DIVISIONS (11,000-375)
      o MECHANIZED DIVISION (11,600-275)     o CAVALRY CORPS
                                                 o CAVALRY DIVISIONS (6,000)
o CAVALRY CORPS                                  o LIGHT CAVALRY DIVISIONS (3,400)
   o CAVALRY DIVISIONS (9,000-64)
                                             o AIRBORNE CORPS (12,000)
o AIRBORNE CORPS (10,400-50)                     o AIRBORNE BRIGADES (3,300)
   o AIRBORNE BRIGADES (3,000)
```

shortly in greater detail. At first, the structure included nine new mechanized corps, but ultimately 29 of these new corps were to be completely formed by the summer of 1942, all reequipped with new KV and T34 heavy and medium tanks. The new mechanized corps were each made up of two tank divisions and a mechanized division. The Soviets retained the cavalry corps and included in them a significant armor capability in the form of a mechanized regiment. They also expanded their airborne brigades into five airborne corps in 1941.

Figure 14 shows the rifle army structure in 1940 and 1941. In theory, the Soviet rifle army was supposed to consist of from four to six rifle corps with a total of 14–16 rifle divisions, and an attached mechanized corps, which, as the mobile group, was designated to conduct operational maneuver. The army had six to eight tank brigades to provide infantry support, two or three air divisions, and a variety of artillery regiments for an overall strength of 1400 tanks and 200,000–300,000 men. This was a shock army, the heavier type army. In reality, the average Soviet army in 1941 possessed a strength of from two to three rifle corps, six to 15 rifle divisions, and a mechanized corps for a total strength of fewer than 100,000 men. The rifle corps itself consisted of three rifle divisions and relatively weak support (see Figure 15). It had some artillery and anti-aircraft support, but very little organic logistical support.

FIGURE 14
ARMY STRUCTURE, 1940–1941

```
Theoretical

      Shock Army
         4-6 rifle corps
            14-18 rifle divisions
            1 mechanized corps (in 1941)
            6-8 tank brigades
            2-3 air divisions
            10-12 artillery regiments

         strength:  200,000-300,000 men
                    1400 tanks
                    2700 guns/mortars


 - - - - - - - - - - - - - - - - - - - - - - - - - - -


 Actual Army Composition 1941

            2-3 rifle corps
               6-15 rifle divisions
               1 mechanized corps (most incomplete)
               artillery regiments
               air divisions

            strength:  60,000-80,000 men
                       400-700 tanks
                       1200-1300 guns/mortars
```

17

FIGURE 15
RIFLE FORCES, 1939–41

1940-41 Rifle Corps

```
3 rifle divisions
2 artillery regiments
1 antiaircraft battalion
1 sapper battalion
1 signal battalion
```

strength: 50,000 men
           966 guns/mortars

- -

1939 Rifle Division

```
3 rifle regiments
  (4 x 76mm guns, 4 x 120mm mortars, 6 x 45mm AT)
2 artillery regiments
1 artillery battalion (16 x 76mm)
1 artillery battalion (8 x 122mm)
2 artillery battalions (12 x 122mm)
1 artillery battalion (12 x 152mm)
1 reconnaissance battalion
1 antitank battalion (12 x 45mm)
1 antiaircraft battalion (8 x 37mm, 4 x 76mm)
1 sapper battalion
1 signal battalion
1 tank battalion
```

strength: 14,483 men
           (18,000 wartime)
              144 guns
               66 mortars
               45 tanks
            1,762 machine guns
               13 armored cars

The rifle division of 1939 had three rifle regiments with its own integrated artillery, two artillery regiments, an antitank battalion, and a strength of just under 15,000 men, expandable to 18,000 in war time. In addition, the 1939 rifle division had an optional tank battalion of 45 tanks. The Soviets however, altered this TOE (establishment) in early 1941 to bring it into line with reality. The strength remained somewhat under 15,000, but, in fact, the firepower of the division was severely reduced (see Figure 16). Few divisional antitank battalions had what they were supposed to have in terms of weaponry. Moreover, when the Soviets created their new mechanized corps, they did so by abolishing their mechanized brigades and by stripping cavalry and rifle divisions of their armor. Thus,

18

FIGURE 16
RIFLE DIVISION, 1941

1941 Rifle Division

```
3 rifle regiments
  (6 x 76mm guns, 4 x 120mm mortars, 6 x 45mm AT)
2 artillery regiments
1 reconnaissance battalion
1 antitank battalion
1 antiaircraft battalion
1 sapper battalion
1 signal battalion
1 tank unit (optional)

strength:  14,483 men
              294 guns
              150 mortars
               16 light tanks
               13 armored cars
```

in the process of creating the mechanized corps, the Soviets stripped armor from just about every other unit in the Soviet force structure. That would have an adverse impact on the Soviets in June 1941.

Figure 17 shows the organization of the mechanized corps, as it originally appeared in 1940 and as it was amended in 1941. It was a true

FIGURE 17
MECHANIZED FORCES, 1940–41

1940 Mechanized Corps

```
2 tank divisions
1 motorized division (1940 TOE)
1 motorcycle regiment
1 signal battalion
1 motorized engineer battalion
1 aviation troop

strength:  37,200 men
            1,108 tanks
```

1941 Mechanized Corps

```
(organization same as 1940)




strength:  36,080 men
            1,031 tanks
            (420 T-34,
             126 KV)
```

19

FIGURE 18
TANK DIVISION, 1940–41

1940 Tank Division	1941 Tank Division
2 tank regiments	(same organization as 1940)
1 motorized rifle regiment	
1 artillery regiment	
1 antiaircraft battalion	
1 antitank battalion	
1 signal battalion	
1 reconnaissance battalion	
1 pontoon-bridge battalion	
strength: 11,343 men	strength: 10,940 men
413 tanks	375 tanks

corps, in terms of size. It was very large and, in fact, too large, initially with 37,000 men and over 1,000 tanks and, ultimately, with 36,000 men and 1,031 tanks, half of which were supposed to be new KVI and II heavy and T34 medium tanks. Each of the corps consisted of two tank divisions and a motorized division with moderate fire support, but with only limited functioning logistical support. The tank division consisted of two tank regiments, a motorized rifle regiment, and a variety of supporting units (see Figure 18). You can see from its strength of just under 11,000 men and 375 tanks that it was not far in size from a contemporary Soviet tank division. There was, however, a very weak logistical structure necessary to keep that division operational, and this fact would have a considerable impact on the fate of those corps and divisions in June 1941.

By mid-summer of 1941 the cavalry forces were about the only mobile units left intact to the Soviets. The cavalry corps and divisions possessed a considerable complement of light tanks and armored cars (see Figure 19). The corps was made up of two divisions, and the divisions consisted of four regiments, although you could find three-regiment divisions and a whole range of mountain cavalry outfits. Most of the armor officers of the Soviet Army came from the cavalry units of the 1930s. As a matter of fact, the mechanized corps were created in 1940 and 1941 primarily on the basis of existing cavalry units and older tank brigades. Hence, when you look at German intelligence reports of May 1941 you will find the Germans carrying the cavalry units and tank brigades in the Soviet order of battle when, in fact, by that time those units had been converted into tank or motorized divisions.

The airborne structure which existed in 1941 supposedly provided the vertical dimension of operational maneuver. An airborne corps consisted of three brigades and a light tank battalion, whose tanks could not be

FIGURE 19
CAVALRY FORCES, 1941

1941 Cavalry Corps

```
    2 cavalry divisions
    1 artillery regiment
    1 tank brigade (light)
    1 signal squadron

    strength:  19,000 men
                 128 light tanks
                  44 armored cars
                 264 guns/mortars
```
- -
1941 Cavalry Division

```
    4 cavalry regiments
    4 cavalry squadrons
    1 machine gun squadron
    1 mechanized regiment (BT-5)
    1 cavalry artillery battalion
    1 antiaircraft battalion

    strength:  9,240 men
                  34 light tanks
                  18 armored cars
                 132 guns/mortars
```

dropped by air, but rather were designed to be airlanded (see Figure 20). The airborne brigade itself consisted of four parachute battalions. As the war unfolded, the Soviets still intended to use these units in an air assault role and, in fact, they did so.

The artillery structure of the Red Army in 1941 was a far cry from the elaborate structure which would emerge by 1945. The basic types of units under *front* and High Command control are shown in Figure 21. They consisted of a variety of gun artillery and howitzer artillery regiments; heavy artillery battalions; heavy gun artillery regiments, and heavy howitzer artillery regiments. In quantity and strength, these forces were relatively weak compared with what would evolve in future years. There is one artillery unit to which I would like to call attention. Ten of these were formed in 1941 to operate with and to support the mechanized corps. This was the special antitank brigade, which consisted of two regiments, each of which possessed a mining capability and complement of trucks to provide mobility. These units proved at least moderately effective in June 1941. As a matter of fact, they provided the only true antitank capability available to the Soviets when the war broke out. Each brigade had 120 antitank guns

21

FIGURE 20
AIR ASSAULT FORCES, 1941

1941 Airborne Corps

    3 airborne brigades
    1 tank battalion (light)
    3 tank companies
    1 long range signal platoon
    1 control aircraft flight
    1 mobile equipment platoon

    strength: 10,419 men
              50 tanks (T37)

1941 Airborne Brigade

    4 parachute battalions
    (6 x 76mm guns,
    12 x 45mm guns,
    6 x 82mm mortars)
    1 bicycle recon company
    1 antiaircraft machine gun
      company

    strength: 3000 men

FIGURE 21
ARTILLERY UNITS, 1941

1941 Gun Artillery Regiment

    12 batteries (122mm, 152mm guns)

    strength: 48 guns

1941 Heavy Gun Artillery Regiment

    6 batteries (152mm guns)

    strength: 24 guns

1941 Howitzer Artillery Regiment

    12 batteries (152mm howitzer)

    strength: 48 guns

1941 Heavy Howitzer Artillery
                 Regiment

    6 batteries (203mm howitzer)

    strength: 24 guns

1941 Separate Heavy Artillery
        Battalion

    3 batteries (210mm guns,
      280mm mortars, 305mm
      howitzer)

    strength: 15 guns

1941 Special Antitank Brigade

    2 antitank regiments
    1 mine sapper battalion
    1 auto transport battalion

    strength: 120 guns
              28 antiaircraft
                machine guns
           4800 antitank
                mines

and roughly 5,000 antitank mines. We shall see some of these units in operation, in particular the 1st Antitank Brigade deployed in the Southwestern Front sector.

The Soviet force structure of 1941 displayed a basic Soviet penchant for largeness – some would say grossness – in terms of size. Units were simply too large. When the Soviets formed these units they tended to safe-side and add to them as much as they could in terms of firepower. In the end, the Achilles heel of most of these units was their utter lack of experienced cadre to command and control them and the comparable lack of effective logistical units necessary to support them in combat.

How did the actual operational concepts of the Soviets change on the eve of war? In theory, they did not change very much in comparison with the theory of 1936. Marshal Timoshenko, the Minister of Defense in 1940, had a speech published, which really resembled a Soviet Field Service Regulation in that it sketched out basic offensive and defensive concepts. Several charts taken directly from that document are shown and since they are in Russian each is described. The first variant portrays a *front* offensive operation involving an attack along one narrow axis (see

FIGURE 22
FRONT OFFENSIVE OPERATION, VARIANT 1:
ATTACK ON A NARROW FRONT

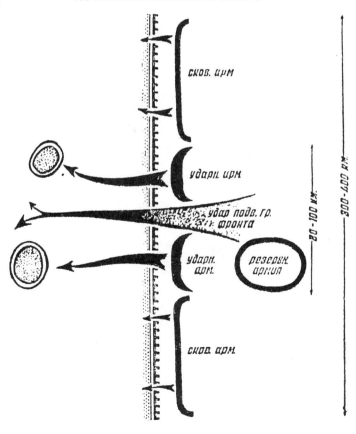

23

Figure 22). On it you can see two *udarnaya armiya* (shock armies) conducting the penetration operation and the *podvizhnie gruppy fronta* (mobile groups of the front) exploiting the tactical penetration into the operational depths. This was but one variation. The second variation represents a *front* offensive conducted across a broad front (see Figure 23). Actually this represents two fronts attacking with their adjoining flanks. Three shock armies from one front and two shock armies from another *front* attack initially, and the mobile groups of both *fronts* then exploit the penetrations to achieve an operational encirclement deep in the enemy's rear. Yet another variation involves multiple strikes along the front designed to achieve multiple penetrations. Shock armies attack in separate sectors, backed up by mobile groups and reserves in the form of

FIGURE 23
FRONT OFFENSIVE OPERATION, VARIANT 2:
ATTACK ON A WIDE FRONT OR AN OPERATION
OF ADJACENT *FRONTS*

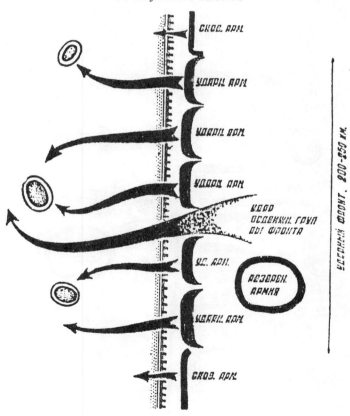

24

several rifle corps. This variant was also designed to produce large multiple encirclements deep in the enemy defenses (see Figure 24).

Timoshenko's speech then graphically illustrated how an army formed for offensive operations in 1940 (see Figure 25). Concentrated rifle divisions conducted the penetration operation, supported by infantry support tanks and backed up by the mobile group of the army. The mobile group, consisting of one mechanized corps, then exploited into the operational depths of the enemy's defense. A last illustration from Timoshenko's speech sums up what the Soviets were trying to achieve by all of this, and perhaps the way it displays the various forces unintentionally reveals a bit of truth about Soviet problems in implementing this

FIGURE 24
FRONT OFFENSIVE OPERATION, VARIANT 3:
SEVERAL ARMY PENETRATIONS ALONG DIFFERENT
OPERATIONAL AXES

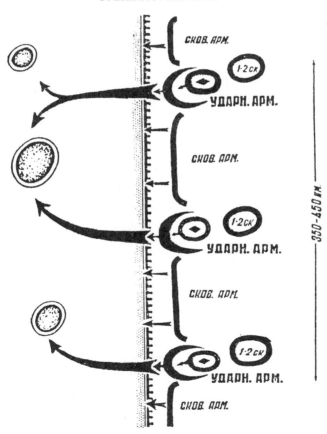

FIGURE 25
ARMY FORMATION IN AN OFFENSIVE OPERATION (ONE VARIANT)

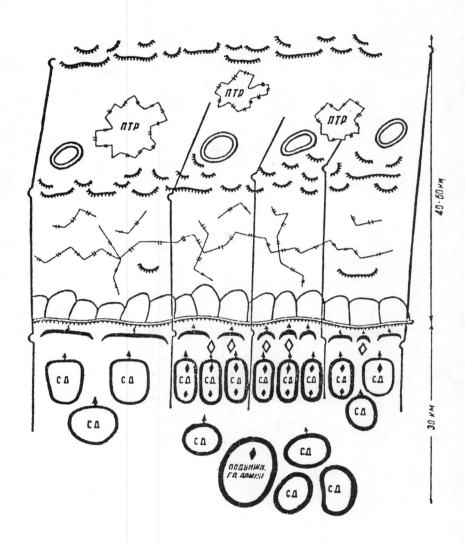

FIGURE 26
FORMATION OF A MOBILE SHOCK GROUP OF FORCES FOR
A PENETRATION (ONE VARIANT)

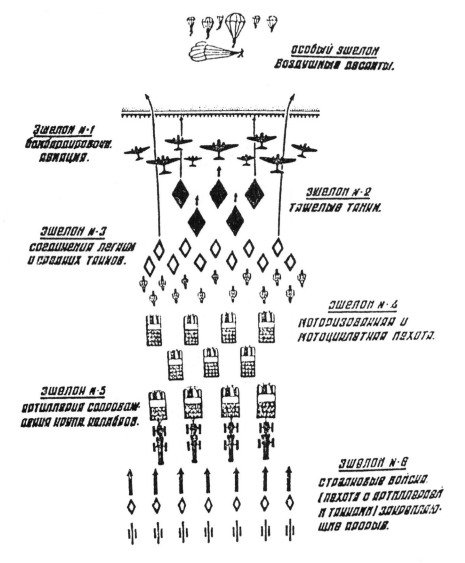

FIGURE 27
SOVIET FORCE STRUCTURE,
JUNE 1941

COMPOSITION

20 Armies
     including: 6 in Far East
                3 partial

```
 62 Rifle Corps
179 Rifle Divisions
 19 Mountain Divisions
 29 Mechanized Corps
 61 Tank Divisions (58 in Mechanized Corps)
 29 Motorized Divisions ( in Mechanized Corps)
  2 Motorized Rifle Divisions
  4 Cavalry Corps
 13 Cavalry Divisions (3 Mountain Cavalry)
  5 Airborne Corps
 15 Airborne Brigades (in Airborne Corps)
 76 Artillery Regiments (howitzer and gun)
 15 Separate High Power Artillery Battalions
 11 Mortar Battalions
 10 Antitank Brigades
 20 Antitank Regiments (in Antitank Brigades)
```

STRENGTH

Operating Forces - 4,900,000 men (2,900,000 in
                                  Western MDs)
Mobilized Force - 9,000,000 men

concept (see Figure 26). It attempts to depict combined arms operations by showing the relationship of aircraft; heavy, light and medium tanks; motorized infantry, towed artillery, and more armor, all tied together in a combined sense to achieve the penetration. Figure 26 actually says more than it intended, because all these force elements appear separately, and that was the way they tended to function in June 1941, with understandably ill effects. The figure even depicts the airborne dimension in the form of parachute landed infantry operating well forward. This then was the actual structure of the Red Army in 1940 and 1941 and the way in which the Soviets projected their forces would be employed on the offense and the defense.

Let me now explain how Soviet forces were actually deployed in June 1941. Figure 27 shows the Soviet order of battle in June 1941. The Red

FIGURE 28
SOVIET ORDER OF BATTLE, JUNE 1941

OB 1941

Border Districts	Covering Armies	Red Army
170 Divisions	56 Divisions	303
	)50 km deep	Divisions
2 Brigades	2 Brigades	(25%
		incomplete)
103 Rifle Divisions		179 RD
40 Tank Divisions		19 Mtn RD
20 Motorized Divisions		61 TD
7 Cavalry Divisions		31 MD
53 Border Guards Detachments		13 CD
9 Border Kommandaturas		

```
20 Mechanized Corps
    8 with some new tanks          27% operable (no parts)
    7 80-100% strength             15,000 Lt Tks
    13 10-25% strength               370 old Med/Hvy Tks
                                   1,475 new Med/Hvy Tks
                                   17,000 total

Rifle Divisions
    8,400-12,000 men
    80-90% weapons
    25-30% of vehicles

Average Strength
    Leningrad        11,985
    Baltic            8,712
    Spec Western      9,327
    Spec Kiev         8,792
    Odessa            8,400
```

Army consisted of 20 armies, 303 division-size formations, and 29 mechanized corps. The mechanized corps, 20 of which were in the forward area, consisted of 58 tank divisions and 29 motorized divisions (there were several separate tank and motorized divisions). The Red Army totalled some 4.9 million men deployed in what the Soviets called the operating forces, two million of which were located in the Western military districts. The Red Army had an estimated wartime mobilized strength of more than nine million men. Of these 303 divisions, 170 were located in the border military districts (Leningrad, Baltic, Special Western, Special Kiev, Odessa and Crimea) (see Figure 28). In addition to this 170 division force there were 53 border guards detachments, nine border komandatura, and 20 of the 29 mechanized corps.

Looking more closely at the actual Soviet force deployment, Figure 29 shows Soviet dispositions on 22 June 1941. What is immediately apparent

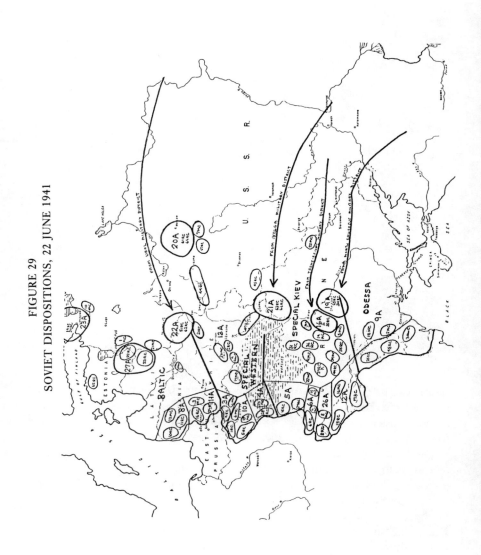

FIGURE 29
SOVIET DISPOSITIONS, 22 JUNE 1941

FIGURE 30
SOVIET DISPOSITIONS IN BORDER MILITARY DISTRICTS,
22 JUNE 1941

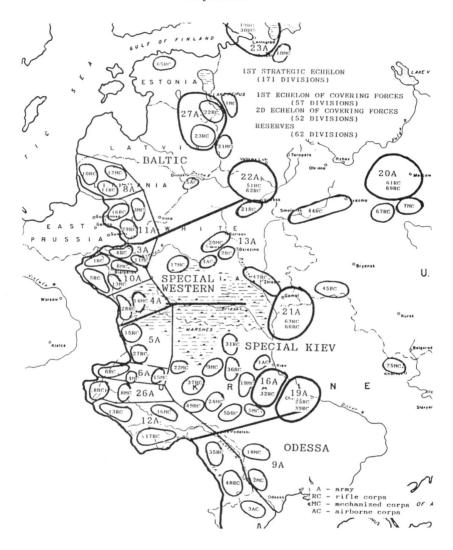

is the fact that the Soviets had been moving forces westward for about two months before June 1941. These were prudent defensive measures designed to create a strategic second defensive echelon. The Baltic Military District consisted of the 27th, 8th, and 11th Armies, each subdivided into rifle corps and mechanized corps (see Figure 30). The Special Western Military District was made up of the 3rd, 10th and 4th Armies deployed forward, and the headquarters of 13th Army deployed at Minsk, but with no units assigned. The Special Kiev Military District had the 5th, 6th, 26th, and 12th Armies with a variety of separate rifle and mechanized corps in the depth of the military district. Finally, the Odessa Military District consisted of the 9th, 18th and Separate Coastal Armies.

During May and June 1941, the Soviets began fielding forward additional armies from the interior military districts: the 22nd Army from the Ural Military District, the 21st Army from the Volga Military District, the 16th Army from the Trans-Baikal Military District, and the 19th Army from the North Caucasus Military District, together with several additional mechanized corps, for example, the 5th. The 20th Army also began forming in the Moscow area and additional units may be seen located in close proximity to the Western military districts.

Soviet war planning will not be discussed extensively here – that is Dr Kipp's subject – but the locations of the greatest densities of Soviet forces should be noted. Look at where the Soviet reserve armies were deployed in May and June 1941, in particular the 21st, 16th and 19th Armies. The southwestern axis was the expected area of the main German thrust, whenever that thrust materialized. Of course, the Soviets did not really expect it to occur in June 1941. The allocation and deployment of the Soviet mechanized corps should also be noted (the mechanized corps are designated by solid circles and the rifle corps by hollow circles).

In general terms, the Soviets considered each of the armies along the border as covering armies in much the same sense that Westerners view covering forces. These were armies designated to absorb the initial shock of the attack, to inflict damage on the enemy, and to set the enemy up for subsequent destruction by second echelon or reserve forces deploying forward. In any case, there was generally one mechanized corps assigned per forward army. To the north, in the Baltic region, were two rifle corps and a mechanized corps in each of the armies. In the Special Western Military District there was also one mechanized corps for each army. In the Special Kiev Military District there was roughly the same pattern, a ratio of one mechanized corps for each rifle corps with the rifle corps deployed forward and the mechanized corps deployed to the rear.

These mechanized corps were themselves deployed in echeloned configuration. The first echelon of mechanized corps supported forward deployed rifle corps from positions 80–100 kilometers to the east of the border. Their task was to blunt the initial German offensive spearheads. Up to 100 kilometers to the east, a second echelon of mechanized corps deployed on a line running from Pskov, Minsk, and Zhitomir to Berdichev. This echelon, along with second-echelon rifle corps would engage and defeat German forces penetrating into the operational depths, and later restore the integrity of the border through offensive action. A third echelon of mechanized and rifle forces, deployed at greater depth, was ready to occupy defensive lines along the Dnepr River, if that was required or, if not, they would join the second echelon in expelling enemy forces from Soviet soil. In essence, the mechanized corps and their rifle counterparts formed a strategic defense in depth, a defense which sought to defeat enemy forces by employing counter-offensive actions of mechanized forces.

The Soviets, however, faced several problems. These mechanized corps had just been formed, command cadre and personnel were untrained, their installational and field support systems were weak, and they lacked the required level of modern equipment, including most significantly, new tanks and trucks. Let me provide just a few examples. In the Western military districts, only eight of the mechanized corps had some new tanks, the T34s and KVs. Seven of them were at roughly 80 to 100 per cent strength and 13 of them were between ten and 25 per cent strength. If we are to believe Soviet sources concerning the condition of these corps, and wartime performance seemed to bear it out, only 27 per cent of the older tanks were operable and there were simply no spare parts available to fix those that were not. There was an overall tank park of over 15,000 older tanks, mostly light, 370 older medium and heavy models, and 1,475 of the new KVs and T34s, or roughly 17,000 tanks in the Soviet armored arsenal in June 1941.

If we focus more closely on the border military districts we can see the pattern of deployment in each district. Colonel General F.I. Kuznetsov's Baltic Military District had 27th Army well to the rear and 8th and 11th Armies located forward. Each of those forward armies had two rifle corps deployed relatively well forward and two mechanized corps (the 3rd and 12th) deployed to their rear. A more detailed look at the deployment will show the tendency on the part of the Soviets to scatter the mechanized corps with individual tank and motorized divisions out of mutual supporting distance. Of course, when the German attack began and the Soviets lost virtually all their supporting air power, the fragmented dispositions of those mechanized corps produced subsequent paralysis. In Lieutenant General D.G. Pavlov's Special Western Military District each of the rifle corps of the 3rd Army was backed up by a mechanized corps; 10th Army had two rifle corps backed up by two mechanized corps, and 4th Army had one rifle corps backed up by one mechanized corps. The same general deployment pattern existed in Colonel General M.P. Kirponos' Kiev Military District.

The Soviets positioned their mechanized corps in virtual triple echelon pattern with a first row of corps collocated with the covering armies, a second row located roughly on a line running from Dvinsk through Minsk and down to Korosten, and a third row positioned east of the Dnepr River. Any projected enemy advance (and obviously the most likely potential enemy was Germany) would have to progress through those rows of rifle armies and through the deeply echeloned mechanized corps. The basic Soviet premise (incorrect as it turned out) was that these covering armies would perform well enough to set up German forces for counter thrusts by the forces deployed in the depths.

Soviet rifle divisions were each supposed to have a strength of 14,483 men. In fact, they averaged between 8,400 and 12,000 men with the weakest being in the Special Kiev and the Baltic Military Districts. The strongest divisions were located in the Leningrad area. The rifle divisions had between 80 and 90 per cent of their weaponry as required by TOE, but a major deficiency was the poor status of vehicles in those divisions. They had only between ten and 25 per cent of the vehicles they were supposed to have, because of the crash program to rebuild the mechanized corps on the eve of war. This program deprived the infantry and cavalry forces not only of their armor but also of much of their mobility.

Since our focus is principally on Soviet armored and mechanized forces, I want to show what that Soviet force of 17,000 tanks meant in terms of the correlation of forces. These correlations have been prepared on the basis of specific military districts, Figure 31 showing the Baltic Military District, which had two mechanized corps deployed forward. There were two additional mechanized corps available to the military district commander, the 1st Mechanized Corps, garrisoned near Pskov and the 21st Mechanized Corps located further to the south. Some of these Soviet mechanized corps were not particularly weak. For example, the 3rd Mechanized Corps at Kaunas had 565 tanks, of which 105 were KVs and T34s, while the 12th Mechanized Corps had 690 tanks, all of the old variety. Generally the corps located further to the rear received lower priority in the assignment of new armored vehicles. They were supposed to receive new tanks by the summer of 1942, but in June 1941 very few new tanks were found in these mechanized corps.

For the sake of comparison, I have shown the armor strength of the German Panzer divisions employed on each axis. In the Baltic, three Panzer divisions are included because I count the southernmost divisions as committed against the Western Military District. In the Baltic Military District I calculated a correlation of roughly 1.3 to one ratio in favor of the Soviets along this axis. In the Western Military District, which became the

FIGURE 31
OPPOSING ARMORED FORCES,
BALTIC MILITARY DISTRICT

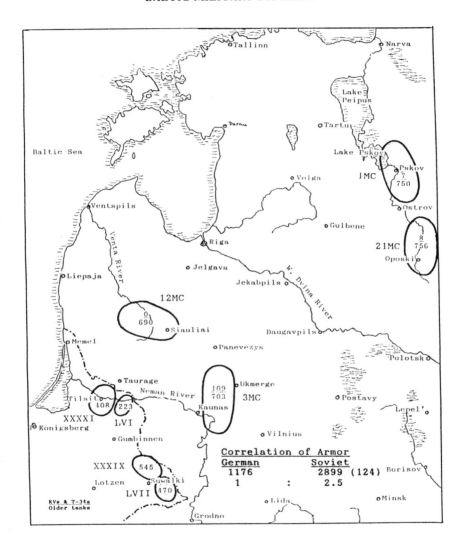

Western Front, there was even greater Soviet armor strength. For example, the 6th Mechanized Corps had just under 1,000 tanks, over 300 of which were new KVs and T34s (see Figure 32). We shall see how prewar deployment problems made it very difficult for the Soviets to bring those tanks to bear during combat. The 11th Mechanized Corps had 300

35

FIGURE 32

OPPOSING ARMORED FORCES, WESTERN MILITARY DISTRICT

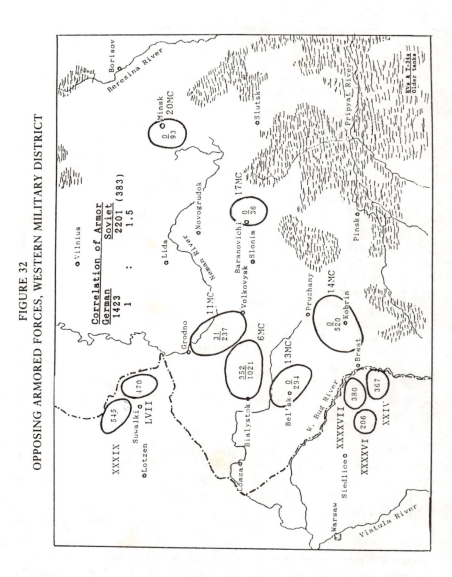

tanks, of which 44 were new, while on the other hand the 13th and 14th Mechanized Corps, located directly opposite where Panzer Group 2 attacked, were equipped only with a total of some 700 old tanks. The mechanized corps (the 17th and 20th), echeloned in depth, each had an average of 300 older tanks. The balance of forces here was roughly 1.8 to one in the Soviets' favor.

The Special Kiev Military District was strongest in terms of armor in June 1941, because this was where the Soviets expected the major effort to be made by any attacking foe (see Figure 33). The strongest of all the Soviet mechanized corps was in this area. Major General A.A. Vlasov's 4th Mechanized Corps, located at L'vov, had over 900 tanks, half of which were KVs and T34s. The 22nd Mechanized Corps, with one tank division. the 41st, located near the border, had 360 tanks, 30 of which were brand new KVs. The 15th Mechanized Corps had over 900 tanks, 150 of which were new, and the 8th Mechanized Corps fielded almost 220 new tanks out of a total strength of 700. These were the corps, the 15th, 8th, and to some extent the 22nd, that would exact the heaviest toll on advancing German forces after 22 June 1941. There were additional mechanized corps to the rear, the 9th, 19th, and 24th, but all were equipped only with significant numbers of older tanks.

This then was the Soviet force structure as it existed in June 1941, together with a brief summary of the expectations the Soviets had considering use of that force structure. We shall essentially be considering the degree to which reality matched these Soviet expectations.

Questions

Question: When the Soviets talk about deep battle and deep operations, do they mention any distances?

Colonel Glantz: Yes, they do mention different distances when they talk about deep battle and deep operations, the two concepts that emerged in the 1930s. The first was a tactical concept and the second an operational concept. They also discussed depths associated with each of those terms. In general terms, the tactical depth meant something less than 50 kilometers, normally about 20 kilometers. The operational depth was greater than 20 kilometers and perhaps as far as 150 to 200 kilometers out. The Soviets, as they have defined the tactical and operational levels, have always maintained indices of depth to correspond with those two terms. The indices have changed with time but you can plot them beginning in the 1930s and running right through the war. Of course, they still maintain the distinction today. The indices help define what is operational and what is tactical in terms of depth.

FIGURE 33
OPPOSING ARMORED FORCES, KIEV MILITARY DISTRICT

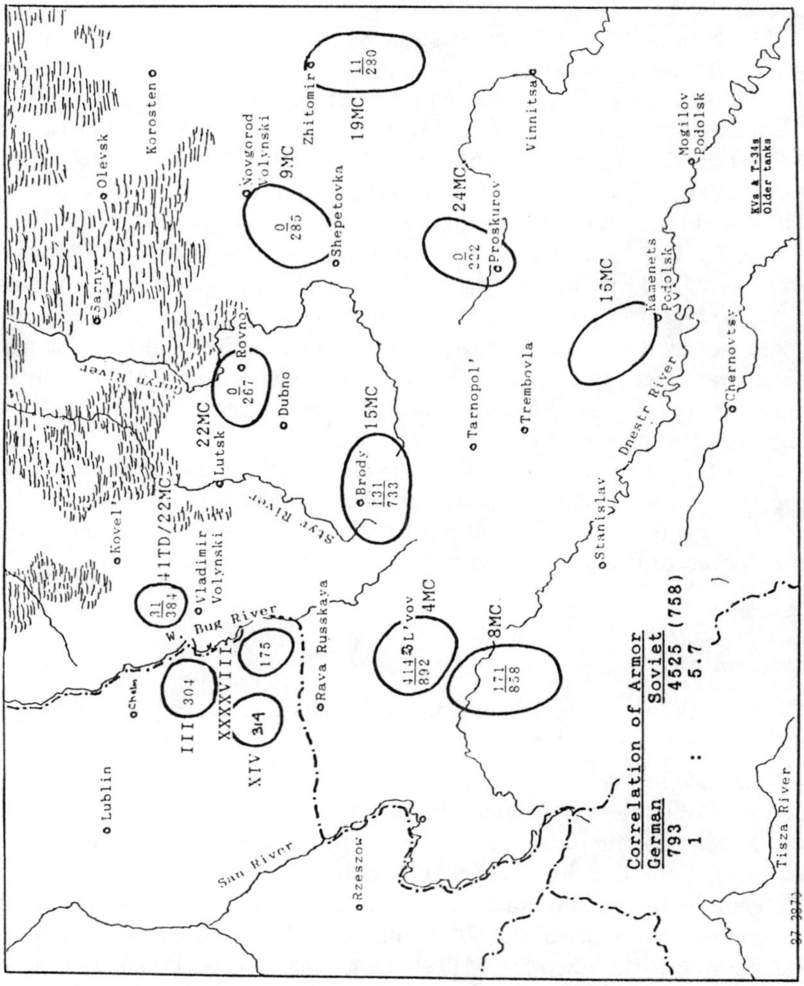

Question: Of the tanks in the mechanized corps, what types were there and how many were operational?

Colonel Glantz: The Soviets claim that 27 per cent of the older light and medium tanks were fully operational. Light tanks included a variety of models, primarily T26s, but many BT5s, or *bystrokhodnye* (fast moving) tanks, as they called them, rapid-moving tanks but with very thin skin. There were some medium T27s and T28s and the T35 models were heavy. Most of the models used in the 1930s had proven relatively ineffective against strong antitank defenses. In other words, the 37mm antitank gun could penetrate them. In fact, even large machine-guns could penetrate some of the smaller Soviet tanks. They tended to retain all older models just as they do today. They retained what they had, but in the full expectation that the T34s and KVs would soon come into the inventory. Soviets have been fairly candid in stating "We let the rest of the stuff [tanks] rot in the expectation that the new tanks would arrive."

Question: How would these facts affect the force ratio you cited?

Colonel Glantz: It is unfair to say the force ratio was 1.8 to one in favor of the Soviets, because as combat would indicate, some of these mechanized corps went from a nominal strength of 600 tanks on 22 June to a strength of only 30 on 28 June. As a matter of fact, most of the corps ended up with about 10 per cent of their original number of tanks left. I would say that at least half of the armored strength of those mechanized corps never made it into combat. They either broke down or never moved in the first place. That is not a new phenomena, because when we get into 1942, the Soviets will study armor attrition and note high attrition rates. They conclude from studying tank corps operations by the newer tank corps formed in 1942, that a mobile corps making a march of upwards of 100 kilometers, not even counting combat losses, experienced a 60 per cent attrition rate for logistical reasons alone. They conducted this type of study through the entire war, and by the war's end attrition rate had decreased to about 13 per cent.

Question: How many tanks were outside the Western military districts?

Colonel Glantz: There were twenty mechanized corps in the Western military districts and nine were located outside. Two of the nine were located in the Far East. Most of those in the interior of the Soviet Union were not manned at levels of over 10 per cent strength. When I say there were 17,000 tanks you must realize that there were some serviceable or rotting tanks in cavalry divisions, and there were some in a rifle division as well. I would say that the 17,000 figure is a minimum figure and the true figure may have been even higher. But again the vast majority were in the West and virtually all the KVs and T34s were in the West.

Soviet War Planning

DR JACOB KIPP

My topic is Soviet war planning in the immediate prewar period. In order to understand that war planning we have to take a slightly longer view of it and understand some of the problems which the Soviet General Staff traditionally had to deal with in terms of its war planning, such as the impact of military experience both in the Russo-Japanese War, the First World War, and ultimately the Civil War on Soviet perceptions about the war planning process, and finally and probably most importantly, Soviet perceptions regarding the nature of armed conflict in the 1930s leading up to and during the first phase of the Second World War and its impact on the perception of the nature, of course and outcome of combat should the Soviet Union be drawn into such conflict.

This is by its very nature a controversial topic. One need only look, for instance, at the recent book by Brian Fugate, *Operation Barbarossa*, in which the author postulates against what is certainly the conventional wisdom, a Soviet defensive plan for a pull back and use of a narrow covering force and the creation of its major defensive line deeper in the Soviet Union, which he describes as "a realistic plan or operative concept" for conducting defensive operations in the initial period of war. This is based on what he believes was Zhukov's adjustments in the last two months before war came. In addition, we have a controversy surrounding Victor Suvorov's article, which appeared recently in RUSI, the Royal United Services Institution journal, which speculates about a Soviet pre-emptive attack in 1941.

If we look at the Soviet experience in war planning, what we will find is that much of what has already been presented sets the context for understanding what the Soviets believed to be the nature of the operational deployments, the interrelationship of that force structure to threat and, ultimately, their concept of operations in the initial period of war. To understand that we have to understand what traditionally have been the dilemmas of Russian war planning. The traditional Russian dilemma since war planning began in 1876, when Deputy Minister of War N.N. Obruchev drew up the first plan for mobilization, concentration and deployment of forces on the eve of the Russo-Turkish War (1877–78), has frankly always been time and space.

Invariably when Russian general staff officers turned to the problem

40

of how they would get forces into contact in the initial period of war, they confronted the fact that their own extensive territory, the relatively weak nature of their rail system and the ponderousness of their force structure made it a race for deployment, a situation in which inherently and by definition they would come in second. This was the situation upon which all war plans in the pre-1914 period, or at least until 1912, were based. The assumption was that Austria, and more importantly Germany on the western border, would deploy more rapidly and therefore Russia would be in a catch-up situation. Given the nature of the Franco-Russian alliance, the need to draw France into war, and help France mount operations in July 1914, this bore heavily on the notion of preemptive mobilization: that is, mobilize first, get a few days on the Germans and thereby win back time and overcome space. The dilemma with that, and parenthetically the reason the Russians were so concerned, was their own experience in 1904 and 1905 when they had found themselves pre-empted by Japan's surprise attack, pre-empted in mobilization, in concentration, and in deployment. Consequently, they spent most of the campaign in the Far East desperately trying to regain the initiative. For Russian officers this meant something had to be done.

In the period 1905–12 they came up with the "magic formula" (ultimately recognized as not magic) of pre-mobilization (*premobilizatsiia*). The problem with pre-mobilization was, first, confusion in the system when various military districts were brought in one at a time, and the problem of disconnection with the war plan, but more importantly, if one went to a whole wide range of measures, what one ended up with was "a duck is a duck if it quacks". All the indicators would then force the other side to say "yes, one is engaged in mobilization".

Therefore, on the eve of the First World War, the Russian position was: "we must mobilize, we must follow our primary war plan and parenthetically, the missions imposed upon us decry any primary concentration on one strategic axis". In 1914 Russia was not only committed to early mobilization, but also to the mounting of early combat operations, which was a violation of preceding war planning on both the Galician axis and into East Prussia. In the one case, it was strategic national interest and, in the other case, alliance considerations: but both were undertaken. Now the impact of that on Russian thinking about war plans is evident.

During the First World War, one of the major studies was a discussion of the nature of operations by a theoretician named Ismest'ev. He noted an Achilles' heel in operational planning. He had been on the General Staff (in the operations section) and, he said they had done a very good job of working on mobilization and concentration but an abominable job on deployment. More importantly, they had assumed that mobilization and concentration and an operational line would define what further combats followed. In fact, as he said, anyone with the slightest experience of combat would know that after the first contact of forces, one must constantly redraft one's plan to deal with the unexpected, both friction within with one's own forces and actions by one's opponent.

In the 1920s, the Red Army picked up the legacies of prewar Russian planning. The problem was relatively simplified for the Red Army. First, one could posit encirclement in absolute hostility, that is, as Frunze wrote in the 1920s, we live in an era of capitalist encirclement. It is not a question of *if* we will be attacked, but rather of *when* we will be attacked. That is, war was seen as imminent and one had to deal with the likelihood of that prospect. On the other hand, however, the configuration of the international arena after the ending of the Russo-Polish War in 1920 seemed to leave the problem of the threat for the next decade relatively simple and relatively clear. Between 1920 and roughly 1931, the Red Army assumed that its opponents in any major war would be the countries of the Little Entente, principally Poland as the close crucial power, and Romania as a probable opponent, with the support of France. What this meant for most of the 1920s was that the Red Army did not anticipate the intervention of the major Western powers with combat forces in a conflict on the Soviet frontier. They expected assistance and arming, but they did not expect the Western states to send troops, partly on the basis of the experience of the Civil War, in which the allies had aided the Whites and the Poles with everything short of manpower. It was an underlying assumption of how the Soviets viewed the nature of the threat.

From 1929 to 1931 three fundamental changes came about to alter Soviet war planning in a fundamental way. First and most crucial, was the emphasis that emerged in that period from people like Tukhachevsky, Triandafillov, Svechin, and Shaposhnikov, who were the most important intellectuals who disagreed over issues, but were at one on this theme. If war should come it would involve total mobilization of the Soviet states. They disagreed as to the exact definition of that mobilization, but they called it *polnaya voennaya zatsiya* (full militarization). Svechin described it as a unification of front rear and state rear. Shaposhnikov talked about the "brain of the army", that is the General Staff working hand in hand with the civilians for the total mobilization of resources for the war effort. Tukhachevsky promoted the idea of military standardization, and did it particularly effectively as Director of Armaments for the Red Army. Everything produced, whether a tractor or a truck or a bed, would have a military standard so that it could be mobilized for the Soviet war effort. Thus, what was emerging in the late 1920s and early 1930s was the notion of total mobilization of the USSR. First, the Stalin revolution took place from the top down in mobilization, and second, the integration occurred of civil military leadership in a fundamental way.

Shaposhnikov, who was not a party member in 1929 when he wrote the book *Brains of an Army*, in essence acknowledged that the military must recognize the superiority of the party and state leadership and work hand in hand with it. In this regard, Shaposhnikov was particularly important because he was literally the model of what in his opinion was the most important characteristic of a general staff officer. He took the notion from Moltke that one must be more than one seems. Now why is that important?

It is important because Tukhachevsky, who was the advocate of mechanized forces in the Red Army and who certainly saw the German threat later on in much more stark times than Shaposhnikov, who only recognized it in 1936, was a very charismatic figure who was a potential military-political rival to Joseph Stalin. Shaposhnikov was never that. Indeed, of all the Soviet political leaders and military leaders, he was the only one Joseph Stalin favored with an intimate form of address, they called him by his *imia i otechstvo* (his first and middle name) – Voroshilov, Zhdanov, Molotov, Malenkov – none of those people were so favored. This meant that Shaposhnikov, who was the architect of the Soviet general staff system, was, first, spared the purges, and second, in a position to continue this notion of total mobilization and, indeed, to practice it to the very eve of the Second World War.

The second fundamental phenomenon after 1929 was the shift in the perception of the threat. Given the nature of capitalist crises, given the growing exasperation of conflict in the Far East, particularly the emergence of Japanese militarism in Manchuria, and given the deterioration of relations in Europe, the Soviets now began to consider the possibility that they would be at war not with the successor states, minor powers, but that they would have to deal with the intervention of the major capitalist powers, in particular Germany. When Germany and Poland signed a non-aggression pact in 1934, in 1935 the Soviet war games were based on a joint German–Polish attack. In the Far East, from 1935 on, the assumption of Soviet war planning was that the possibility of the extension of conflict outside of Manchuria was high and the likely avenues of Japanese attack were two: against China, which they desperately preferred, and against the Soviet Far East, which they desperately feared.

In 1937, in connection with the third Five Year Plan, a threat assessment was made by the Soviet General Staff. Shaposhnikov was responsible for drawing it up. It is crucial to note that the preeminent point of that assessment, which went into war planning over the next two years, was the possibility of threat from both East and West and the need to delineate the balance of forces regarding what was the immediate probable threat, and what was the most vital threat. The decision was made that the immediate probable threat was, in fact, Japan, and Soviet mobilization and shifting of forces in the Far East was dictated along these lines. Regarding the situation in western Europe there was still the hope that efforts towards collective security, notably the Franco-Czech-Soviet Treaty, would inhibit German aggression or at least create a potential coalition in which the Soviet Union could play a preferred role and check German ambitions.

This situation was very interesting because in the third Five-Year Plan from 1938 to 1942, which, of course, was never completed, was an interesting balancing of Soviet forces. One of those intriguing aspects of it was a rearmament cycle, which was agreed upon on the basis of experience in Spain, particularly, to create aircraft and armor. The fruits of that were to appear in 1941 in the new tanks (both KV1s and T34s), in new aircraft, a new generation of further aircraft, which were comparable with those enjoyed by the Western powers including Germany, and new bomber and ground attack aircraft, notably the IL2, which would become the most produced aircraft of the Second World War (over 35,000 units).

In addition, however, there were some other intriguing commitments: a commitment to an oceanic navy, which was strange, and a commitment to capital ships. There was also a commitment to assets outside coastal defense (the Soviet navy, until that time had been primarily interested in coastal defense, submarines, motor torpedo boats, etc.). Its capital ships commitment was extraordinarily short-lived. It lasted roughly from the beginning of the plan in 1938 to the middle of 1940. With the victory of Germany in the West, the construction of capital ships was suspended. The hulls were there, but the emphasis in naval resources radically shifted to mine and antimine warfare. This was one of the most crucial indicators that the probability of conflict in the summer of 1940 shifted from Japan to Germany in terms of Soviet General Staff planning.

Furthermore, if we look at the situation with regard to the Far East, we can see that Soviet management of conflict in that particular part of the world had been reasonably successful. There were conflicts, with the large-scale conflict in 1938 at Lake Khasan and then full-scale warfare on the Mongolian People's Republic border from May to September 1939. It was in this period that one can argue there was a fundamental reassessment of the Soviet geo-strategic position. In April, the British offered their blank check to Poland. In May, they began negotiations (not very seriously) in an attempt to draw in the Soviet Union to counter the German threat to Poland, and simultaneously, the Soviet Union found itself engaged in large-scale fighting in the Far East.

It is noteworthy that during this period the Soviet military efforts were concentrating on two issues. One was an accurate assessment of the correlation of forces in Europe. The second was an accurate assessment of the course and outcome of conflict in the Far East. To take the Far East first, there the situation had stabilized by July. The Japanese attacking forces had been contained and the Soviets essentially wrested the initiative

44

from the Japanese. In western Europe there was a reassessment – I would argue a fundamental reassessment – of both the will and intention of the Western allies. Munich had, to all intents and purposes, killed collective security as a policy on the part of the Soviets *vis-à-vis* France and Britain. In the case of Poland, the Soviets had their own perceptions about Poland as a successor state, as a victor against the Soviet Union in the Soviet–Polish War of 1920, and as a natural area for Soviet expansion. When Germany offered the opening, the Soviets were willing to accept it, with the fundamental understanding that they would, under the cover of the negotiations of the Molotov–Ribbentrop Pact, be able to deal with the situation in the Far East, having isolated Japan from its most important ally, Nazi Germany, and having created a situation where they anticipated a prolonged war in western Europe in which the correlation of forces would favor neither a coalition of the Western Entente Powers nor Germany and its allies. A knock-out blow to Poland, if it was followed by Soviet advances along its east European frontier to create a protective zone, was seen by the Soviet leadership and the military as apropos. In 1939–40 the question was how long would that conflict in the West continue: that is, would there be a continuation of war or would there be unexpected developments?

Several things deserve note in the fall of 1939. First, Soviet military operations in the Far East were highly successful. The Soviets annihilated a Japanese corps at Khalkhin Gol. The young commander, Georgi Zhukov, came back covered in glory and was promoted to prominent positions, including head of the Kiev Military District, over a number of senior officers. Second, the Soviets were able to advance into the areas of the collapsing states of eastern Europe; not only eastern Poland, but it also put pressure on Lithuania, Estonia and Latvia who, without the guarantees of the Western powers and without German intervention – which at this time was concentrating on the west – felt that they had to make concessions to the Soviets, and thus were ultimately incorporated.

Finally, of course, there was the question of the Soviet provocations against Finland and the launching of a war against the Finnish state, which quite clearly in conception and execution was highly flawed. There was a fundamental fight within the Soviet leadership as to how that war should be fought. Marshal Shaposhnikov, one of the few experienced military commanders with staff experience in Soviet circles in 1939, and a survivor of the purges, but also a protector of many junior officers who survived the purges, including K. Rokossovsky, found himself at odds with Stalin and what might be called the Tsaritsyn Mafia, the people from Stalin's entourage who had served with him in the 1st Cavalry Army in the fighting in Tsaritsyn. They believed that it would be a walkover. Soviet military writings in the 1930s had postulated that wars would begin with provocations, that partial mobilization of forces, if carried out appropriately, and with the advantage of surprise would make it possible for relatively quick and decisive victories in frontier battles. In the case of Finland, Shaposhnikov, looking at the terrain and at the forces of the Leningrad Military District, fundamentally opposed a partial mobilization and the provocations against Finland, suggesting indeed that it would take a large scale mobilization and the dispatch of substantial forces.

The beginning of the Finnish War was a disaster. The Soviets were totally unprepared for the conduct of winter offensive operations. Their committed mechanized corps ended up as a circle of wagons as opposed to a combat formation, and Soviet casualties were horrendous, with about half a million killed, wounded and missing. The situation was so bad that politically the leadership had to carry out major changes. Shaposhnikov, who was head of General Staff, and Voroshilov, who was head of the Commissariats of War, were dismissed, and a new leadership was brought in, although responsibility lay with Comrade Stalin. Primary responsibility for the defeat clearly belonged with Voroshilov, Budenny and Stalin, who underestimated the ability of the Finns to resist.

What was the situation in 1940? First, a new command team was emerging in late spring and summer, until the German military successes occurred in the west. The debate about large mechanized formations ended with the German victories in the Low Countries and France. The advocates of smaller formations had based their analysis largely on Spain, including General Pavlov, who commanded the Western Special Military District and who was to become a victim of German armored attacks in 1941. His position was undermined and the commitment to the creation of the first nine mechanized corps was accepted.

There was, however, a fundamental tension now in the Soviet military situation. Timoshenko came in as Commissar of War. He identified the primary problem of the Soviet military coming out of Finland as basic small unit problems, and suggested that the summer of 1940 must be spent in intensive training to deal with those problems. The military districts were told: "That is your focus, that is your interest, work it out". Simultaneously there was a new Chief of the General Staff, Meretskov, who had done reasonably well in Finland, but who had none of the background of Shaposhnikov. In the spring of 1940, a new war plan had been under consideration. That war plan addressed the probability of a German attack and in it Shaposhnikov had assumed that the primary German attack would indeed come through the Bialystok salient down the Minsk–Smolensk–Moscow axis. Shaposhnikov had based his analysis here on the vulnerability of that sector of the front and on the correlation of forces which Germany could achieve in that sector given the nature of the road and rail network, and the vulnerability of Soviet forces in that region, because that theater had not been prepared to accept the Soviet forces which would move into it. A simple matter: the rail gauge had not been changed. Eastern Poland still had narrow gauge and the Soviets were only in the process of re-laying their lines in 1940–41.

After Shaposhnikov's removal in the fall, a major reconsideration of that proposed war plan went forward and Stalin, on getting a brief from Meretskov, suggested on his own volition that the main axis of attack be changed. The axis that mattered was that of Kiev, the Donbas and the Caucasus. Stalin's argument, which he had pounded into his head for over a decade now, was the notion that the next war would be a protracted conflict involving successive operations, and that in order to continue those operations one had to talk about the mobilization of the national economy for total war effort. Given the vulnerability of Germany to economic strangulation, if Russian war materials were cut off, prudent German military planning would involve as primary objectives, in its initial operations, the seizure of the Ukraine, the Donbas and, if possible, the north Caucasus and the Caucasian oilfields. This perception and this analysis became the foundation of the general war plan which was accepted for 1941.

Each of the military districts was handed the responsibility for positioning its forces according to that war plan, and the primary axis of threat was to be covered by the concentration of forces in those areas – that is in the south, in the Ukraine – to deal with that situation.

In December 1940, the Soviet Main Military Command hosted a conference of commanders. This was a usual conference held to complete the summer maneuvers and exercises to lay out plans and prospects for the next year. It was on this occasion that Timoshenko made the address which has already been mentioned. However, included in this particular meeting was a cycle of war games in which the political leadership took an intense and immediate interest. The heads of the two main forces were selected on the basis of the commander of the Special Western Military District and the Special Kiev Military District. In the two games played, the command of blue forces against the Special Western Military District was put in the hands of Zhukov, while the red forces, the Soviet defending forces, were put under Pavlov. In the attack in the south the roles were reversed.

Zhukov, in his memoirs, talks about his being able to achieve a correlation of forces and get the required breakthroughs roughly equivalent to what, in fact, the Germans would achieve over a longer period of time. Reflecting gaming considerations, the exercise went according to plan and the underlying Soviet assessment was surely that the frontier battles would essentially be battles of covering armies. The outcome, however, was unpleasant because the Germans did achieve breakthroughs and they did achieve encirclement. In the south Pavlov also had success although not nearly as great.

In the post-conference discussions Stalin specifically asked the participants to come to the Kremlin and, with members of the Politburo, make an assessment of the war game. Stalin gave Meretskov short shrift and did not let him finish his presentation. In general, he treated him like a man doomed, not to extermination, although that with Joseph Stalin might be understood, but rather to removal as Chief of the General Staff.

Stalin did however, raise a series of questions. First, what assumptions were made regarding the correlation of forces? One of them was that one Soviet division was clearly superior to one German division. Stalin said, "Forget that; that's for propaganda purposes among ourselves and we have to deal with what the real world is". The second problem was mechanized warfare, and in a very heavy-handed way, Stalin pushed his military commanders into addressing the question, "If you have to deal with this threat what do you need? Do you need mechanized corps?" Those who answered "no" were mostly cavalry types or older commanders whom Stalin shut up immediately. The other side said "yes", and he asked how many. In that session there was a kind of boosterism. Stalin pressed this notion of how many corps would be created.

This was January 1941; they had been in the process of raising nine corps in about six months and suddenly the figure of 20 more arose – 20 additional mechanized corps to be created for a total of 29. All the military districts were to get them including those in the Trans-Caucasus. Everyone was supposed to get his mechanized corps. The General Staff were horrified. In 1938, Kadishev, in a series of lectures at the General Staff Academy, had said there was one fundamental mistake one could make if war was imminent. That was to begin a major restructuring of one's forces, because one would find oneself with neither A nor B, but with some intermediate form which would not be adapted to combat. Such was, indeed, the situation in the spring of 1941. The formations were in the process of being raised and a rearmament cycle was under way, a rearmament cycle in which not only had the vehicles not arrived, but the crews had not been trained.

When Kirponos, new commander of Kiev Military District, visited one of the tank training grounds he was shown one tank that was particularly good, a new T34. It ran all over the field and it was wonderful. He went over and found a lieutenant running it, and he said, "All right, find me an NCO and let's see what he can do." They could not find an NCO who could drive the new T34. That was anecdotal, but it was also suggestive of the problem which was indeed emerging. As increasing indicators showed that war was more and more imminent, the political leadership was slow to respond to them, partly because they wanted the war to be delayed psychologically and partly because they were fearful, given their conception of provocations from the 1930s, that responses would be seen as pre-mobilization and therefore provoke a German attack, when one might not actually be imminent. Soviet leadership was politically divided between those who saw the redeployments coming and said, "What we are faced with is German pressure, a political ultimatum and then some sort of concession," and those who said, "Yes, but it will be an attack".

For most of May and early June the Soviet leadership was quite unclear as to which that would be. It was, in fact, not until the second week of June that the Soviets mounted their own provocation: the infamous Tass news release in which they announced rumors about German deployments along their western border, adding, "Of course there is no deterioration of German–Soviet relations, and by the way, our own summer deployment should not be taken as any hostile move towards Germany". As Marshal Vasilevsky pointed out in his memoirs, a clear element of provocation was involved here. Germany's political leadership was in effect being asked to deny beating their wives – that is, any response by Germany had to be a giveaway of their intentions. And the longer there was no response from Germany the more committed the Soviet military leadership was to the reality of the attack.

That context coincided, first, with the major reorganization of Soviet forces; second, with the advance into a theater of war which had been unprepared; third, with the major expansion of Soviet manpower so that they were moving from a territorial to a cadre system and having all sorts of problems with basic military training; and fourth, with the digestion of military lessons from the war so far, and I would argue that at that level the Soviets were doing very well. Soviet authors on the eve of the war were talking about operational surprise, they were talking about the role of German mobile groups, and about a new concept of how to fight encircled, because given the nature of mobile warfare and maneuver, it was anticipated that formations would find themselves encircled and they were concerned about what they would do to stabilize that combat power.

All of these things were transpiring in a context. The Soviet leadership did not want to provoke hostilities at a time of complex secrecy in the Soviet system, so that there was fundamental disfunction – a cybernetic disfunction – between two Soviet systems of information. One was among the initiated, and that included a good portion of the General Staff and certainly the political leadership who thought that war was coming, although how close they could not say. The second was an attitude among the rank-and-file that war was not close and therefore should not be anticipated.

Where does all of this come into play? It comes into play at the lowest level of the military. It comes into play in terms of force deployments, the fact that Soviet divisions on the frontier, to avoid provocation, were kept either in their camps and under strength, so that they were not in a position to meet the initial blow. In short, the Soviet Union was drifting towards a war, attempting to anticipate what could be the threat, attempting to mobilize, but in such a fashion that they would not provoke the contest, and informed in their concept of mobilization by what I call the dialectic of deep battle and deep operations. It was the notion of trying to create a second strategic echelon. Initially (and the Soviets are very forthcoming in this), the covering forces were to stop the German offensive and the second strategic echelon was to counterattack or occupy positions to form a second strategic belt should the frontier fighting go badly.

The Soviet Union's conception of the war was that if it came, it would be a long one. They grossly underestimated the impact which surprise and German premobilization and deployment would have upon their forces. Furthermore, the initial deployments along the western borderlands left that first strategic echelon without immediate support and, in fact, in no position to carry out what would become the demands from Moscow for immediate and decisive counterattacks.

Question: Could you comment on the border defenses?

Dr Kipp: One of the major problems with the border defenses was that the Soviets had the concept of what they call fortified regions. On the basis of the experience of the First World War and their experience in the Civil War they did not believe in the idea of an uninterrupted fortified belt. Instead, they took primary axes which they believed were fundamental to their defensive positions and turned those into fortified regions. One of the problems with the situation from 1939 to 1941 was that by moving the state border forward they created a need to build new fortified regions out in advance. The assets to build those regions had to be gotten somewhere and what did they do then? First, they stripped the older ones back on the old state frontier. Second, because the construction battalions and units did not have construction assets, they stripped out supporting transports, trucks, and tractors and put them into the construction battalions building the new fortifications.

As a result, when the war came the Soviets had large numbers of artillery parks in divisions and corps which had no prime movers. If you will, they were robbing Peter to pay Paul. There was also a major fight over where the fortified regions were, and how they were located (too close to the borders was Zhukov's assessment). In general, given what was supposed to happen with those (that is, they would be manned and brought up to strength before the initiation of hostilities), they contributed very little to initial combat power because the garrisons had not been mobilized.

I did not mention a related point about the Kiev axis. On the eve of war, 21 June, the Main Military Council made the decision to create a new *front*. The 9th Army was turned into a *front* to deal with the Romanians, a clear indication that they wanted Kirponos and the Southwestern Front to concentrate upon the threat coming towards Kiev from the Lublin area. The interesting thing about the situation was that while the army staff was there, the *front* staff was taken to the Moscow Military District. So when the war came there was the anomaly of a *front* created with its headquarters and personnel back in Moscow and finding enormous problems in getting down and conducting the operations.

Analogous to the situation with the fortified regions was that of the border guards. Supposedly, before hostilities began the Soviet border guards were to be mobilized into the contingents of the military districts. The only place where that took place, interestingly enough, was south of Kiev and that was on the volition of any army chief of staff and commander, not a *front* commander. He did it on his own. Along the rest of the border, the frontier guards essentially remained outside the Soviet chain of command until after the attack began.

Question: Can you connect in the Soviet spy system before the attack?

Dr Kipp: One of the problems in this period was that Stalin had a system without a system. What he did was concentrate the collection of raw intelligence into a few actors who reported directly to him, and then it went essentially to the Politburo and out. The officers in the operations sections of the General Staff claimed that they did not know about important pieces of intelligence coming in, therefore they could not respond to them. There was one case concerning the order which was issued for mobilization of forces and the intelligence assessment that went with it. Golikov, who was head of intelligence, was tricked into signing the document. His deputy did what any staff officer might do, although in the Stalin system, he would have to be brave. He sent out copies of a supposedly signed covering order calling for mobilization on a basis of threat, said the original copy was in the safe of the chief of GRU, then handed Golikov the release that had been sent out and said, "Sign this one". Golikov signed it, because he was done for either way, but he relieved the officer and sent him off to a curious sanitarium down in Odessa, in which, according to the fellow's comment, the only people there seemed to leave on a regular basis, never to return, leaving their luggage behind. It was thought to be a GRU collection point for those who were going to places from which people did not return.

It was a very bad intelligence system; I call it cybernetic crises. It concentrated everything in Stalin's hands; he manipulated the information, and it was very difficult for the next level of decision-makers to have a full picture of what was happening. Some did; for example, Kuznetsov, the head of the navy. The navy had a whole set of indicators which meant war was imminent. And the Germans gave them that full set of indicators. One was the movement of all merchant ships out of Soviet ports. When Kuznetsov picked that one up he gave orders for the navy to move out in a war-imminent posture, both in the Black Sea and in the Baltic.

So, if they had the right indicators and were in the right place, they could pick them up but for the General Staff there were untold problems. Part of the problem was the paralysis that Stalin had induced. The purges did not end in 1938. Although we speak of 1937 and 1938 as the worst years, people were still being picked up and provocations being arranged in 1941. Trusted general staff officers would have someone ask them provocative questions. They would give answers and then the person would disappear. So the system created its own gaps in intelligence. Thus the Soviets were quite vulnerable in that area.

Question: Why did the Soviets concentrate such forces in the Southwestern area?

Dr Kipp: The basic expectation was that the initial German attack would be launched there. If they could parry it, they anticipated a counterstrike out of Western Military District down into the flank, and the rest of these forces would be part of a follow-on for a pincer. The objective, however, was double, because the Soviets also had an appreciation of the strategic vulnerability of Germany down in Rumania. It was interesting that in June, July and August the Soviets mounted pinprick attacks in Rumania by raids of naval aircraft. In fact, there was one amphibious landing on some islands in the Danube and shelling of other points. None of these actions was able to disrupt oil production seriously or offer any major threat, but they are part of the notion of provocation, to draw the opponent's attention to an area and get him to respond, essentially in an area that would draw his combat power away from where, certainly by July and August, the major threat had developed.

The original raid in Rumania was an interesting one. I have read one Soviet article where the naval aviators laid out the ordnance mix that went into that attack. It was quite clear it was preplanned. They had a mix of fighter aircraft, they had heavy ordnance incendiaries and they knew what they were going after. Clearly that was seen as a vital target. The primary aim was to bring the two military districts together and if possible cut off the main weight of the German force.

Question: The figure of Stalin is so riveting that it is hard to extract him. If you look at the abstract problem as Nekrich does it seems the intelligence is flowing in massive quantities. The problem seems not to be with its I&W [indicating and warning] system, but rather with the assessment by Stalin.

Dr Kipp: Yes, but the problem was that the Soviets looked at the source and they said, "That's what they want us to believe. You are provoking us into a war in which you, in fact, would like to involve us". One of their major problems was the penchant for Stalin to deal with "collection" rather than analysis. He did not deal with digested intelligence. He essentially wanted raw stuff which was understandable. Political leaders have that weakness by definition. Raw materials look very attractive. On the other hand, the most crucial question from 15 to 22 June was not whether war was imminent or not imminent. It was how many days. The Soviet assumption – and blame Shaposhnikov, not Stalin, for this – was that the indicators which appeared in terms of troops deployment, particularly of the German mechanized forces, would give the Soviets ample time to continue this process of mobilization, and yet reasonably reach their destination. In fact, they were talking about a two week window before those land indicators (mechanized forces) would mean that attack was imminent.

My reading, primarily of the memoirs, accounts of the period and Nekrich, is that the "warning war imminent" date was 20 June, and rather than 15 days they got two. The creeping up to war, essentially beginning in early May, was only a first stage and there were a whole set of measures which were to follow, but it was too late.

Question: The Russians were really surprised by the date of the attack. Would you agree?

Dr Kipp: In terms of the response time they must have been surprised by what was happening. But you have to add to that the fact that they also fundamentally misguessed where the main weight of the German attack would be. The two coincided and they became multipliers. And then add on this horrendous force restructuring problem. We had a bridge in Washington, in which the various engineering problems were individually quite manageable. But when you put them all together this span would essentially levitate about 60 feet in high winds. I think here we have a case of 60 foot levitation and destruction, because so many things were wrong simultaneously that one is talking about multiplier upon multiplier creating crisis. So I would agree with you on the day of the attack.

Question: Nekrich talks about their forward positioning of personnel and equipment. How did that fit in with their planning?

Dr. Kipp: It was not so much the forward positioning as the centralized nature of the rear service. You have to understand that from 1929 to 1941 there was a real fundamental debate going on inside the Soviet military about the nature of rear services of the Red Army. In his book *The Nature of Operations of Contemporary Armies*, Triandafillov said, "In eastern Europe one has a peasant rear". By that he meant a lack of paved roads, a very thin network of rail lines, and a reliance ultimately on moving from within divisions and down on horse transport, if you were moving goods and services (logistical support). In the 1930s there were those in the Red Army who argued that they had solved that problem, and had created an industrial, and therefore, a mechanized rear.

In fact, the nature of rear services was absolutely and utterly chaotic. It was not only that they were forward, but there was no effective command and control of them. Resources which were quite far back in the first week of the war, that is as far as Minsk, did not get evacuated because there was no mechanism to carry it out. In fact, in many cases they were not even destroyed. They were captured intact.

What followed was a major shift in the reorganization of Soviet rear services. A much more effective system began to evolve in July, not right away, but the beginning of the organization of a more effective one. One of the problems was that all rear services came under the responsibility of the General Staff, and in 1940–41 the General Staff let that responsibility slip badly. The response and the reform was to create a separate rear service to make it co-equal in that area with the General Staff, and to take the General Staff out of the day-to-day movement of supply and forces. It is a highly centralized system, it unites front and rear very closely, and it brought in industrial management, but it created someone directly responsible for managing those services.

Obviously, then, there was a problem, but it was more than just forward deployment. There was a whole system that was not very responsive to the needs of maneuver war. One can ask oneself, however, given the nature of eastern Europe whether it was reasonable to anticipate, given the situation in 1939–41, that there would be much mobility outside of rail mobility for logistical stores. The Soviets just did not have the trucks or the road system to do much movement outside of it. As for the shortage of vehicle parts, all the collective farms that were supposed to provide the trucks, they never reached the units.

The German Army in 1941

KENNETH MACKSEY

Introduced by Colonel Paul Adair

The distinguished English historian Kenneth Macksey joined the British Army in 1941 and took part in the armored fighting in northwest Europe, both as a troop leader in a tank troop and as a liaison officer to the 1st Polish Armored Division. After the war he remained in the British Army in the Royal Tank Regiment. He has written extensively on armored warfare and, in particular, has written a biography of General Guderian.

My aim is to outline the state of the German Army (*das Heer*) in June 1941 with particular emphasis on the fast troops, that is, the panzer and motorized divisions in the four panzer groups involved.

First of all, the general structure of the German Army was quite different from the the Russian Army. It consisted of the mass of the marching infantry on horse and foot. A number of vehicles were involved, of course, to tow anti-tank guns, and every now and again assault guns would be attached to them. But by and large they were marching infantry, they were horse-drawn artillery, and much of the transport was horse-drawn. They were quite different, not only in their structure but also in their way of thinking, from those of the fast troops, the panzer divisions particularly, which began to be formed in the 1920s and reached fruition in 1939, principally directed by General Guderian.

The other services that are fundamental to this whole campaign are the logistical services. The logistical services on the Russian side broke down completely, and complaints are sometimes heard from the Germans, of how difficult their logistical services were. They were in paradise compared with what was going on in the east. It is well to bear in mind, however, that, first of all, there was a feeling, based on a certain amount of study, that the campaign would only last about six weeks. Remember that before the Germans went into Russia in June 1941, no campaign of theirs had lasted much more than six weeks. So the depth of the logistical services had not in any way really been tested, and certainly not in a long campaign. Remember too that the logistical services depended on two basic methods of movement. First by rail, but after the Russian frontier the rail could not be used because it was a different gauge from that of the

Germans. Second, resupply by road and road transport had been pretty well developed and I will return to that.

First of all let us consider the fast troops and how they came into being. After the First World War, the Germans realized that one of the things that had gone seriously wrong was that they had no tanks, or at least not many. Most of those they had, in fact, were captured British ones. Something had to be done. At that time, too, there was a general movement towards mechanization, as there had to be, if only because the horse population was in decline because they were in less demand commercially. This was becoming quite a problem. As you know, by virtue of the Treaty of Versailles, the German army was reduced to 100,000 men. Germany was not allowed to have tanks or anything like that, and in their opinion, and for a good reason, they were surrounded by enemies. A 100,000-man immobile army could not defend Germany. For that reason the movement to highly mobile troops was accelerated.

Most people probably know that when the German General Staff was abolished after the Versailles Treaty, they formed the *Truppenampt*, which was like the German General Staff, a select band of officers who got together and planned for the future, when they could have the necessary equipment. They looked at every new idea, including airborne troops and tank troops. They also brought in a man called Guderian, then a major and a German General Staff officer of the highest grade, to look at mechanization.

Guderian was a controversial figure. He was a light infantryman, which meant he fought a bit faster than ordinary infantrymen. Ordinary infantrymen may disagree, but it is one of the things that goes with light infantry and with the Jaegers. More importantly, he was also a signaller, who had been trained in radio in 1911. His father, who was his commanding officer, had sent him off to a course so that he could cool down over the girl he was going to marry. So he went off to learn about signalling. Soon he was an expert signaller and he later took a signal detachment to the battle of the Marne. He knew how command and control worked and he was something else as well. He was a man of very firm ideas, unafraid of standing up to senior officers, no matter how senior. As a junior officer, after the battle of the Marne, when he disagreed violently with the way he had been treated and deployed, he had a flaming row with his division commander, who then posted him away to quieter places on the Ypres salient.

By bringing a man in like that, who in a way was an early model of a technical staff officer, the *Truppenampt* had somebody who was going to look at new ideas and push them forward. The more Guderian read and the more he studied and experimented with things that were not tanks, but different models, the more he became convinced that not only was the tank important and dominant in its way, but it had to be combined with other arms in a different way from that being by other armies. In other armies the tank was being subordinated to the infantry. Guderian developed the idea of combat teams which led to panzer divisions made up of tanks, artillery, motorized infantry, and motorcyclists, all working together.

He was helped in a way by the British, who were carrying out similar experiments and had tanks with which to do it. They experimented in public and published their manuals in public, at nine pence a copy. The Germans could read these and did. So in the early stages Guderian was very largely copying British ideas.

Then there came a time, about 1932–33, when he went off on his own. They were his ideas, nobody else's. For example, concerning vehicles, he went, as the British did, for three types of armor-fighting vehicles: a light tank for reconnaissance; a medium tank for tank versus tank action, with something like a 37mm gun; and a close support tank, which would fire smoke and high explosive. He would have liked heavy tanks very much indeed, and said so, but, in fact, he could not have them and knew it. There was no great priority being given to this. There was no money and no manufacturing capability at that time. So he had to shelve his plans.

Thus he was producing the tanks he had developed towards 1941. There was armor protection on the medium tanks of about 30mm, which, in fact, would not keep out very much. But it kept out shell fire, and it kept out bullets, and it gave them a pretty good chance of survival. The Germans also tried very hard to make those tanks reliable, not entirely successfully, but they were better than others. They looked at the gun problem and their tendency seemed similar to that of the British: to mount a gun which would defeat their own armor without necessarily using the gun to defeat the armor of the enemy they might meet. That was, and is, a very dangerous philosophy.

I must also mention the vehicles used for logistics, the "B" vehicles. Clearly what was needed was a cross-country vehicle. Instead they had forced upon them the ordinary commercial vehicles, 4 × 2s, which were all right when there were plenty of roads, as in Western Europe. But in Russia they were not very good. Nevertheless, they were developing a useful family of vehicles which would do extremely well and be reasonably reliable. Towards the end of the first phase in France, in 1940, they still had 50–60 per cent of tanks running. Most of those out of action were, in fact, only broken down; within a few days they had been repaired and put back into the line.

The most important aspect of the German organization of panzer divisions and like formations was their command, control and communications. In the 1920s the Germans made a deliberate effort to produce far better radio sets than ever before. They produced a first-class range of sets

German Battle – Tanks , 1937 – 41

Deutsche Panzerkampfwagen 1937 – **41**

Pz. Kpfwg. I mit 2 MG

Pz Mk-I

(2-MG /
(1941 used in
(2 nd(arm'd)Coy/
(Arm'd EngBn 37)

Pz Mk-II [*Ausf. 'G'*]

(1– MG 34/ +
(1– 2o mm/ Tk gun)

(1941 used in:
(light Tk Plts./
(+ Arm'd EngBn-s).

(Used also for
(Recce-Teams of
(Arty Rgts ,
(Arm'd Recce Bns/
(PzDiv's/motInfDiv)

PzKw II mit KwK 20mm 38/L-40

Pz. Kpfwg. III mit 5 cm KwK 39L/42

Pz Mk-III

(2-MG 34 / +
(1– 5o mm / Tk gun–L/42
((shortbarreled) –

(2., 3., 6., + 7./Pz1 ≡
(17 Pz Mk-III/Tk gun–5omm
(from Oct/Nov'4o on   )

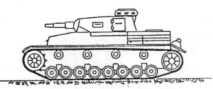

Pz. Kpfwg. IV mit 7,5 cm KwK L/24

Pz Mk-IV

(2 MG-34 / +
(1 75 mm / Tk gun – L/24)
((shortbarld.)   )

(4. and 8./PzRgt 1 =
(14 Pz Mk-IV-L/24 :
(from 1936/37 – 1942)

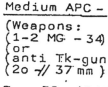

Medium APC –

(Weapons :
(1-2 MG – 34)
(or
(anti Tk-gun
(2o -/ 37 mm)

June 39 - 1945

m. SPW (Sd.Kfz. 251/1)

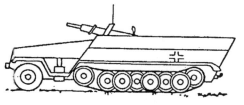

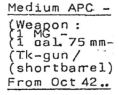

Medium APC –

(Weapon :
(1 MG –
(1 cal. 75 mm–
(Tk-gun /
(shortbarrel)
From Oct 42 ..

m. SPW (Sd.Kfz. 251/9) mit 7,5cm StuK L/24

Light
Arm'd Recce-
(Scout) Car

(1-2 MG and/
(or 2omm/Tk-
(AA-gun- 39)

le.Pz.Sp.Wg. (Sd.Kfz. 222) mit 2cm KwK 38 L/55

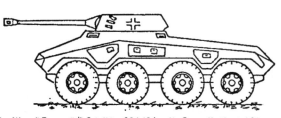

Heavy Recce
(Scout-/Gun-)
Tk(Achtrad)-
(2 MG + / or
(1 - 5o mm/
(Tank gun)
From 1943 on

s. Pz.Sp.Wg. "Puma" (Sd.Kfz. 234/2) mit 5cm KwK L/60

which, when introduced into service in the 1930s, proved excellent, mostly in the high frequency range. They also insisted that commanders command from the front, take advantage of fleeting opportunities, make quite sure that their orders were being obeyed, and generally have an impact instead of sitting in a command room just giving orders at the end of a telephone. This, I suggest, was about the most important contribution made by General Guderian. He certainly had an impact on the technical side with the vehicles, but he lost out very often on getting what he wanted, except signal-wise, and it worked.

He was also extremely keen to have good reconnaissance, which was vital. Good ground and air reconnaissance were important because his concept of panzer divisions was that they shot out in front, drove deep into the enemy lines, did not necessarily wait for anybody else to catch up, and therefore had exposed flanks. He calculated that you could do this and get away with it, providing you had information about what was coming into your flanks or elsewhere, so that you could redeploy quickly to meet the threat. Thus he emphasised the need for reconnaissance and he got it in the shape of armored cars, light tanks and good cooperation from the Luftwaffe with aircraft, which, incidentally, had very heavy casualties finding the information he wanted.

Regarding fire support, there is now a tendency to think that the Luftwaffe were the major elements of fire support for the panzer divisions. To a certain extent, of course, that was true but, on the other hand, one must not belittle the contribution made by the artillery. Deployed well forward, they made a considerable contribution, and Guderian's only major regret was that he could not persuade the gunners to do away with towed artillery. He wanted them, right from the start, to have self-propelled artillery with the gun pointing forwards. He always maintained that it was too much for the gunners, after 300 years of having them pointed back, to change overnight to having their guns pointed forwards. He made a lot of friends among the gunners by saying it.

When Hitler came to power in 1933 he began to see the embryo of panzer divisions and made enthusiastic remarks. Now Guderian in his book made great play of Hitler saying: "This is what I want and this is what I'm going to have!" Of course, Hitler did say it. No doubt Hitler was after something impressive to suit his political bluff with the military background. I do not think that at that time that Hitler, or a great many other people in the German Army, really understood Guderian's plans. I would suggest they did not begin to understand it until the end of the Polish campaign.

At any rate, Guderian was able to get the support he needed from within the army and from Hitler to develop panzer divisions ahead of everybody else. Whereas the British had an embryo in the first one in 1934, the

Germans had three proper panzer divisions, although admittedly without much equipment, in 1935; and they had developed the techniques of how to use them up to a point. That point, of course, expanded when they began to get involved in wars. Just as the Russians learned from the Spanish Civil War, so too did the Germans with the detachment they sent with the Condor Legion. They only had those little Mark I training tanks, useless in combat, so that there really was not a fair test. But the commander, a man called von Thoma, thought they were only useful supporting infantry, and furthermore that they did not need a radio in every tank. Of course that did not go down well with Guderian, who was trying to sell radios in every tank around the Ministry of Defense. That was not going to help his case. However, he still got what he wanted.

Rehearsals followed to see whether the panzer divisions could advance without breaking down over a long journey and arrive at the other end in fairly good condition with their logistical system working. The first rehearsal was in Austria, the second was in the Sudetanland, and the third the takeover of Czechoslovakia in the spring of 1939. As a result of those three experiences, without a shot being fired, the panzer divisions and the panzer corps (which had been formed but not under that name) managed to smooth out the wrinkles. They had the command and control system working quite well, they had the traffic under control (after solving a few problems), and the logistical system kept them supplied. They reached their various destinations in good order, and made an enormous impression.

That really was a turning-point as far as the panzer divisions were concerned, because during this period, when Guderian was pushing his line very hard, he was meeting fierce opposition in the higher echelons of command. The Commander-in-Chief, the Chief of Staff, and numerous other people were against him. They thought he was creating an army within the army. They saw in him a man of, at times, quite explosive temperament, as ambitious as they were and seeking to be commander-in-chief, which he could have been. Numerous attempts were made to sidetrack him, and in the end they did manage to sidetrack him just before the Polish campaign. He had enough influence, however, to come back and command a corps in Poland.

Let us now look at those two major campaigns that took place before the Russian campaign began. In Poland, the panzer corps and the panzer divisions were extremely short of tanks. There were only 2,800 tanks and the vast majority were only light tanks. Only a few were PZ-3 and PZ-4. Nevertheless, against an opposition which was immobile and which had very poor command and control they drove through. They completely outsmarted the Poles, they were far too fast for them, and, in fact, the Poles collapsed because of the sheer speed and momentum of the panzer divisions leading the marching army. That proved the point. Guderian was to say later that from the reception to the plan to go into France, one would have thought nothing had been learned from the advance into Poland. However, the lesson had been learned and when the issue was rammed home, it worked and he got what he wanted.

France was probably the most celebrated campaign in the world, because here was a victorious army by no means at full strength. After all, the German army went to war faster than was intended and without the equipment it should have had. Here was Germany, taking on France, the biggest, most powerful and most respected military power in western Europe, aided by Britain. France had many more tanks than the Germans, in many ways better tanks (certainly better armored), and the Germans took them on and defeated them. They defeated them, by going through fast, by engaging the enemy armor at a distinct disadvantage within the frontier, and then by going straight ahead, as Guderian wanted, certainly not waiting (although they tried to make him wait) and aiming straight for the English Channel.

Now let us look at the panzer technique. There was a tendency to say that tanks joined with the infantry assault and bored holes through, with artillery support. That was often true. Guderian's technique, however, as I have always understood it and other people have confirmed this to me, was not to force the tanks into a direct assault against antitank gun screens and artillery, and for a very good reason. With 30mm of armor you were going to be in trouble. The idea was to blast a hole through, and better still, by excellent reconnaissance to find that hole, push your armor through with some infantry, get on to vital ground, bring the infantry forward on to that vital ground, and place antitank guns there. If the enemy was then obliging enough to attack them at a disadvantage, they were shot at, while the tanks stood back and waited for the opportunity to do the next movement. This was the essence of how panzer divisions operated. Furthermore, it was done by these very effective battle groups, which could be tailored quickly and respond by radio control to the situation.

So by 1940 Guderian had produced a very powerful offensive weapon which could and did upset the whole military balance of thinking. Almost accidentally, certainly unexpectedly, he gave Hitler the feeling that he had a weapon which could help him conquer far more than was actually possible. It was as a result of that feeling that Hitler went into Russia in 1941.

The panzer division of 1941 was totally different from the one the Germans had in 1940. The tank element had been halved in order to double the number of panzer divisions. In May 1940 there were ten, while in June 1941 there were 19 available in Russia. There were also one and a half or two in North Africa. The infantry component had been increased to some extent, and equipment had certainly been improved. For example, they had nearly all medium tanks and only a few light tanks, primarily PZ-3 and PZ-4s. Transport had improved to some extent, but not much. The infantry, most of whom in 1940 had traveled in lorries, were now traveling more in half-tracked armored vehicles, but not enough. Although the composition of the panzer division going into 1941 was criticized, I do not think it was all that bad. It was very similar to those that most armies adopted and the British Army adopted later in the war.

Each panzer division had a tank regiment. Of the 19 regiments in the divisions, one per division, nine of them had three battalions of tanks, and 11 of them had two battalions of tanks. So a panzer division was between 150 and 200 tanks. The infantry regiments varied, in fact, things always varied in the German Army. There was no standard organization at all, largely because of the non-availability of the right kit, but for other reasons as well. Basically there were rifle brigades with two lorried infantry battalions and one motorcycle battalion; sometimes there would be what was called a mechanized battalion of infantry which rode in half-tracks. Similarly, antitank guns were tacked on to them. Sometimes they belonged to the regiment, sometimes they came from the outside. The interesting thing was that the German infantry at this time were getting a much more powerful antitank gun than the armor. The PZ-3 tanks still had the short 50mm gun while the infantry began to get the long 50mm gun. You will begin to realize the significance of this, because in addition to that long 50mm gun the infantry had the 88mm gun. But surprisingly, when the Germans came up against the Russian KV1 tank, none of those guns penetrated it and that became fundamental.

The artillery regiment had three artillery battalions of 105mm howitzers and 10cm guns. The 10cm guns were interesting. They developed later as a useful antitank weapon in various difficult conditions, when they could be fired over open sights, very often with no shield. Often they were the only guns that could cope with the KV1.

Now I want to discuss the layout of the Barbarossa attack. Army Group North went up north towards Leningrad and contained Panzer Group 4 under General Hoepner. Towards Minsk and Smolensk in Army Group Center there were two panzer groups, No. 3 under Hoth and No. 2 under Guderian. These groups made first for Minsk and then for Smolensk, where this study will terminate, although they later went well beyond. In Army Group South under von Rundstedt there was Panzer Group 1 under General von Kleist.

The details of how they were made up will come out much more clearly from the other contributions. But there was a lot of flexibility and considerable regrouping that continued all the time, very quickly and effectively. This was the beauty of the command and control system, which enabled them to conduct this operation. Sometimes, too, there were panzer groups consisting of panzer corps containing panzer divisions. These groups were virtually armies, but they were not called armies. They were often placed under armies and obviously the feeling here was "For goodness sake let's not lose our grip of them because if we lose them completely they will shoot on ahead and we will have lost command of them". In the central area, towards Smolensk, Panzer Groups 2 and 3 were under the control much of the time of an ordinary infantry army, Fourth Army under von Kluge. This would create friction, which you will hear about later on.

Finally, there were two or three critical factors that affected the operation of those panzer groups. First was the quality of intelligence available. It was rather poor in places, but rather good in others. For example, they had a much better idea in some sectors of where the Russians were and what they were. They had severe problems in understanding the terrain because the maps were of variable quality. Some of the German-made maps were very high quality, while the Russian maps were extremely misleading and almost blank in places. Thus there was no uniform coverage on maps and anything could happen.

Another major factor in intelligence was the incomplete knowledge of the awful state of the Russian roads. They were quite appalling, and furthermore, they went through difficult country. In the south, however, it was wide open steppe and there was a certain amount of easy movement. The farther north you go, the more you move into forested areas, and here the roads became absolutely vital because they were the only means of moving. When they began to break up it created logistical problems.

Let us now move to the logistical problems. The major method of logistical resupply was by rail to railhead and then by truck along the roads. The range of truck transport limited sustainment of the initial offensive. Without the railway being pushed forward at all, supplies could safely be moved forward by truck for about 300 miles, as far as Minsk. To go beyond that to Smolensk in strength, 500 miles, help would be required from the railways. But there were choke points on the railway, the first choke point being where the gauge changed from German to Russian, and I gather chaos reigned here. Therefore, more and more load was being put on road vehicles. But then the problem arose of how far those road vehicles, and the stores they held, would go. In fact, panzer divisions were stocked to move for four days without replenishment. They carried four days' petrol and ammunition to scale. It did not work out that way because as they ran into bad roads that four-day period became two days and things became more and more stressed. Then, as they moved into the forested areas, Russian soldiers, who had disappeared into the trees, started coming out behind and ambushing the columns. Thus a considerable number of logistical problems built up particularly in the northern and central sectors. It did not stop the Germans completely and there was no complete collapse. Nevertheless, things were not good and momentum was sometimes lost.

Finally, there was a question of tank maintenance, and general vehicle maintenance. A mechanized army must not break down. Up to this moment the Germans had managed quite nicely with a centralized system. That is, when a tank needed a major repair or even minor repairs, it would be taken back to Germany, reworked in workshops, or even in factories where they were built. This worked well if they were only operating over six weeks. Light repairs were done by workshops out on the ground and, of course, they needed covered accommodation. If covered accommodation had been burned down or was unavailable, that made life difficult and maintenance fell off.

This was exactly what happened. Gradually the centralized system failed because they could not get the vehicles back, owing to problems on road and rail. In any case, the workshop companies out in the field were not coping. Within the period under study that was not a very strong factor, although it was beginning to affect tank strengths. Later, however, that central organization seemed to have broken down (and in fact did break down in many ways), and therefore other problems occurred, resulting in the loss of vital tank forces.

Armored forces were the main spring of the German attack into Russia. The infantry followed and did marvelously. But it was the tank force upon which everything focused and just as the Russians had problems, so too did the Germans.

Plan Barbarossa

LIEUTENANT GENERAL GERD NIEPOLD (retired)

Introduced by Colonel Paul Adair

General Niepold, who started life as an infantry soldier and then went on
to the staff, spent this interesting period on higher staff. He later served as
a staff officer with the 12th Panzer Division, then as a staff officer at a
panzer corps, and finished the war as a teacher at the armored school.
During his time as the principal staff officer in 12th Panzer Division in
1944, he was concerned very much with operations trying to restore the
balance after the attack in June 1944. He wrote a very good book on the
collapse of Army Group Center.

Fortunately for us, to understand the story in 1941, General Niepold, as
a young staff officer was the ordnance officer, or personal staff officer to
General Paulus, then the *Oberquartiermeister I* at supreme headquarters.
As such he was responsible for planning in Barbarossa.

The Objectives of Operation Barbarossa and
Points of German Main Effort In 1941

I witnessed the first year of the Eastern Campaign in the *Oberkommando des
Heeres* (OKH – Army High Command). On 1 April 1941, in my first
assignment as a general staff officer, I was appointed aide de camp to
Major General Paulus, *Oberquartiermeister I* (Deputy Chief of the General
Staff for Operations) in the General Staff of the Army.

Up to 1939 five *Oberquartiermeister* were subordinate to the Chief of
Staff. They were the chiefs of the 12 divisions of the General Staff of the
Army. By 1941, their number had been reduced to three, plus the
Oberquartiermeister I, who was responsible for the logistics of the army.
The *Oberquartiermeister I* was permanent deputy of the then Chief of Staff,
General Halder, and at the same time his closest assistant and advisor,
mainly in command and control matters. Moreover, the *Oberquartier-
meister I* was frequently assigned special missions, such as traveling to
Groups of Armies, to allies or even to Field Marshal Rommel in Africa.

On 31 July 1940, Hitler, in front of the highest-ranking officers of the

Wehrmacht announced his decision, already considered for a long time, to eliminate the Soviet Union as quickly as possible. That operation was to begin in May 1941. He developed the basic lines of the operation which included, with equal priority, a thrust towards Kiev and attacks through the Baltic States and towards Moscow. A secondary operation towards Baku was to follow later (see Figure 34).

Consequently, Major General Marcks, Chief of Staff of Eighteenth Army, prepared an operational plan which, in accordance with Halder's directive, placed the main effort in the central sector of the offensive. Halder thought that the campaign would be won by seizing Moscow after several devastating blows against the Red Army. Thus, the Wehrmacht would have to advance towards that objective along the shortest possible route. According to Marck's plans the line Rostov–Gorki–Arkhangelsk was to be reached not later than 17 weeks after the seizure of Leningrad and the eastern Ukraine.

Early in September 1940 Lieutenant General Paulus took over the coordination of all planning for Operation Barbarossa. In the first days of December he conducted a map exercise with the chiefs of division of the General Staff and other officers. The planning for the first part of the campaign may be summarized briefly as follows:

- The Soviets will eventually try to occupy defensive positions along the line Dnieper-Berezina-Polotsk-Riga.
- On the German side, three Groups of Armies will be formed, one to the south and two to the north of the Pripet Marshes lying between them.
- The Southern Group of Armies will attack with its main effort from Poland in the direction of Kiev and will afterwards cut off enemy forces east of Kiev.
- The Central Group of Armies will aim at a large-scale battle of encirclement around Minsk; to this effect it will be provided with strong infantry forces and with the bulk of the mobile formations.
- The Northern Group of Armies will attack Leningrad through the Baltic states.

Rapid envelopment of the enemy forces and the seizure of Moscow could only be achieved if protection of the flanks of the rapidly advancing Central Group of Armies was the main task assigned to the Southern and Northern Groups of Armies. An attack against Leningrad depended upon the success of the offensive against Moscow. Thus, in the opinion of the General Staff, and in particular of its chief, the center of gravity of the entire campaign had to be placed on the quick seizure of Moscow. The view was held that the Soviet state would collapse totally once its capital and center of all railway and communication links was eliminated.

FIGURE 34
OPERATIONAL PLAN FOR BARBAROSSA

On 5 December Colonel General Halder presented the army concept of operations to Hitler. He stressed his view that a particularly strong thrust force would have to advance from the Warsaw area towards Moscow. The Southern Group of Armies was to advance towards Kiev and the Northern Group of Armies towards Leningrad. In spite of Moscow being the initial center of gravity, due to the funnel-shape topographic form of Western Russia the conduct of operations inevitably had to be eccentric.

On the whole, Hitler consented to the OKH concept of operations, but he already said that the Red Army would have to be defeated in several large-scale battles of encirclement. He left open the question of the thrust towards Moscow and also did not consider the overall strategic objective, the so-called A-A-line between Astrakhan and Arkhangelsk.

But what was remarkable about this conference on 5 December was Hitler's hint, and, in fact, his plan that the Central Group had to be so strong that the bulk of its forces could turn north in order to encircle the enemy forces in the Baltic Provinces, which, in Halder's opinion, was only a secondary operation. Hence, Halder's most important strategic idea, to make the seizure of Moscow the center of gravity of the entire Russian campaign, had become questionable. Thus, Hitler got lost in *operational* thoughts instead of determining a binding *strategy*.

Hitler's thoughts took clearer shape in the plan of Lieutenant Colonel, G.S. von Lossberg, which the OKW (High Command of the Armed Forces) presented in December 1940. In that plan, the center of gravity was maintained with the Central Group of Armies, but after the disruption of enemy forces in front of the Dnepr–Dvina line, mobile forces were to be diverted north to seize the coast of the Baltic Sea, Leningrad, and Kronstadt (Kronshtot) to ensure the supply of ore from Scandinavia. Only then was the operation to seize Moscow to be continued. Turning forces south towards the Ukraine and the Donets Basin in the second part of the campaign was also considered.

The roots of the conflict between Hitler and Halder about the further conduct of operations, which later became even more violent, had already begun at this point.

On 18 December 1940 the period of planning came to an end. Hitler issued his decisive Directive No. 21, which was based on the plan of the OKW and provided bindingly for the turn of strong mobile formations from the center to the north, once the enemy had been beaten in front of the Dnepr–Dvina line. It also became manifest that Hitler regarded the seizure of war-essential economic centers as the main objective of the campaign, whereas Halder considered this as a dissipation of forces which would then be lacking for the decisive thrust against Moscow.

In two big conferences with the highest-ranking officers of the

Wehrmacht on 9 January and 3 February 1941, Hitler, in a well-conceived sequence, named the most important missions as: "cutting off the Baltic area, annihilation of the Russian army, seizure of the most important industrial regions, and destruction of the other industrial areas". If the Red Army succeeded in withdrawing on a large scale, the Baltic Provinces and Leningrad would have to be taken with priority in order to gain the most favorable supply basis for subsequent operations. Then operations in the center of the front would have to be stopped in order to outmaneuver the enemy from the flanks. Of course the final, repeatedly revised version of the Army Initial Deployment Directive Barbarossa of 8 June 1941 had to follow the OKW Directive No. 21 of 21 December 1940: Moscow would be a later objective and would no longer be the crucial objective from the start.

The Eastern Campaign began in the early hours of 22 June 1941. How much time would it take? I can still recall exactly the following event. On 23 June 1941 Field Marshal von Brauchitsch entered the room of General Paulus at OKH headquarters in Angerburg, East Prussia. After Paulus's briefing on the course of operations on the first day, von Brauchitsch asked: "Well, Paulus, how long will the campaign be?" Paulus, after brief consideration, answered: "I think six to eight weeks, sir". Then von Brauchitsch replied: "Yes, Paulus, you may be right, we shall probably need six to eight weeks for finishing Russia".

The campaign took exactly four years minus six weeks. I would like to add that most of the general staffs in the West also thought that Russia would be defeated within ten weeks.

Already at the end of June and in early July the decision to continue the campaign had to be made, which Hitler called "perhaps the only crucial decision in this war at all".

On 13 July the differences in Hitler's and Halder's views again became apparent. Halder expected only an odd conglomerate of enemy resistance groups without any operational coherence in front of Leningrad and therefore wanted to advance south towards Kholm with the mobile troops deployed in the northern sector of the Central Group of Armies. Hitler intended a substantially stronger employment of forces against the Leningrad lines of communication.

While the operations division of the General Staff had already considered the first measures for the occupation of Russia and for the reduction of the German Army, the command and control directives to the Groups of Armies were already varying in accordance with tactical developments.

On 23 July Hitler once more emphasized his three objectives to the GHQ of the Army Command. They were the Leningrad area, the Moscow area, the Ukraine and the industrial and oil centers in the south.

He also expressed the view that after the battle for Smolensk Panzer-gruppen (Armored Groups) 2 and 3 of the Central Group of Armies would have to deploy to the right and left to support the Southern and Northern Groups of Armies. "The Central Group of Armies must advance towards Moscow with its infantry divisions", he said.

The OKH and the commanders of the Central Group of Armies made alternative proposals which, however, were only partially considered. Hitler repeatedly spoke against operating with long-range objectives, and pleaded instead for the destruction of minor pockets. Moreover, he came back to the concept of reinforcing the Southern and Northern Groups of Armies at the expense of the Central Group of Armies. Halder constantly tried to convince Hitler of the viability of his (Halder's) basic strategic concept to thrust against Moscow as long as the mobile formations were not too worn down, in order to eliminate the second front in the east completely. For, in Halder's opinion, this was, after all, the purpose of the entire Eastern campaign.

At the end of July the decision between an attack against Moscow and operations on the wings was postponed anew (see Figure 35). On 4 August 1941, one day before the end of the successful battle of encirclement of Smolensk, Hitler met Field Marshal von Bock, commander of the Central Group of Armies, and Generals Guderian and Hoth, commanders of Panzerguppen (Armor Groups) 2 and 3. All generals agreed among themselves and almost implored Hitler that the attack against Moscow was decisive and that it would be possible to start on 20 August after a short period of regeneration. (It would be interesting to examine the effects the enemy's threat against the two flanks would have had.)

Hitler and the OKH, in particular Halder, continued to exchange their views till 21 August, when Hitler wrote bluntly to the Commander-in-Chief of the Army: "The proposal of the Army does not meet my intentions. The most important objective, still to be reached before the beginning of winter, is not the seizure of Moscow but the occupation of the Crimea, of the industrial and coal region on the Donets, and the blocking of the Russian oil supply from the Caucasus Mountains, the isolation of Leningrad in the north, and joining forces with the Finns." General Guderian, again in a talk with Hitler, pleaded uncompromisingly but in vain for the attack against Moscow and against the thrust towards Kiev. Hitler answered: "My generals know nothing about the economic aspects of war". He issued the strict order to attack Kiev as the next strategic objective without delay, and subsequently, the attack began on 25 August. I still remember exactly the excitement in OKH caused by Hitler's decision.

On 13 September, only 13 days after Hitler had committed the already weakened armor formations to attack targets 600 km away in the south and

FIGURE 35
GERMAN OPERATIONAL PLAN, AUGUST 1941

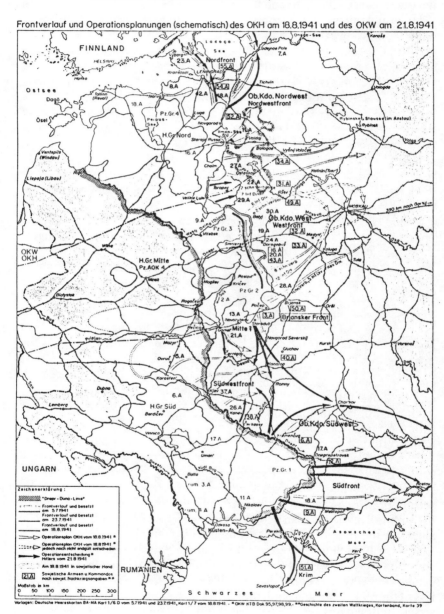

Frontverlauf und Operationsplanungen (schematisch) des OKH am 18.8.1941 und des OKW am 21.8.1941

in the north, targets which those formations had failed by far to reach, he declared that the war objective Leningrad had been reached and could thus be regarded as secondary.

Hitler did not want to seize Leningrad. Rather he wanted to starve it. It is hard to tell whether Field Marshal von Leeb, Commander of the Northern Group of Armies, and General Reinhardt, Commanding General of XXXXI Armeekorps (Army Corps) were right in saying: "The city lies in front of the German troops and nobody prevents them from entering it". In any case, the Northern Group of Armies had to detach three panzer divisions and two motorized divisions to the Central Group of Armies. At that moment, Hitler had practically taken over control of the operations from the OKH. However, his logic was incomprehensible.

On 10 September the OKH issued an order for the destruction of enemy forces east of the line Roslavl-Smolensk-Belyi and for a subsequent advance towards Moscow. The highest stake had to be risked by employing an army still possessing a large offensive capability, but only 34 per cent of its tanks. On 26 September the battle of Kiev ended in a victory. Then an attack along the entire front was ordered for 2 October. It must be remembered that the Central Group of Armies was forced to be inactive, just 320 km from Moscow, from the beginning of August until 2 October.

In the order of the day, Hitler declared that conditions had finally been created to deal the enemy a crushing blow before the beginning of winter. "This year's last big battle is beginning today." This, however, also implied that the Russian campaign would last longer. The attack against Moscow, codenamed Typhoon, had begun when it was already too late. Soon it was gradually halted by mud and frost. On 5 December 1941 the easternmost line in the war was reached in the center of the Eastern Front. German troops were 25 km north and 35 km west of Moscow and 90 km east of Tula. On 8 November the Northern Group of Armies seized Tikhwin, but had to abandon it on 8 December. Joining German forces with the Finns was not possible. The German troops had made superhuman efforts and the subsequent retreat was to be just as self-sacrificing.

Historians are right in saying that the Russian campaign was definitely lost already before German forces had reached Moscow. But, having served for two-and-a-half years on the front in Russia, I think that the seizure of Moscow would not have broken the Soviet resistance owing to the strength of the Russian people and the material support from Russia's allies. At the time the campaign would have continued.

It is hard to tell to what extent the permanent disputes between Hitler and the OKH, as well as the frequent changes of the objectives, of the center of gravity, and of the distribution of forces, have contributed to the loss of the 1941 campaign and, thus, to the loss of the entire war. The most serious mistake was that Hitler changed his strategy too often in order to react to the enemy's tactics.

Let me add a few words concerning Field Marshal Paulus. His state of health was not too good, which may have affected his initiative and his steadiness. But, in spite of it all, he was a master of the operational art.

I remember how, in the autumn of 1941, tasked by Halder, he drafted the plan for the 1942 campaign by just drawing a few lines on a map of Russia and adding a calculation of forces. To this he added a written comment: "In 1942 we can either reach the Volga or enter the Caucasus Mountains. Trying both means the destruction of one of the two groups of forces." Tragically his own prophecy was fulfilled at Stalingrad early in 1943 thanks to Hitler's leadership.

Going on from what was said before one could for a long time discuss the question: "When it comes to executing an agreed strategy, where must the line between politicians and soldiers be drawn?"

Questions

Question: A lot has been made about the delay in the beginning of the Russian campaign because of the diversion of forces into the Balkans. Could you comment on the significance of this?

General Niepold: If we had started the campaign into Russia six weeks earlier we would have been able to take advantage of better weather and better terrain conditions and could have had better results.

Professor von Luttichau: I cannot believe this was so. First of all, 15 May was a tentative date. At that time there had been considerable rain and the rivers were overflowing. There was no possibility at that time of attack. The second point is that the armored forces used in the Balkans were shipped only ten days before the attack. Consequently they were still in place in time. The third point is that the army headquarters used was a reserve headquarters not used initially in the attack on Russia.

General Niepold: I don't know what the weather was like in May 1941. But even if we assume that on 15 May the attack could not commence, there was still the possibility of postponing the attack for two days or two weeks. Even if the attack could have commenced at the end of May or during the first part of June, it would still have been a gain of time that would have enabled us to reach Moscow before the winter came. The German High Command was flexible enough to postpone the time gradually in a similar way as they did in 1940 in the attack in France.

German Colonel: We were company commanders in Yugoslavia and Greece. And we were constantly pushed forward to hurry up in order to be available for the campaign in Russia. Even the period for refreshing the troops after the Balkans campaign was reduced to make these forces available for the campaign in Russia.

Question: Can you address the question of the internal makeup of the panzer divisions and the degree to which they were dependent on French equipment, and that there were more then 2,000 types of vehicles in the East. Second, we should clarify the structure of the German infantry divisions because there was a very clear organization as to which division would have two or three regiments, and so forth. This was not mass confusion on the part of the infantry divisions.

Answer: The German panzer divisions were organized in only one way, according to their establishment. After the campaign in France, we converted approximately ten motorized divisions into panzer divisions. The original panzer divisions were more experienced than the new divisions.

Regarding infantry, already during the campaign in France there were several types of division. That is to say, the first organization was in place. The second and third organizations were of lower quality while the fourth group were considered to be good divisions. All the four organizations could be rated as sufficient. By the end of the French campaign and in the Russian operations the quality of the infantry divisions became lower and lower.

Question: Can you comment on the morale of the German soldier as opposed to the morale of the Soviet soldier and how that morale changed in the first eight months?

General Niepold: Morale qualities did influence the campaign. Normally and basically there was no difference between Soviet and German soldiers. But you must consider that the German soldiers, by the time they advanced into Russia, did have experience and did have the experience of successful campaigns in the West. This gave them great confidence and a good quality of soldiering. On the other hand, the Soviet soldier was a fierce fighter who had experienced defeat after defeat, which lowered his morale. So that on the whole, morale was higher on the German side and did influence the campaign.

This is one of the very important tasks of soldiers today. Their training and equipment must be excellent so that they can have this feeling of superiority.

Question: Earlier Dr Kipp mentioned a comparison process on the Soviet side. The Russians were equating one German division to one Russian division but then Stalin said let's not pay attention to this, since this does not really reflect reality. In the planning process for Operation Barbarossa, when the German staff officers were working on what would happen if the invasion was initiated, what kind of assumptions were being made regarding the equivalency of German infantry and panzer divisions to Soviet formations?

General Niepold: I did not take part in the first planning period and war games and operational conferences. However, the development and the thought that Russia would be defeated within eight weeks led me to the conclusion that the German operational or supreme command was convinced of German superiority concerning operational command and control of men and equipment and of the quality of the troops.

General Thilo: I belonged to the operational division of the Supreme Command of the Army and two days after the beginning of Barbarossa, we were clearly told not to underestimate the enemy because he fought excellently.

General Niepold: Even the American General Staff assumed that Russia would be defeated within ten weeks.

General Thilo: There were eight panzer divisions deployed from the Balkans (the 2nd, 5th, 8th, 9th, 10th, 11th, 14th, 16th), also the infantry regiment Grossdeutschland and the 1st and 2nd SS Divisions. Of all these, only the 2nd and 5th Divisions belonged to the reserve of the supreme command of the army. So, in other words, there were at least eight divisions which had to be refreshed and regenerated ready for the Russian campaign.

Question: Earlier in the war the German Army used paratroops and airborne troops, for instance, at Rotterdam and Crete. I wonder if there was planning in Operation Barbarossa for a combined operation of armored troops and paratroops and airborne troops?

General Thilo: There was only one airborne division and it engaged in only three smaller tactical encounters but not in real operational missions.

Colonel Ritgen: In my opinion the basic reason for not using paratroopers in the first part of the Russian campaign was that they had sustained such heavy losses in Crete and had not been regenerated by the beginning of Barbarossa.

Question: A question must be asked about the potential effect of an earlier beginning for Barbarossa. Whether the difference made by the Balkans campaign was six weeks or four weeks or even three weeks, what was the significance of the extra time? Perhaps it would have been the capture of Moscow. But our speaker has already said that in his opinion the capture of Moscow would not have caused the collapse of the Soviet state.

General Niepold: I think it would have been possible to capture Moscow if we had started six weeks earlier. But having become acquainted with the Russian soldiers and with the Russian people, and having considered the fact that the Russians had already removed their industry and their resources far eastward, in addition to the vast American support, I believe that the Russians would never have given up.

2

The Border Battles on the Siauliai Axis
22–26 June 1941

Overview

COLONEL D. M. GLANTZ

Let us now begin examining the operations that took place during the opening days of war in late June and July 1941. I will present an overview of operations focusing principally on Soviet actions during the first week of war in all sectors of the Eastern Front. In addition, I will provide considerable detail from the German side concerning what the Soviets call the *pogranichnaia srazheniia* (the border battles) of 1941. Those battles resulted when German forces, early on the morning of 22 June, began Operation Barbarossa. We are going to look at the developing border battles from north to south, keying on the operations of the four German Panzer groups and also on the actions or lack of actions, of the twenty Soviet mechanized corps deployed in the border military districts.

We will first look at action in the Baltic Military District, along what I call the Siauliai axis, which principally involved the operations of German Army Group North and the corresponding actions of Soviet 12th Mechanized Corps and one tank division out of 3rd Mechanized Corps. Subsequently, we will look at operations along the Vilnius axis, essentially involving operations by the remainder of Soviet 3rd Mechanized Corps. These two cases correspond to the operations of German Panzer Groups 4 and 3. We will then look at the very complicated battle which occurred north of Bialystok, along the southern flank of Panzer Group 3, and the battles which took place near Brest, south of Bialystok, in the sector of advance of Panzer Group 2. Here we will look at the immediate reaction of four Soviet mechanized corps and the subsequent reaction of two mechanized corps deploying forward from the interior of the military district. Last, we will look at the most extensive and successful Soviet mechanized operations, realizing that successful is a relative term, those against Panzer Group 1 which advanced along the Lutsk-Rovno axis. This involved operations by initially three, and subsequently three more Soviet mechanized corps.

In this overview I will focus principally on Soviet actions. I will, however, mention, in general terms, the German order of battle just to provide a context for my description. As a matter of course, I will begin with an intelligence assessment: a picture of what German intelligence saw on the eve of 22 June. I will then look at Soviet organization for combat along each axis. Finally, I will track through the developing operations day by day by employing German archival operational records depicting the situation on the evening of each day and then by looking at summary maps which reflect the daily progress of both Soviet and German forces.

Figure 36 shows the overall German intelligence map revealing Soviet dispositions opposite Army Group North (*Heeresgruppe Nord*). Notice the locations and nomenclature of Soviet divisions as German intelligence detected them before 22 June. It shows the Soviet divisional numbers (125 for example) and, in the case of divisions that the Germans had not been able to identity, it shows the number 1 plus a questionmark. It also identifies a Soviet army headquarters (the 8th) and a corps headquarters (the 16th). Some Soviet divisions are shown in the depths and, interestingly enough, two Soviet tank divisions, the 2nd and 5th, are identified. This was an unusual phenomenon, for German intelligence did not, as a matter of course, detect most of the Soviet mechanized and armored units in the border military districts.

I reduced and simplified the German archival map into the clearer Figure 37. German intelligence determined that the approaches into the Baltic Military District were defended by two Soviet armies, the 8th and the 11th. German intelligence, however, failed to detect the rifle corps within those armies, but did determine the identity of the rifle divisions deployed along the border and in the depth. They also detected Soviet armored units, including three tank brigades near Salantai, and a tank division located at Kedenai.

Let us now compare the German assessment with actual Soviet dispositions on 21 June 1941 (See Figure 38). Soviet forces covering the border in the Baltic Military District included Major General P.P. Sobennikov's 8th Army, which in turn was subdivided into Major General I.F. Nikolaev's 10th Rifle Corps, and Major-General M.M. Ivanov's 11th Rifle Corps. Each of the rifle corps contained rifle divisions; the 10th Rifle Corps with the 10th and 90th Rifle Divisions and the 11th Rifle Corps with the 125th and 48th Rifle Divisions. To the south was deployed Major-General V.I. Morozov's 11th Army.

The chief mobile force available in the northern sector of Colonel

FIGURE 36
GERMAN INTELLIGENCE ASSESSMENT (ORIGINAL)

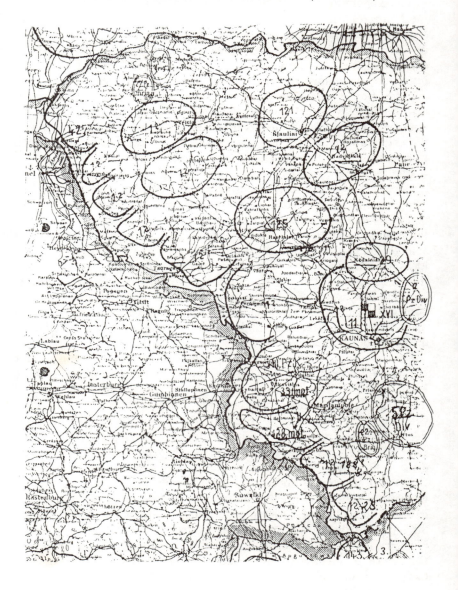

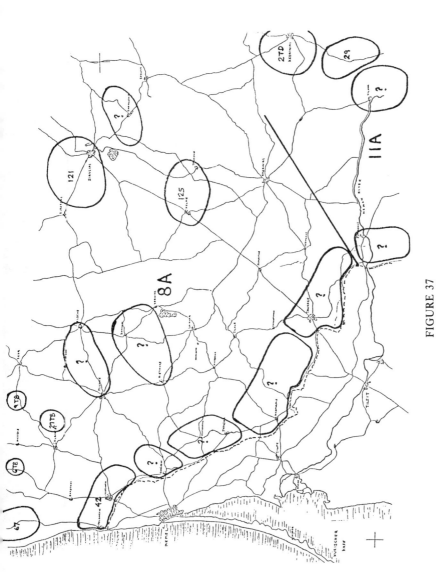

FIGURE 37
GERMAN INTELLIGENCE ASSESSMENT (SIMPLIFIED)

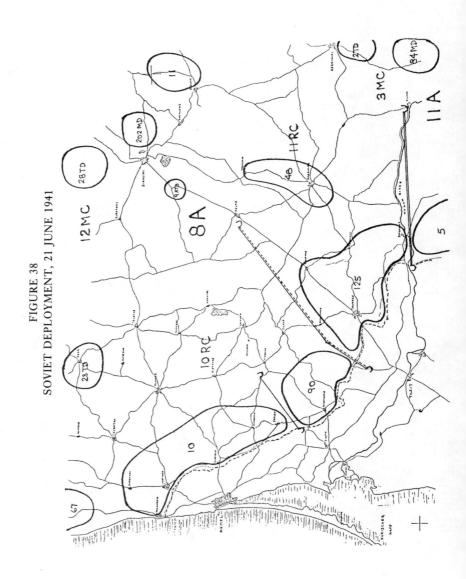

FIGURE 38
SOVIET DEPLOYMENT, 21 JUNE 1941

General F.I. Kuznetsov's Baltic Military District was the 12th Mechanized Corps. Major General N.M. Shestapolov's 12th Mechanized Corps consisted of the 23rd and 28th Tank Divisions and the 202nd Motorized Division. As the map shows, these units were somewhat spread out throughout the depth of the military district.

Whereas German intelligence had determined that upwards of nine Soviet rifle divisions were deployed in the Baltic Military District, in fact, there were roughly half that number present on 22 June. This intelligence gap will be further discussed when we look at the second case study along the Vilnius axis. In general terms, German intelligence did not pick up the existence of 12th Mechanized Corps' two tank divisions. They did, however, detect existence of the 3rd Mechanized Corps' 2nd and 5th Tank Divisions located further south. The explanation for this dichotomy is fairly simple. German intelligence collection out of the city of Kaunas (Kovno) was quite efficient since the Soviets had recently occupied the area, the population was friendly to the Germans, and a German intelligence station was in the area. Hence, the Soviet mechanized units in that region were fairly easily identified, whereas in most other regions they were not. Many of these mechanized corps had been formed between February and May 1941 on the basis of existing cavalry divisions and tank brigades. It is very likely that the tank and cavalry brigades noted on German intelligence maps were, in fact, the base units from which those tank divisions had been created.

Figure 39 shows both German and Soviet deployments on the eve of the attack. German forces consisted of Eighteenth Army, organized into the XXVI and XXXVIII Army Corps, the XXXXI and LVI Motorized Corps, and elements of X Army Corps, as well as Panzer Group 4, which would spearhead the operation through the Baltic region toward Leningrad. The most significant units from the standpoint of mobile operations were 1st, 6th, and 8th Panzer Divisions followed up by the 36th and 3rd Motorized Divisions. Except to indicate where they went, I will not describe the operations of these units, leaving the details to the German veterans from those units.

First, a few words about Soviet force strength and deployment. The rifle divisions of the Baltic Military District averaged roughly 8,700 men each, when mobilized. In other words, they began operations in June at about 60 per cent strength. Most of the divisions had their full complement of artillery, but the majority were short of trucks; most of those trucks and vehicles had been used to create mechanized corps and for other purposes. The general deployment of rifle forces was in single echelon configuration. The two rifle corps, 10th and 11th, were positioned side by side. The 10th Rifle Corps had its two divisions deployed forward, although the bulk of the troops of those divisions were in lagers, or camps, on the morning of

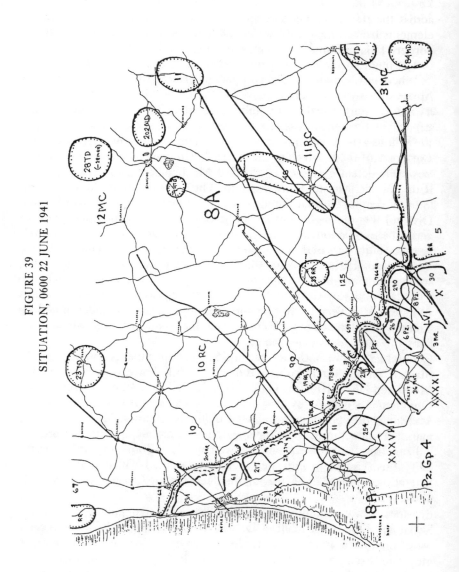

FIGURE 39
SITUATION, 0600 22 JUNE 1941

22 June. The 10th Rifle Division had all its regiments in camps on line across the front at a depth of about 10 to 15 kilometers, with scattered elements from company to battalion strength actually deployed along the border. This amounted to roughly an 80-kilometer front for the division.

The main Soviet defenses along the border were manned by ten border guards detachments, whose positions ran the entire length of the border. Apparently there were no *ukreplennyi rayon* (fortified regions) present. These were distinct combat fortifications units of roughly division strength deployed in most of the border military districts. The 90th and 125th Rifle Divisions deployed with elements of two regiments forward and one regiment well to the rear. On the night of 21–22 June, several hours before the German attack, General Sobennikov ordered his 11th Rifle Corps commander to move the 48th Rifle Division, which had been located north of Siauliai, southward into positions behind the 125th Rifle Division. That movement was in progress at the time of the German attack and the 48th Division was spread out along the road, with its lead elements near Raseinai and its rear elements somewhere north of Siauliai. There was one additional rifle division, the 11th, located in reserve positions southeast of Siauliai.

Let me add a few words about the 12th Mechanized Corps, to remind you of the resulting balance of forces in terms of armor (see Figure 40). Colonel T. S. Olonek's 23rd Tank Division, deployed near Seda, had 300 light and medium tanks, most of which were T26 with some BT models. Colonel I. D. Cherniakhovsky's 28th Tank Division, located just north of Siauliai, also had about 300 light and medium tanks. The 202nd Motorized Division of Colonel V. K. Gorbachev (no relation to the current Gorbachev) was much weaker, with only about 90 light tanks. Thus 12th Mechanized Corps, which was viewed by both the *front* and army commanders as the principal *front* counterattack force, totally lacked KVs and T34 tanks.

The 3rd Mechanized Corps, headquartered further south near Kaunas, had its attention split in two directions, looking westward toward Raseinai and southward toward Alytus on the Neman River. It had two tank divisions and a motorized division as well. Major General E. N. Soliankin's 2nd Tank Division was located at Kedenai. It was a relatively powerful force with 55 T34s and KVs, roughly a battalion of each, and 145 older tanks. Major General P. I. Fomenko's 84th Motorized Division, also located near Kedenai, was equipped with roughly 60 older light and medium tanks. These were the forces which would actually confront the German divisions advancing along the Leningrad axis. Even this representation does not provide an adequate view of the dispersion of Soviet forces. The 28th Tank Division, for example, had its two tank regiments north of Siauliai, but its motorized rifle regiment was over 100

FIGURE 40

ARMORED CORRELATION OF FORCES: NORTHWESTERN FRONT, BALTIC MILITARY DISTRICT

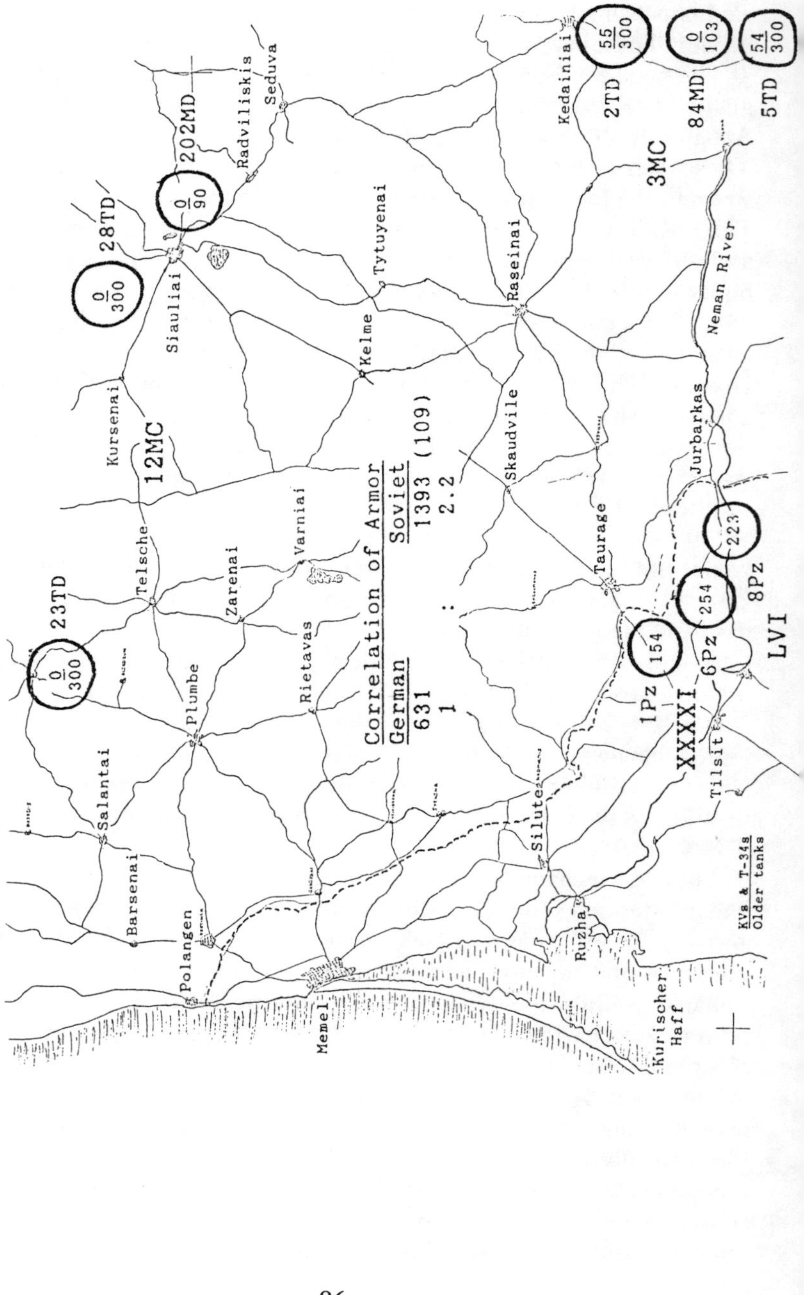

Correlation of Armor

German	Soviet
631	1393 (109)
1	:	2.2

KVs & T-34s
Older tanks

kilometers to the north at Riga and did not participate in the initial battles. Thus, that division went into combat almost tank pure.

The German attack began early on 22 June. Figure 41 shows a German situation map from Army Group North records that summarized action on the first day of combat, a very chaotic day from the Soviet standpoint. The map eloquently portrays the extraordinary speed and depth of the initial German advance. By the end of the first day of combat, the Germans had correctly identified the 90th and 125th Rifle Divisions, which by the end of the day had already been smashed by the initial attack. The Germans certainly identified growing Soviet armor concentrations, including that of the 23rd Tank Division moving into assembly areas near Plumbe. The Germans also detected the forward movement of Soviet armor in the Kursenai area, which probably involved lead elements of the 28th Tank Division and the antitank brigade stationed at Siauliai, and also the advance of Soviet armor towards Raseinai. These latter units were probably light tanks out of the rifle divisions because the 2nd Tank Division, which ultimately moved to Raseinai, did not begin its march until very late in the day.

There was very rapid German forward progress, in particular by the armored elements. Lead elements of 8th Panzer Division were already disappearing off the map by the end of the first day of the offensive. You can clearly see 1st and 6th Panzer Divisions beginning their dash northward to Raseinai. The next map (Figure 42) shows both the Soviet and the German movements, and again, I will focus principally on Soviet movements. There was a considerable amount of confusion in the Northwestern Front (former Baltic Military District) headquarters after the attack began. This confusion reigned throughout the Soviet Union and in all border military districts. Generally the confusion could be characterized first, by disbelief; and second, by conflicting reports from the border areas; and finally, by conflicting orders from higher headquarters. Along the border, units suffered heavy initial losses and issued desperate cries for help, while confusion reigned at army and *front* level as commanders sought in vain to obtain guidance from Moscow. Generally the guidance from Moscow at this stage was to "do nothing, and do not provoke the Germans". By late evening, the "do not provoke" orders changed into orders "to launch counterattacks and expel the Germans". Of course, at this point, the orders to launch counterattacks were virtually futile as we shall see.

Late on 22 June, Kuznetsov ordered Sobennikov to move his 12th Mechanized Corps forward. That movement began late on 22 June. You can see on the map the planned movements of Olonek's 23rd Tank Division and Cherniakhovsky's 28th Tank Division. Given the logistical state of those divisions, it was indeed miraculous that they were able to

FIGURE 41
ARMY GROUP NORTH SITUATION MAP:
EVENING, 22 JUNE 1941

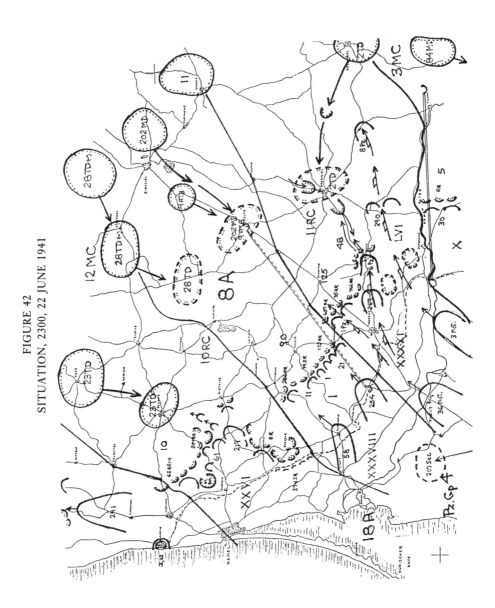

FIGURE 42

SITUATION, 2300, 22 JUNE 1941

move at all. But, in fact, they did hit the road. The general plan was to move those two divisions southward into concentration areas southwest and southeast of Telsche in order to strike at the left flank of advancing German forces. The distances involved in 28th Tank Division's movement from its initial assembly area north of Siauliai to its ultimate assembly area was roughly 70 kilometers. The movement distance of 23rd Tank Division was somewhat less (about 50 km).

At the same time, late on 22 June Kuznetsov ordered the 3rd Mechanized Corps commander to move his 2nd Tank Division westward toward Skaudville by way of Raseinai to participate in what they hoped would be a joint attack against the flanks of the German advance, which seemed to be along the Taurage-Kelme-Siauliai axis. Those Soviet armored movements began early on 23 June, although in general terms the armored forces deployed forward in piecemeal fashion. A major problem for the moving Soviet forces was total dominance of the air by the Germans. This not only made armored movement very hazardous and costly, it quite often drove Soviet armored units off the road and hence, the many stories which later circulated about divisions driving into swamps and bogs. The most severe impact however, was on logistics, because the soft-skinned ammunition and fuel vehicles simply could not make it forward with the mechanized corps through the gauntlet of fire. Most mechanized corps that went into action did so with only one day's worth of ammunition, if that, and with one day's supply of fuel. Thereafter, the tanks became stationary pill boxes.

Now let us track the action as it developed. A German intelligence map from 23 June (Figure 43) demonstrates that the intelligence picture was beginning to clear. If we analyse these German intelligence records carefully over a period of eight or nine days, they basically confirm what the Soviets have said concerning the units deployed into the region and the subsequent fate of these units. On the maps 12th Mechanized Corps is labeled as one unidentified panzer corps (see Figure 43). New numerical designations also emerge for Soviet rifle divisions. These designations accorded well with reality. Late on 23 June, German intelligence began detecting the growing Soviet armored concentrations. By then the Germans had fully identified the remnants of those Soviet divisions which had defended along the border and which had suffered such heavy casualties early in the operation.

Late on 23 June the Soviet armored counterattacks began to materialize (see Figure 44). The 9th Antitank Brigade and the 202nd Motorized Division were ordered to hold German forces at Kelme, and the 2nd Tank Division began its march toward Raseinai. Simultaneously, the 23rd Tank Division began its movement southward. While on the move it collided with advancing elements of the German 61st and 217th Infantry Divisions

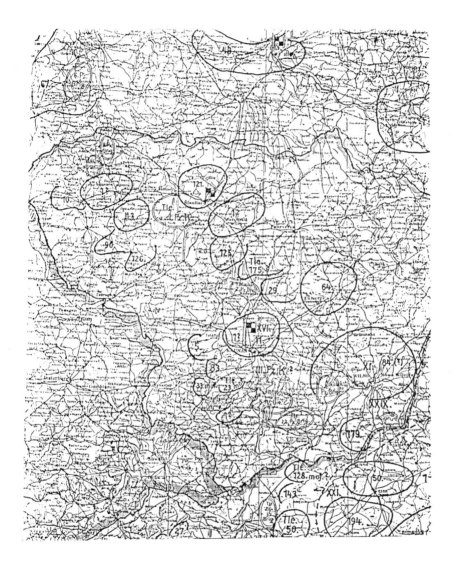

FIGURE 43
GERMAN INTELLIGENCE MAP, 23 JUNE 1941

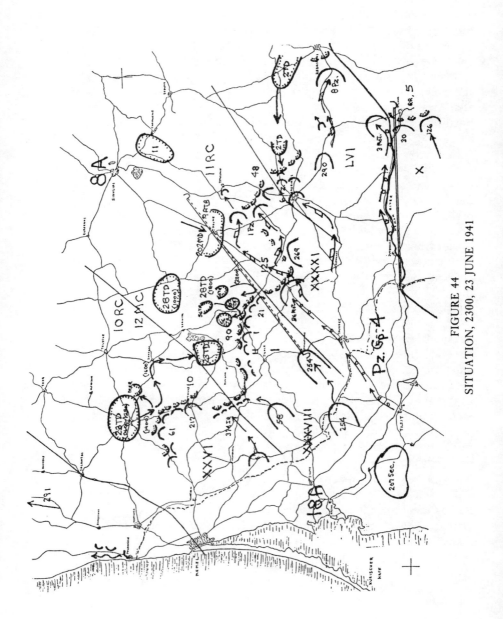

FIGURE 44
SITUATION, 2300, 23 JUNE 1941

and in the ensuing battle its motorized rifle regiment was cut off from the division's tank regiments. While the motorized rifle regiment withdrew to the north, the two tank regiments changed their course and continued moving south to try to join forces with the 28th Tank Division. Late in the day at roughly 1800 hours, 28th Tank Division's two tank regiments finally reached assembly areas west of Kelme. At 2200 they launched an attack against elements of the German 21st and 1st Infantry Divisions, but the attack was repulsed by about 0100. Out of the 300 tanks in each of those Soviet tank divisions, probably less than 100 actually made it to the battlefield.

Figure 45 is a blow-up map of the developing action on the night of 23 June. The bitterest fighting took place between lead elements of 6th Panzer Division and the forward deploying Soviet 2nd Tank Division's 2nd Motorized Rifle Regiment. A subsequent German intelligence map prepared on 24 June clearly shows where the severest fighting was occurring, in the area east of Laikuva, where the Germans identified a Soviet panzer brigade attacking, which was, in fact, the 28th Tank Division, and near Raseinai, where Soviet 2nd Tank Division elements, and a possible 5th Tank Division were identified, the latter erroneously. At the time the 5th Tank Division was actually operating further south, attacking German forces near Alytus.

Figure 46 outlines the course of battle on 24 June, when there were heavy attacks by Soviet 2nd Tank Division's newly assembled units at Raseinai. These attacks drove back lead elements of 6th Panzer Division and threatened them with destruction. The Soviets used some of their new medium and heavy tanks but in a rather interesting fashion. The remnants of the 48th Rifle Division, which earlier had been smashed in a meeting engagement west of Raseinai, provided, or at least tried to provide, flank security for the 2nd Tank Division. As the map shows, 2nd Tank Division needed the flank security because the Germans were attempting to envelop the Soviet concentration at Raseinai with 1st Panzer Division, and later, 36th Motorized Division.

Further to the northwest, the Soviet 28th Tank Division sat immobile throughout the entire day because of a lack of fuel. Its two tank regiments were unable to join the armored units of 23rd Tank Division, which did, in fact, launch small probing attacks to the west. There was a great deal of poor coordination on the Soviet side during this stage of the operation. The 23rd and 28th Tank Divisions never had direct contact with one another and the orders they received were conflicting. Late in the day, while 28th Tank Division was ordered to hold fast and attack the following day once it had received fuel, the 23rd Tank Division received orders to withdraw and begin a retrograde operation back to the Siauliai area. The map shows that at this time the remnants of the forward deployed Soviet

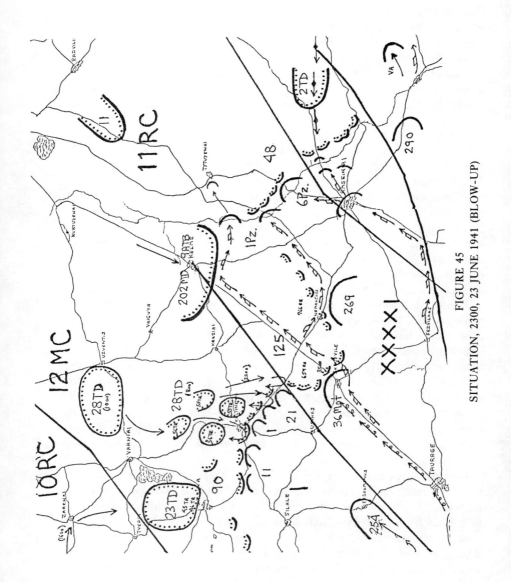

FIGURE 45

SITUATION, 2300, 23 JUNE 1941 (BLOW-UP)

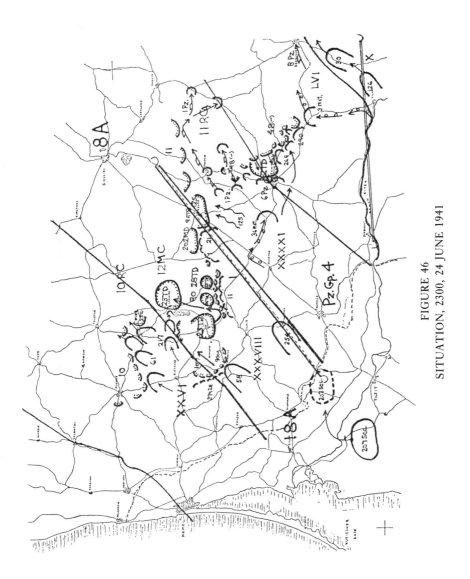

FIGURE 46

SITUATION, 2300, 24 JUNE 1941

95

rifle divisions, now organized in small groups, just clung to defensive positions along the flanks of the Soviet mechanized forces.

June 25 was the climactic day in terms of armored fighting on the Siauliai axis during this initial stage of war (see Figure 47). On this German situation map you can see the northward withdrawal of the Soviet 23rd and 28th Tank Divisions; the encirclement of 2nd Tank Division, and the German recognition that 2nd Tank Division had, in fact, been formed from the 5th Cavalry Division. (Both names are used on the German intelligence map.)

Now let us look at the actual situation map (Figure 48). On 25 June the 28th Tank Division initially launched fairly heavy attacks on German positions with its remaining light tanks, but by late in the day it had been enveloped by the German 11th and 58th Infantry Divisions. Consequently, the army commander, Sobennikov, ordered Shestopalov to withdraw the remnants of his mechanized corps. The orders went out to both the 23rd and the 28th Tank Divisions, which began a slow retreat northward towards Siauliai, there to join with Soviet forces that had erected a rather fragile defense line just south of the city. The Soviet 2nd Tank Division was less fortunate. After its initial success against lead elements of 6th Panzer Division and heavy fighting throughout the day, by nightfall the division ran out of fuel and ammunition. The tanks became pill boxes and, at the same time, 1st Panzer and 36th Motorized Divisions enveloped the ill-fated division. Eventually the division was destroyed and its commander killed in the operation.

The last day of combat under observation, 26 June, marked the general withdrawal of Soviet mechanized forces, a withdrawal that ultimately extended all the way to the Western Dvina River (see Figure 49). We can also observe the final destruction of Soviet 2nd Tank Division and the very rapid subsequent advance of 1st Panzer and 6th Panzer Divisions which left that unfortunate Soviet division behind as a mass of tanks, now converted into pill boxes which German sappers would have to destroy in a long and arduous process.

What was the cost of these border battles to the Soviets in the Baltic Military District? 12th Mechanized Corps went into combat on 22 June with a paper strength of about 690 tanks. By 29 June the corps' tank strength was down to 50, or 10 per cent. About half these losses were caused by mechanical faults, probably sustained during the approach march to the battlefield. The remainder were destroyed in combat. Most of those combat losses, in particular those of the 23rd and 28th Tank Divisions, occurred because they simply ran out of fuel and ammunition. Cherniakhovsky's 28th Tank Division decreased from 220 to 22 tanks. It is interesting to note that examination of the experiences of all of these mechanized corps, not just those in the Baltic Military District, reveals

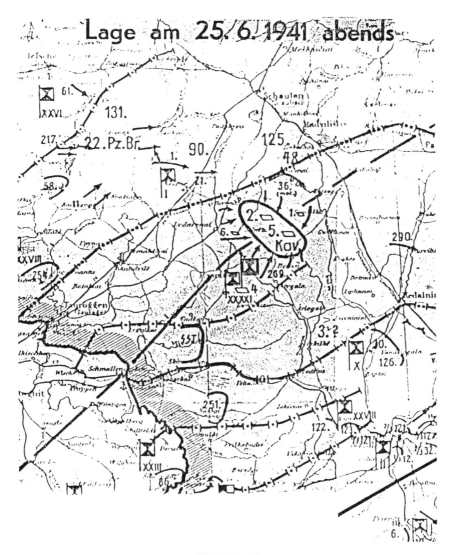

FIGURE 47
GERMAN SITUATION MAP: EVENING, 25 JUNE 1941

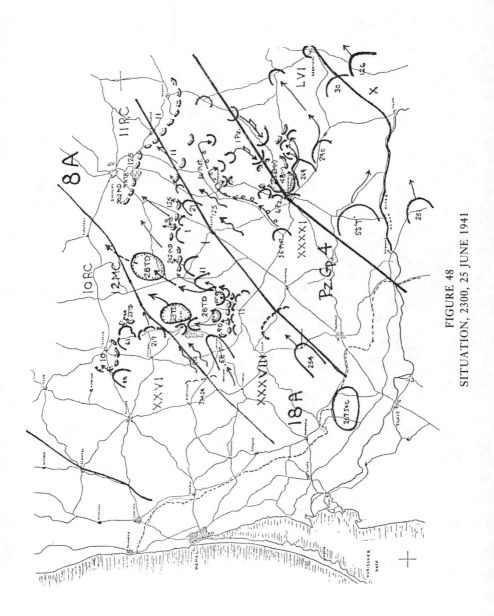

FIGURE 48
SITUATION, 2300, 25 JUNE 1941

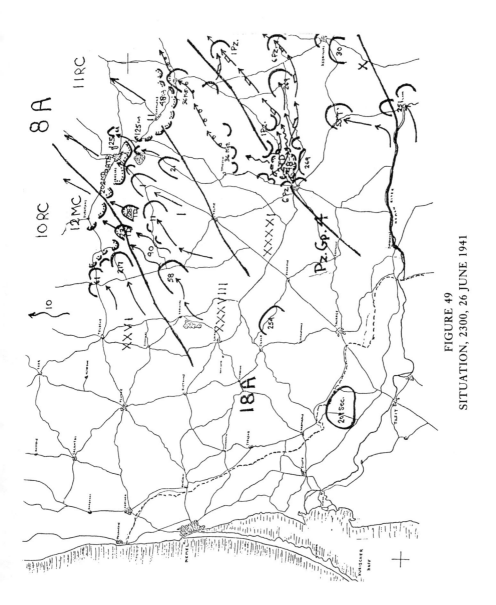

FIGURE 49

SITUATION, 2300, 26 JUNE 1941

99

that virtually every corps lost about 90 per cent of its strength in a period of from four to seven days.

The fate of the commanders typify the situation. The 90th Rifle Division commander, Colonel Golubev, died on 22 June during the initial attack. The 67th Rifle Division commander, Colonel Dedaev, died on 27 June. The 12th Mechanized Corps commander, General Shestopalov, was wounded on 27 June and died on 6 August. The 202nd Motorized Division commander, Colonel Gorbachev, died on 18 August of wounds inflicted in the initial fighting. However, not all of the key personalities taking part in the border battles disappeared from the scene. Many were to surface in later operations. General Sobennikov, the 8th Army commander, survived to become, later in the war, the deputy commander of several armies, including 3rd Guards Army. The 10th Rifle Corps commander, General Nikolaev, later became commander of a number of armies, among them 42nd and 70th. Colonel Cherniakhovsky of 28th Tank Division, was the same Cherniakhovsky who was later to command 3rd Belorussian Front. And last, but not least, Colonel Rotmistrov, Chief of Staff of 3rd Mechanized Corps, was to rise to 5th Guards Tank Army command later in the war. There would be more battles for some but, of course, the losses overall were quite catastrophic.

German Operations in the Baltic Region: The Siauliai Axis

GENERAL GRAF VON KIELMANSEGG (retired)
and
COLONEL HELMUT RITGEN (retired)

Introduced by Colonel Paul Adair

We now learn the German side of this operation. The first unit we will consider is the left flank corps, XXXXI Panzer Corps, of General Hoepner's 4th Panzer Group, and we begin with the right flank division of that corps, which was 6th Panzer Division. It is presented by General Graf von Kielmansegg, the senior general staff officer of the division. Shortly afterwards he went to the operations staff of the Army headquarters, OKH, remaining there until after 20 July, when he was sent back to command an APC regiment in the 11th Panzer Division. After the war he was one of the officers instrumental in forming the Bundeswehr. He finished his distinguished military career as CINCCENT.

To assist him in the presentation of 6th Panzer Division operations is another officer, Colonel Helmut Ritgen who, at this time was adjutant in a battalion of the panzer regiment of 6th Panzer Division. He ended the war commanding a battalion in Panzer Lehr Division and fought extensively on the Western front. After the war, he took part in the Bundeswehr and did much of his service in Washington, and later he was on the staff looking at the options for the main battle tank.

Overview of 6th Panzer Division Operations

General Graf von Kielmansegg

I will start with a broad survey of the mission of the panzer and army groups. Before the start of the offensive, we really did not know too much about the enemy (see Figure 50). Intelligence, and we have already seen the comparisons of intelligence, was much worse than in the Polish and French campaigns. Intelligence was completely incorrect, even down to the details on the maps we had. These were Russian maps and they were deliberately wrong and misleading. We knew, however, or at least believed, that the Soviet border forces were not too strong in contrast to the Soviet forces in front of our Army Groups Center and South. The

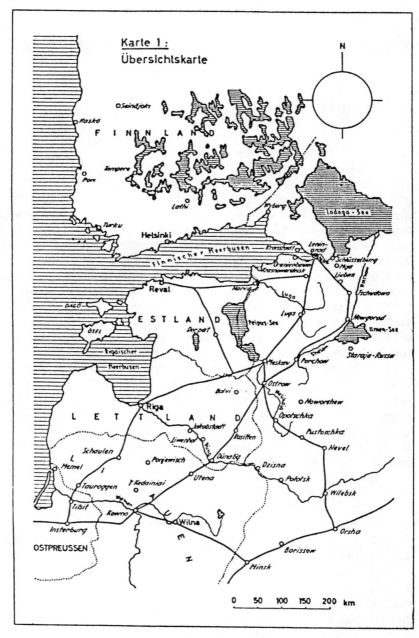

FIGURE 50
AREA OF OPERATIONS, BALTIC REGION

enemy forces in the northern sector were very deeply deployed in between the new border of the Soviet Union and the old Russian border with the Baltic states. That meant the line Narva–Lake Piepus. More or less parallel to this line ran the so-called Stalin Line.

This poor picture of the enemy that we had in the Northern Army Group was the main reason why the army group planned a very quick breakthrough and subsequent deep penetration in the form of a wedge (a *kiel* in German) in the middle of the sector (see Figure 51). And it was a very different plan from that of the other army groups, as you will see. The spearhead, Panzer Group 4, would advance ahead, with 16th and 18th Armies following on the right and left to protect the flanks of the panzer group. It is interesting to note that the first order to the army group already gave, as a final objective, Leningrad, 800 kilometers distant. This was in the first order issued before the start of the war. The first objectives were bridgeheads over the Dvina River 300 kilometers away, and the second objective was the line Narva–Lake Piepus, 550 kilometers away. A motto was given to us, not just in the form of an order, but it was hammered into the minds of all soldiers of the panzer group from private to general. This motto was "Surprise and then forward, forward, forward".

6th Panzer Division was within Panzer Group 4, commanded by General Hoepner, who had been divisional commander of our division since 1938. Later on, as you may know, Hitler dismissed and degraded him in front of Moscow because he had not followed the Führer's orders exactly. Hoepner was executed in August 1944. Panzer Group 4 consisted of two panzer corps (see Figure 52). We, of 6th Panzer Division, were in XXXXI Panzer Corps, commanded by General Reinhardt. The corps consisted of 1st and 6th Panzer Divisions, 36th Motorized Infantry Division, and the 269th Infantry Division. Its mission was to break through the border positions north of Tilset and to reach the Duna [Dvina] River between Dunaberg and Jacobstadt. The second corps of Panzer Group 4 was the LVI Panzer Corps, commanded by General von Manstein. The corps consisted of 8th Panzer Division, 3rd Motorized Infantry Division, and the 290th Infantry Division. It was, you may remember, the corps on the right flank of both the army group and the panzer group. This corps reached its first objective, the bridgehead at Dunaberg, within four days. Having found a weak spot, it reached its objective without too much heavy fighting, and the Soviet 2nd Tank Division, while marching westward, slipped just north of the advancing 8th Panzer Division with the mission to stop our 6th Panzer Division and XXXXI Panzer Corps as well. Both Soviet 2nd Tank Division and 8th Panzer Division ignored each other.

This development required Colonel General Hoepner to make a difficult decision, which General von Plato will touch upon. Another difficult decision had to be made later, concerning the further advance of

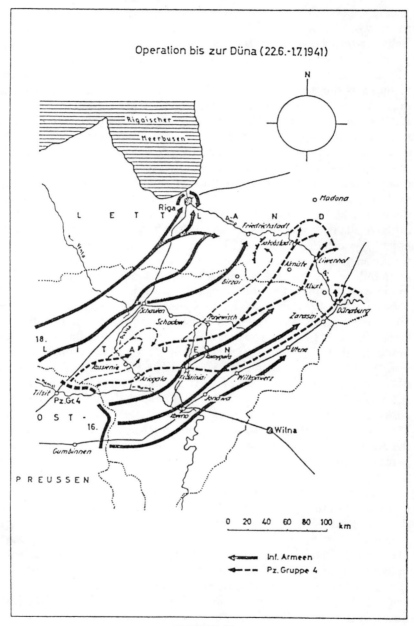

FIGURE 51
OPERATIONS TO THE DÜNA (DVINA) RIVER,
22 JUNE TO 1 JULY 1941

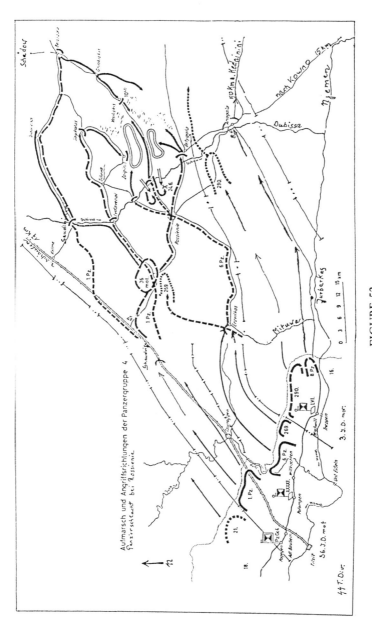

FIGURE 52

PANZER GROUP 4: COMBAT AT ROSSIENE

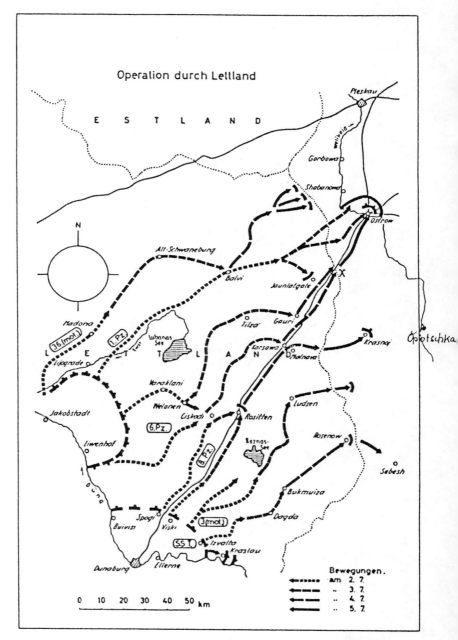

FIGURE 53
OPERATIONS IN LETTLAND, 2–5 JULY 1941

the panzer group out of the Duna bridgehead (see Figure 53). This did not belong to the border battles, but rather originated as a consequence of those battles.

Here, I would like to highlight one point, because it is one of the most interesting points concerning this advance to the north. If you compare Manstein's book, *Lost Victories*, with what in my view is the best description of the advance of Panzer Group 4 to Leningrad, written by Hoepner's Chief of Staff, General Charles de Beaulieu, you will detect rather significant differences and contradictions. These were not so much about the facts, but rather about the ideas as to how to conduct the advance further north. Manstein's recollections are sometimes a bit subjective and not always fully correct as far as this operation is concerned. These differences may have resulted from the fact that Hoepner and Manstein, both excellent leaders, were rather different in nature and character. The personal relationship between leaders is always of importance.

6th Panzer Division Operations

COLONEL HELMUT RITGEN (retired)

The 6th Panzer Division was one of the oldest German armored divisions. Formed in 1937 as 1st Light Brigade, it was later called 1st Light Division and then became a panzer division with the attachment of 11th Panzer Regiment, although it was not redesignated 6th Panzer Division until December 1939. It had been committed during the campaigns in the Sudetenland in 1938, Poland in 1939, and France in 1940.

In June 1941 (see Figure 54), Panzer Regiment 11 had three battalions, each with two light and one medium tank companies, and totaled 220 combat tanks, including 42 Mark IV tanks with a short-barrelled 75mm gun. The low muzzle velocity of this gun (420 meters per second and a high-angled trajectory) allowed a maximum armor penetration of only 41mm. HEAT ammo was not yet available. The bulk of the division's tanks were 105 Czech tanks (35T) with a 37mm gun. These tanks became useless below freezing-point, since their power and steering controls were pneumatic. They had been out of production since 1938 and, although extremely reliable, were at the edge of their system-life and had been declared "no longer suitable for combat" some months before. However, owing to the low tank production in Germany, no replacement tanks were available.

General von Kielmansegg: 6th Panzer Division was the only division in the German Army which had such equipment. That compelled us, from the very beginning, to fight only in mixed combat groups. That was the rule at this time.

Colonel Ritgen: 6th Rifle Brigade consisted of the 4th and 114th Motorized Rifle Regiments, each with a headquarters, two motorized infantry battalions and a support company with six 75mm infantry guns. Only one rifle company had received the new half-track APC (SPW). As a fifth battalion, there was the 6th Motorcycle Battalion, called K-6 and mostly mounted on motorcycles.

The 41st Tank Destroyer Battalion had received not more than 12 50mm antitank guns. The rest had to make do with the obsolete 37mm guns, nicknamed the "Door-knocker".

108

FIGURE 54
6TH PANZER DIVISION ORGANIZATION

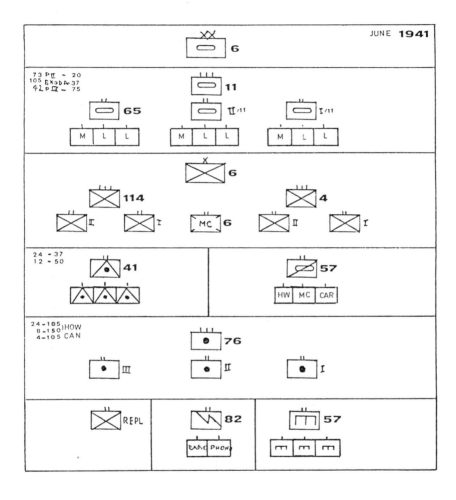

The 76th Artillery Regiment consisted of a headquarters and two light (105mm) and one medium (155mm) battalions, each with three batteries of four guns.

In retrospect, the armament and vehicles of 6th Panzer Division were really poor. It was a miracle that the division reached the outskirts of Leningrad and Moscow, in spite of an enemy superior in numbers and material. This achievement was the result of supreme leadership combined with excellent morale and training.

Nobody in the division wanted a war with the Soviet Union, but if war came, nobody was particularly worried by the thought of the Red Army, which was believed to be "far from a modern army", on the basis of its poor showing in Finland. Nevertheless, the idea of Russia's vast plains, poor road and rail communications, and its geographical character was most troubling: Napoleon's fate had not been forgotten!

I was adjutant of 2nd Battalion, 11th Panzer Regiment and I was most optimistic. At school I had been regarded as a good mathematician. So I tried to compute the duration of our campaign by the duration of the past campaigns in Poland and France in relation to the strength of the opposing forces, distances, and other factors. My conclusion was that the war would be over at the end of July. Thus I set my wedding-day for 2 August. Unfortunately, I had failed to consider an unknown factor in my computation. So my fiancée had to wait two more years!

The only special training we received for Russia were lessons in the Cyrillic alphabet to enable us to read Russian maps and road signs.

General von Kielmansegg: I would add that on the division staff we were not as hopeful as Colonel Ritgen. But it was very significant what was provided to the soldier regarding the meaning of the operation. We saw, I would say, a little more clearly the danger of a two-front war for Germany and the danger of space and time in endless Russia.

Colonel Ritgen: Now let me review the situation prior to the operation and German plans (see Figure 55). 6th Panzer Division, commanded by Generalmajor Landgraf, had the mission of breaking through the border positions in the forest zone south of Tauroggen and advancing via Kongayly and Stegvilai, to Rossinie in order to gain bridgeheads across the Dubyssa River. This was the objective for the first day. Thereafter, it was imperative to cross the Dvina River as soon as possible to prevent the enemy organizing a strong defense line there. Our right flank neighbor was the 269th Infantry Division, reinforced by a tank company of my battalion, and our left flank neighbor was 1st Panzer Division.

The Enemy: It was believed that the border position, as assessed by air reconnaissance and marked on this map, was defended by only weak

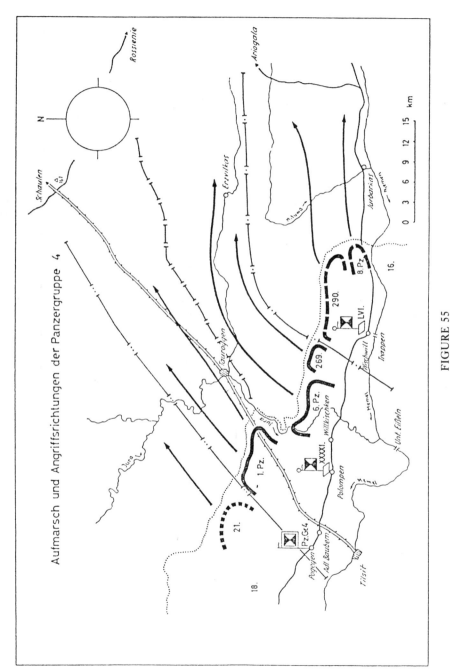

FIGURE 55

GERMAN PANZER GROUP 4: OPERATIONS TO ROSSIENIE

enemy forces. The east bank of the Dvina River could however, offer a strong line of resistance. An early crossing of this river would be essential to prevent enemy fortification of this position. The existence of enemy mechanized corps in the area was known, but we had no knowledge of the new enemy heavy tanks.

The Terrain: The border zone was heavily wooded and partly swampy. East of the border there were sandy plains up to the Saltuona River valley. East of it, the deeper-cut Dubyssa River valley could be used by the enemy as an obstacle. Movement and supplies would be severely impeded by the total lack of roads and highways, all the more so since the division's supply trucks were commercial ones unable to travel cross-country.

Weather: The operation would depend heavily on dry weather, since marching 300 km to the Dvina River along sandy or swampy tracks would be a problem.

General von Kielmansegg: Here, I would like to put in one remark about what Colonel Ritgen is about to describe, regarding our first fighting against the heavy tanks, KV1 and KV2. It was a complete surprise, just as it was a surprise to meet the T34 tank. Nobody in Germany knew anything about these tanks, even that they were under construction.

The terrain, as he mentioned, was woody and swampy. We had to overcome this terrain all the way up to Leningrad with the exception of XXXXI Panzer Corps between Duna and Ostrag. I can only say you should have seen this terrain which was thick green jungle. We could see only a short distance ahead. The lack of roads was equally bad.

Colonel Ritgen: This is how the operations unfolded. On 22 June (D-Day), to achieve surprise, the division crossed the Neman River on engineer bridges during the last night before the attack and proceeded to attack from the march at 0300. An artillery preparation of five minutes on known targets proceeded the infantry attack. Enemy resistance in our sector was much stronger than expected. Up to six antitank ditches in a series had been dug and these were stubbornly held by riflemen supported by snipers in trees. Fortunately no enemy antitank guns or mines were in position. Since nobody surrendered, almost no prisoners were taken. Our tanks, however, were soon out of ammunition, a case which had never happened before in either Poland or France. Resupply depended on the arrival of supply trucks which were unable to overtake us as they tried to cope with the traffic jams on the narrow track.

On a motorbike I tried to assemble the ammunition trucks. Driving was exciting because of the presence of snipers, which could not be located. Their victims were hit primarily by gun-shots in the head. A few hours later I witnessed an incident which characterizes the fanaticism of the

Soviet soldier. Beyond the forest we were waiting for resupply for at least two hours near a cornfield. Suddenly two Russians jumped out of the field with their hands raised. A sergeant waved to them to come to us. At that moment they dodged, while one threw a hand-grenade and the other fired a pistol at the sergeant, who was wounded. The Russians must have hidden motionless in this field for three or more hours.

By noon the forest had been cleared. From now on progress was hindered more by the deep sandy track and the lack of supplies than by enemy action. No bridges had been blown up but their low load capacity forced tanks and heavy trucks to ford the streams. At night we crossed the Saltuona River but owing to the delays in the forest we did not reach our objective for the day, the Dubyssa River. During the first day we captured only a few prisoners and almost no weapons.

That night everybody felt that this campaign was quite different from previous campaigns. The air had been quiet but for a few reconnaissance planes and two Soviet bombers, which soon fell victim to our flak (antiaircraft). We were also warned of possible airborne landings by the enemy.

On 23 June we continued our attack towards the Dubyssa River with two battle groups abreast; Group Seckendorff on the right, and Group Raus on the left. My tank battalion had been relieved by the 1st Battalion, and 65th Battalion was now attached to Group Raus. By 1500, against light resistance, Group Seckendorff had taken Rossinie, a small town, and at 1700 it seized a small bridgehead. A short while later Group Raus secured a second bridgehead further north. At nightfall Seckendorff's bridgehead was attacked by Soviet infantry supported by tanks but they were repulsed. During darkness however, the Soviets attacked again and the bridgehead had to be evacuated. Division ordered the recapture of the bridgehead west of Rossinie the next morning at 0800. For this operation, 2nd Battalion, Panzer Regiment 11 was ordered to concentrate at 0600 west of Rossinie.

General von Kielmansegg: I will add another cruel experience of our division. Colonel Ritgen mentioned a second bridgehead. This one was not given up during the night. In it were about two platoons and these were overrun by a Soviet attack during the night. The next day we found all the personnel shot, that is murdered, and atrociously mutilated. Eyes had been put out, genitals cut off and other cruelties inflicted. This was our first such experience, but not the last. On the evening of these first two days, I said to my general, "Sir, this will be a very different war from the one in Poland and in France."

Colonel Ritgen: On 24 June, at first light, Soviet tanks in great numbers crossed the Dubyssa River supported by artillery (see Figure 56). Some of our riflemen were cut off by the assault (as General von Kielmansegg mentioned).

These hitherto unknown Soviet tanks created a crisis in Battle Group Seckendorff, since apparently no weapon of the division was able to penetrate their armor. All rounds simply bounced off the Soviet tanks. 88mm flak guns were not yet available. In the face of the assault some riflemen panicked. The super-heavy Soviet KV tanks advanced against our tanks, which concentrated their fire on them without visible effect. The command tank of the company was rammed and turned over by a KV and the commander was injured.

I suppose the Soviet tank crews had no time to familiarize themselves with the guns of their tanks or zero them in, since their fire was very inaccurate. Furthermore, the Soviets were poorly led. Nevertheless, the appearance of these heavy tanks was dramatic. One of our reserve officers – today a well-known German author – lost his nerve. Without stopping at the headquarters of his regiment, the division, or the corps he simply rushed to the command post of General Hoepner to report that "everything was already lost!"

A KV tank had reached the northern Dubyssa River bridge, thereby blocking it and cutting contact with Battle Group Raus in its bridgehead. All attempts to destroy this tank failed, including the fire of an 88mm gun and, during darkness, the use of an engineer patrol with explosives. Owing to the heavy fire, the patrol was unable to approach the tank.

At 1230 2nd Battalion of the Panzer Regiment advanced from its assembly area to form a firing line east of Rossinie. We soon made contact with the heavy Soviet tanks. Despite their thick skin we succeeded in destroying some by concentrating fire on one tank after the other. "Aim at the hatches and openings!" we ordered. Then we were forced to stop because our Mark IV tanks had to be resupplied with ammunition.

At 1500 we resumed the attack and drew nearer to the Dubyssa River bank, within 1000 meters. Some enemy tanks were set on fire and others blinded. If they turned around, we found it was possible to knock them out from the rear. During this attack we were supported by a battery of *Nebelwerfers* ("Moaning minnies" engineer mortars). Since its barrage was a new experience – never heard before – we were as frightened by it as the enemy! Again our advance was stopped by the thickening enemy fire. An attempt to resume the attack at 2100 failed. In spite of heavy artillery fire our tanks were resupplied during darkness. During the whole day we had received no air support.

General von Kielmansegg: I will only add a word about the early panic. It was mastered, finally, only by the attitude and discipline of the officers. At the division level we saw, for the first time in the war the danger of a serious

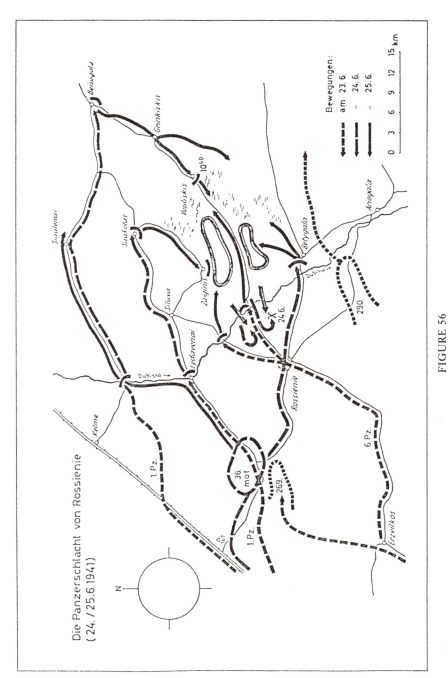

FIGURE 56
BATTLE OF ROSSIENIE, 23–25 JUNE 1941

defeat. This was one of the heaviest strains I ever experienced during the war. The redemption came after having seen these monster tanks with my own eyes while going forward on a motorcycle. The message came that the first one was made immobile by a mine placed by a lieutenant under the track. In the early afternoon an 8.8 cm battery sent by the corps arrived. The 8.8 was the only weapon which could penetrate the armor of the KV1 and KV2, the exception being the front side of the turret.

Colonel Ritgen: The past day had changed the character of tank warfare. The KV tanks represented a wholly new level of armament, armor protection and weight. Hitherto we had used tanks mainly to fight infantry and their supporting arms. From now on the main threat was the enemy tank itself. The need to destroy it at as great a range as possible led to the design of longer-barrelled guns of larger calibre and of more effective antitank ammunition.

The night of 24–25 June passed quieter than expected (see Figure 57). The Soviets had withdrawn from the west bank of the river. Our advance commenced at 0900 on 25 June. We crossed the Dubyssa River and gained a bridgehead without significant enemy resistance. Our path to the east offered a dreadful picture of smashed vehicles of Motorized Rifle Regiment 114, rolled over by tanks, and of burnt Soviet tanks, trucks and equipment. We also found our riflemen who had been cut-off two nights before. They had been killed and horribly mutilated.

These were not the only losses we had suffered. In my battalion one officer had been killed, several were wounded, and a few NCOs and two men had become casualties but we had not as yet totally lost any tanks. Only two had received hits. One cannot read the captured war diary report of Soviet 3rd Mechanized Corps without smiling. It read "2nd Tank Division fought tank actions in the region of Skaudvila, destroying 100th Motorized Regiment – (should read 114th Regiment) – and up to 40 tanks and 40 guns. In the evening entered Rasiniai area without fuel." We had regained morale and confidence! We had been better than the enemy although he had superior tanks.

Beginning at first light on 25 June Battle Group Raus also widened its bridgehead and its commander observed the approach of 1st Panzer Division from the northwest (see Figure 58). At 1100 Panzer Regiment 11 proceeded to reach the Dvina River and exploit our success. The Soviets were in full flight. At Pikciunai however, our spearhead was fired upon and the platoon commander killed. The enemy was encircled in a forest, which he held on to firmly. At 1900 a planned attack was conducted against some stubbornly defended strongpoints but soon the attack had to be halted because of darkness. While our riflemen attacked, the tanks were resupplied.

On 26 June contact was reestablished with 1st Panzer Division. The battlefield was mopped-up and all our elements were resupplied. On 27 and 28 June against slight resistance, the division advanced to the Dvina River and was enthusiastically welcomed by the Latvian civil population. Early on 28 June the Dvina River was reached and on 29 June we crossed the river to establish a bridgehead near Livenhof.

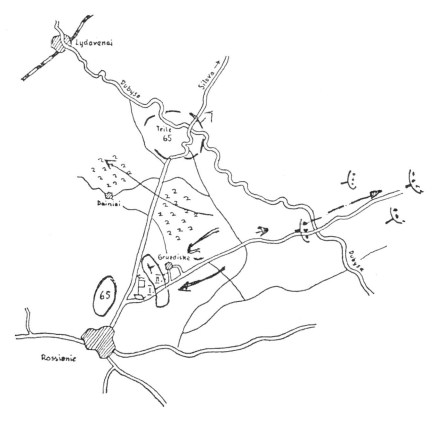

FIGURE 57
BATTLE OF ROSSIENIE, 25 JUNE 1941

Conclusion

General Graf von Kielmansegg

Colonel Ritgen gave you his experiences as an adjutant. An adjutant in the German Army was quite different from an aide-de-camp as you know it.

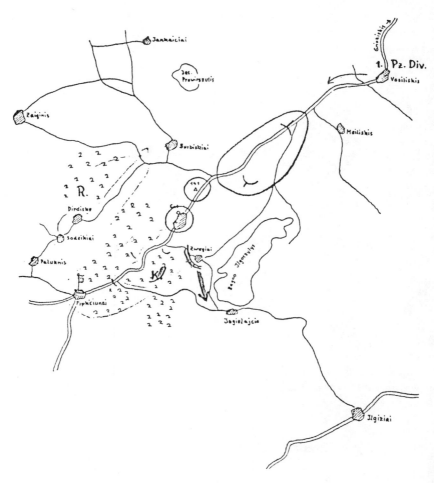

FIGURE 58
BATTLE OF ROSSIENIE, 25–26 JUNE 1941

An adjutant was an S-1, S-2, S-3 and S-4 all in one person. The tank battle at Rossinie was the first great panzer battle in the entire eastern campaign. The XXXXI Panzer Corps conducted this battle as a classic battle of encirclement in Cannae style. 6th Panzer Division had to bear the entire burden of the Soviet counterattack as long as the other divisions were making this outflanking maneuver on the right of the right and the left. It was 100 per cent successful. More than 200 Soviet tanks, and we

118

could count them, were destroyed and the Soviet 2nd Tank Division was smashed to pieces. After this XXXXI Corps and 6th Panzer Division reached the Duna River between Livony and Jacobstadt, north of Dunaberg, rather fast and seized a large bridgehead. Together with the bridgehead at Dunaberg, the first objective of Panzer Group 4, 300 kilometers from the border, was reached on the sixth day of the campaign. The Soviets' counterattacks could not stop the advance.

The events after crossing the Duna River do not belong here, but I would like to give just a hint. In the coming days there were three very difficult and interesting decisions to be made by General Hoepner: first, how to advance from the Duna River through the Stalin Line to the line Lake Piepus-Ostrog; second, how to conduct the attack against and across the Luga River, south of Leningrad, at the Luga woods; and third, how to proceed afterwards.

This war against the Soviets was a new experience for us and was very different from fighting Polish, French and British forces, and later on Americans. The main difficulty in the advance against Leningrad, with the exception of the few days at Rossinie and later on at Luga, was not so much the enemy, but the terrain, with almost no roads. And the main problem, often more than combat, was logistics. Although we have spoken about the surprise of the Russians, these two points were a surprise for us.

In the end, the border battles in the north had no special lessons – I emphasise special – with the exception of Hoepner's decision to continue the advance north of Dunaberg without regard to the pending danger of counterattack on the right flank. Figure 59 shows the relationships of time and space, in relation to the advance of Panzer Group 4. As you can see, within three weeks XXXXI Panzer Corps had advanced 750 kilometers and LVI Panzer Corps 675 kilometers. That is more or less the distance from our present (1987 East-West German) border on the east to the European Atlantic coast, especially in the north of the AFCENT area. These figures mean a daily average of about 30 km.

Speaking for a moment as former CINCCENT, that is what we have to stop definitively. It is the responsibility of our politicians to enable the military to fulfill this task successfully.

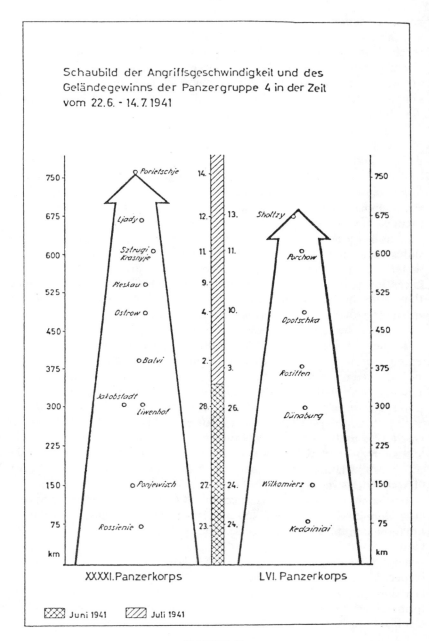

FIGURE 59
PANZER GROUP 4 OPERATIONS, 22 JUNE TO 14 JULY 1941

1st Panzer Division Operations

LIEUTENANT GENERAL A. D. VON PLATO
and
LIEUTENANT COLONEL R. O. STOVES

Introduced by Colonel Paul Adair

In looking at the operations of XXXXI Panzer Corps and, in particular, those of 1st Panzer Division, our two witnesses are Colonel Stoves and Lieutenant General von Plato. Colonel Stoves was a commander of a tank platoon in 1st Panzer Division. After the war he joined the Bundeswehr and finished his career as a liaison officer with the I British Corps at Bielefeld. General von Plato, at that time second staff officer of 1st Panzer Division, went on to become the first staff officer of 5th Panzer Division in 1944. After the war he had a distinguished career, finally becoming Chief of Staff to NORTHAG and commander of the territorial command.

Employment of 1st Panzer Division During the Initial Stages of the Russian Campaign, June 1941 – July 1941 (The Border Battles of Panzer Group 4)

Lieutenant Colonel Rolf O.G. Stoves (retired)

Introduction

During the first three months of the German offensive against the Soviet Union our Thuringian-Hessian 1st Panzer Division (from Weimar) served under HQ Panzergruppe (PzGrp) 4/Heeresgruppe (AGrp) Nord of General von Leeb.

1st Panzer Division fought as the left flank element of Hoepner's two armored corps together with 6th Panzer Division, 36th Motorized Infantry Division and the 269th Infantry Division. Headquarters XXXXI Panzer Corps arrived from Yugoslavia at the end of April 1941. The commander general, General (Armor) Hans Georg Reinhardt, was known and highly respected as the former commander of 1st Armored Infantry Brigade (1.PzDiv) from 1936 to 1938, as was Colonel General Hoepner, our former Commanding General in XVI Panzer Corps during the Polish Campaign of September 1939.

1st Panzer Division had been organized in 1934 and 1935 and took part in the Polish Campaign in 1939, and the French Campaign of 1940 when it fought under Panzer Corps and later Panzer Group Guderian (see

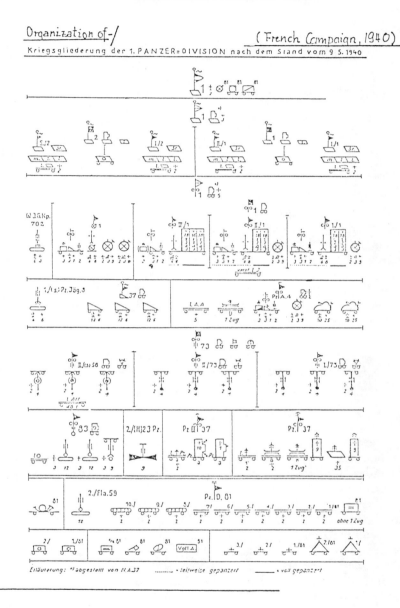

Organization of -/ (French Campaign, 1940)
Kriegsgliederung der 1. PANZER=DIVISION nach dem Stand vom 9 5. 1940

Guderian: Erinnerungen eines Soldaten, Anlage 24

FIGURE 60
1ST PANZER DIVISION ORGANIZATION,
9 MAY 1940

Kriegsgliederung der Panzerbrigade 1   1935/40

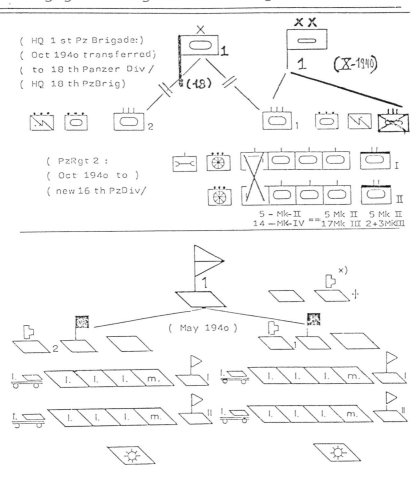

(HQ 1 st Pz Brigade:)
(Oct 1940 transferred)
(to 18 th Panzer Div /
(HQ 18 th PzBrig)

(PzRgt 2 :
(Oct 1940 to)
(new 16 th PzDiv/

5 - Mk-II   5 Mk II   5 Mk II
14 - Mk-IV == 17Mk III 2+3MkIII

(May 1940)

xx) 2 Coy's (1./-+ 6./Pz1)
   formed Sept'39: 1/2 of
   Tk-Replacemt-Bn 1, Erfurt
x) from PzNachrAbt 37 /

FIGURE 61
1ST PANZER DIVISION ORGANIZATION, 1935–40

123

Figures 60-61). In September 1940 our division, along with Headquarters Eighteenth Army (Army Group B), was transferred by rail-transport to East Prussia. From 15 September to June 1941 our units were garrisoned in the area of Zinthen (Panzer Regiment 1) Sensburg (Headquarters, 1st Panzer Division), and Allenstein/Rastenburg (the rest of the division). These nine months were used to reorganize and refill the battle worn units and to receive new and better weapons and equipment as well as additional new units of infantry. The large nearby training areas of Arys allowed us to begin an extensive period of intensive combat training from April to June 1941. During this training we organized our battalions and support units into two or three freshly formed Combat Groups. Thus 1st Panzer Division utilized and trained their soldiers according to experience gained during many exercises and four months of hard fought combat. As a result of the division's panzer raids towards the Vistula River south of Warsaw, and via Sedan on the Meuse River to Amiens and south of Dunkerque (in May 1940), and later from the Aisne southward towards Belfort near the Swiss frontier, the division had learned to organize and fight in two or three mixed Combat Groups, depending upon the area and countryside, the enemy situation and our own troop availability.

The state of 1st Panzer Division in June 1941

From November 1940 through March 1941 1st Panzer Division had been thoroughly reorganized. An order of the OKH required formation of 21 plus three (by October 1941) panzer divisions (with tanks) from ten existing armored divisions, and ten motorized infantry divisions (without tanks) plus Motorized Infantry Regiment Grossdeutschland (Brigade), as well as three SS-motorized infantry divisions, and motorized SS-Rifle Brigade LAH (Leibstandarte Adolf Hitler), from two motorized infantry divisions, and eight infantry divisions (horse drawn) (see Figure 62). Consequently, by October 1940 Headquarters 1st Panzer Brigade, Panzer Regiment 2 and two tank companies of Panzer Regiment 1 left 1st Panzer Division to organize and form the freshly created 16th and 18th Panzer Divisions. 2nd Squadron (PzSpah) of Armored Reconnaissance Battalion 4 (PzAA-4) was transferred to the newly organized 19th Panzer Division. One company of Motorcycle Battalion 4 (K-1) left the *1st Rifle Brigade* (1.SchtzBrig) to form the new motorcycle battalion of 4th Panzer Division. Many experienced armored officers, NCO's and specialists left 1st Panzer Division to help reorganize those new units in the next nine months. Instead of the previous four battalions of motorized infantry, 1st Panzer Division now commanded five battalions.

From units of 1st Rifle Brigade (2dBn, Rifle Rgt 1, parts of Motorcycle Rifle Bn 1 and units of Replacement Battalion of Rifle Regiment 1) a 2nd Motorized Rifle Regiment (No. 113) was formed by February 1941. The

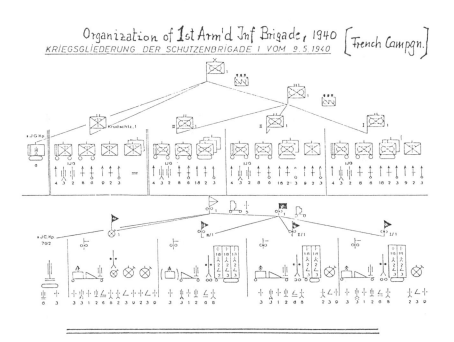

Organization of 1st Arm'd Inf Brigade, 1940 [French Campgn.]

KRIEGSGLIEDERUNG DER SCHÜTZENBRIGADE 1 VOM 9.5.1940

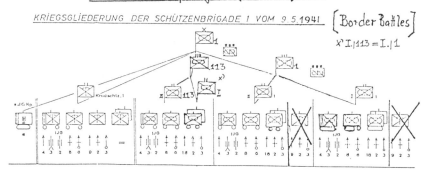

1st Arm'd Inf Brigade (1. Pz Div) '41

KRIEGSGLIEDERUNG DER SCHÜTZENBRIGADE 1 VOM 9.5.1941 [Border Battles]

x) I.|113 = I.|1

FIGURE 62
1ST PANZER DIVISION ORGANIZATION, 1940–41

125

1st Battalions of Rifle Regiments 1 and 113 were each organized and mounted on APCs (four companies each on SPW/SdrKfz.251/1). The 2nd Battalion and supporting weapons were transported on trucks behind halftracks (in parts slightly armored). Heavy infantry Gun Company 703 (15mm) was now integrated and contained six heavy infantry guns (150mm self-propelled on Mk I or II chassis).

In March 1941 1st Panzer Division received 15 antitank guns (50mm). Motorized Artillery Regiment 73 received, for each battery, a couple of light APCs (Sdr.Kfz 250/5) for artillery reconnaissance and Armored Engineer Battalion 37 (PzPiBtl 37) received Mk 1 – II tanks (2.1Pz). 2nd Battalion, Artillery Regiment 56 (heavy) finally became *IIId* Battalion, Motorized Artillery Regiment 73 (heavy) (III(s)/ArtRgt 73 (mot)). Panzer Regiment 1 now received for its four medium tank companies 17 Mk III tanks (PzKw III/KwK-50/L42 each) and five Mk II tanks. A few Mk II tanks and Mk 1 command tanks were passed on to our artillery regiment, the armored reconnaissance battalion and the armored engineers. Shortly before June 1941 light Antiaircraft (AA) Battalion 83 (GAF) (le Flak-Abt.83/mot(LW)) once more became attached to 1st Panzer Division and was now reinforced by two AA-Combat Teams (two Flak-88mm on halftracks each). Helmut Schmidt, future German Minister of Defense and Chancellor of the Federal Republic from 1969 to 1982, served as a lieutenant and commander of a light Flak Platoon with le.Flak-Abt.83 until February 1943.

Colonel Stoves: Let me present to you the well known organization of 1st Panzer Division (state of 1939–1940) with one tank brigade and an armored infantry brigade with a total of 250 tanks.

When we returned from France, as mentioned earlier, 21 German panzer divisions were formed from ten, which meant that the regiments had to be split. Most tank brigades were dissolved and the division gave up Panzer Regiment 2 to newly formed 16th Panzer Division which dissolved in Stalingrad two years later.

When we prepared for the Russian campaign our strength was as follows:

– one armored infantry brigade with five battalions

– two armored rifle regiments, 1 and 113, each with one armored battalion with four APC companies, one motorized armored infantry battalion and regimental heavy weapons (antitank guns)

– one tank regiment with two battalions each with two light tank companies of five Mark II tanks, 17 Mark III tanks with a tank gun of 50mm short barrel. The one heavy tank company had tank guns calibre 75mm short barreled with low velocity (good for infantry support but ineffective against new Soviet monster tanks)

Total: 125 APCs
75 Mark III tanks (50mm)
28 Mark IV tanks (75mm)
45 Mark II tanks
Some 15 Mark I tanks with machine-guns given to Armored Engineer Battalion 37

General von Plato: I would mention here especially the air reconnaissance squadron in the division. This was very important for us, these nine planes which looked over our flanks and sought enemy and friendly force movements. We also had very good connections with the air force fighter squadron through the recce squadron. They were very important. The aircraft were old Henkel models. There was an Air-Liaison-Team attached to HQ 1st PzDiv (one air controller/GAF on an APC).

Colonel Stoves:

Planning: During the first three months of Operation Barbarossa 1st Panzer Division fought under Panzer Group 4 and HQ XXXXI Panzer Corps (see Figure 63). It was the task of General Reinhardt's XXXXI Panzer Corps (Chief of Staff LTC(GS) Hans Roettiger) (Inspector Army/BW 1958) to pierce and smash the Soviet border fortifications around and east of Tauroggen (Taurage). After that was accomplished it was to thrust as fast as possible against the Dvina River in the Daugave sector and gain bridgeheads on the eastern banks of that river around Jakobstadt (Jakavpils). 1st Panzer Division (Commander Lieutenant General Kirchner and CS/Ia LTC (GS) Wenck) was ordered to assault and thrust northeastward across the River Jura, crossing in sectors on both sides of Tauroggen (Taurage). 1st Panzer was to gain the big highway northeast of Tauroggen, head towards Schaulen and then continue the advance immediately via Skaudvila and Kelme against the city of Ponjevits, which was the first objective of the assault.

Lieutenant General Kirchner now organized under commander Panzer Regiment 1 Armored Combat Groups with approximately 150 tanks (plus 10 in reserve), organized into two tank battalions (see Figure 64). Each battalion had two medium tank companies, each with 17 Mk III tanks (50mm/L42) and five Mk II tanks (20mm), and one heavy tank company with 14 Mk IV tanks (75mm/124) and five Mk II tanks. Together, the division had 45 Mk II (20mm), 75 Mk III (50mm), 28 Mk IV (75mm/ short), and eight command tanks Mk III (two machine-guns but no gun),

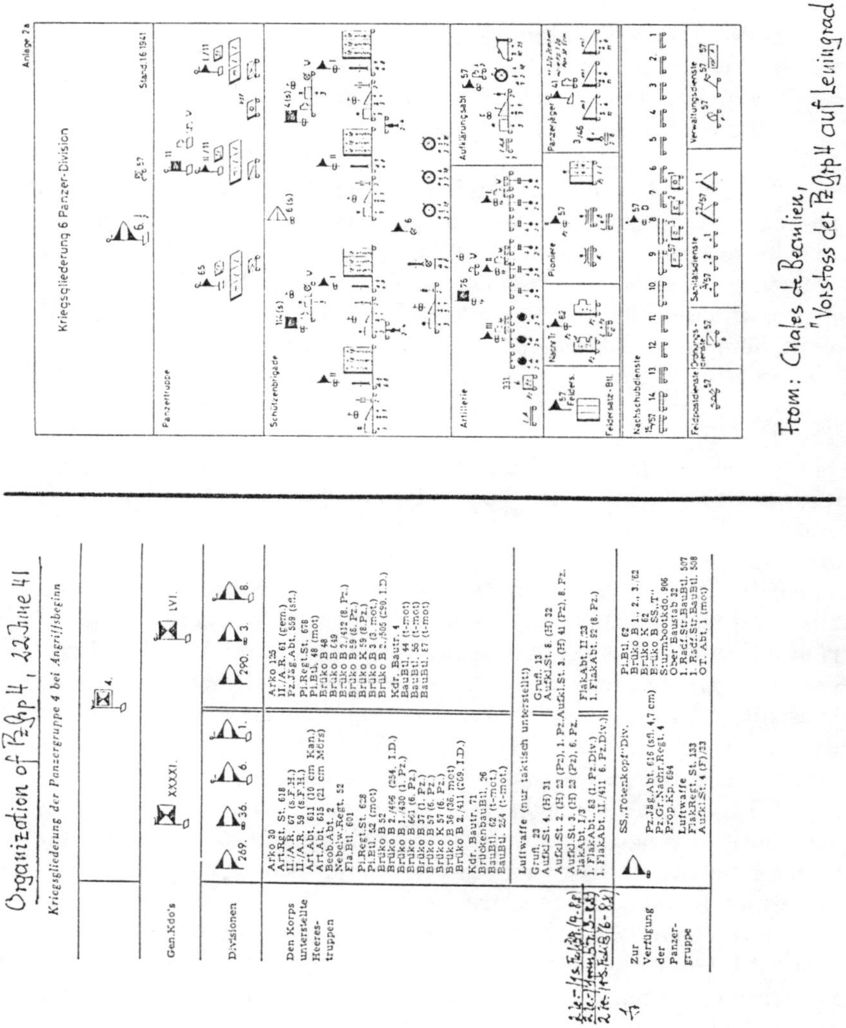

From: Chales de Beaulieu,
"Vorstoss der PzGrp 4 auf Leningrad"

FIGURE 63

PANZER GROUP 4 ORGANIZATION (22 JUNE 1941) AND 6TH PANZER DIVISION ORGANIZATION (1 JUNE 1941)

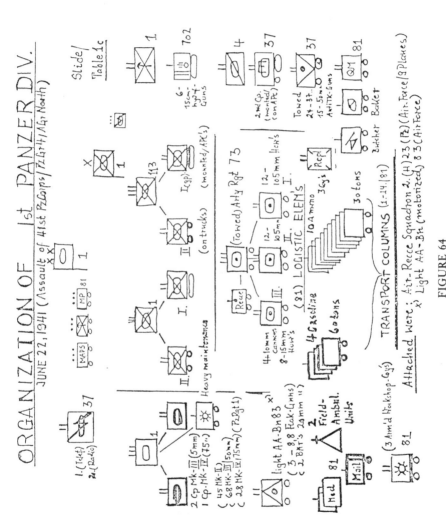

FIGURE 64

1ST PANZER DIVISION ORGANIZATION, 22 JUNE 1941

and 125 APCs (for combat) of both motorized rifle regiments (I./1 + I./113), plus six heavy infantry guns (150mm SP) and one armored reconnaissance company.

The forward detachments of 1st Panzer Division marched from 16 June into the Eighteenth Army assembly area west and northwest of Tilsit along the Memel River (in Lithuania called the Njemen River). Panzer Regiment 1 with approximately 160 tanks (including the reserve squadron), left its garrison at Zinthen, 50 km west of Konigsberg, on 17 June. All armored units were ordered to march only during the night. Officer reconnaissance teams, clad like civilian hunters or farmers, were dispatched into the countryside to take a short look at the area east and southeast of Tilsit and west of Tauroggen. However, the area three miles west of the former German/Lithuanian border remained strictly "off limits!" A few selected advance assault teams moved into the frontier section during the night of 21 June through 22 June. No armored movements were permitted after the initial assembly of the division. There we waited calmly for the final orders to arrive.

HQ, 1st Panzer Division, covered by a deep forest, was located near the small village of Kullmen. Now everything was thoroughly prepared and organized.

On 21 June, at about noon, HQ 1st Panzer Division received the final attack order by special liaison officer: "D-Day 22 June 1941. Start of the assault Zero-Five minutes past 3 o'clock, a.m."

The Panzer Encirclement-Battle Northeast of Rossieni (Rassainiai): *21–26 June*

Phase One: Breaking through Border Fortifications near Tauroggen and Capture of Tauroggen by XXXXI Panzer Corps of Panzer Group 4, 22 June: On 22 June 1941, Lieutenant General Kirchner's 1st Panzer Division advanced into the assault with three mixed combat groups, across the old Lithuanian/German border east and northeast of Tilsit. While the enemy situation was more or less uncertain, the first assault was organized as follows (see Figure 65):

Right (wing): one reinforced infantry regiment of the 102nd Infantry Division (Commander Colonel Badnski)
Center: Motorized Combat Group Westhoven (Commander, HQ, and the bulk of reinforced Rifle Regiment 1 plus one mixed tank company under Lieutenant Fromme).
Left (wing): Armored Combat Group Kruger (Commander and HQ, 1st Rifle Brigade with the bulk of Rifle Regiment 113, Panzer Regiment 1, and one artillery battalion)

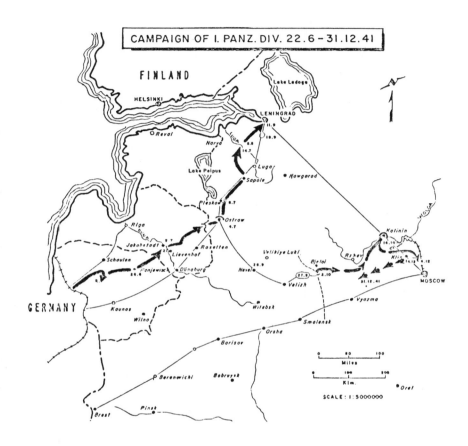

FIGURE 65
1ST PANZER DIVISION OPERATIONS,
22 JUNE–31 DECEMBER 1941

THE INITIAL PERIOD OF WAR

The organization of our mixed combat groups and their strength as tank or motorized infantry heavy corresponded to the area/terrain, the enemy and our own strength. It was the result of long, bitter experience during three campaigns.

During the early hours of 22 June, Motorized Combat Group Westhoven (in short: CbtGrp.We.) attacked by surprise with the reinforced 2nd Battalion, Rifle Regiment 1 (II./S.R.1) in the vanguard and advanced against heavy enemy mortar and artillery fire. After strong, severe and stubborn fighting against Soviet infantry it reached the Jura River sector along and around the well known border town of Tauroggen. Fourteen APCs of 1st Battalion, Rifle Regiment 1, supported by mixed Tank Company Fromme of Panzer Regiment 1 crossed the steep river banks in this sector at about 1300 and forced their way into the city. Thus, the reinforced APC battalion Krieg (I.(gp)/S.R.1) with APCs and 18 Mk II and Mk III/IV tanks under Lieutenant Fromme of Panzer Regiment 1, after seven hours of swift assault and hard fighting, seized two of the three most important Jura River bridges. Later in the afternoon strong, stubborn and cunning Russian infantry, fighting with antitank guns and light tanks, were thrown back. They defended from house to house and road block to road block, until German assault-troops using flame-throwers and demolition charges, cleared the passage. By midnight the Russians were thrown back northeastward beyond the northeastern ridges of Tauroggen. Tauroggen and its vicinity were cleared of the last enemy groups by the motorized 2nd Battalion of Rifle Regiment 1 (2dBn/S.R.1)

A partly damaged road-bridge across the Jura River at Tauroggen was soon captured and quickly repaired by engineer platoons of S.R.1 and Motorcycle Battalion K-1 supported by army engineer units. These arrived soon on the explicit orders of General Reinhardt, who followed closely the attack of his old 1st Rifle Brigade. From midnight on, that important Jura River crossing was available again for all transports and other vehicles, including heavy tanks.

Shortly after midnight motorized CbtGrp.We. reached the area around Lapurvis (six miles northeast of Tauroggen). Here the soldiers took a well deserved rest of four hours, ordered by Lieutenant General Kirchner, who followed the assault in his command APC, along with Colonel Westhoven's armored Forward HQ (six APC and four Flak-20mm(SP). Shortly after, forward logistical teams, which were transported by a few APCs, appeared for resupply of gasoline and ammunition. By 0100, our master-sergeants showed up with food, cigarettes and repair teams.

Armored Combat-Group Kruger (in short: CbtGrp.Kr.) advanced toward the Jura River with two assault groups organized as follows: reinforced Rifle Regiment 113; and reinforced Panzer Regiment 1 with reinforced 1st Battalion, Rifle Regiment 113 (Major Dr. Eckinger) ahead. Major General Kruger with the bulk of 1st Rifle Brigade and Panzer Regiment 1 attacked across the Lithuanian border at about 0400. Their vanguard, the reinforced 3rd Company of S.R.113 with 16 APCs, two AA-Flak guns (20mmSP), ten Mk III and two Mk IV tanks, and one light 105mm field howitzer battery had already crossed the border at about 0300 and reached the Jura River after a short march and forced the steep river by means of a newly discovered ford. They opened the way for the follow-on armored combat group of 1st Panzer Division. Armored CbtGrp.Kr. advanced toward the river, thrust by surprise against unprepared enemy border-guards and gained the Jura River north of Tauroggen by 1200 against slowly stiffening enemy resistance. The APC battalion of Dr Eckinger (I./S.R.113) forced that steep river sector after removing masses of Soviet mines (achieved by their own regimental sappers among the first assault-wave). Then they quickly smashed through wire obstacles in front of a row of concrete pillboxes along the first line of border fortifications around Tauroggen. Captain "Schorsch" Feig's reinforced 3rd (APC) Company/S.R.113, reinforced by 30 medium tanks of I./PzRgt.1, then stormed ahead. Behind them the first border defense line was cleared of stubbornly defending enemy infantry by the advancing motorized elements of 2nd Battalion/S.R.113 (II./113), reinforced by several companies of Motorcycle Battalion 1 (K-1).

Motorized CbtGrp.Kr. with APC-Bn-Eckinger (I./113) operating far ahead, advanced across the big road running from Tauroggen via Skaudvila to Siauliai (Schaulen), giving the defeated and dispersed enemy no chance to reorganize their defenses.

Phase Two: Pursuit through Lithuania 23–24 June: On 22 June 1941 1st Panzer Division had successfully broken through the Soviet border defense lines around Tauroggen, but only after hard fought skirmishes using all type of weapons. On 23 June the division continued its advance in a northeastward direction (see Figure 66). At about 0400 its two combat groups stormed ahead in pursuit of Russian forces which by midnight had been thrown out of Tauroggen. Motorized CbtGrp.We. and armored CbtGrp.Kr. advanced against the area around Skaudvila–Kelme (17km southwest of Siauliai (Schaulen)). In the meantime, Armored Reconnaissance Battalion 4 (PzAA4), along with elements of Motorcycle Battalion 1 (K-1), undertook to protect 1st Panzer Division's wide open left flank. Motorized 36th Infantry Division had just received orders to move up behind XXXXI Panzer Corps' left flank.

The following were the soldiers who led the assault against the Russian Baltic Special Military District:

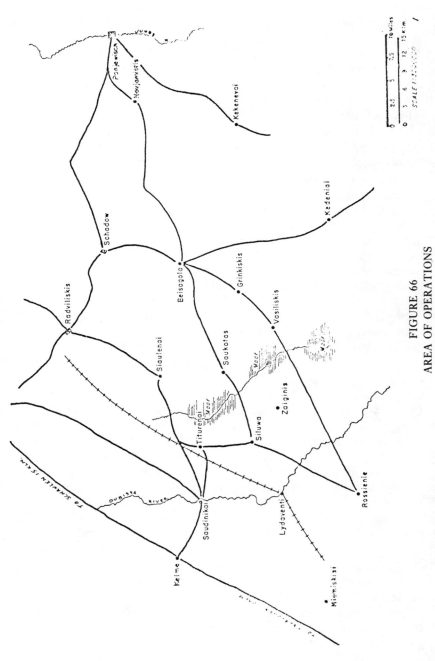

FIGURE 66
AREA OF OPERATIONS

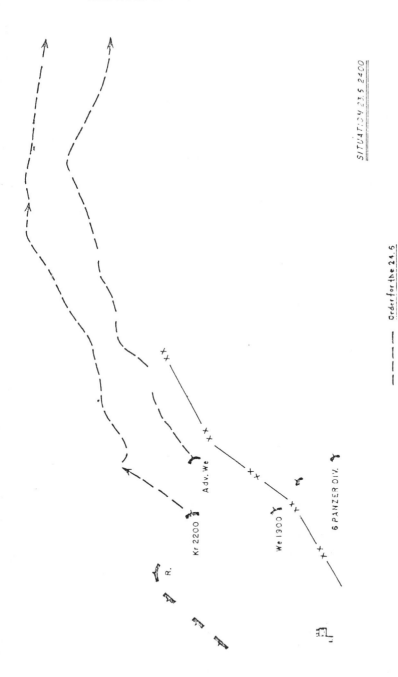

SITUATION 23.5 2400

Order for the 24.5

FIGURE 67

COMMAND AND CONTROL STRUCTURE, XXXXI PANZER CORPS

Command and Control Structure, XXXXI Panzer Corps

Cdr. Army Group North:	Field Marshal Ritter von Leeb
CS:	Lt Gen. (GS) Brennecke
Cdr, Panzergroup 4:	Col. Gen. Hoepner
CS:	Colonel (GS) Charles de Beaulieu
Quartermaster-General (G4):	Major (GS) von Metzsch
Cdr. 6.Panzer Division:	Maj General Landgraf
CS:	Major (GS) J.A. Graf von Kielmansegg
Cdr. 6th Rifle Brigade:	Colonel Erhard Raus
Cdr, 36th Infantry Division (mot):	Lt Gen. Ottenbacher
CS:	Major (GS) Runkel
Cdr 1.PanzerDivision:	Lt Gen. Friedrich Kirchner
CS:	Lt Col. (GS) Walther Wenck
G-4:	Major (GS) Anton Detlev von Plato
Cdr 1st Rifle Brigade	Maj General Walter Kruger
Cdr. 1st Rifle Regiment	Colonel Franz Westhoven
Cdr. 113th Rifle Regiment	Colonel G. v. Heydebrand und der Lasa
Cdr. 1st Motorcycle Battalion	Lt Col. Wend v. Wietersheim
Cdr. 1st Panzer Regiment	Lt Col. Arthur Kopp
Cdr. 73rd Artillery Regiment	Colonel Rudolf Holste
Cdr. Armored Recce Battalion 4:	Lt Col. Alexander von Scheele
Cdr. Armored Engineer Battalion 37:	Lt Col. Wilhelm Knopff

Eight hours after the continuation of our advance on 23 June, Lieutenant General Kirchner, leading the assault behind motorized CbtGrp.We. from his command APC was informed by his CS, Lieutenant Colonel Wenck (HQ/Main 1.Pz), about new orders from General Reinhardt which stated that XXXXI Panzer Corps wished to change the present direction of its attack. Instead of reaching the area around Kelme (17km southwest of Schaulen) as soon as possible and then advancing further toward the northeast, 1st Panzer Division was now directed by General Reinhardt, who arrived at HQ (Main), 1st Panzer shortly afterwards, to wheel from positions south of Kelme and move directly eastward in order to secure a safe crossing site over the steep Dubyssa River in the section near Lydavenai, where there was a 300 meter long railroad-bridge. After that, 1st Panzer Division was to advance further eastward against the Ponjewisch (Ponjevits) area by using two march routes. (Later these were called Panzer Rollbahn or Panzer Highways).

After new orders had quickly been passed out, 1st Panzer Division's motorized CbtGrp.We. thrust forward successfully against enemy strongholds around Nemaksciai, approximately 25 km west of Rossieni, where 6th Panzer Division was fighting. They had to cope with elements of the Russian 125th Rifle Division.

Motorized CdrGrp.We. was then organized in the following manner:

Commander and HQ, 1st Armored Rifle Regiment 1 (Kdr and S.R.1) with:

– APC Battalion 1 (gp)/S.R.1 (reinforced by 15 Mk II tanks and three Mk III/tanks under Lt. Fromme);
– one tank destroyer company of Tank Destroyer Battalion 37 (Major Kaundyna) (three guns – 50mm and nine guns – 37 mm);
– motorized 2nd Battalion, S.R.1 (transported by trucks). Heavy weapons carried behind halftracks, and three antitank guns
– 2nd Battalion, Motorized Artillery Regiment 73 (II./AR 73) with 12 light howitzers (105mm) and halftracks
– 1 battery, AA-Flak Battalion (mot) 83 (GAF) (two Flak 88mm and three Flak 20mm guns.
– 1 light platoon of Field Hospital Company 1./83 (plus a Medical Transport Group).

By midnight on 23 June the vanguard of motorized CbtGrp.We., the reinforced APC Battalion 1, S.R.1 (without one APC Company), had advanced into the area south of Tituvenai, 20 kms east of Kelme on the eastern banks of the Dubyssa River. Meanwhile CbtGrp.Kr. reached Saudinikai. For Colonel Westhoven's force, as well as for the advance of the northern wing of XXXXI Panzer Corps' armored units, the capture of an undemolished, safe railroad bridge across the steep Dubyssa River near Lydavenai, was of decisive importance. Almost the entire logistical support, transported by heavy trucks or trains, had to use that bridge. Therefore, immediately after receiving the new orders to turn eastward, Colonel Westhoven ordered a preplanned, surprise raid against that most important object, to be executed at once.

For that purpose, 1st Lieutenant Wichmann of Rifle Regiment 1, who had planned and prepared that bold action ahead of time, formed a special assault team (supported by a troop of Regiment 800 Brandenburg zbv). Lieutenant Wichmann received orders to seize that railroad bridge near Lydavenai by a surprise assault and hold it until the bulk of motorized CbtGrp.We. had arrived and crossed the Dubyssa River.

Figure 68 shows the result of a dashing diversionary raid. Lieutenant Wichmann and his men reached the 300-meter long railroad bridge across the Dubyssa near Lydavenai at 1830. The crossing was intact and safe for

137

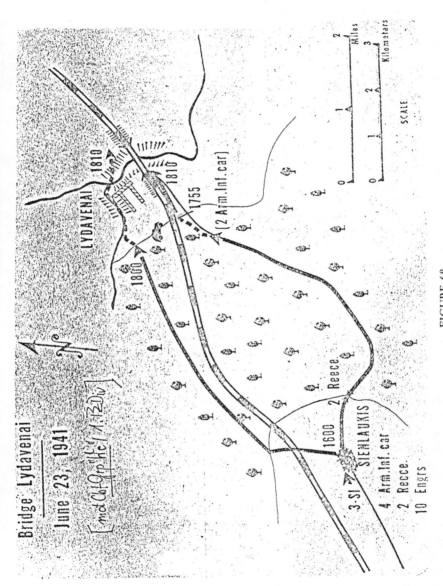

FIGURE 68
SEIZURE OF LYDAVENAI BRIDGE, 23 JUNE 1941

undisturbed transport of all types of German armored vehicles and supplies. A few hours later Motorcycle Battalion (K-1) secured a large bridgehead around Lydavenai.

After passing out orders for the continued advance on 24 June, at 0030 HQ, 1st Panzer Division was informed by the Chief of Staff XXXXI Panzer Corps (Lieutenant Colonel (GS) Roettiger) about the situation further south (see Figures 69–70). At the same time, 1st Panzer Division was informed of newly changed boundaries between it and 6th Panzer Division on the right and 36th Infantry Division, moving up on the left. Lieutenant Colonel Wenck, Chief of Staff, 1st Panzer Division, now received more information about a strong force of enemy tanks in LVI Panzer Corps sector south of Kedeiniai. Therefore Wenck had to plan out and designate new routes of advance for all three combat groups. At about 0130 the combat groups' liaison officers received orders by radio to thrust ahead at 0440. Accordingly motorized CbtGrp.We., fighting on the right flank of 1st Panzer Division, was ordered to assault via Saukotas (approximately 30km northeast of Rossienie, where 6th Panzer Division was engaged) and Baisogala against Ponjewish. Armored CbtGrp.Kr. was to advance via Siaulenai (northeast of Kelme) and Schadow (southeast of Schaulen) against Smilgai (southwest of Ponjewisch).

All occurred as ordered. Shortly before 0700 on 24 June CbtGrp.Kr. reached the area around State Farm Gut Murai, a wide farm-site southwest of Siaulenai. There, by a rapid surprise assault, APC Battalion Eckinger (I.(gp)/113) thrust against and broke through strong Soviet infantry combat groups, which were supported by effective antitank guns (cal./7, 62) and strong groups of medium tanks (types T-26 and Christie). Eckinger pushed ahead further northeastward for the more heavily wooded areas southwest of Schadow.

During the course of 24 June, motorized CbtGrp.We, advancing more or less without strong enemy interference, reached the large village of Baisogala, 12 km south of Schadow on the main road to Rossieni. Our advance also went on as planned (see Figure 71).

In the meantime, further south the right flank neighbor, the Westfalian 6th Panzer Division had been engaged in heavy, bloody tank skirmishes with strong Soviet tank and armored rifle brigades from Soviet 3rd Armored Corps. At about 1330 General Reinhardt, Commanding General XXXXI Panzer Corps, arrived at the forward HQ of 1st Panzer Division near Niaimaxiai, southwest of Saukotas. After a short briefing during which it was stated, "Russian antitank gun 37mm is as useless against our new tank armor plating as our 50mm/L42 tank cannon and 50mm antitank gun was against the armor of medium Russian tanks. The Soviet heavy antitank gun (7, 62mm?) is a frightful weapon", General Reinhardt then issued the following order to 1st Panzer Division:

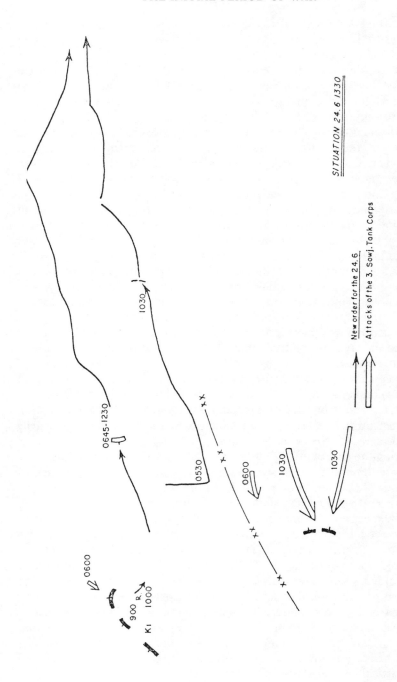

FIGURE 69
SITUATION, 1330, 24 JUNE 1941

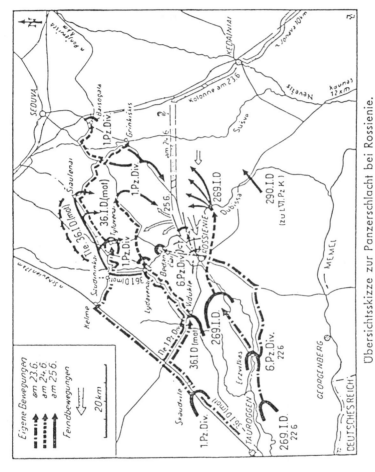

Übersichtsskizze zur Panzerschlacht bei Rossienie.

FIGURE 70
BATTLE OF ROSSIENIE, 23–25 JUNE 1941

141

6th Panzer Division [is] fighting a severe defensive battle against strong armored Soviet combat groups, with many heavy tanks, in the area east and northeast of Rossieni (Rasainiai).

1st Panzer Division is moving up in the area Vosiliskis-Grinkiskis. Units must be prepared to wheel either in the westward direction, in order to destroy the enemy armored brigades in front of 6th Panzer

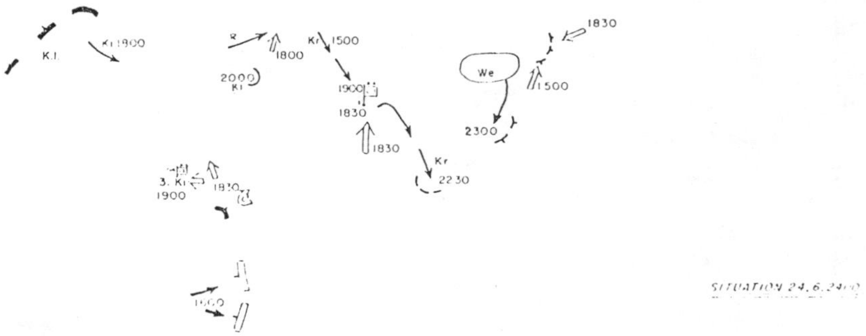

FIGURE 71
BATTLE OF ROSSIENIE, 2400, 24 JUNE 1941

Division, *or*, following new orders of HQ XXXXI Panzer Corps, to advance further eastward and break through (against the area around Ponjewisch/south of Riga).

By radio-message, at 1350, HQ 1st Panzer Division ordered motorized CbtGrp.We. to wheel in, while defending Baisogala with parts of 2nd Battalion, S.R.1, and assault Grinkiskis (1km southwest of Baisog.) and the junction of the three main roads northeast of Rossieni. CbtGrp.Kr. was tasked with cleaning up the battleground around State Farm Gut Murai, while the bulk of General Kruger's force would turn southward to advance via Saukotas (25km northeast of Rossieni) against enemy forces in the area of Vosiliskis, Zaiginis, and southeast of Siluva. Because of very bad road conditions and marshy countryside, the vanguard of CbtGrp.Kr. (reinforced armored Rifle Battalion 1 (113)) did not reach Saukotas until 1900.

Meanwhile, CbtGrp.We. repulsed repeated enemy assaults against Baisogala, which was successfully defended, although units of 36th Infantry Division, ordered to relieve S.R.1 around Baisogala, did not arrive until the next morning. By late evening, CbtGrp.We. had reached Grinkiskis and had fought off repeated enemy attacks by infantry riding on trucks. At the same time, reconnaissance teams tried to discover what was happening further to the southwest

The forward headquarters of 1st Panzer Division (Lieutenant Colonel Wenck and his aides) reached the new Forward Command Post around State Farm Gut Saukotas by 1830. In the meantime, the advance element of CbtGrp.Kr., reinforced Panzer Regiment 1 (with APC Battalion Eckinger/-I./113), marched southward, repeatedly delayed by bad roads and sandy, marshy grounds. The countryside was barren and, in some instances, impassable. Moory, wet grounds slowed the advance because advance elements were quite often busy rescuing bogged-down tanks. They were nearly lost while trying to find a way around the moory terrain along the axis of advance. Weak enemy units, primarily infantry with a few antitank guns and light tanks (T-26) had to be defeated along the way. When the first tanks of Panzer Regiment 1 arrived near Saukotas they had to support the forward headquarters of 1st Panzer Division against marauding enemy groups with tanks, which were trying to escape northward from advancing 6th Panzer Division. Lieutenant Colonel Wenck soon ordered a reinforced AA flak battery of Light AA-Flak Battalion 83 (with two 88mm guns) to protect headquarters against these attacks. When the G-4 of 1st Panzer Division arrived later that night at Saukotas to clear up urgent questions of resupplying forward elements, Wenck and von Plato discussed with Lieutenant General Kirchner the experience of the first three days of attack. They concluded:

> The Soviet soldier fought bravely and stubbornly and was easily satisfied [fed]. The defense in the sector of our division appeared "disorganized". Their infantry defended their positions until the last, often very skillfully using all advantages of the rolling terrain.
>
> As far as our German Combat Groups were concerned, fighting during the nights, or late evening hours, which went on during this period without much interruption, was mainly done by our infantry and rifle units because our tanks were severely handicapped at that time, and because fighting in darkness, our drivers and gunners could not see much. The lenses of the tank rangefinder equipment of most of our armored vehicles only permitted us very poor visibility between 2100 and 0500. Therefore the riflemen often climbed onto, and rode on top of our tanks, sitting beside the driver. They advised tank drivers, and often tank commanders, from behind the turret by using handsignals or by simply shouting about the right way to drive or the proper direction to fire (called shooting "over the thumbs").

During that night and the following morning at Saukotas and Vosiliskis, both combat groups were ordered to use new advance routes. This occurred without causing "too much trouble". Since 1st Panzer Division had been ordered to turn about and head south and southwest, it became necessary to move Panzer Regiment 1 from the left (northern) flank of XXXXI Panzer Corps to the right, or western flank of 1st Panzer Division in order to assault, with the support of tanks, against enemy positions at Vosiliskis, south of Saukotas (where most enemy tanks were expected). Lieutenant General Kirchner, aware of what might happen, ordered that quite difficult maneuver, and sent all available officers and NCOs to all crossroads to direct the advancing columns which crossed during the night under fire from different sides. The maneuvers worked well despite the constant heavy fighting.

The advance guard of CbtGrp.Kr., threw back and dispersed a couple of already scattered and weak enemy detachments and at 2300 reached Vosiliskis and the area four kilometers northeast of Vosiliskis. Here they linked up with the forward units of CbtGrp.We. By reaching and securing the line Vosiliskis – Grinkiskis, 1st Panzer Division had secured positions which threatened the rear of strong Russian forces attacking the lines of 6th Panzer Division. Both combat groups were now ordered to hold that line against enemy counterattacks.

Phase Three : *The Tank Battle near Rossieni, Saukotas and Vosiliskis, 25 June 1941*: Major (GS) von Plato, G-4 of 1st Panzer Division, during the night 24–25 June moved the advanced logistic units forward to a wooded area near Lydavenai (see Figure 72). During that same night, the G-2, HQ 1st

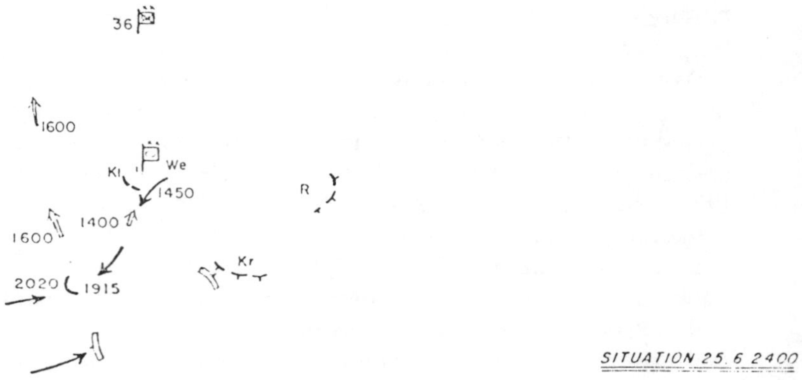

FIGURE 72
BATTLE OF ROSSIENIE, 2400, 25 JUNE 1941

Panzer Division received reports from his own reconnaissance aircraft, as well as from the G-2 of XXXXI Panzer Corps, informing him about the unloading of enemy railroad transports near Radviliskis (15 km southwest of Schaulen). To take care of enemy elements arriving from that area, the bulk of Armored Reconnaissance Battalion 4 (PzAA 4) received orders to seize and cover the area from Siaulenai to north of Tituvenai. Motorcycle Rifle Battalion 1 (K-1) moved into the area north of Lydavenai to cover that important Dubyssa River crossing against enemy assaults. The G-4 of 1st Panzer Division felt quite relieved when Lieutenant Colonel Wenck informed him about the new situation. He also received information that the quartermaster of Eighteenth Army, who was responsible for the logistic support of Panzer Group 4 during the first phase of our advance in the Dugave sector, had now directed the first supply columns eastward.

The early morning hours of 25 June brought another assault against the forward headquarters of 1st Panzer Division at State Farm Gut Saukotas. Again the General, his Chief of Staff, officers, NCOs, as well as most of their staff personnel had to grab their guns and sub-machine-guns and defend themselves against another surprise assault by Russian infantry and medium tanks. Again the Russians were repulsed and all tanks were knocked out by the 88mm flak combat teams of AA Flak Battalion 83 (Air Force), which had deployed south of the command post. Then HQs, 1st Panzer Division received several other alarming messages. The most important read:

> Russian tank assaults with super-heavy armored fighting vehicles, KV-I and KV-II tanks, have overrun the 2nd Battalion of Armored Rifle Regiment 1. Neither the infantry's antitank guns nor those of our own panzer Jaeger platoons (six antitank guns 50mm/1g), nor the tank cannons of the medium and heavy German tanks are able to pierce the plating of the heavy Russian tanks! What can be done to stop those heavy Russian tanks?

Even elements of Panzer Regiment 1, covering the main road towards Rossieni, south of Vosiliskis, failed to stop those super-heavy tanks advancing north against Saukotas. Major General Kruger, commander of 1st Rifle Brigade, was ordered to meet the Russian tank assault with his own counterattacks. In the meantime, the batteries of Artillery Regiment 73 had to depress their barrels and fire in the horizontal position, thus eventually stopping that dangerous enemy attack by direct fire from open firing positions. The 100mm field cannons of 3rd Battalion, Artillery Regiment 73 knocked out a couple of threatening Russian tank packs equipped with T-26 and KV-I tanks. They were supported by a few 88mm AA flak combat teams (from the AA Battalion 1 of Flak Regiment 3 and from light AA Battalion 83 /Air Force), which General Reinhardt had directed to the battleground near Saukotas and Vosiliskis (from CbtGrp.Kr.).

At 0820, the tanks of reinforced Panzer Regiment 1 launched a decisive counterattack which pressed the strong enemy assault groups back and turned the fortunes of the day. The enemy was finally thrown back. Only because of their greater speed, more skillful handling, and superior radio communications systems were the German tanks of Panzer Regiment 1 able to throw the enemy back two miles. Shortly after, however, another pack of Soviet heavy tanks appeared.

Those new Russian tanks, which made the surprise appearance near Saukotas, were unknown types of tanks named the Klim Voroshilov series (the KV-I and KV-II tanks weighing 43 and 52 tons respectively). A combat report of 2nd Battalion, Panzer Regiment 1, 1st Panzer Division, described that tank battle which occurred between Vosiliskis and Saukotas:

> The KV-I and II, which we first met near Saukotas, were really something!
>
> Our companies, the 6th and 7th companies of Panzer Regiment 1, opened fire at about 800 yards but the fire remained ineffective! We moved closer and closer to the enemy, who for his part continued to approach us unconcerned. Very soon we were facing each other at from 50 to 100 yards. A fantastic exchange of fire took place, without any visible German success! The Russian tanks continued to advance undisturbed. All armor-piercing shells simply bounced off their plating.
>
> Thus we were presently faced with the alarming situation of the Russian tanks driving through the ranks of reinforced 1st Panzer Regiment towards our own infantry, riflemen from Rifle Regiment 1. (S.R.1), and on into our rear area with all of its logistic installations. They also headed toward our combat groups and divisional headquarters and threatened to interfere with our own supply columns!
>
> Panzer Regiment 1 therefore about-faced and rumbled back along with those KV-I and KV-IIs, roughly said, rolling in line with them! At last we were able to outmaneuver them and knocked out many. In the course of this astonishing operation we finally succeeded in immobilizing some with special-purpose shells (so-called Rotkappchen) at a range of 30 to 60 yards.
>
> Later a counterattack was launched and the Russians were finally thrown back. A protective front was then established around Vosiliskis and Saukotas. Severe defensive fighting went on for some time.

During the severe and bloody fighting, CbtGrp.Kr. succeeded in advancing another three miles and ten Russian heavy tanks were destroyed by different means. While German tanks threw back the Russian infantry, our own riflemen and armored engineers (from Pioneer Battalion 37 (Pi 37)) knocked out many other enemy tanks by throwing bundles of explosives (demolition charges) against tank tracks or tank turrets. Thus, the infantry often succeeded in at least turning the dangerous tanks into immobile machine-guns carriers.

The dominant sector of that rolling countryside was Hill 139 (139 meters high). It was a very close embattled spot, which was finally conquered by 2nd Battalion, Rifle Regiment 113. A short time later strong Russian infantry forces with many medium and heavy tanks launched repeated counterattacks.

The defensive positions around Hill 139, under attack until midnight, were only held with the assistance of two light batteries and one heavy battery of the 3rd (heavy) Battalion of Artillery Regiment 73. The battle of CbtGrp.Kr., west of Vosiliskis, went on until late in the night. All Russian attempts to break through to the northeast failed. Saukotas and Vosiliskis were successfully defended against dangerous assaults from all sides. For the protection of the forward headquarters of 1st Panzer Division from enemy elements repeatedly advancing against State Farm Gut Saukotas, two reinforced companies of Motorcycle Battalion K-1 marched from Lydavenai to Saukotas, while one reinforced company of K-1 remained at Lydavenai to cover the forward elements of the G-4 of 1st Panzer Division and to defend the important railroad bridge near Lydavenai. Smaller enemy units, testing the security guards located there, were repulsed repeatedly.

At about 1100 on 25 June, another Russian tank force was reported to be assembling south of Saukotas. Lieutenant General Kirchner therefore ordered CbtGrp.We. to move from Grinkiskis to Saukotas. Since one reinforced motorcycle rifle company of Armored Reconnaissance Battalion 4 (which was to relieve the rifle companies covering Grinkiskis) was slowed tremendously by bad, sandy roads, Colonel Westhoven left weak defensive units at Grinkiskis and Baisogala. Then, at about noon, reinforced Armored Rifle Regiment (S.R.1) about-faced and marched back into the area due south of Saukotas along the old well-known routes of advance used two days before. Immediately after its arrival and while it was waiting for artillery and armored support, a severe enemy attack struck against the lines of CbtGrp.We. However, the combined firepower of four batteries of Artillery Regiment 73, which had arrived just in time, and a few 88mm AA flak guns of 1st Battalion, Flak Regiment 3, repulsed that last enemy counterattack.

Thereafter, CbtGrp.We. launched another counterattack and at 0700 reached the crossing over a tributary of the Dubyssa River near Zaiginis.

One hour later Colonel Westhoven's men linked up and shook hands with advance units of 6th Panzer Division located southwest of Vosiliskis and south of Zaiginis!

CbtGrp.Kr., which had been halted after reaching the area around Sargeliai, by evening repulsed repeated attacks by Russian tank units and rifle battalions trying to escape final encirclement. All attempts to break out by forces of the Soviet 3rd Mechanized Corps (with elements of 2nd Tank Division, 125th Rifle Division, and 48th Rifle Division) failed. By midnight the enemy was encircled from the west by the reinforced 6th Panzer Division; from the north and northeast by the 1st Panzer Division; and from the south by the 269th Infantry Division. The combat groups of 1st Panzer Division reported another eleven KV-I and II tanks and 25 medium tanks destroyed.

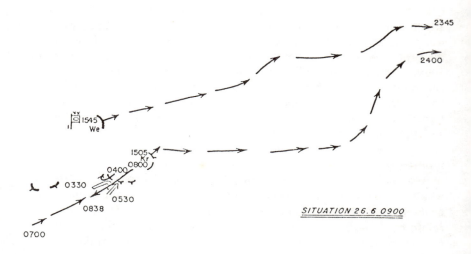

FIGURE 73
SITUATION, 0900, 26 JUNE 1941

Phase Four : Assault toward the Duna (Dvina) River, 26 June 1941: Combat GroupKr. was hit again by strong Russian counterattacks near Sargeliai during the early hours of 26 June (see Figure 73). All assaults were repulsed, mostly by batteries of Artillery Regiment 73 firing from open firing positions along the hills around Sargeliai. The counterattack of Panzer Regiment 1 against Hill 52, south of Sargeliai, supported by APC Battalion I/113 and 1st Battalion, Artillery Regiment 73, reached the hills south of Sargeliai by 0830. Panzer Regiment 1 reported approximately 500 Soviet medium and heavy tanks destroyed. It then linked up with 6th Panzer Division south of Sargeliai. Again many heavy Russian tanks were knocked out, one showing 70 hits by tank or antitank guns. None of these hits however, had pierced the armor plating. Most tanks had run onto mines and lost parts of their tracks.

Logistical support for forward elements of all armored units proved quite difficult during these battles. Transport columns of the G-4 of 1st Panzer Division sometimes reached their units only under the protection of tank platoons. Urgently needed ammunition and gasoline were brought forward by using APCs. The enemy repeatedly interrupted truck traffic along the road from Lydavenai to Saukotas by using strong infantry marauding teams with light tanks. The G-4 of 1st Panzer Division, in person, led one of these supply columns from Lydavenai to Saukotas, where the most urgent supply of ammunition and gasoline was required. On the night of 24–25 June, Eighteenth Army formed a "Forward-Supply-Post" for ammunition and gasoline at Saukotas.

General Reinhardt visited the headquarters of 1st Panzer Division, as well as the headquarters of both combat groups, a couple of times during those days. The appearance of his command APC and his well known tall figure were of tremendous support for the fighting morale of 1st Panzer Division.

The Exploitation

After destroying the Russian 3rd Mechanized Corps south of Saukotas and around Vosiliskis, XXXXI Panzer Corps again turned eastward (see Figure 74). In accordance with orders received on 26 June, 1st Panzer Division ordered its combat groups, after reorganizing and resupplying, to form two columns (*marschgruppen*) to reach the Juodo River by midnight. CbtGrp.Kr. was to advance from Vosiliskis via Juodeliai-Krakenava to Upite, while CbtGrp.We. would advance from Saukotas via Baisogala-Neujamietisto-Ponjewisch. Armored Reconnaissance Battalion 4 (PzAA-4), protecting the northern flank, was to reach Huta via Baisogala. By midnight on 26 June, 1st Panzer Division had reached Donjewisch with the advance units of CbtGrp.We., where it seized a big gasoline depot fully intact. The vanguard units of 1st Panzer Division reached the Dugave River bank south of Jakobstadt (Jakawpils) on 28 June. There the 2nd Battalion, S.R.113 seized a bridgehead on the eastern bank around Kreuzburg, by 1000 hours.

By 4 July, CbtGrp.Kr. had conquered an undemolished bridge across the Welikaja River at Ostrov but heavy tank battles raged at Ostov and south of Pleskov. By 17 July reinforced APC-Battalion Eckinger (I./113)

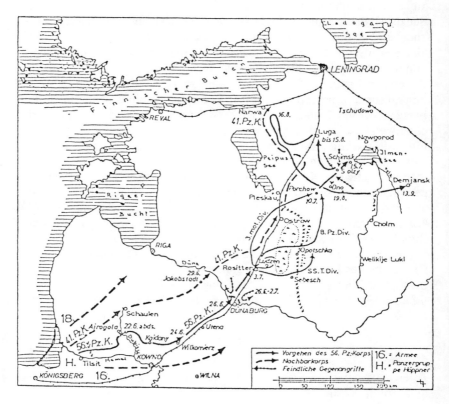

FIGURE 74
XXXXI PANZER CORPS EXPLOITATION

had captured a bridgehead across the Luga River at Ssabsk, north of Luga
and 75 miles west of Leningrad. 1st Panzer Division held that bridgehead
across the Luga until 8 August when the final assault of XXXXI Panzer
Corps of Panzer Group 4 against Leningrad began.

That operation, which reached Rechkolovo-Pushkin by 18 September,
has been described in our war diary 1. Panzer Division, 1935–45.

During these battles we heard and saw nothing of our famous air aces.
So the Chief of Staff of 1st Panzer Division said, "Let's do something".
He asked the High Command, as well as the Commanding General,
whom he saw every day, "What can we do about this business?" General
Hoepner said "Don't worry, they will appear". Nothing happened, so he

sent a radio message to his superior and said there "were only Red aces demonstrating their talents." He did it in rhymes so it was interesting to see the signals people translate it into a typical barren message such as "Go there and do this". The answer came "Don't bother, take it easy, be aware that it is only temporary. In a short time you will see our wonderful air aces, who can do anything." Wenck's answer, hours later, was, "There were no Nazi flyers!"

Well, they turned up, but the width of the Russian area and the size of its sectors was something that changed all manner of fighting. At that time things were discovered in the line and in combat which later provided a basis for the creation of battlegroups of the first combat commands of NATO.

Let me finish with one remark. The Russian soldier fought very bravely. He was stubborn. You had to really knock him down before you were able to go on. He was brave and tough. To be prepared today men need the same type of training we had in the eight months between the French and Russian campaigns. We were lucky. We were prepared and we must remain prepared. I hope today's generation will not have to do the same bloody business we did 40 years ago.

Reflections on XXXXI Panzer Corps Operations

LIEUTENANT GENERAL A.D. VON PLATO

I wish to underline a few points of Colonel Stoves which dealt with the northern wing of General Reinhardt's XXXXI Panzer Corps.

1. The importance of those air-reconnaissance squadrons (German Air Force – GAF). Nine air-reconnaissance aircraft were attached to each panzer division with the task of watching developments along our open flanks, as well as all movements of enemy tank formations (e.g. of the Soviet 3rd Mechanized Corps coming in from the area around Kovno).

2. Difficulty in the first deployment of the two armored corps during the night of 21–22 June, 1941.

The Memel River (Njemen in Lithuania) divided the area into two parts. The part north of Memel River was very small; only three armored divisions (1st, 6th, and 8th Panzer) could move into the northern part of the assembly area behind the infantry division already on line. The three motorized infantry divisions (3rd, 36th, and SS-T) had to remain south of the Memel River during daylight before the day of assault. Nevertheless, it remained uncertain whether our surprise action would succeed or not. Requested supply depots for ammunition and gasoline north of the Memel River, which we found necessary for our fast movements, were not approved by the Army Group North HQ.

3. Inadequate picture of the enemy. We knew, in general, of the presence and positions of the three Soviet mechanized corps. (1st Mechanized Corps was at Pleskau-Ostrow, 12th at Schaulen, and 3rd at Kowno.) However, we did not know the definite number of enemy infantry divisions available on the other side. More or less, we were convinced that the Soviet High Command planned a surprise attack. Only the time and date of such an attack was uncertain to most of us. The interrogation of prisoners of war revealed later that the bulk of the Russian troops deployed along the frontier sector opposing Panzer Group 4 (Hoepner) and Eighteenth Army, had been withdrawn a few days before.

4. The consumption of fuel was much higher than was provided for in advance of those first six days of attack. Bad roads, sandy, dusty roads or field lanes, and moory, marshy sections of countryside in the northern part of XXXXI Panzer Corps' axis of advance encompassed more territory

than we expected and led to the consumption of more POL than anticipated. On several occasions during those first days of attack the consumption rate was at least three times higher than was provided for.

5. A very interesting operational situation developed on 24 June for headquarters, Panzer Group 4, while the tank battle near Rossieni was under
way. Colonel General Hoepner, Commanding General of Panzer Group
4, had to ask himself the question whether he could leave the task of
destroying reported enemy armored forces to XXXXI Panzer Corps
alone, or should he halt the bulk of LVI Panzer Corps (von Manstein),
advancing rapidly towards Dunaberg to deploy it against enemy forces in
the North?

Colonel General Hoepner decided to stick to his orders that LVI Panzer
Corps should move forward in the direction of Dunaberg. (That situation
was later played very often during map-exercises of our Kriegsakademie as
an operational problem).

6. A decisive situation occurred 14 days later. On 10 July the assault of
XXXXI Panzer Corps continued northeast from Pleskau to Luga, towards
Tschudowo, approximately 100 kilometers southeast of Leningrad.
Already, during the second day of that renewed attack against Leningrad,
enemy resistance increased. The small, sandy and marshy roads, often
leading through large wooded areas, did not permit rapid thrusts and
bypassing of enemy strongholds, as had been done between Duna and the
Stalin Line, south of Pleskau.

While consultations with Colonel General Hoepner went on, General
Reinhardt, Commander of XXXXI Panzer Corps, decided to shift the
direction of his assault. Shortly after Salpolje, southwest of Luga, had
been seized following heavy and bloody combat, General Reinhardt
ordered 6th, and later 1st Panzer Division, to turn from its old axis of
advance and wheel to the north. Reinhardt now wished to reach the dry
ridge south of Kingisepp for the last attack towards Leningrad, heading
from the southwest. This did not correspond with the plans of the Chief of
the General Staff of the German Army, Colonel General Halder, who
wanted to keep Northern Army Group forces closely attached to Army
Group Center (Mitte), in order to support the attack against Moscow.
Now the width of the Russian front grew wider. As a result the coherence
within Panzer Group 4 was lost between XXXXI Panzer Corps, fighting
southwest of Leningrad, and LVI Panzer Corps, advancing via
Tschudowo and southwest against Leningrad.

7. Our initial intelligence picture in the beginning was better in the north
because the Russians had taken over Lithuania one year earlier and the
people disliked the Russians. For this reason we had a better picture of the
enemy. I repeatedly received complaints as G-4 over the fuel shortages in
the front. On one occasion on 24 June the enemy was sitting between the

fighting units and the supply depots. So I took three tanks out of my workshop company and drove with two columns (one of gasoline and one of ammunition) to Colonel Wenck, Chief of Staff, 1st Panzer Division. We arrived after some fighting. This was the kind of business the G-4 got into.

Another interesting situation developed at the time General Hoepner ordered his LVI Panzer Corps to go on to Dunaberg. General Reinhardt of XXXXI Corps had the same decision to make and he ordered 1st Panzer Division to stop, turn, and attack the Russians in the rear on 24–25 June. I think it was the correct decision because 6th Panzer could not have defeated the Russians alone. Colonel Wenck, who later taught at the Staff Academy, used this case to teach students the decision-making process.

3

The Border Battles on the Vilnius Axis
22–26 June 1941

Overview

COLONEL D. M. GLANTZ

From the Soviet standpoint, if there was any area where the battle was over before it began, it was along the Vilnius axis. The German intelligence view was fairly accurate, probably because the city of Kaunas was an excellent intelligence collection point, for the reasons already stated. The Germans assessed that there were a number of Soviet rifle and motorized divisions along the border, backed up by 2nd and 5th Tank Divisions and several separate tank brigades (see Figure 75). These were assessed to be organized as part of 3rd Mechanized and 16th Rifle Corps. As may be seen from the actual situation (Figure 76), that portrayal was fairly accurate.

There were, however, some aspects of Soviet deployments which differed sharply from Soviet dispositions further north and that caused German intelligence to assess greater Soviet strength along the border than actually existed. Major General V.I. Morozov, Commander of 11th Army, deployed his 16th Rifle Corps' divisions in camps west and southwest of Kaunas. His 29th Rifle Corps (the so-called Lithuanian Rifle Corps) deployed in deeply echeloned positions south of Kaunas. The 3rd Mechanized Corps of Major General A.V. Kurkin, consisted of the 2nd Tank Division we have already looked at, located near Kedenai, Colonel F.F. Fedorov's 5th Tank Division, stationed north of Alytus, and Major General P.I. Fomenko's 84th Motorized Division located near Kaunas.

Thus the Soviet defense was slightly deeper here than was the case to the north. The bulk of forward deployed Soviet rifle divisions had only one regiment near the border (5th, 33rd, 188th, and 126th Rifle Divisions) or only two battalions forward (23rd Rifle Division), while the divisions' main

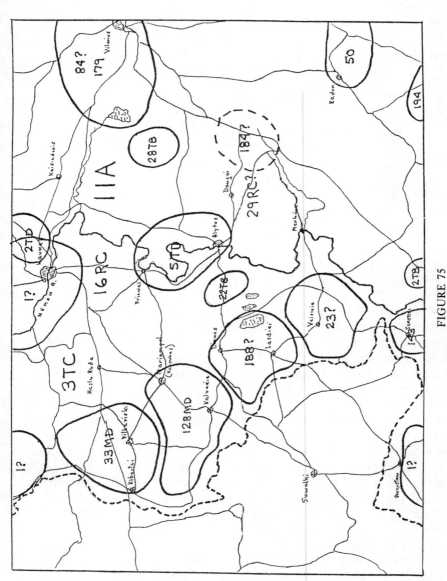

FIGURE 75

GERMAN INTELLIGENCE ASSESSMENT

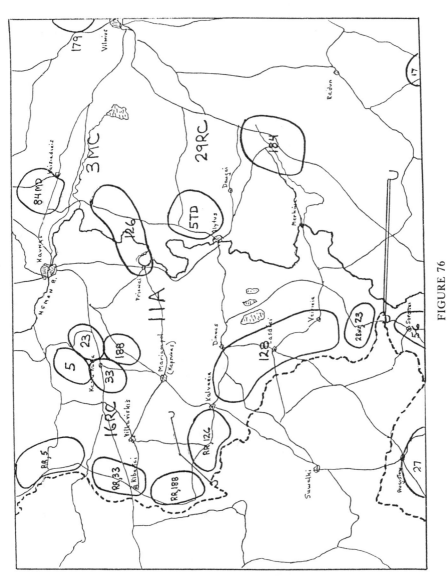

FIGURE 76
SOVIET DEPLOYMENT, 21 JUNE 1941

forces were in large camps near Kaslu Ruda. These divisions would have to deploy forward in the event of an attack, and in most cases they did so on 22 June.

Figure 77 shows the opposing force dispositions as they existed early on 22 June 1941. German forces consisted of German Ninth and Sixteenth Armies with the XXVIII, II, V, VIII and XX Army Corps and General Hoth's Panzer Group 3 with XXXIX and LVII Motorized (Panzer) Corps. The assault was to be spearheaded by 20th and 7th Panzer Divisions advancing eastward towards Alytus and by 12th Panzer Division which would advance towards the Neman River at Merkine. It was to be literally a race to the Neman River between the panzer spearheads and Soviet forces attempting to erect defenses along that river line.

Operations in this sector developed very rapidly. By the evening of 22 June, virtually all Soviet rifle regiments along the border had been engaged, fragmented, encircled or destroyed (see Figure 78). Many small pockets remained as a hindrance only to German logistical activity. The 5th, 23rd, and 188th Rifle Divisions attempted to move forward to reinforce the border positions under a hail of aerial bombardment which decimated their logistical trains. As the harried remnants raced westward they ran into advancing German infantry. After a series of very intense meeting engagements which resulted in heavy Soviet losses, Soviet troops attempted to conduct a delaying action.

Meanwhile, Morozov ordered the 23rd Rifle Division to establish defenses around the camps at Kaslu Ruda, while the 126th Rifle Division erected defenses along the Neman River south of Kaunas. The 84th Motorized Division was also supposed to occupy strong defensive positions southeast of Kaunas. The key Soviet maneuver of the day, but one which did not succeed, was the movement of Fedorov's 5th Tank Division southward either to blow up the bridge at Alytus or seize the bridge to prevent the Germans getting across the Neman River. Only small elements of 5th Tank Division reached Alytus in advance of German Panzer Regiment 25, elements of an artillery battalion and a small portion of a tank regiment. These Soviet units were quickly driven off and the Germans seized control of Alytus, a very key location, very early in the operation.

From this point on 5th Tank Division split, with a portion of the division fighting its way back to the north, while another portion dodged 12th Panzer Division, which had also conducted a very rapid advance, and thereafter made its way southeast until it eventually joined the so-called Minsk pocket. The maps show the encirclements that resulted on the first day throughout the entire sector. Meanwhile the Soviet 11th Army's second echelon division of 29th Rifle Corps tried in vain to assist 5th Tank Division along the Neman River.

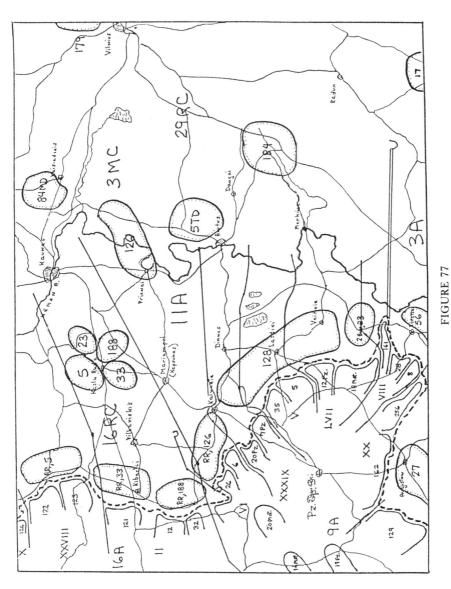

FIGURE 77
SITUATION, 0600, 22 JUNE 1941

159

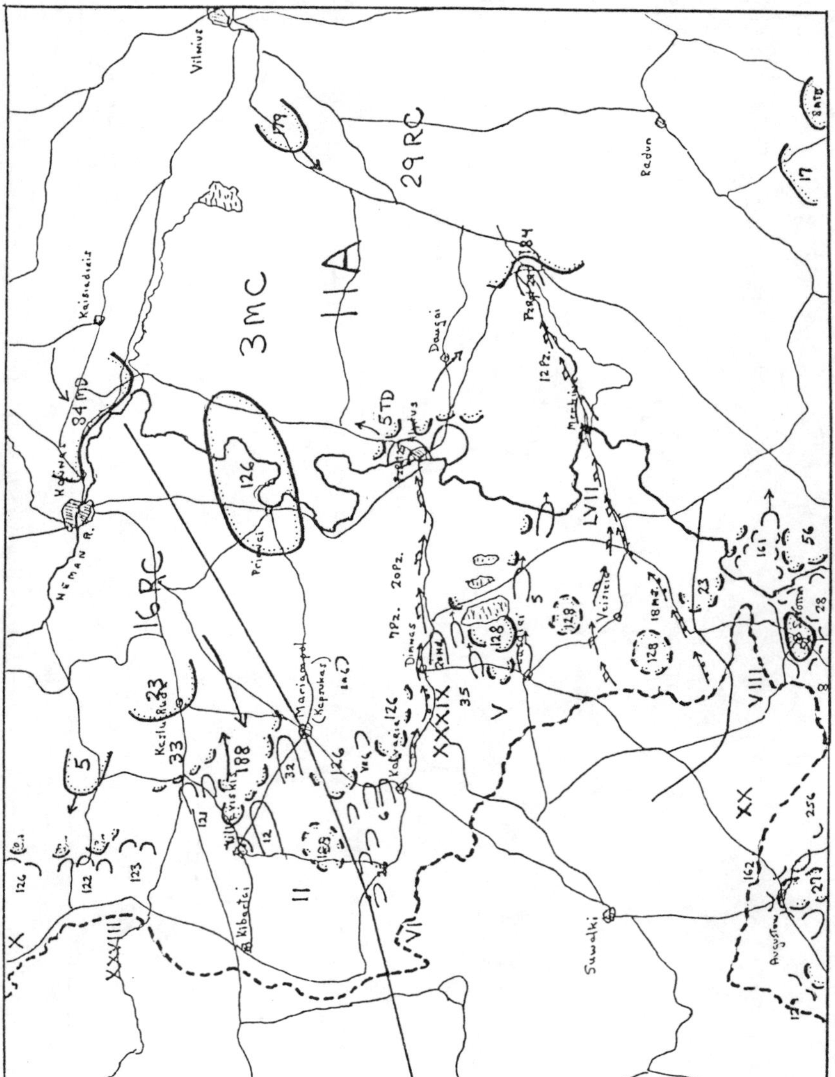

FIGURE 78
SITUATION, 2300, 22 JUNE 1941

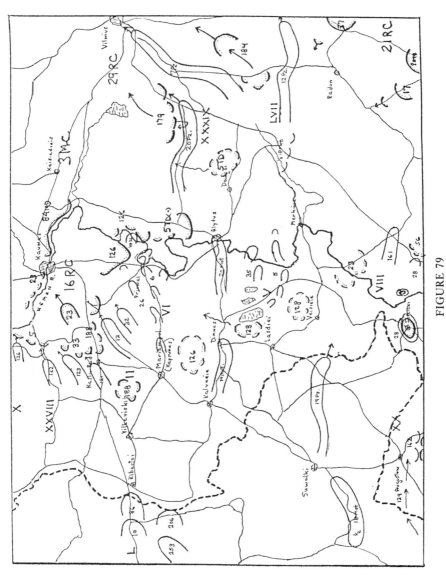

FIGURE 79
SITUATION, 2300, 23 JUNE 1941

On the second day of the attack, 23 June, the German panzer spear-heads literally disappeared off the map heading east via Vilnius towards Minsk (see Figure 79). 7th Panzer Division reached Vilnius and then swept southeast towards Minsk with 20th Panzer Division hard on its heels. 12th Panzer Division did likewise further south and advanced toward Radun. 20th and 14th Motorized Division formed a moving corridor following 20th Panzer's path as did 19th Panzer Division in the wake of 12th Panzer. All this German armored movement would soon become the northern pincer ultimately forming the great encirclement of the Soviet forces at Minsk.

Meanwhile Soviet defenders along the Neman River attempted to erect defensive positions around Kaunas anchored on a bridgehead on the eastern bank of the Neman River, using the remnants of 16th Rifle Corps and 84th Motorized Division, while the latter continued receiving repeated orders to assist the beleaguered 2nd Tank Division further north. At the same time the Soviets began erecting strong defenses south of Radun anchored on units of the newly arrived 21st Rifle Corps and 8th Antitank Brigade. In the center it was all chaos, with German panzer and motorized units heading deep into the Soviet rear, while fragmented Soviet forces tried to find their way out, either to the north or to the south. There was almost total loss of command and control on the Soviet side.

By late 24 June, the bulk of German panzer units had disappeared off the map in the east, either advancing toward Minsk or pressing against Soviet forces south of Radun (see Figure 80). On this date the North-western Front commander, Kuznetsov, ordered a counterattack to be launched from the Kaunas area southward. The order went primarily to the harried 84th Motorized Division and to remnants of 5th Tank Division, as well as to the rifle divisions defending the city. Ironically, a similar order reached 2nd Tank Division already decisively engaged at Rasienai further north. The counterattack understandably never materialized.

By 25 June the Soviet situation had deteriorated further (see Figure 81). German forces seized Kaunas and cleared the west bank of the Neman River, while Soviet forces conducted a slow and agonizing withdrawal from the area between Vilnius and Kaunas. By 26 June Soviet units had been almost totally eradicated from this sector as German infantry and motorized infantry pressed Soviet forces further north and south away from the axis of the main German thrust (see Figure 82).

Finally, 3rd Mechanized Corps, which went into combat with about 460 tanks on 22 June, by 26 June had been reduced to about 50 tanks. The 5th Tank Division did manage to extricate some of its units from the fighting east of Alytus. Its commander survived the battle, and brought remnants of the division back to Minsk. There it became involved in equally harrowing

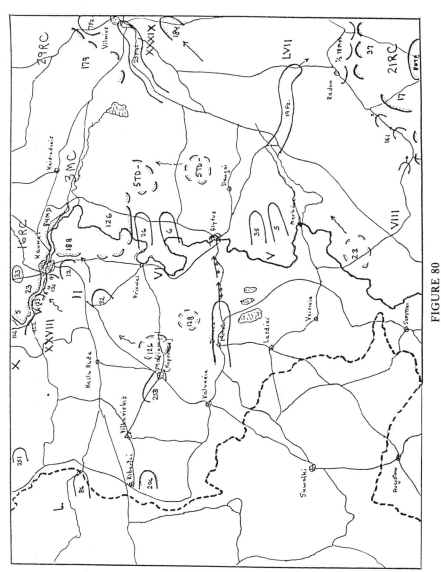

FIGURE 80
SITUATION, 2300, 24 JUNE 1941

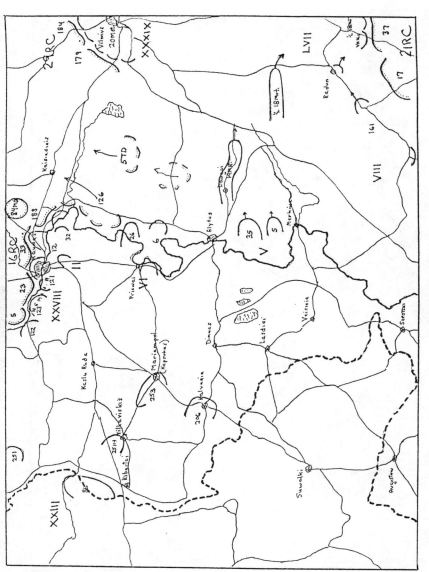

FIGURE 81
SITUATION, 2300, 25 JUNE 1941

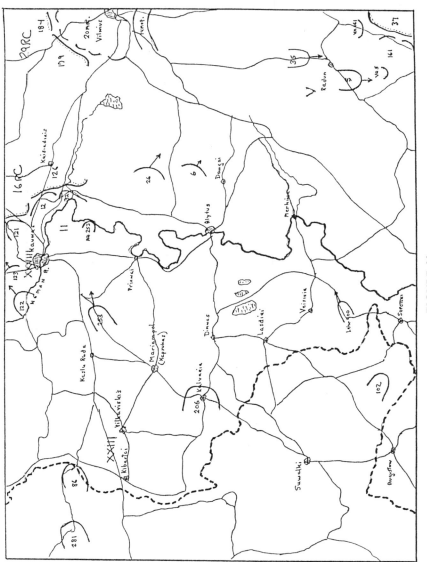

FIGURE 82
SITUATION, 2300, 26 JUNE 1941

and desperate combat. According to the roster of 11th Army commanders who fought in this sector, a number of the rifle division commanders were killed in early operations as were a number of motorized and tank division commanders. Some did survive. For example, Colonel Fomenko of 84th Motorized Division rose to command the Soviet 18th Tank Corps later in the war.

XXXIX Motorized Corps Operations

MAJOR GENERAL HORST OHRLOFF (retired)

Introduced by Colonel Paul Adair
General Ohrloff and Colonel Rothe were participants from Panzer Group 3. They served in the left flank Panzer Corps, the XXXIX, and their division, 7th Panzer, was the right flank division of that corps. General Ohrloff was a company commander in the panzer regiment of that division. Later in the war, he had a most interesting career as a staff officer in the headquarters of the Supreme Commander, West. After the war he joined the Bundeswehr and was deputy commander of I German Corps at Munster.

Colonel Rothe was the signal officer of another battalion in the same panzer regiment. After the war he spent much time in the Bundeswehr as a liaison officer in the US. I am privileged to be a member of the old Comrades' Association of the same division.

Major-General Ohrloff: As you know my name is Russian. The name was important at the time of Empress Catherine II, for Catherine II had two friends, one a general and one an admiral. One of them killed Peter III, and both fathered children by Catherine the Great. There is no relationship however, between relatives of mine and that particular Ohrloff.

My comments are divided into the following sectors:

1. Some facts about 7th Panzer Division;
2. Special training before Barbarossa began;
3. Information on the enemy and his intentions;
4. Conduct of operations of XXXIX Panzer Corps and especially of 7th Panzer Division, preceding the encirclement of Minsk.

Since I was a member of Panzer Regiment 25 of 7th Panzer Division from the beginning of the war against Russia until the relocation of the division in France in spring 1942, I shall pay special attention to the combat actions of this regiment.

Some Facts about 7th Panzer Division

In May and June 1940, the division had fought in Belgium and France under its then commander Wustenfuchs (Desert Fox) Rommel, who later became Field Marshal. Because of its rapid advances and its surprise attacks, 7th Panzer Division received the nickname the "ghost division".

The organization of 7th Panzer Division was almost identical to that of 6th Panzer Division already mentioned. The only significant difference was that the panzer battalions had four, not three panzer companies, three light companies with 17 tanks each and one heavy weapons company with 14 Type IV tanks. The advantage of this organization was that the battalions had more combat power, greater command and control flexibility, and additional equipment in the third company to function as a reserve. The most important tank was the 38T, a Czech combat vehicle which, like the 35T, had a 37mm gun. Its mobility, however, was superior to that of the smaller tank.

Special Training before Barbarossa began

After the relocation of 7th Panzer Division from an area south of Bordeaux, France to Bonn, west of Bad Godesberg, in February 1941, training emphasis was on:

1. training and advanced training of junior military leaders, especially their ability to act independently and responsibly.
2. instruction in the cooperation of all weapons in combat situations as taught by the experience of the Western Campaign.
3. close cooperation of tanks, armored infantry, motorcycle infantry, engineers and artillery at company and platoon level.

From the experience of the past campaigns in France and Poland, the units had learned that the cooperation of tanks with armored infantry, both in a mounted and dismounted combat mode, was very important. Therefore this type of operation had been practiced frequently.

As far as live firing was possible on the shooting ranges, it concentrated on engaging antitank weapons and tanks with guns, and on acquiring machine-gun experience. Night firing with many different illuminants provided a great impression of weapon effectiveness. In addition to the instructional activities we had to spend much time on logistical support. Replenishing military supplies, repairing weapons, equipment and vehicles, and providing spare parts and new types of weapons all led to a high degree of operational readiness. One technical detail seemed to be important. In the future it would be necessary to march long distances. To enable the tanks to do this we constructed an installation to transport four gasoline canisters upon the engines of the tanks. It was an addition of 18 liters of gasoline. This development was later very useful.

My 11th Company, which was attached to 3rd Battalion of Panzer Regiment 25, was established in spring 1941, just a few months before the beginning of the attack. 11th Company became combat-ready in a very short time because some other companies provided it with a platoon of five tanks each. My principal tasks in this company were:

1. Psychological preparation of the subunits for a possible offensive against Russia although nobody knew when this offensive was to begin or whether it would take place at all.
2. Getting to know the soldiers, especially the officers and NCOs, and winning their confidence.
The training of the different platoons did not vary much because they had all gone through the Western campaign.

Information on the Enemy and his Intentions

Most of the details about the organization of the different Russian units and formations were known and passed on to the soldiers. This, however, was not done in connection with Barbarossa because neither this password nor the intention to attack Russia was known. The panzer battalions were surprised to hear that Russian tank companies were equipped with only ten tanks and that a platoon consisting of three tanks apparently had one radio set only which was in the platoon leader's tank.

Unlike the Russian tanks, those of the Wehrmacht all had radio sets. Every platoon consisted of five tanks so that it could be divided into subunits of two squads each. In addition to providing more combat power, the German panzer company with its 17 tanks had the big advantage of being less liable to lose strength through losses or breakdowns caused by technical problems. Another important advantage for the German armored forces seemed to be that usually Russian infantry could not follow the tanks on APCs (armored personnel carriers) or ICVs (infantry combat vehicles). Therefore the speed of an attack was determined by the speed of infantry soldiers fighting in a dismounted combat mode, not by the speed of the tanks. This meant that the Russian attacks were slowed down considerably.

Russian soldiers were known to be tough and extremely skilled in terrain exploitation and camouflage, whereas the junior military leaders were not flexible enough to act on their own initiative.

Although the Russians had a greater number of tanks, this quantitative superiority was countered by qualitative deficiencies. However, we knew nothing about the famous T34 or KV1 tank. The greatest advantage for the German armored forces seemed to be that the Russian infantry could not accompany tanks on armored vehicles.

I want to stress again: this information was in no way directed toward Barbarossa or toward the intention to attack Russia because at that time political and especially economic relations between Russia and the German Reich were normal.

Conduct of Operations of XXXIX Panzer Corps, especially of 7th Panzer Division, Preceding the Encirclement of Minsk

The objectives of XXXIX Corps were:

– to break through the enemy forces close to the border;
– to achieve the prerequisites for destruction of enemy forces between Bialystok and Minsk by rapidly advancing through the area north of Minsk. This was to be done in close cooperation with Panzer Group 2, which was to attack Minsk from the south.

On the night of 18–19 June the three divisions of XXXIX Corps were transferred from their assembly areas to marshaling areas northeast of Suwalki (see Figure 83). For the first day of attack, 7th Panzer Division was given the following tasks: Covered by 20th Infantry Division (motorized) on the right flank and by 20th Panzer Division on the left flank, the division was to:

1. break through the border fortifications (we knew no details about them),
2. turn eastward south of Kalvaria,
3. advance on Alytus through the gap of Sinnas,
4. succeed in forcing the Neman River as the day's objective.

On 21 June, starting at 0630, the Russians repeatedly carried out demolitions, especially in their rear area which suggested that they were preparing a defense against a possible attack. The attack began on 22 June at 0305; however, the German assessment of the enemy turned out to be wrong (see Figure 84). Opposition in the border area was weak and there was only minor artillery resistance. After five hours, at about 0800, Schutzen (Rifle) Brigade 6 had reached Kalvaria.

Panzer Regiment 25, which was reinforced by Kradschutzen (Motorcycle Infantry) Battalion 7, also marched to Kalvaria. Near the eastern fringes of the town the regiment encountered the first enemy, Russian infantry. The enemy was obviously surprised by the attack and withdrew. The panzer regiment advanced on Alytus so rapidly that the units and subunits were mixed up. Tanks that dropped out temporarily because of technical problems were unable to rejoin their units, and tanks moving too slowly were overtaken by faster vehicles. A tank race also occurred in 3rd Battalion of Panzer Regiment 25 (of which my 11th Company was a part),

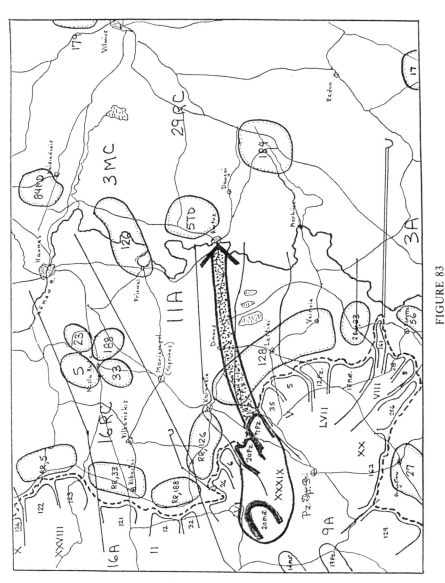

FIGURE 83
SITUATION, 0600, 22 JUNE 1941

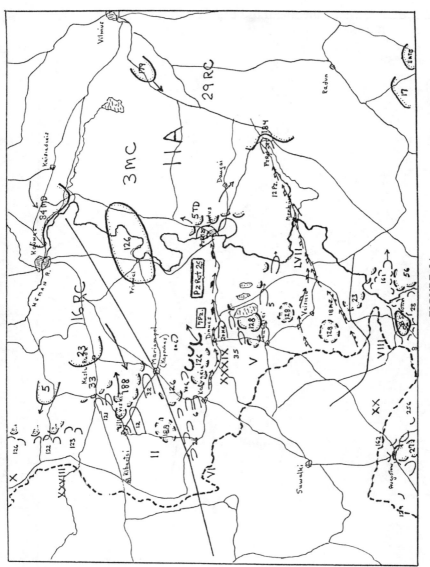

FIGURE 84
SITUATION, 2300, 22 JUNE 1941

which had been committed against the southern Neman River bridge (see Figure 85). However, during this deployment the regimental commander ordered the battalion to make for the northern bridge. The aide de camp of 3rd Battalion did not know about this change and therefore, on reaching the fork in the road that divided the northern and southern route, he directed the tanks following him to the original objective of 3rd Battalion, the southern bridge. Despite the fact that operations were then carried out by different units at both bridges, the German forces succeeded in seizing these two important bridges undamaged.

After about 20 tanks of 3rd Battalion had crossed the northern bridge, the 21st tank was hit by a Russian tank which was in a well-concealed position near the bridge and could not be detected by the German tanks.

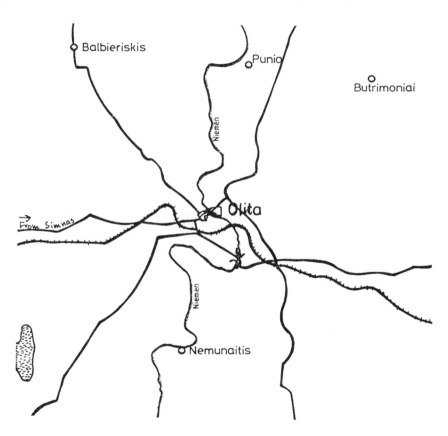

FIGURE 85
THE OLITA (ALYTUS) REGION

173

The commander of the German tank, a second lieutenant, was killed and the Russian tank rushed back to its unit by passing approximately 30 German tanks which were dispersed throughout a large area. Several tanks including mine, tried to destroy the enemy tank using our 37mm gun. These attempts, however, had no effect on the T34 which we were observing for the first time.

The German forces did not succeed at first in expanding the northern bridgehead because it was impossible to destroy the Russian tanks standing in hull-down positions on the reverse slope (see Figure 86). East

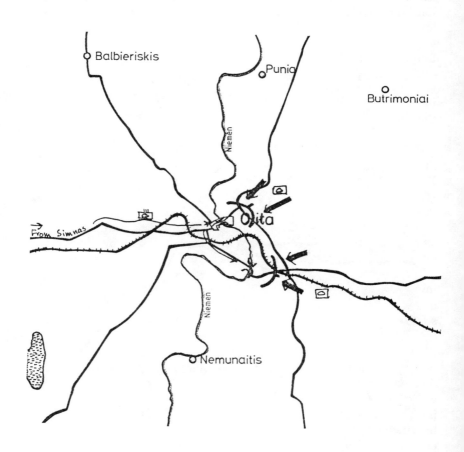

FIGURE 86
7TH PANZER DIVISION COMBAT AT OLITA, 22 JUNE 1941 (AM)

of the southern bridge some German tanks were ambushed, and six were lost to antitank gun fire. However, in the course of several counterattacks 15 Russian tanks were destroyed. The Russians launched a counterattack with many tanks plus artillery and infantry support. In the course of the ensuing battle between Russian and German tanks, more than 70 enemy tanks were destroyed.

Panzer Regiment 21 of 20th Panzer Division had followed Panzer Regiment 25 to Alytus on the same march route (see Figure 87). This regiment was attached to 7th Panzer Division and was directed to the northern bridgehead where it arrived at 1930 hours. Regiment 21 was ordered to take over the defense of this bridgehead to facilitate the detachment of 3rd Battalion of Panzer Regiment 25, which was to be available for an attack. Therefore, Regiment 21 had to hand over 30 per cent of its ammunition to Regiment 25 because that amount of ammunition had been used.

3rd Battalion of Panzer Regiment 25, supported by strong artillery, broke out of the northern bridgehead on the east bank of the river towards the southern bridgehead, thereby allowing the German forces to expand the area gained so that the Panzer regiment could assemble all three battalions on the east bank.

The tank battle near Alytus between German tanks and those of Soviet 5th Tank Division was probably the hardest combat ever conducted by 7th Panzer Division in the Second World War. The Russians, however, seemed to be almost beaten: several villages in the rear area burst into flames indicating that the Russians intended to break off the encounter.

After the units had been marshaled and provided with the necessary supplies during the short night, the division left the southern bridgehead on 23 June to reach the heights surroundings Vilna (see Figure 88).

Panzeraufklarungs (Armored Reconnaissance) Battalion 7 seized an important undamaged bridge 10 kilometers west of Vilna in a surprise attack, thereby enabling Panzer Regiment 25 to bypass the town from the south in its attack and push through to the north at nightfall to encircle the town and place its eastern fringes under tank control.

On 24 June at about 0500, the motorcycle battalion succeeded in occupying the airfield of Vilna from the south and advancing on the town. The houses were decorated with Lithuanian colors and on entering the city the soldiers were received most enthusiastically. German security installations and march columns were repeatedly attacked from the south by enemy armored battle groups, but they were all fended off. The enemy's lines of defense in front of Vilna and around the town were obviously broken through at that point; resistance was to be expected only in the large wooded area to the east and to the southeast of the town.

On 25 June the division intended to advance upon the enemy lines of fortification along the border between Poland and Russia via Molodeczno (see Figure 89). However, Schutzen (Rifle) Regiment 6, which had been committed in advance and started at 0600 for a direct attack on Molodeczno, met tremendous resistance so that the route of advance could not be seized until nightfall. In the meantime, Schutzen Regiment 7 and Panzer Regiment 25 had reached the area east of Radoskovice.

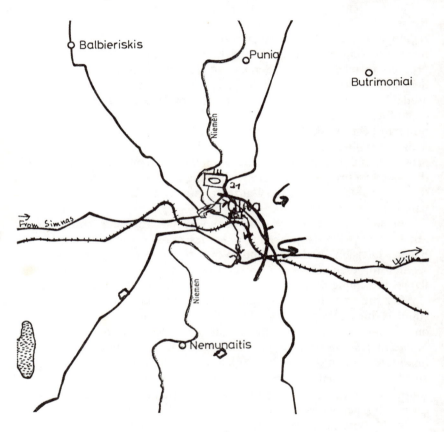

FIGURE 87
7TH PANZER DIVISION COMBAT AT OLITA, 22 JUNE 1941 (PM)

However, in total darkness they met massive resistance which could not be broken.

Throughout the day the division was attacked by Russian aircraft; particularly affected was Schutzen Regiment 6 in Molodeczno. The bridge in Radoskovice was damaged and repaired several times, as was the division's headquarters. German assessments of the enemy indicated that

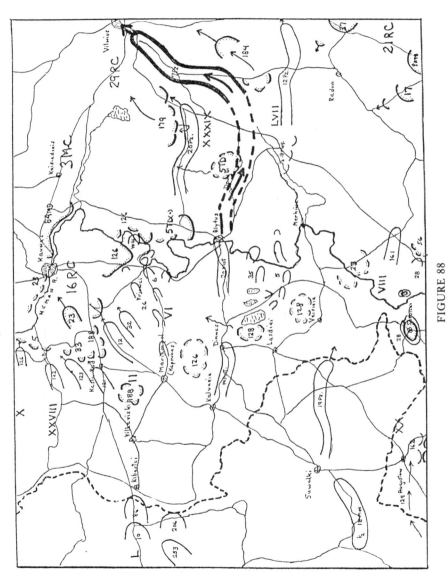

FIGURE 88
SITUATION, 2300, 23 JUNE 1941

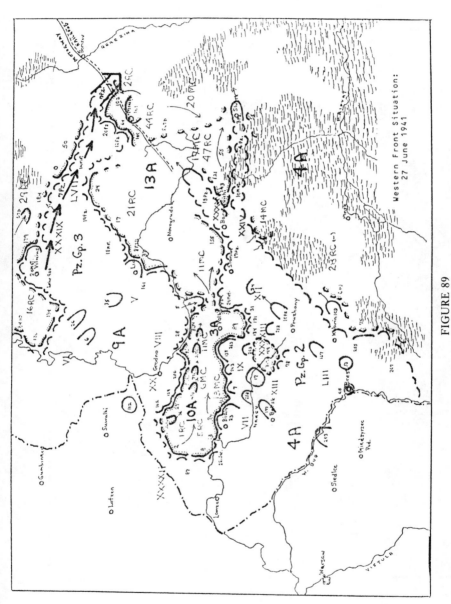

FIGURE 89

7TH PANZER DIVISION OPERATIONS, 24–27 JUNE 1941

the Russians knew that their lines of defense had been broken through but were unable, in spite of numerous single centers of resistance, to form a coherent line of defense. Terrain reconnaissance revealed that there were no modern fortifications in the combat sector of 7th Panzer Division. The enemy had obviously withdrawn in the face of fierce and determined attacks.

The overall assessment led to the decision to commit Panzer Regiment 25 to the motorway and the railroad line Minsk–Moscow on 26 June (see Figure 90). The regiment was reinforced by an armored infantry battalion. 3rd Battalion of Panzer Regiment 25 was ordered to spearhead the regiment's advance in its attempt to gain the forest east of Smolewiecze

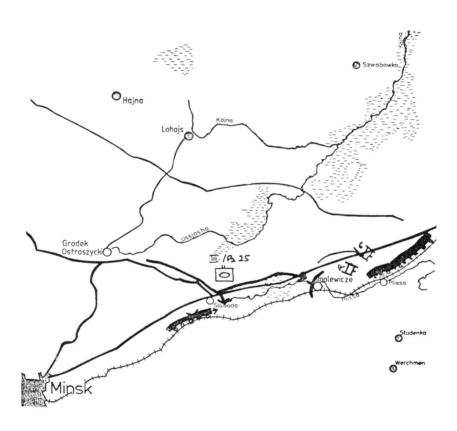

FIGURE 90
7TH PANZER DIVISION OPERATIONS EAST OF MINSK, 26–27 JUNE 1941

and to secure the northern and southern regions there. 3rd Battalion reached the motorway north of Slopoda at about 1700. It made no contact with the enemy but encountered frequent air attacks. The battalion's next step was to seize Smolewiecze, 20 km northeast of Minsk, at nightfall. Here the unit met only minor resistance on the part of snipers. Just south of the motorway, I myself stopped a freight train with supplies from Minsk by firing at it with my tank gun. The remaining four tanks of another company of the battalion had to engage a tank transport train which came from the east and stopped one kilometer west of the small railroad station of Plissa.

At sunrise on 27 June the tank transport train discovered these four tanks and combat ensued in the course of which the company commander's tank was destroyed. However, another supporting panzer company consisting of six tanks and several antitank guns managed to silence the Russian train. In the course of this battle the regimental commander, Colonel Rothenburg, was seriously injured by a shell fragment. The joy at our great success was damped by the fact that this much revered commander was killed by snipers on the way back through the rear area.

The northern part of the ring around Minsk was then closed (see Figure 91). XXXIX Corps, and especially 7th Panzer Division, had fulfilled their tasks. At that time, Panzer Regiment 25 had only about 50 per cent of its Type II and 38T tanks left, and a mere 25 of its Type IV tanks. Therefore, a panzer battalion was deactivated temporarily.

Since attacks from the east, south and west had to be expected, the division prepared a defense by allocating defensive areas to the two Schutzen (rifle) regiments and to the *Panzeraufklarungs* (armored reconnaissance) battalion. Part of the panzer regiment was kept available as a reserve. Since the Russians had disrupted the division's supply routes in several places, only local attacks were possible. Supply vehicles had to be escorted by tanks, and detachments with flatbed trailers sent out to recover tanks damaged during the march had to be protected by armored vehicles. The great importance of the Minsk–Moscow road became evident when a new Russian division moved forward on 27 June to clear this road.

From the beginning of hostilities, the command of *Heeresgruppe* (Army Group) 3 had paid special attention to the Orsha-Smolensk-Vitebsk triangle so as to give the enemy as little time as possible to prepare a defense or to set up defensive installations. The command was even prepared to neglect the encirclement of Minsk or to spend less time on it to avoid endangering its real objective. The *Oberkommando de Heeres* (OKH) (Supreme Army Command), however, did not share this view.

In order to continue the attack as soon as possible, XXXIX Corps ordered 7th Panzer Division on the evening of 28 June (see Figure 92):

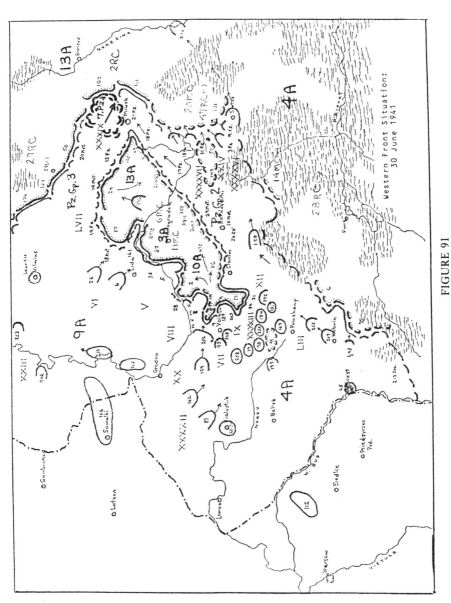

FIGURE 91
7TH PANZER DIVISION OPERATIONS, 27 JUNE 1941

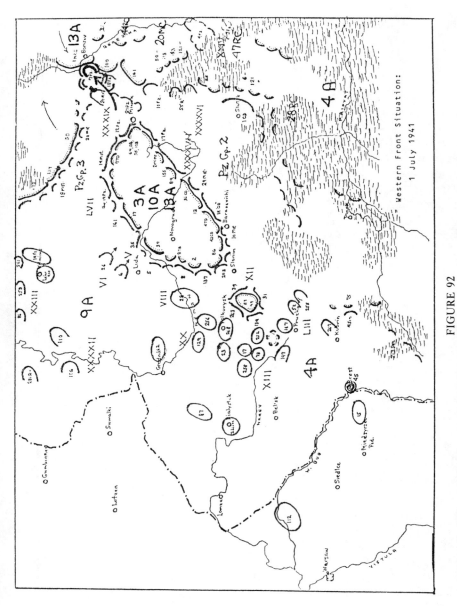

FIGURE 92
7TH PANZER DIVISION OPERATIONS, 28 JUNE–1 JULY 1941

– to organize a battle group prepared to attack Borissow, which was in the northeast, on call, in order to force a crossing over the Beresina River there, and
– to form a bridgehead.

Since the roads in the Borissow area were in a very bad state, a panzer battalion was ordered to execute this mission. The battalion was 1st Battalion of Panzer Regiment 25 which was reinforced by other units for the mission.

On 28 June, the day on which the attack was to be continued, Minsk was seized by 12th Panzer Division. On the morning of 29 June the Corps repeated that the mission to attack Borissow was of critical importance, that it was still effective, and that the beginning of the attack would be announced in good time. This information was the prelude to the battle for Smolensk.

4

The Border Battles on the Bialystok–Minsk Axis: 22–28 June 1941

Overview

COLONEL D. M. GLANTZ

Let us look at the sector where the Soviets expected the heaviest armored combat to occur. Indeed, it did turn out to be most intensive in the south where they expected it. But it was also intense where they did not expect it, in the Western Front sector. We will consider the Western Front first, and then the Southwestern Front.

The overall German intelligence assessment prepared on 17 June 1941 (see Figure 93) is very similar to the one referred to earlier concerning the Baltic region. This is the German intelligence appraisal showing where the Germans judged Soviet units to be located on 17 June. They had identified correctly the Soviet army designations; 3rd, 10th, and 4th. The Germans noted rifle divisions, motorized units, cavalry units, and one tank corps, the 6th, which was a correct identification. Figure 94 is a simplified version of this map. If you compare the German intelligence assessment with Soviet units actually in the Soviet Western Front order of battle in June 1941, a distinctive feature emerges very similar to that which we saw in the Baltic Military District. There was a big difference between the intelligence assessment and reality.

In general terms, across the breadth of the entire eastern front, German intelligence counted roughly 40 per cent more Soviet rifle forces than were actually there. Conversely however, German intelligence counted only roughly 20 to 30 per cent of the Soviet mechanized forces actually present. I think there is enough evidence to indicate that the Soviets probably consciously postured larger forces in the immediate border districts than they actually had, at least in terms of rifle forces. It is also very probable that the Soviets deliberately hid, as much as possible, the mechanized

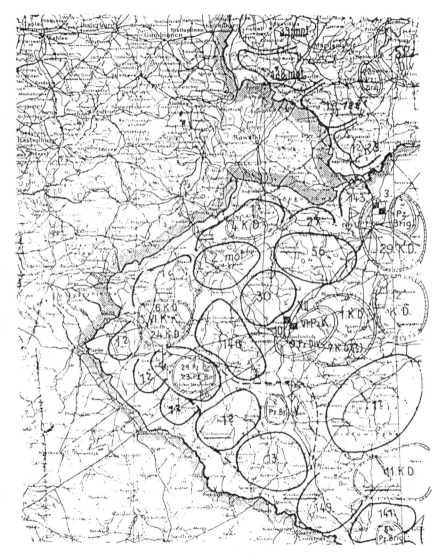

FIGURE 93
GERMAN INTELLIGENCE MAP, 17 JUNE 1941

185

forces in those regions. This tracks very closely with Soviet deception efforts conducted from 1942 to 1945, which I have looked at quite closely during the past three years.

Of course, the most important question is: to what end did the Soviets erect that false image? It may have been, in fact, a part of the overall Soviet defensive scheme, perhaps a desire to reinforce German perceptions that more forces were in the border military districts than was actually the case.

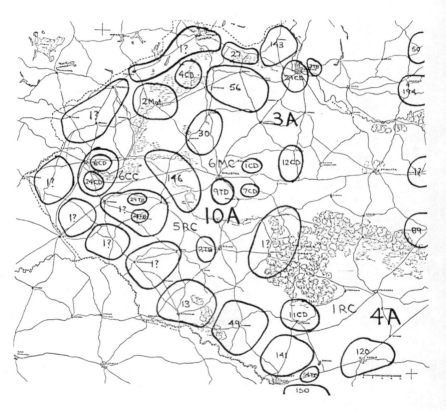

FIGURE 94
GERMAN INTELLIGENCE ASSESSMENT
(simplified)

This measure could have been designed to deter German action. Soviet attempts to hide their mechanized corps could have been designed to deal with the Germans should deterrence fail. In any case, the net effect was to convince the Germans that they would destroy more Soviet forces along the borders than would actually be the case.

Of course, the Soviet force deployment was much deeper than the Germans had expected. In general terms, German intelligence detected more Soviet cavalry units than actually existed and that was because most of those cavalry units had provided the base for the new undetected Soviet mobile formations. German intelligence continued carrying panzer or tank brigades on the map, when in fact, those brigades had either become mobile divisions or elements of mobile divisions, in the new Soviet mechanized corps. The map (Figure 94) provides the clearest illustration of that larger German image of rifle forces than actually existed. The region extending from Lomza southeast toward Brest indicates seven Soviet rifle divisions carried on German intelligence maps, when in fact there were only four.

Let us now look a little more closely at the Soviet order of battle in the Special Western Military District, (see Figure 95). Lieutenant General D.G. Pavlov commanded the Special Western Military District which in wartime became the Western Front. He had under his command three armies, the 3rd, 10th, and 4th, which were deployed from north to south. The 3rd Army covered the northern flank of the Bialystok bulge, the 10th Army anchored the central portion of the bulge, and 4th Army covered the southern flank of the bulge. These were relatively untenable positions given the routes that the German panzer groups ultimately took. The route of 3rd Panzer Group was north of this bulge and the route of 2nd Panzer Group south. It was this geographical position that led almost inevitably to rapid bypass, envelopment, and encirclement of Pavlov's force.

Lieutenant General V.I. Kuznetsov's 3rd Army consisted of one rifle corps, the 4th, with two divisions forward (the 27th and 56th) and one division, the 85th, in second echelon. He also had one mechanized corps (the 11th) located just south of Grodno. 11th Mechanized Corps of Major General D.K. Mostovenko consisted, as did all mechanized corps, of two tank divisions and one motorized division. Its general deployment evidenced the same sort of mal-positioning that other mechanized corps experienced. Colonel N.P. Studnev's 29th Tank Division was located at Grodno, Colonel M.F. Panov's 33rd Tank Division was located south of Grodno, and Colonel A.M. Piragov's 204th Motorized Division was located basically a full day's road march to the rear. The 11th Mechanized Corps was a strong corps, as we will see, and did have some new KV and T34 tanks. The 4th Army of Lieutenant General A.A. Korobkov was deployed in the same general configuration as 3rd Army with one rifle corps (28th) and one mechanized corps (14th) deployed forward. 28th Rifle Corps had two divisions deployed north and south of Brest backed up by Major General S.I. Oborin's 14th Mechanized Corps' 30th Tank Division and 22nd Tank Division. Its motorized division (the 205th) was actually located somewhat further to the east, again a day's march from the tank divisions which it was to support. One additional rifle division, the 49th, not within the corps structure, but rather under direct army control, was located on the army's right flank.

The 10th Army of Lieutenant General K. D. Golubev was positioned in the center of the Bialystok bulge. It consisted of two rifle corps (the 1st and the 5th) backed up by the 6th and 13th Mechanized Corps. In 10th Army,

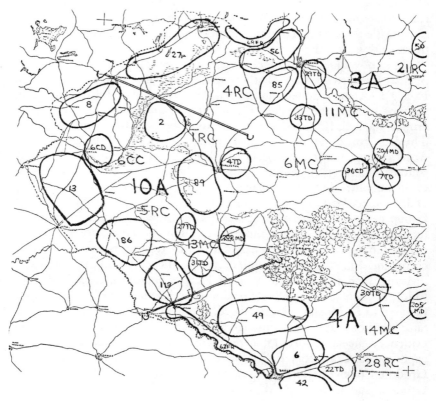

FIGURE 95
SOVIET DEPLOYMENT, 21 JUNE 1941

the rifle and mechanized corps were paired with a rifle corps forward and a supporting mechanized corps to the rear. The army's 1st Rifle Corps had the 8th Rifle Division forward and the 2nd Rifle Division to the rear. 5th Rifle Corps had two divisions (the 86th and the 13th) forward and the 89th Rifle Division to the rear.

The 6th Mechanized Corps of Major General M.G. Khatskilevich had its 4th Tank Division just east of Bialystok and its 7th Tank Division further east near Volkovysk. Its 29th Motorized Division was located even further east at Slonim. It was very poor deployment and a tremendous scattering of forces in that corps. This mechanized corps, incidentally, was the heaviest on the Western Front, with a total strength of around 960 tanks, including KVs and T34s, as we shall see. Major General P.N. Akhlyustin's 13th Mechanized Corps, with 27th and 31st Tank Divisions and the 208th Motorized Division, was designated to support 5th Rifle Corps. It was, however, a weak corps equipped with only older model tanks. In addition, Pavlov had at his disposal one cavalry corps, the 6th, with one division forward at Lomza (the 6th) and one division to the rear (the 36th).

German forces were assembled for the attack as shown on the map (see Figure 96). Ninth Army operated from the north, with VIII, XX and XXXXII Army Corps. To the south the Germans deployed Fourth Army with Panzer Group 2, XII, XXXXIII, XIII, and VII Army Corps. Panzer Group 2 consisted of XXXXVII and XXIV Motorized Corps.

One armored force correlation (see Figure 97) provides a more detailed view of Soviet armored force deployments as they existed on 22 June. First, notice the scattered nature of Soviet armored units. None of the Soviet mechanized corps had all their forces at a single location. The 11th Mechanized Corps had its two tank divisions forward, and one of those tank divisions (the 29th) was quite strong. The 29th Division was located at Grodno and had 28 KVs and T34s and 200 older tanks. However, the 30th Tank Division was quite weak with only two KVs and 30 T34s. The 6th Mechanized Corps was quite heavy. Its 4th Tank Division, stationed near Bialystok, had 163 KVs and T34s and 212 older medium and light tanks. Its 7th Tank Division located at Volkovysk had 163 T34s and KVs and 212 older models. (Recent Soviet articles cite 7th Tank Division strength as: 51 KVs, 150 T34s, 125 BT 5/7s, and 42 T26s.) Thus, this corps had 960 tanks, roughly half of them new models. However, these new tanks were received in April and May 1941, their drivers were assigned in late May and early June, and many of the drivers simply had not been trained. Also, many of the new KV tanks, in addition to not being bore-sighted, could not fire their guns because there was no ammunition. For example, the 41st Tank Division, which we will look at an action in the Southwestern Front area, went into combat with no ammunition whatever.

The weakest of the mechanized corps (the 13th), did have its units in close proximity to one another, but it made very little difference because the total strength of that corps was roughly 300 older tanks and no T34s or KVs. The 14th Mechanized Corps, which was the corps which Guderian's Panzer Group 2 ran straight into and through, also had no new medium or heavy tanks, which largely explains the ultimate fate of the Soviet 22nd Tank Division, the first engaged, which, by the end of the first day of combat, had lost most of its tanks as well as its commander.

The overall armor ratios, again realizing that many of these Soviet tanks were not in particularly good shape, was roughly 1.6 to 1 in the Soviets' favor. Incidentally, the damage figures, or the figures for the destroyed Soviet tanks up through 10 July in this sector just about matched the strength losses gleaned from Soviet sources: that is, somewhere in the neighborhood of 80 per cent of their original strength.

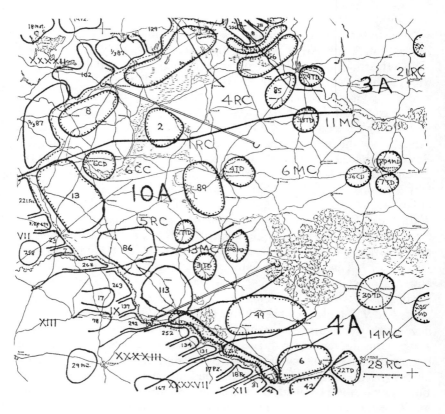

FIGURE 96
SITUATION, 0600, 22 JUNE 1941

190

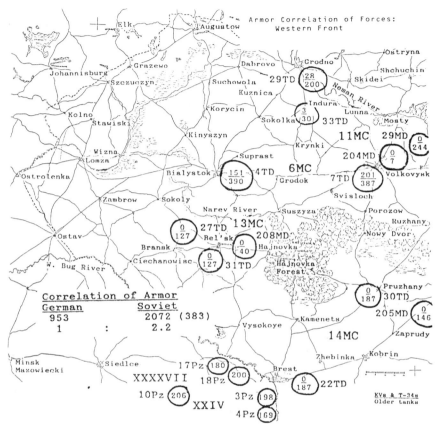

FIGURE 97
ARMORED FORCES, SPECIAL WESTERN MILITARY DISTRICT

One particular sector, near Grodno (see Figure 98) was, from the Soviet standpoint, where the heaviest and most successful armored fighting took place. Obviously, there was also heavy fighting east of Brest, but that fighting was not successful since the Soviet 14th Mechanized Corps was simply rolled over by Panzer Group 2. In the area near Grodno however, the Soviets attempted to carry out a planned and coordinated counterattack. They did, in fact, launch counterattacks, although they were not particularly well coordinated. German sources confirm that these attacks were quite heavy.

This was the configuration of Soviet forces defending near the city of Grodno, located on the Neman River just east of the little beak of East Prussia which protruded into the Soviet Union. The defensive positions of

191

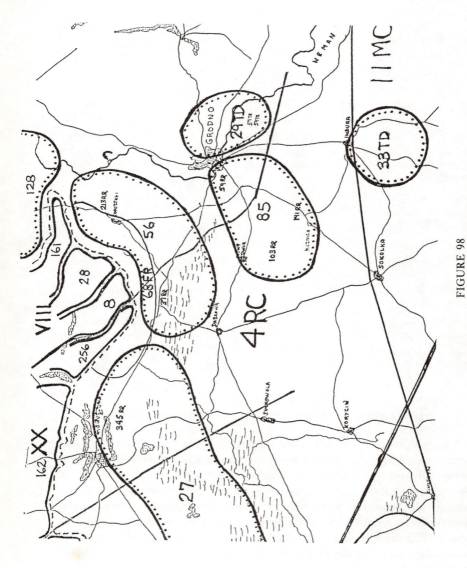

FIGURE 98
GRODNO SECTOR, 0600, 22 JUNE 1941

Soviet 3rd Army in this sector were manned by the 56th Rifle Division, which had two regiments positioned forward and one to the rear. There was also a fortified region defending along the border, the 68th Fortified Region, which was basically a rifle, machine-gun, and artillery outfit made up of separate battalions. In essence, it was a heavy border guards type defensive unit. It occupied positions along the border from the Neman River north of Grodno westward to Augustov. To the west, the 27th Rifle Division had a regiment defending in Augustov, a regiment further south, and one regiment well to the rear. The 85th Rifle Division had its three rifle regiments in camps southwest of Grodno, the 29th Tank Division had half its strength north of the Neman River and half south, and the very light 33rd Tank Division was located south of Indura. We will look at this area closely as the Soviets tried to orchestrate some kind of coordinated counterattack amidst the confusion which reigned after 22 June.

The map (Figure 99) moves a little bit further into the Soviet operational depths. You cannot understand what was occurring around Bialystok unless you look back at the Minsk area as well, because this was a battle occurring simultaneously along the border at Bialystok, back at Volkovysk, around Minsk, and ultimately, toward Borisov on the Beresina River. It reflected the essence of deep operations unfolding, only of course in this case it was German deep operations.

Backing up Soviet 3rd, 10th, and 4th Armies were the other combat elements of the Special Western Military District. These included Major General M.P. Petrov's 17th Mechanized Corps based at Baranovichi and Major General A.G. Nikitin's 20th Mechanized Corps based at Minsk. Both these corps were woefully under strength with roughly 300 tanks each and very few new models. When 17th Mechanized Corps deployed forward its armored force numbered only 36 tanks, while 20th Mechanized Corps fielded only 93. Apparently the fielding of new armor into the Soviet mechanized forces was proceeding with priority going to the mechanized corps deployed forward. Then, as time passed, the Soviets planned to fill up the mechanized corps to the rear. The 21st Rifle Corps consisted of the 17th, 37th, and 24th Rifle Divisions, and on 22 June its divisions were moving southward towards Lida. These divisions, along with the 50th Rifle Division, were the forces that 7th Panzer Division ran into on the road to Minsk. The 44th Rifle Corps consisted of the 100th Rifle Division, located west of the Berezina River, and the 161st, 108th, and 64th Rifle Divisions stationed east of the Berezina. These were the units that raced towards Minsk to try to stop 7th Panzer Division's approach to that city. The 47th Rifle Corps had its units strung out from Baranovichi through Slutsk to Bobruisk. These units would hasten forward and collide with Panzer Group 2 near Baranovichi.

Thus, Soviet defenses and separate units of various size were deployed

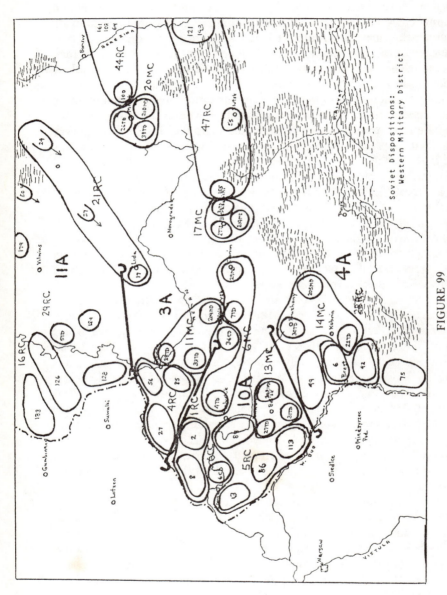

FIGURE 99

SOVIET DISPOSITIONS: SPECIAL WESTERN MILITARY DISTRICT

throughout the depth of the military district. As this German deep operation developed, with Panzer Group 3 thrusting along the northern axis and Panzer Group 2 thrusting along the southern axis, a series of battles occurred along the border, and simultaneously, another series of battles erupted along the routes of advance of those panzer groups. These battles were, in essence, meeting engagements in which it was very difficult to maintain control of units, especially if you were being attacked successfully.

Now let us turn to the conduct of the operation, which was similar in some respects to events in the Vilnius sector where 3rd Panzer Group thrust rapidly forward towards Minsk (see Figure 100). There would be very rapid development of deep operations by Panzer Group 2, which

FIGURE 100
SITUATION, 2400, 22 JUNE 1941

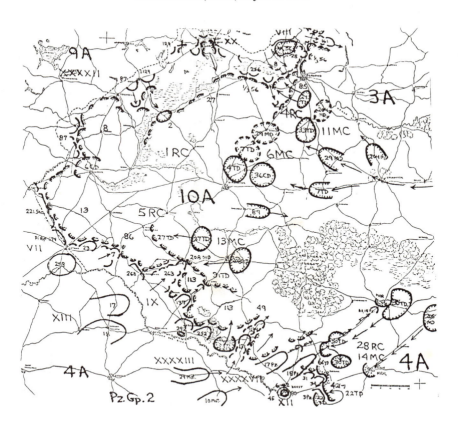

advanced along two axes, spearheaded respectively by 17th and 18th Panzer Divisions and by 3rd and 4th Panzer Divisions.

Very early on the morning of 22 June and soon after the German attack had begun, elements of the Soviet 42nd and 6th Rifle Divisions were surrounded and isolated in Brest by the German 45th Infantry Division. The 17th and 18th Panzer Divisions, side by side and supported by 31st Infantry Division, rapidly attacked to the east, north of Brest. Meanwhile, 3rd and 4th Panzer Divisions began an attack eastward south of Brest on a route of advance parallel to the routes taken by 17th and 18th Panzer Divisions.

The attacks of 18th and 3rd Panzer Divisions ran into the Soviet 14th Mechanized Corps' 22nd Tank Division, which was equipped only with older tanks. That division tried to halt the German advance but was very severely smashed up in the process. Thereafter, the division attempted to fight a delaying action through successive positions. As it withdrew, command and control deteriorated and the division essentially dissolved. In fact, the initial German artillery preparation produced 20 per cent casualties in the division and destroyed all corps communications. The division commander was killed on 23 June while trying to launch a counterattack.

After news had arrived of the German attack, 30th Tank Division quickly deployed forward from its camp at Pruzhany, in so doing striking lead elements of 18th Panzer Division late on 22 June. It then withdrew southeastward to join the remnants of 22nd Tank Division and the portions of the two rifle divisions which had not been encircled in Brest. The 205th Motorized Division, itself weak in armor and lacking many vehicles, simply created a reinforced battalion-size group under one of its regiments and sent it forward to assist the mechanized units. Ultimately, this battalion task force provided security around the city of Kobrin in the hope of covering the withdrawal of 30th and 22nd Tank Divisions, when that became necessary.

Throughout the entire process of defense in the Western Front sector, there existed the same pattern of uncertainty and conflicting orders which characterized fighting elsewhere. The first orders sent down by higher commands were to hold fire and do nothing to provoke the Germans. These were followed by routine orders to counterattack, and then, after an extended period, during which it became clear what was happening, there were finally orders to withdraw. These withdrawal orders often came too late. During the entire period there was lack of communication between headquarters at all levels, in particular between *front*, army, and corps commanders.

On 22 June in the northern sector, Panzer Group 3 swept on eastward to Alytus, leaving the task of clearing Soviet forces from their southern flank to the German VIII and XX Army Corps, which were primarily infantry forces. These were the forces that fought their way into the Grodno area, surrounded one Soviet rifle regiment near Sipotski, and drove the remainder of the Soviet 56th Rifle Division back through the city of Grodno.

From Grodno in the north to just north of Brest in the south, the entire German effort around the Bialystok Salient was an economy of force operation. Elements of XXXXII Army Corps, specifically the 129th and 87th Infantry Divisions, covered the wide expense from Augustov to Lomza, while German main attack forces thrust eastward north of Grodno. The VII Army Corps pressured Soviet forces in the section southeast of Lomza. Aside from the assaults of Panzer Groups 2 and 3, perhaps the most devastating attacks, in terms of the Soviets' inability to defend against them, occurred in the area southeast of Bialystok. There the Germans IX, XIII and XXXXIII Army Corps struck across the Bug River and engaged elements of Soviet 4th Army's right wing and 10th Army's left wing. Faced with disaster along the border, the 10th Army commander ordered Akhlyustin's 13th Mechanized Corps forward to launch counterattacks or establish a new defense line. This was the mechanized corps that lacked a significant number of tanks of any type.

Upon receipt of these orders, 27th and 31st Tank Divisions moved forward and established a defensive line along a river west of Bel'sk to act as a rallying point for forces which had been routed along the border. It appears that many of 13th Mechanized Corps' tanks never reached the river and perhaps only 100 tanks participated in the defense. Hence, this line inexorably moved northward under pressure from the German advance.

Offering a closer look at combat in the Grodno region, Figure 101, a map from the records of German VII Army Corps, portrays events on 22 June up to 2400. The Neman River is on the right and the city of Grodno. Notice the surrounded Soviet rifle regiment at Sipotski which held out for 48 hours. On the bottom half of the map are elements of Soviet 11th Mechanized Corps' 29th Tank Division going into action. As in the Baltic region, these counterattacks tended to be uncoordinated and conducted in piece-meal fashion. That was the first major Soviet problem. The second was the logistical problem of a lack of fuel and ammunition, caused both by the Soviet poor logistical system and by the heavy German air attacks which blanketed the roads.

A more detailed look at combat on 22 June in the Grodno sector shows the rapid advance of the German 161st Division which seized a bridgehead across the Neman River (see Figure 102). The 161st Infantry Division advanced parallel to Panzer Group 3, while the German 28th and 8th Infantry Divisions swept around the defenders of Sipotski and forced Soviet troops back toward Grodno. In response, the Soviets brought the

FIGURE 101
GRODNO SECTOR, VIII CORPS SITUATION MAP:
2400, 22 JUNE 1941

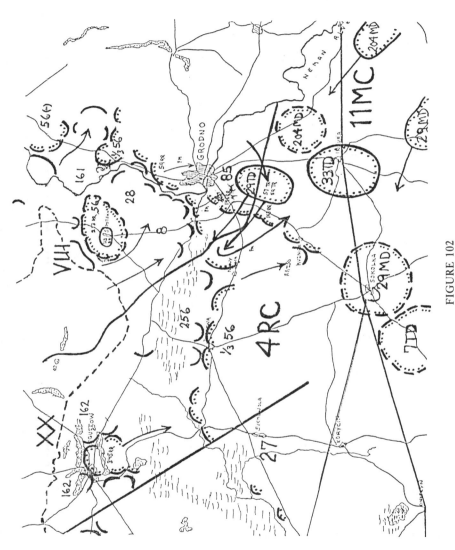

FIGURE 102

GRODNO SECTOR, 2400, 22 JUNE 1941

85th Rifle Division forward with orders to back up remnants of 56th Rifle Division and establish a defense line running roughly southwest from Grodno. The 29th Tank Division's two tank regiments went into action late in the afternoon of 22 June, counterattacking against the right flank of the German 8th Infantry Division, in part successfully, and probably causing some consternation in that division. Meanwhile, the 33rd Tank Division moved northward towards Grodno from Indura under heavy German air attacks.

Late on 22 June Pavlov, the *front* commander, ordered 6th and 11th Mechanized Corps to concentrate northeast of Bialystok and then strike northward in a major counterattack, apparently in concert with pre-war operational plans. Pavlov sent Lieutenant General I. V. Boldin, his deputy, forward to coordinate the effort. Given the great distance the mechanized corps had to travel and the narrow time constraints, it would be at least 24 hours before such a counterattack could hope to materialize. The German intelligence picture of 23 June reinforced a tendency seen earlier in the Baltic Military District (see Figure 103). After a full day of combat the Germans now identified Soviet units more correctly and the frontline trace after two days of combat may be seen as well.

Many written accounts reflect the chaos reigning in the Soviet Western Front headquarters at this stage of the operation. General Pavlov clearly did not have control over events, or his own destiny for that matter. He lacked communications with his army commanders and, in fact, there was an almost total breakdown of communications throughout the sector. Radio communications failed and within 48 hours of the start of the operation commencing most wire land lines had been cut by combat itself or by German divisionary forces.

Late on 22 June Pavlov sent Boldin from *front* headquarters to 10th Army headquarters to ascertain what was occurring and to organize the planned counterattacks. Boldin has written a book and several articles on his subsequent experiences. They are revealing and are perhaps the most graphic accounts of what was occurring. His accounts capture the absolute chaos reigning supreme in Soviet command channels throughout the first few days of war. His initial orders were to fly to Bialystok to find General Golobev's 10th Army headquarters. Boldin's flight, at low level through skies dominated by German aircraft, was harrowing at best. He landed at the Bialystok airstrip just as it came under attack by German fighters. Fuel dumps blazed on all sides. He found 10th Army headquarters huddled in dugouts near the airstrip, but Golubev was away trying to locate some of his subordinate units.

In essence, Boldin's task was to assemble the forces of 6th Mechanized Corps, the heaviest mechanized corps, and launch it, in concert with 11th Mechanized Corps and 6th Cavalry Corps, in a concerted attack to the

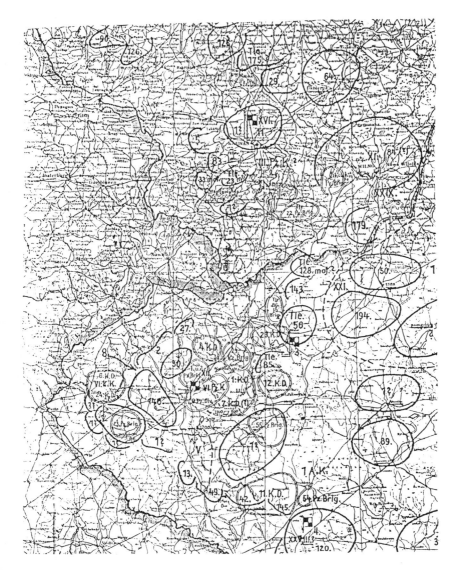

FIGURE 103
GERMANY INTELLIGENCE MAP, 23 JUNE 1941

north towards Augustov, to sever the communications of German forces thrusting eastward toward Vilnius and Minsk (Panzer Group 3). The original plan was to have 29th and 33rd Tank Divisions of 11th Mechanized Corps strike northwest of Grodno and 4th and 7th Tank Divisions of 6th Mechanized Corps assemble northeast of Bialystok and then attack northward toward Augustov. The 29th Motorized Division would fill the gap between the attacking corps and 36th Cavalry Division was to cover the forces' left flank. The counterattack, if executed properly, could have produced a real crisis for German XX and VIII Army Corps.

Major problems immediately surfaced as Boldin tried to assemble his force. The assembly of Khatskalovich's 6th Mechanized Corps took place slowly since some units had to march forward from positions east of Volkovysk. The road network was under constant attack by German aircraft and since the Soviet air force had been destroyed on the ground there was no air protection. 7th Tank Division lost 63 of its 368 tanks and all its rear service units in its 14-hour march. Sixth Cavalry Corps units, especially 36th Cavalry Division, suffered severe casualties (between 60 and 80 per cent of its strength) even while attempting to assemble. Because of these problems, assembly of the counterattack force had been only partially completed by nightfall on 23 June. While Boldin worked on assembly of 6th Mechanized Corps under pressure of higher head-quarters, 11th Mechanized Corps continued to throw its two tank divisions at German positions west of Grodno.

On 23 June German Panzer Group 2 made rapid progress against diminished opposition (see Figure 104). 17th and 18th Panzer Divisions brushed aside remnants of Soviet 14th Mechanized Corps and raced on to Baranovichi. 3rd and 4th Panzer Divisions, attacking in tandem, crushed Soviet resistance west of Kobrin and drove the task force of 205th Motorized Division from the city. 14th Mechanized Corps tried in vain to defend from several positions, but by days end its remnants were forced to begin a rapid withdrawal eastward. That corps had begun combat on 22 June with 478 tanks. After two days of fighting it was down to a strength of 250, and after two more days only 30 tanks remained. This tremendous loss rate typified attrition within Soviet mechanized units.

Meanwhile, German forces of VII, IX, and XIII Army Corps continued to gnaw their way into Soviet defenses south of Bialystok, in several sectors seizing key bridgehead positions across the main Soviet river defense line. The defending 13th Mechanized Corps used its depleted armor force in a vain attempt to halt the advance. German XXXXII Army Corps' lead elements drove into the dense Hajnowka Forest, severing Soviet communications between forces operating in the Bialystok and Brest sectors. Within two days Soviet 10th Army forces gave up their attempts to defend and withdrew into the forest. Thereafter it became a difficult task for the

Germans to root them out of this swampy, heavily wooded, and generally nasty region.

As complete deterioration beset Soviet defenses in the south, further north the Soviets continued to attempt to assemble their counterattack force. Only in the Grodno area did that counterattack materialize. The blow-up map details combat in that area on 23 June (see Figure 105). The

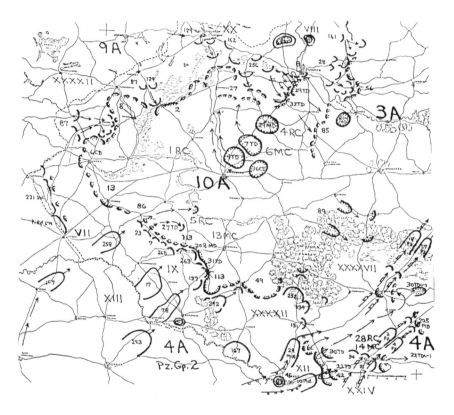

FIGURE 104
SITUATION, 2400, 23 JUNE 1941

3rd Army commander, Kuznetsov, issued withdrawal orders to 85th Rifle Division, which had gone into battle only the day before, to move back and occupy new defensive positions running north and south along a river southeast of Indura. However, the 29th and 33rd Tank Divisions remained south of Grodno with orders to continue their attack, ultimately in cooperation with 6th Mechanized Corps' 4th and 7th Tank Divisions

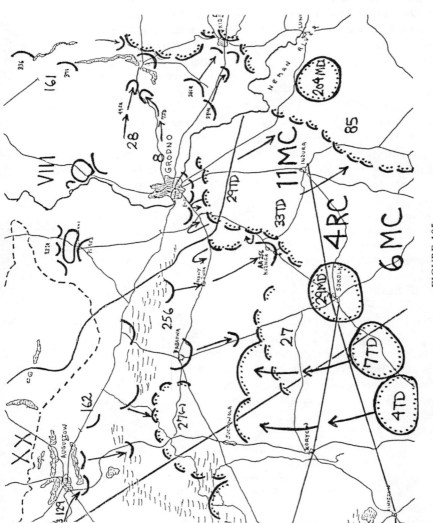

FIGURE 105
GRODNO SECTOR, 2400, 23 JUNE 1941

and 29th Motorized Division, which by nightfall were just arriving in designated assembly areas.

By nightfall on 23 June, the lead elements of 4th and 7th Tank Divisions staggered into the area west of Sokolov and began a night march northward towards Augustov. Elements of 36th Cavalry Division, which had survived the treacherous road march, covered the tank divisions' left flank. At about midnight Boldin received new orders. Given the time involved in launching an attack northward toward Augustov and the position of cooperating forces of 11th Mechanized Corps, which were still held up by German defenses southwest of Grodno, Boldin was told to shift the axis of his two-division attack to the northeast, that is, directly parallel to the main highway running from Sokolov to Grodno. Consequently, during the night 6th Mechanized Corps lead elements, in a 140-kilometer march, retraced their steps and reassembled in positions from which they could launch an attack along the new axis. The impact of this maneuver was felt primarily in the wear-and-tear on the equipment and in the high consumption of precious and dwindling fuel supplies.

The German Fourth Army situation map of 24 June (Figure 106) shows the relationship of all combat elements on that day, as German panzer forces thrust towards Minsk and as important but futile battles raged in their rear, combat which was virtually irrelevant to the larger issue of strategic victory. The deterioration of the Soviet position throughout the Bialystok bulge is readily apparent.

By the evening of 24 June, for all practical purposes there was no longer any organized Soviet resistance east of Brest (see Figure 107). Remnants of the Soviet 42nd Rifle, 22nd and 30th Tank, and 29th Motorized Divisions were now conducting a slow delaying action back eastward south of Slutsk and Bobruisk. In fact, the entire southern flank of the Bialystok bulge had now begun to cave in. Elements of 13th Mechanized Corps and cooperating rifle forces withdrew into the Hajnowka Forest and pursuing German units attempted to bypass the forest (134th and 131st Infantry Divisions) while follow-on forces from XIII and LIII Army Corps assembled to do the nasty job of clearing Soviet troops from the forest. Meanwhile, Soviet defenders west and south of Bialystok strove to hold the city by shifting forces eastward from Lomza.

While all of these disasters mounted for Pavlov's forces, Boldin continued to orchestrate his counterattack west of Grodno. (see Figure 108). You can see the eastward turn of Soviet 4th and 7th Tank Divisions and the advance of 29th Motorized Division. Together they launched very heavy attacks on the salient defended by the German 256th Infantry Division, whose left flank was already under heavy attack by 11th Mechanized Corps' armor. At this juncture, or a short time before, these heavy Soviet assaults forced the Germans to shift, first the 162nd and then

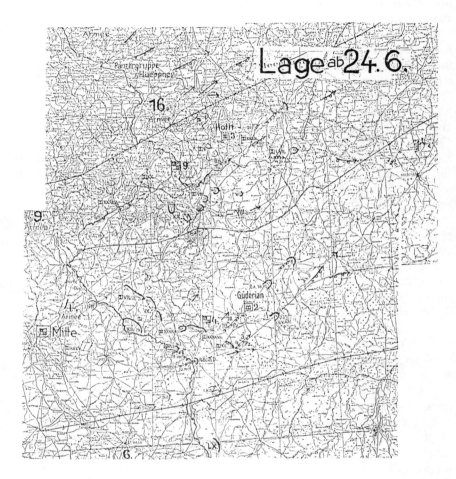

FIGURE 106
GERMAN FOURTH ARMY SITUATION MAP, 24 JUNE 1941

the 129th Infantry Divisions southeastward to assist the beleaguered 256th Infantry in its fight. Meanwhile the Soviet 29th and 33rd Tank Divisions continued to launch heavy attacks southwest of Grodno and the Soviets again changed their mind and threw the 85th Rifle Division forward into combat in an attempt to commit every force they possessed into the struggles against the three German infantry divisions. The

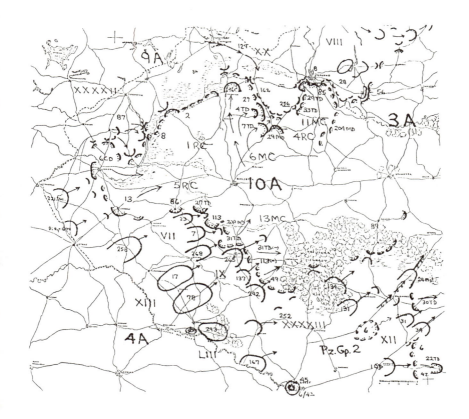

FIGURE 107
SITUATION, 2400, 24 JUNE 1941

supposedly immense armored counterstroke missed its intended target of Panzer Group 3, which was, by now, off the map 100 kilometers to the east. The immense counterstroke, by virtue of Soviet command and control difficulties as well as logistic problems, never came close to living up to its name or its expectations.

A German VIII Army Corps situation map, which recounted action in

207

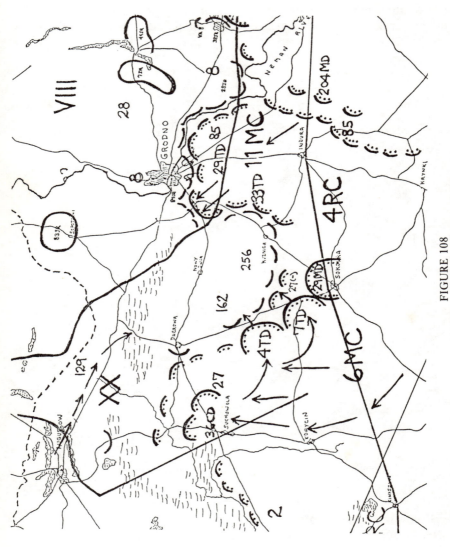

FIGURE 108

GRODNO SECTOR, 24 JUNE 1941

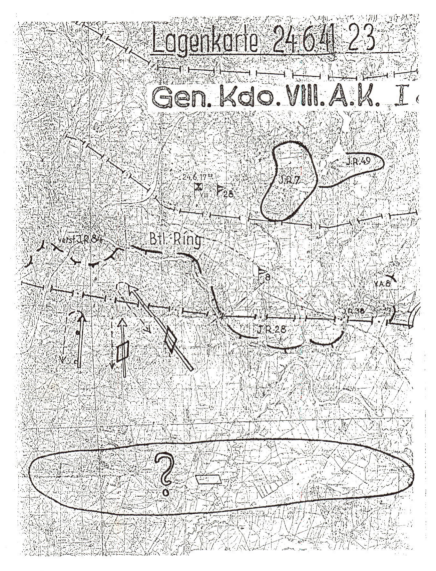

FIGURE 109
GRODNO SECTOR, VIII CORPS SITUATION MAP,
24 JUNE 1941

the Grodno area on 24 June, accurately reflected the Soviets' intent (see Figure 109). Notice the assembly of Soviet armor as detected by the Germans and the heavy attacks already under way. The actual situation map of combat in the Grodno areas clearly shows the situation. The 85th Rifle Division attacked Grodno proper, while the remaining tanks of 29th Tank Division pounded German infantry defenses southwest of the city. The heaviest fighting occurred between Soviet 4th and 7th Tank Divisions and German forces defending along and north of the Sokolov–Grodno road.

The next composite map (Figure 110) shows the situation on the evening of 24 June to the depth of the Western Front. While heavy combat raged at Grodno, Panzer Groups 3 and 2 continued their advance toward Minsk. The Soviets now began committing their *front* reserves to stem the tide of the German advance. 21st Rifle Corps elements duelled with, but could not halt, the 7th and 20th Panzer Divisions' forward movement and then shifted southwest to establish new defenses facing north near Lida.

The 47th Rifle Corps, having deployed westward from Bobruisk, cooperated with understrength 17th Mechanized Corps in an attempt to halt Panzer Group 2 at Slonim and later Baranovichi. Further to the rear, the newly activated Soviet 13th Army, commanded by Lieutenant General P.M. Filatov, assembled the 44th Rifle Corps and the slowly arriving 2nd Rifle Corps to prepare to defend Minsk proper.

On 25 June the Soviet front continued to cave in, particularly along its southern flank (see Figure 111). By this time Panzer Group 2 had cleared Slonim and its advanced elements were fighting for possession of Baranovichi. The group now detached 29th Motorized Division and sent it northwestward against Volkovysk, in the rear of Soviet 10th and 3rd Armies. Other follow-on German infantry divisions (134th, 131st, 31st, and 34th) wheeled northward between Pruzhany and Slonim to entrap Soviet forces operating to the north. Volkovysk was a particularly important target, for its road network controlled all Soviet lateral and forward movement, as well as resupply, between Bialystok and Minsk.

By this time Soviet forces from southeast of Bialystok to Pruzhany had withdrawn into the forests, and German infantry were following in after them. To the west, Soviet forces clung desperately to their positions south and west of Bialystok, while simultaneously dispatching units (including elements of 86th Rifle and 6th Cavalry Divisions) eastward to keep the road through Volkovysk open.

But even as all this was occurring, the heavy Soviet attacks continued south and west of Grodno as Boldin steadfastly attempted to carry out his counterattack orders. Again, we have a German VIII Army Corps map showing the situation on the evening of 25 June (see Figure 112). It reflects the continuing heavy Soviet attacks on Grodno proper and to the

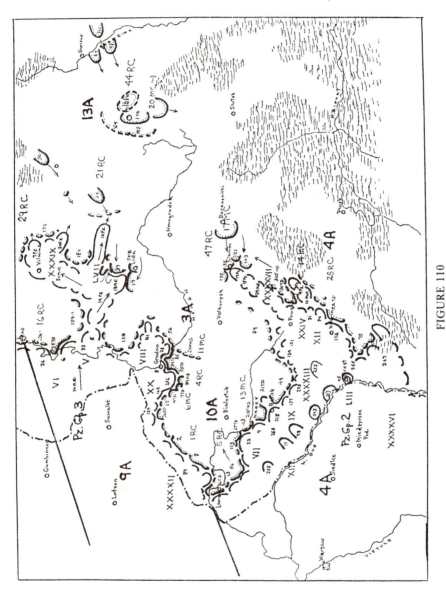

FIGURE 110

WESTERN FRONT SITUATION, 24 JUNE 1941

southwest. All the while, German forces of the 28th and 161st Infantry Divisions were gnawing through Boldin's right flank north of the Neman River. Soon they would threaten the Neman River in Boldin's rear and his communications with the rear as well. In these vicious attacks the Soviet mechanized corps were using up their last drops of fuel.

The composite situation map on 25 June shows the last day of heavy

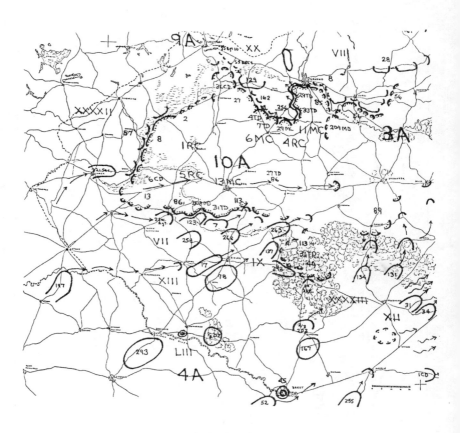

FIGURE 111
SITUATION, 2400, 25 JUNE 1941

Soviet attacks in the Grodno area (see Figure 113). By nightfall, having achieved very little, Soviet units began to run out of fuel and ammunition. The first divisions to do so were the 29th and 33rd Tank Divisions. Very shortly after remnants of those units were ordered to the rear in order to try to keep open the lines of communication. Soon, 6th Mechanized Corps

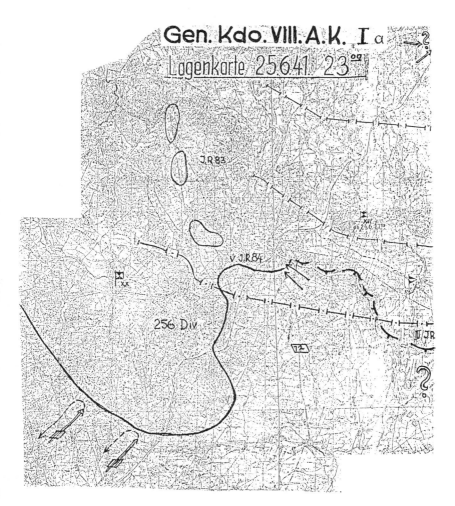

FIGURE 112
GRODNO SECTOR, VIII CORPS SITUATION MAP,
25 JUNE 1941

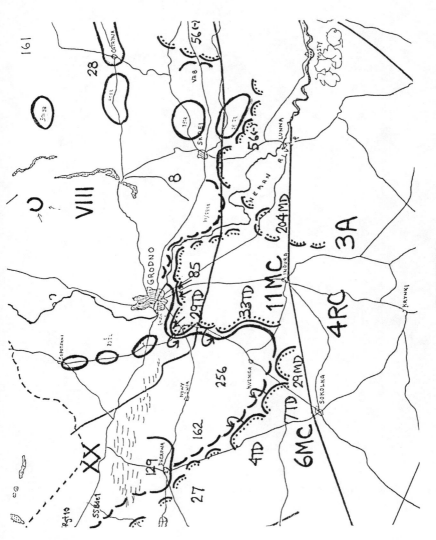

FIGURE 113
GRODNO SECTOR, 25 JUNE 1941

FIGURE 114
GERMAN SITUATION MAP, 26 JUNE 1941

received similar orders to move to the rear. Unfortunately, they could not move their equipment because fuel supplies had been exhausted.

This German summary map shows the situation on the evening of 26 June (see Figure 114). The most important point is that Minsk was now under attack by 12th and 20th Panzer Divisions with 7th Panzer Division ranging far to the northeast toward the Berezina River. Notice the lead elements of 3rd, 4th, 17th and 18th Panzer Divisions moving past Baranovichi towards Slutsk and Minsk. The German trap was about to slam shut at Minsk.

On 26 June all Soviet hopes for a successful counterattack evaporated (see Figure 115). Consequently, *front* headquarters issued a general order to all forces to withdraw. The Western Front now hoped to use the

FIGURE 115
SITUATION, 2400, 26 JUNE 1941

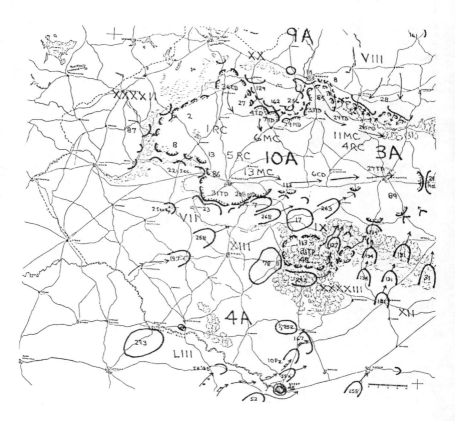

remnants of its mechanized forces to help clear a pathway to the east. Even that hope however was frustrated by the German 29th Motorized Division's seizure of the highway east of Volkovysk. This left in Soviet hands only a small corridor running westward along the southern bank of the Neman River, by the village of Mosty. Even this corridor was threatened as German VIII Army Corps' 28th Infantry Division was pushing Soviet 56th Rifle Division remnants south towards the river.

Some of the Soviet mechanized forces made it eastward out of the pocket, but it was only one of several successive encirclements and they did not make it out of the major new encirclement which subsequently formed west of Minsk. Already pockets of Soviet resistance remained in the Hajnowka Forest. Germans now had to chop each pocket into smaller ones and then digest each of those subpockets in its turn. As catastrophic as it seemed for the Soviets, this process took considerable time. The more time it took, the further eastward the German panzer groups moved without proper infantry support. Ultimately, that had a telling effect on German prospects for achieving success days and weeks later in battles around Smolensk. The battles east of Bialystok severely taxed future German capabilities to continue to mount true combined army operations as they advanced eastward. It would also have a telling effort on the future strength of the panzer divisions.

In the Grodno area on 26 June, the Soviets attempted to implement withdrawal orders. Boldin created a small operational group of commanders and staff officers and moved east in what turned out to be an interesting but arduous hegira (see Figure 116). He fought his way out of the Volkovysk pocket only to enter the Minsk pocket. Ultimately, after more than 40 days' march through the German rear, Boldin broke out through German lines near Smolensk. Shortly thereafter, Boldin was given command of 50th Army which he would command until early 1945.

The situation map of 27 June shows the desperation of the Soviet situation with both flanks of the Western Front almost totally collapsed (see Figure 117). German forces, consisting primarily of infantry, emerged from both sides of the Hajnowka Forest, seized Bialystok, and then pressed against Soviet forces in the pocket, now numbering over 100,000 men. For an indicator of the ferocity of combat, take, for example, the case of the 11th Mechanized Corps, which had begun the initial counterattack at Grodno and which had persisted in the attack day after day from 22 to 25 June. During this period the corps' armored strength fell from 305 to 30 tanks in five days, while its personnel strength fell from 32,000 to about 600 men.

The detailed map of action in the Grodno area on 27 June demonstrates that the Soviet escape corridor was indeed a narrow one (see Figure 118). German 28th Infantry Division forces crossed the Neman River in some

217

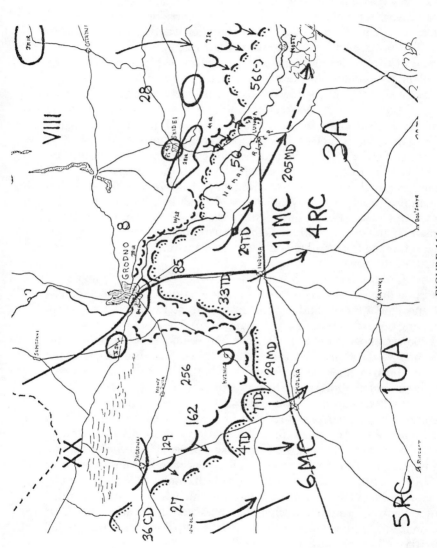

FIGURE 116
GRODNO SECTOR, 26 JUNE 1941

sectors, while 29th Motorized Division troops pressed down the highway westward toward Volkovysk. Now German XX Army Corps began its own advance southward from Grodno, counting along the way the numerous carcasses of abandoned Soviet tanks. Soviet forces raced, or more properly, plodded eastward through the gauntlet of fire. Those who made it succeeded only in reaching yet another encircled pocket west of Minsk.

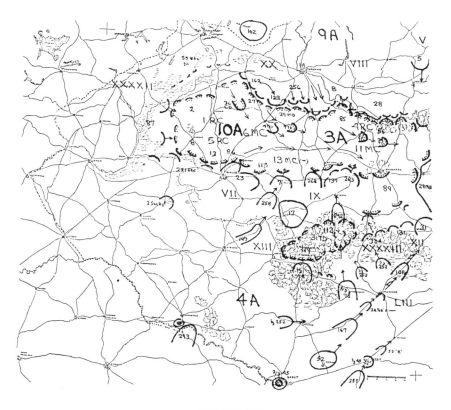

FIGURE 117
SITUATION, 2400, 27 JUNE 1941

The broader view of the situation on 27 June vividly portrays the deteriorated Soviet position (see Figure 119). German 7th, 12th, and 20th Panzer Divisions were bearing down on Minsk from the north. To the south 18th Panzer had seized Baranovichi and 3rd Panzer had secured Slutsk. They now moved on towards Minsk and Bobruisk respectively. You can see the multiple Soviet pockets emerging. The following day

219

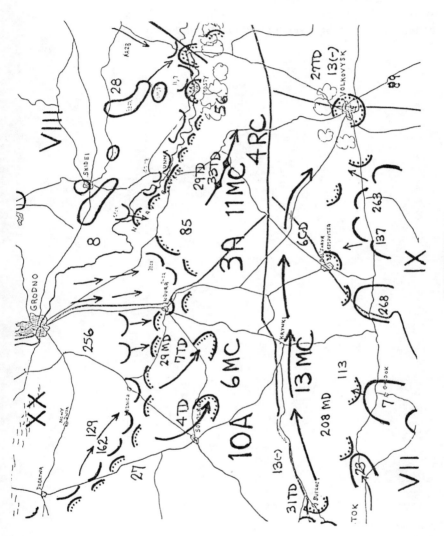

FIGURE 118
GRODNO SECTOR, 27 JUNE 1941

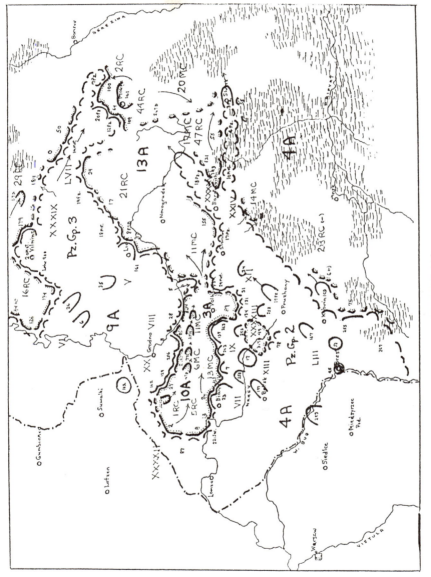

FIGURE 119
WESTERN FRONT SITUATION, 27 JUNE 1941

these pockets were fragmented further as VIII Army Corps' 28th Infantry Division seized the town of Mosty on the Neman River (see Figure 120). Both the 28th Infantry Division and the newly arrived 5th Infantry Division severed the last Soviet withdrawal routes from the Volkovysk pocket, just as remnants of Soviet 10th Army were being liquidated north of Bialystok.

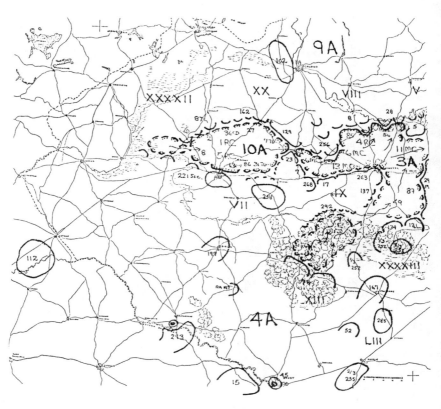

FIGURE 120
SITUATION, 2400, 28 JUNE 1941

On 29–30 June German forces seized Minsk, thus forming the huge Minsk pocket which contained the bulk of the remnants of Soviet 3rd, 10th, and 13th Armies. The Soviet 2nd Rifle Corps, the only portion of 13th Army remaining outside the encirclement, tried in vain to erect new defenses along the Berezina River between Borisov and Bobruisk (see

222

Figure 121). By nightfall on 30 June however, 3rd Panzer Division had secured Bobruisk. The next day 7th, 18th and 4th Panzer Divisions approached the river and, in some instances, breached the Soviet defenses (see Figure 122). This, in essence, set the stage for the next phase of the operation, the advance to Smolensk and the series of battles around it.

By 1 July the remnants of Soviet 3rd, 10th and 13th Armies were in a sack surrounded by a cordon of German infantry divisions. Soviet 4th Army was a mere shell of its former self, and most of the mechanized corps had vanished from the scene. The next act of the play would see the entrance of new players. Perhaps surprisingly however, many of the older Soviet divisions which had fought their way eastward from the border, and even some which had disappeared into the large encircled pockets, would reappear in subsequent battles. These were remnants of the former units, which often numbered only 1,500–2,000 men. Their ability to survive and fight another day bore mute testimony to their tenacity and the porousness of German lines around those large pockets.

Regarding the border battles on the Western Front, one can draw several conclusions. First and foremost, the impact of German surprise was apparent. The surprised Soviet commanders lost all command and control over their forces in general, and responded by launching what, in essence, were knee-jerk counterattacks in accordance with prewar defensive plans, which were by now irrelevant. The most important Soviet counterattack developed inexorably along the Grodno axis while collapse was occurring in all other sectors. As a result of this disastrous fighting the Soviets lost the bulk of their forces defending the Bialystok salient.

As a footnote, many of the several hundred thousand Soviet troops encircled west of Minsk survived to form partisan units which would have their day in 1944. Nevertheless the German pocket produced a huge toll of prisoners. Within two weeks, however, the German infantry divisions would have to abandon their task of gathering up prisoners as their Panzer comrades, then engaged in heavy fighting around Smolensk, called for their assistance.

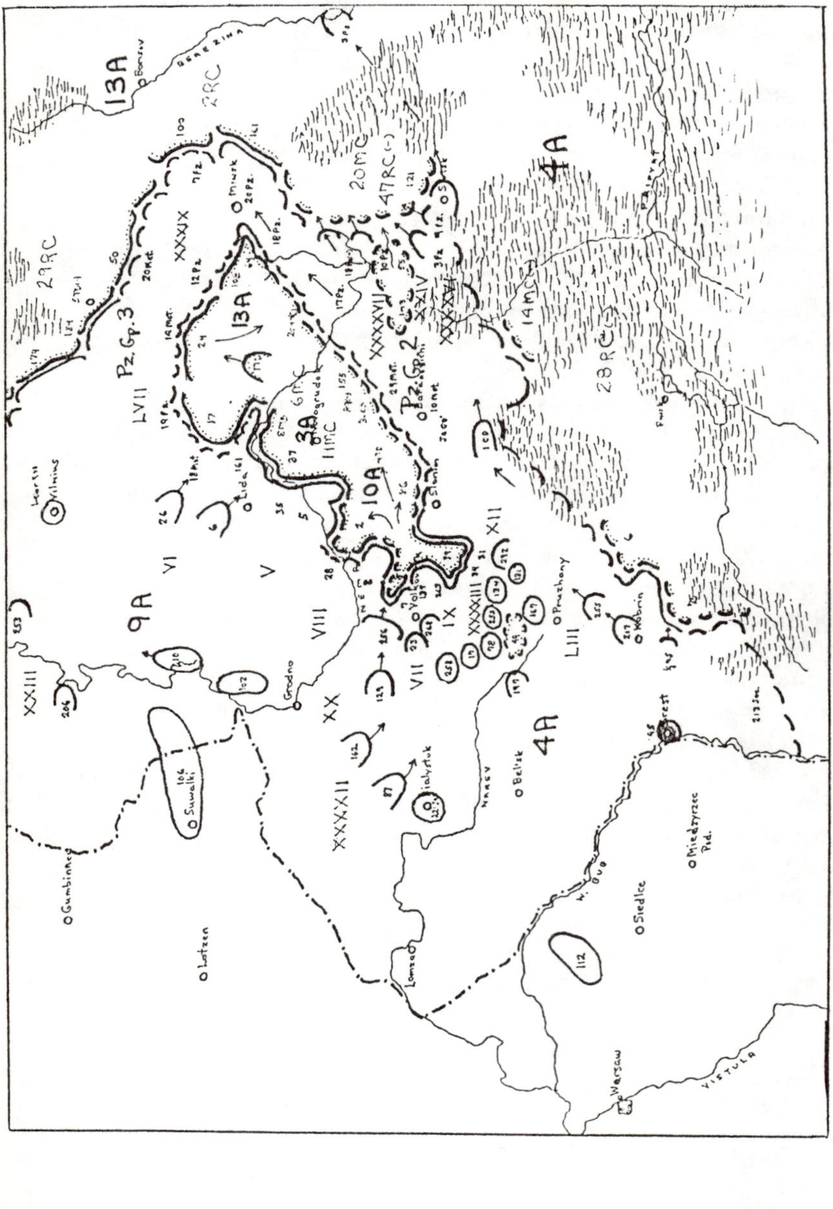

FIGURE 121

WESTERN FRONT SITUATION, 30 JUNE 1941

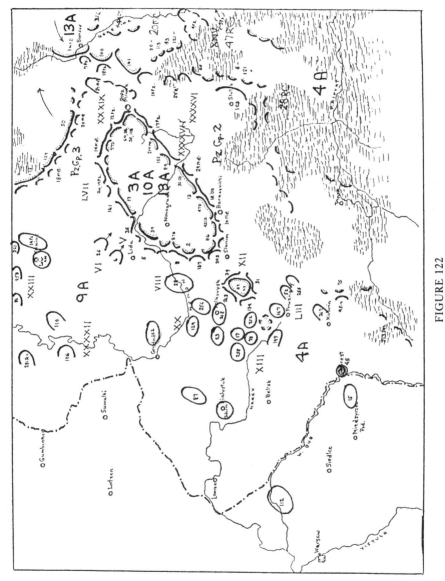

FIGURE 122

WESTERN FRONT SITUATION, 1 JULY 1941

12th Infantry Division Operations

LIEUTENANT GENERAL HEINZ-GEORG LEMM
(retired)

Introduced by Colonel Paul Adair

So far we have been concentrating on the Panzer divisions on the German side. Now General Lemm will recount what a follow-on German infantry division experienced. General Lemm started the war as a platoon commander of 12th Infantry Division and he ended up commanding a regiment in the same division. He was with that division all through the war on the Eastern Front, which is almost unique. After the war General Lemm joined the Bundeswehr and later served as the Chief of the *Heeresampt* in Cologne.

The initial situation within the Northern Army Group provided for an attack by the Eighteenth Army in the north, the 4th Panzer Group (Hoepner) as the main thrust force in the center, and the Sixteenth Army on the right. The Sixteenth Army consisted of three infantry corps, the X, XXVIII and II. The II Corps on the right flank was to be the first force to reach the Njemen River south of Kovno. At the same time it would protect the expected rapid thrust of the Panzer Group and maintain contact with Ninth Army of the Central Army Group advancing further south. Finally, it was to cross the Dvina River near Dvinaburg. Within the II Corps, 12th Infantry Division and 32nd Infantry Division were to be employed to accomplish those tasks in addition to the follow-on 121st Infantry Division. All were well-trained divisions, and the 12th and the 32nd had already proved themselves in Poland and France. At that time I was a member of the 12th Infantry Division as company commander, 2nd Company in Fusilier Regiment 27.

My regiment was fully manned. It had three battalions with three rifle companies each and one mixed machine-gun company equipped with heavy machine-guns and medium mortars. As supporting weapons each regiment had one infantry gun company with six light and two heavy infantry guns as well as one tank-destroyer company equipped with 3.7 cm and 5 cm antitank guns. Finally, the regiment had one platoon of engineers, one cavalry platoon for reconnaissance tasks, and one platoon for radio and telephone communications. Except for the tank-destroyer company, the entire regiment was mobile – although it consisted only of vehicles pulled by horses. The personnel strength of one infantry regiment was about 60 officers and 2,300 to 2,500 NCOs and lower ranks.

On 14 June the 12th Infantry Division, which had come from Holland and had arrived by rail in East Prussia in the first days of June, was given an order to protect the border in the area east of Gumbinnen. On 16 June the division commander, Major General von Seydlitz, was briefed on the division's mission during the Barbarossa attack at the headquarters of II Corps, which was commanded by General of the Infantry von Brockdorff-Ahlefeldt. Two days later, field units down to company level received the first orders for the attack and map documentation on the zone of attack.

The field units themselves were positioned in the woods, close to individual farmsteads, camouflaged against air reconnaissance; the artillery moved into firing positions 2–4 km west of the border depending on the terrain. Officer observation posts were set up to observe the area on both sides of the border by means of scissor telescopes. The atmosphere among the soldiers was good, especially since all movements and missions were declared to be "border protection measures". On 21 June, at 1410 the encrypted codeword for the initiation of the attack was transmitted to all units and in the evening the units formed up for the attack. Field units received verbal orders which were passed to the company commanders. It was remarkable that the notorious "Commissars' Order" was read out to all personnel. Immediately after that, however, the order of the division commander was read out which said that the "Commissars' Order" was not valid for the division.

We received only poor information on the enemy and terrain in the area of attack. We had been able to recognize that the Russians had high wooden guard towers; we had been able to observe the relief of the sentries and their supply procedure, and furthermore we could see vivid entrenching activities about 800–1,000 meters behind the border. From aerial photographs some firing positions of Russian field artillery were known. The division expected a troop strength of about one to two Soviet regiments in front of its sector which would presumably fight a delaying action in their field positions and developed bases. The maps we received were poorly printed and provided hardly any information on altitudes, road conditions, and forest vegetation.

In the morning, at 0305, we began the attack without preparatory time-on-target artillery fire. In the beginning of the attack the resistance of the Russians was weak and consisted of individual fire with guns, light machine guns and the irregular fire of a light artillery battery. My company advanced well, but the very great physical efforts required for passage through the roadless, sometimes sandy, sometimes swampy terrain, the wading through several swampy brooks with all our weapons and ammunition boxes in a sun now standing high, exhausted many soldiers. All were very thirsty. The village of Debiliniai, in Lithuania, was conquered at 0450. The first Russian prisoners appeared happy that for them the war, although hardly begun, was over. From the population nobody was to be seen and the cattle were gone as well. At the village well I had my men fill their canteens. Soon enemy resistance with gun and machine gun fire became stronger. At 0730 the regiment was able to report the capture of Kunigiskiai. Here, in the sandy hilly terrain, the Russians had built bunker positions reinforced with wooden timbers and had dug fox-holes and ditches on both sides of the village. They defended those fortifications tenaciously and bravely. Despite its frontal attack, our 3rd Battalion remained immobile for almost one hour and encountered its first notice-able losses, whereas the 1st Battalion, to which also my 2nd Company belonged, was able to advance past the village, turn in and enter the village from the rear, thus blocking the way for Russians who attempted to make a fairly orderly retreat.

The Russian losses were very high and about 60 prisoners were taken. Many Russians – primarily Uzbeks and Tartars – surrendered voluntarily, and Ukrainians also threw away their weapons and left their well-camouflaged combat positions. The losses on our side were numerous as well. As far as I can remember they amounted to ten or eleven killed and more than 20 wounded. During the last minutes of the assault, while we were already seizing one house after the other in the village of Kunigiskiai, a Russian battery moved into an open firing position about 800–1,000 meters away and opened rapid fire from all six guns which, however, hit the Russian defenders more than us and decisively contributed to the accomplishment of our mission. Yet we were happy when the artillery observers who advanced with our infantry companies concentrated the fire of three of our own batteries on the Russian guns which were completely visible targets and destroyed that enemy battery within a few minutes. I report on that first heavy border fight for Kunigiskiai in a little more detail since it was there that we gained our first experiences with the Soviet enemy.

This and other experiences permit me to make the following observations:

1. The Soviets were not to be underestimated as enemies. The individual soldier fought tenaciously and was personally brave. I often saw how wounded Russians, even in hopeless situations after the attacking German infantry had swept across them, resumed the battle from the rear area.
2. The Soviets knew about the value of the spade. As soon as they moved into a position every soldier took his spade and, as quickly as he could, he dug himself a fox-hole or a combat position which he also camouflaged

immediately in an excellent manner, in order to adjust to the terrain. He also slept in that hole and was able to survive in it with only a little dried bread, a handful of millet, and a bottle of water.

3. Russian armaments were good, and in some cases superior technically to ours. Above all, the weapons were all weather proof and robust. The Russian machine pistol could be fired even after it had just fallen into the mud. I have already mentioned the 7.5 cm gun which appeared in great numbers everywhere as supporting artillery for the infantry. Our side rapidly recognized the value of that weapon in an antitank role. When the lack of penetrating power of the small German antitank guns became clear, hundreds of captured Russian 7.5 cm guns were successfully employed as antitank guns following minor technical modifications.

4. The Soviet leadership showed great weaknesses, especially at the middle command and control levels of battalion, regiment and brigade. From the very beginning, the Soviets counted on the great Russian potential of men and the width and depth of the Russian territory to assist their defensive efforts. Their headquarters were over-organized. For every special branch there was a deputy commander. It could happen that the deputy commander for engineer matters laid mines or constructed barriers at the very point where one hour later the deputy commander for the artillery wanted to have his artillery move into firing positions. Without the approval of the political deputy, the actual commander of the formation was hardly able to enforce an order and, in many cases, there was also a lack of coordination in terms of the interaction of different forces and weapons.

5. For reasons of distrust, the Russians initially had a distinct mix of personnel in their formations with regard to ethnic origins. Of course, an Uzbek or Azerbaijan, for instance, felt desperately unhappy among only Russians or Ukrainians. Thus, the first to desert in masses were the members of Turkish people, Georgians, and the Caucasian tribes.

6. Logistics on the Russian side functioned very poorly during the first days of war. The Russians did, however, compensate for their deficiencies as a result of several factors including:

– the frugality of the individual Russian soldier;
– the reckless employment of their population, including women and children for military purposes. I myself observed how the civilian population of a village, driven by mounted soldiers, with their bare hands rolled hundreds of barrels of fuel to the front;
– the capability to improvise which is characteristic of many Russians;
– finally, the threats and execution of draconian punishments.

Once again let me return to the first day of attack. After the battle of

Kunigiskiai, during which three and a half German rifle companies had wiped out two reinforced Soviet battalions except for small elements, (in this connection the excellent support rendered by the batteries of Artillery Regiment 12 must not be forgotten), the physical powers of our soldiers were strongly reduced. Therefore, the division commander ordered several hours of rest for Regiment 27. He had Infantry Regiment 48, which had so far followed-up as the reserve of the division, move forward in order to continue the attack. The third regiment of the division, Infantry Regiment 89, had to fight a hard battle east of Galeriske in the afternoon.

In the afternoon, my regiment again became active. The division objective was to pursue the withdrawing enemy during the night and if possible establish a bridgehead across the small Szeszupa River. On this occasion it was the terrain and the condition of the roads rather than enemy resistance which rendered that night march, with permanent contact with the enemy, a very tough task. At 0230 on 23 June, the formations reached the Szeszupa River and crossed it with their lead combat patrols. In the plain words of the division's war diary the following assessment was made of events on 22 June: "On the first day of the campaign against Russia, the Division has fully met the ordered objective of the attack. The air distance from the border to the areas reached is about 50 km."

The course of the action in the following days was similar in most respects to action during the first two days of the campaign. During that period of time the attack of Panzer Group 4 proceeded rapidly forward. Its forces reached the Dvina River, crossed it and advanced into the area of Ostrov. The infantry corps on the right flank of the Panzer Group attempted to maintain communications by all means while negotiating incredible march distances. The infantry experienced severe problems regarding its mobility including the following:

- many horses were lost,
- supply was often interrupted,
- the terrain was very swampy.

Yet, despite these problems, the infantry achieved daily march distances of 30–40 kilometers. Consequently, march and combat groups were established. They consisted in most cases of one battalion infantry, a battery of artillery, engineers, and an advance party with tank destroyers and reconnaissance subunits. In order to render the infantry companies more mobile, the advance party was given all captured trucks. The Russians had left behind a great number of 1½-ton vehicles, which were constructed like the American Ford model and which – having large tires – were fairly suited to cope with bad roads and terrain. Our overwhelming intention was: Don't give a single chance to the Russians to reorganize. Keep them running.

By the beginning of July, 12th Infantry Division had crossed the old border between the Soviet Union and Latvia. In front of it, on high ground in the Sebesh-Osweja area, lay a well-developed system of field fortifications called the Stalin Line.

On 12 July, Fusilier Regiment 27 attacked those positions with two battalions. The division's war diary described the attack:

> The high ground around point 166 is dominating. It gradually ascends to point 166, offers little cover and must be considered unfavorable for an attacker. The mountain massif was constructed in a step-like manner. Many flanking positions, it took the enemy 10 days to construct it. The positions are deep in the ground ...
>
> Around 0600, the village of Usborje was conquered. At 0800, I Battalion/27 was located 300 meters in front of the edge of the massif. Position after position had to be overpowered in the depth of the field of the defense. Effective support by 3 batteries of Artillery Regiment 12. At 0845, the 2nd Company succeeded in conquering the highest elevation, 166.

Since I was the commander of that 2nd Company, let me make an additional remark. The last 80 meters in front of the Russian positions were on a steep grade. None of us would still have enough breath left to cry out the loud and continuous "Hurra", traditionally in the German infantry used to demoralize the enemy before penetrating into the Russian ditches and bunkers. Therefore, I had called to our three buglers, the platoon messengers in those days, but who still carried signal horns, and ordered them to remain lying on the ground where they were, on my sign to blow the old Prussian signal of attack continuously with all their might. The sounding of the horns obviously had such an enervating effect on the Russians that many tried to run away, while others threw away their weapons and raised their hands. Thus the mountain massif was in our hands.

This operation taught me as a young officer these essentials:

– Develop phantasy even in the midst of combat.
– Be aware of the emotional conditions of your soldiers in such situations so that you can take quick measures to motivate the soldiers again, even if only with the trumpets of Jericho. It will help also to overcome depression and fear, especially when running up a steep slope into strong enemy fire.

Finally, remember always your knowledge of war history and the Bible. Both are useful for young infantry officers.

28th Infantry Division Operations

COLONEL DR ALFRED DURRWANGER (retired)

Introduced by Colonel Paul Adair

Colonel Dr Durrwanger was in the 28th Infantry Division, which you will remember was heavily committed in the area around Grodno and faced some of the most pressing Soviet counterattacks. At this stage Colonel Durrwanger was a company commander. Later in the war he became a general staff officer in an infantry division and also served in Supreme Army Headquarters, OKH. After the war he joined the Bundeswehr and later served at the German Embassy in Paris.

Let me first draw your attention to two principal points, two elements of the war in Soviet Russia, as explained by some special and personal experiences. These points are: first, how to become conscious of the particular nature of war in the Soviet Union, this in only abbreviated form; and second, in more detail, the practical use of a fundamental principle of our warfare, the so-called *Auftragstaktik* – those tactics which work by giving only the framework of an order, and by leaving all the details to the subordinated officers and men. (I shall explain this expression in more detail later.)

The war began for the entire German Army on 22 June 1941, at 0305 in the morning, as well as for my regiment, which was located in the Suwalki area, in the southern parts of East Prussia (now part of Poland), where we, together with other divisions, were jammed into the woods near the frontier. When the battle began, we found the Soviets surprised, but not at all unprepared. I repeat: not at all unprepared.

At the beginning of the Soviet campaign I was company commander of the 13th Company of my regiment. In each infantry regiment there were three battalions, each with four companies, and a 13th and 14th (antitank) company. The 13th Company was composed of four platoons with eight pieces, six of which had a caliber of 7.5 cm and two of which had a caliber of 15 cm. Our comrades in the heavier artillery called us "gypsy" (Zigeuner) artillery. This Infanterie-Geschutz Kompanie (company of light guns), equipped with about 130 horses, 110 men and eight artillery pieces was placed directly under the command of the regiment. This is one fact I should underline. The second fact is that this company could be divided up in several parts and each platoon could be added, in case of combat, to one of the three battalions. If all battalions were involved in fighting, the company commander would be out of work and free for other tasks according to the wishes of the regimental commander.

Ideas about the War in Soviet Russia

What were our thoughts as we crossed the Soviet border?

– First, there was *no* enthusiasm, not at all! It was rather a deep feeling of the immensity of that enterprise and the question immediately arose: Where and at which place would there be an end to the operations?

– Second, we had to remember Clausewitz, who at the beginning of the nineteenth century had served for some years in the Russian Army and who had said (in the eighth chapter of his famous book *On War* (*Vom Kriege*)):

> The Russian Empire is no country to be conquered formally [in due form], that is to keep it occupied ... Such a country could only be mastered by its own internal weakness [debility] and only by the effects [results] of an interior discord [schism]. To hit the weak points of the political existence, a violent shock of the state is indispensable, a shock that strikes its heart.

– Third, we learned in school after World War I, when I entered the first class, that Woodrow Wilson, the famous President of the United States during the First World War, said, among other things, when addressing Congress to declare war against the Central European Powers – among them Germany (1917): "We don't want any conquest [in Europe] ... We are only the protagonists, pioneers for the rights of mankind ... But the right is more precious than peace...We will fight for the rights and for the freedoms of little nations ...".

– And last, there was a general idea among the German soldiers according to the famous phrase "Germany expects everyone to do his duty".

The Border Battles

After having crossed the Soviet border, the two other regiments of our division, believed to be confronted with the main forces of the enemy, advanced very quickly. Our regiment, considered to be a reserve, first remained on our side of the border. Only one battalion, accompanied by one of my platoons, had to cross the frontier, but only to protect the open flank of the other regiments. This battalion had to advance through a large forest and was then stopped unexpectedly by strong Soviet forces that fought vigorously. Here was the first indication that our knowledge of the enemy forces, even along the border, was inadequate.

At that moment my place as company commander of the 13th Company was near the command post of the regiment. The regimental commander, becoming a bit nervous because he had heard nothing about the progress of his battalion, ordered me to take a motor-bike, with a cyclist, to contact the battalion and find out what was going on. I remember very well the vast woods we both had to cross, with thinly scattered trees and a little brushwood on either side of a broad sandy road. You could not use this road with the motor-bike because there was so much sand. On both sides of the road however, there was a small path with solid, firm soil, so that the driver could proceed along it slowly. Both the driver and I had our loaded submachine-guns wrapped tightly around our shoulders.

While proceeding little by little forward, we saw now and then a German dispatch rider or runner or an ambulance. Finally we found the staff of the battalion and the commander explained the situation to me. Unexpectedly, there was very vigorous, strong opposition from an adversary who fought obstinately inside and outside of bunkers (pill-boxes), none of which had been marked on our maps. Therefore the situation was a surprise for both sides. The commander told me that a Soviet infantry company had marched some hours before along the road we had just used, but the Soviet company was not at all aware of the German soldiers in front of them.

After an hour we returned by the same broad road with the motor-cyclist ahead of me guiding the cycle slowly forward meter by meter along the small sandy path. We focused our attention only on the path but not on any enemy. Suddenly a Red Army soldier stood five steps before us, aiming his Sten gun at us. He was, I remember well, a young man, well dressed, with a keen face, a pink collar patch, and only with a cap (no casquet). In our confusion the cyclist and I remembered only one Russian word: *Stoi* (stop)! The Russian soldier stopped abruptly without doing anything. The cyclist discontinued and we both put our left foot on the ground. One second later the cyclist let go of the steering – unexpectedly for me – and the cycle fell to the ground, dragging me to the ground as well, unaware of this action of my soldier, who fled behind some trees. Now the Russian soldier only had to aim, first at the flying cyclist, then calmly at me who was lying under the cycle. I tried eagerly to reach the trigger of my Sten gun, but it seemed to me an entire eternity before I got to it. My subsequent shots went into the blue sky and nothing happened! The Russian soldier, perhaps frightened by the shots, quickly disappeared and my cyclist came back and helped me to lift up the cycle and get out from under it. Carefully we proceeded several meters into the forest, but our Soviet acquaintance had disappeared completely. Whether he was hidden in a tree (that often happened in Russia), behind a tree or under the leaves or in a pit, we never discovered. This was perfect camouflage on his part, an evident sign of his great ability to adapt to the surroundings.

This was my first encounter with a Soviet soldier. I had to realize that we were confronted with another type of combat, that is, fights behind the front and behind the forward line. The German soldier was neither accustomed nor trained to accomplish such malicious procedures.

My soldiers told me afterwards that they had observed a Soviet soldier who made signs of surrender. He was subsequently shot down by his own people. Another Russian soldier lying heavily wounded in a trench which had just been taken by us, put a hand-grenade below his back and was blown apart at once. It even happened that some stragglers (*Versprengte*) occupied the recently destroyed bunkers anew and fought to their final extermination.

All this proved that physically, as well as psychologically, the Soviet soldiers were extremely tough. Where did this come from? I think it was based in the first place on their ideological conditioning. We never expected nor were we trained for that kind of adversary.

While the other regiments of my division advanced very quickly without facing great resistance, it took my regiment three days to overcome the Soviet units in front of us. They defended a line of bunkers and fortifications, partly incomplete but protected by trenches, with utmost tenacity and, let me say, with cruelty as well. The Soviets had just occupied this line some days before and when attacked they had not retreated. They were very brave soldiers. Our losses were 25 soldiers killed and 125 wounded within one battalion in these three days.

Evidence from prisoners confirmed that our regiment had attacked crack units (*Elite-Einheiten*) and a camp of officer candidates. In their camp they were very well equipped (soap, towels, map cases, etc.).

Battle in Crossing the Neman River

My regiment, after being detained by the resistance of crack Soviet units during the border battles, subsequently followed the two other regiments of my division and gradually approached the wide Neman River, about 90 kilometers away from the German border. During the night and the early morning of 28 June the units of the regiment reached the little village of Holynka, about 10 kilometers distant from the Neman. The regiment was the reserve of the division behind the two other regiments, which were now involved in combat with the Soviets.

I would like to draw attention now to one element of German warfare that had great success, especially in Soviet Russia, the so-called *Auftragstaktik* (this word had never been used before or during the war and

235

had not been mentioned, as a word, in German regulations). *Auftragstaktik* is a short description of the way to make units function. In short, it means that the order to fulfill a certain military mission is only given within broad parameters and all further details regarding its fulfillment are left to the subordinate. This principle can be applied to all forces. It is the result of long experiences and especially of a belief that better know-how in warfare decides the issue of who will prevail in battle.

Let me give you a practical example of *Auftragstaktik*. After having arrived at that little village during the night, the regimental commander ordered me in the early morning, and also the commander of the 14th Company, to contact the other regiments of our division (the 7th) in the frontline. We were to explain to the other regimental commanders the situation in our regiment and ask for their respective situations. My regimental commander had acted according to his own decision that it would always be good to be informed concerning the present situation although not being in the frontline: *Auftragstaktik*!

On two motor-bikes with side cars, I took my company staff with me. At last I found the regimental commander of the neighboring regiment (Colonel Boge) in a stand of bush. He explained his regiment's situation to me. It had been heavily attacked the day before and this evening and he marked on my map the position of the enemy as far as he knew it. He warned me that the Soviets in front of his regiment would be very dangerous. This regimental commander had the reputation in the whole division of being a rather prudent man.

I sent my collected information immediately to my regiment and reflected what could be done now, knowing that I had executed and finished my orders, which were to establish contact with our neighbor. It was a sunny and very hot morning and there was no noise of battle, absolutely nothing. Beside the warbling of some birds, nothing could be heard.

Finally I resolved to approach closer to the Neman River with my little company staff (three or four men) to become more informed about the situation. Our feelings were a mixture of curiosity and fear, no doubt, but there was also a certain zealous desire to profit by the situation, which was obviously favorable to us. Therefore, knowing the personality of my regimental commander so well, I added to my first report to the regiment our intention to proceed. I asked the regiment to send us a platoon of infantry, transported by the vehicles of the 14th Company, and a platoon of light guns from my own company, as soon as possible. I ordered the dispatch rider to rush back to my regiment as quickly as possible.

So we did take the risk and prudently approached the village of Mosty near the banks of the Neman River along a major road. We went on and nothing happened. Before reaching the village we saw a Soviet antitank gun at the first house, surrounded by three or four dead Soviet soldiers who had been left behind. Proceeding slowly we were rewarded by a threefold stroke of luck. First, the little village had been given up by the Soviets and was not occupied as it had been the night before. Second, near the bank of the river, we discovered a high observation post made of wood that permitted good observation to the other side of the Neman. Third, from that observation tower we perceived a sturdy bridge over the wide Neman River leading from the end of the village to the other bank, and – thank heavens – it seemed to be intact. That bridge was not marked on our poor and inaccurate maps. Therefore, it could be of tremendous benefit for the rapid advance of my division, for the river here was about 70 to 80 meters wide. When we finally approached the bridge, we found it not prepared for demolition.

Immediately, I sent another report to my regiment telling all what we had found and how favorable it would be to have some reinforcements in order to take the bridge and create a bridgehead on the south side of the river. After a short period the requested reinforcement arrived and we briefed them on the situation and told them how to proceed. My regimental commander himself arrived with these soldiers. He told me that he had mobilized a whole battalion to profit from this situation and to gain, if possible, the other side of the river. Meanwhile, the Soviets on the opposite side of the river began to realize what had happened and started to shoot across the bridge. The regimental commander was the first to shoot from our antitank gun, positioned to shoot near the bridge.

The bridgehead on the other side of the Neman River was established by our regiment in the course of the afternoon. The little resistance we faced was probably from the enemy rearguards. Possession of the bridge, of course, provided an enormous advantage for the quick advance of our division. The regimental commander had pushed his units forward without any direct or specific order of the division, but only motivated by the will to make use of that recently discovered weakness on the Soviet side. That is the essence of *Auftragstaktik*.

3rd Panzer Division Operations

COLONEL HORST ZOBEL (retired)

Introduced by Colonel Paul Adair

To continue our study of this axis Colonel Zobel will examine 3rd Panzer Division, which was the left hand division of XXIV Motorized Corps of Guderian's Panzer Group 2. Colonel Zobel was concerned with training at various levels. He was a troop commander at this time and remained in panzer units throughout the war. When he joined the Bundeswehr after the war he became the inspector of armored troops as his last appointment.

At the beginning of the Russian War, I was a young platoon commander in the 2nd Battalion, 6th Panzer Regiment. I can say very little about operations on a higher level, but I can, perhaps, say something about the nature of a tank battle and its atmosphere. In this context I will sometimes mention Corps and Panzer Groups to put the subject on a higher level in order to make it easier to understand the whole situation.

I will concentrate on four principles involved in leading motorized troops which were applicable to operations in those times, and which apply to contemporary operations as well.

These principles are:

1. Motorized, especially armored troops, have to be led from a position well forward.
2. Leading on the battlefield has to be carried out by short orders, primarily orally or by radio and, below battalion level only orally or by radio.
3. German motorized troops were organized to fight in battle-groups with constantly changing organizations – sometimes even daily.
4. During an attack over a longer range, logistic echelons should be thoroughly integrated into fighting echelons. This includes ammunition, fuel, and food as well as medical support.

There were five distinct stages of our operations, each delineated by the crossing of major rivers:

1. The crossing of the border and the attack across the Bug River.
2. The attack on Bobruisk and the crossing of the Berezina River.
3. The attack on Slobin on the Dnepr River.
4. The crossing of the Dnepr River and the breakthrough of the Stalin Line.
5. The crossing of the Ssosh River at Kritschev south of Smolensk.

At the end of each section I will summarize by mentioning some noteworthy points. First, as a sort of introduction, here is the organization and mission of Panzer Group 2.

THE ORGANIZATION OF PANZER GROUP 2 AND ITS MISSION

Commander:	Generaloberst Guderian
Chief of Staff:	Oberstleutnant Freiherr von Liebenstein
XXIV Panzer Corps:	General der Panzertruppen
	Freiherr Geyr von Schweppenburg
3rd Panzer Division:	Generalleutnant Model
4th Panzer Division:	Generalmajor Freiherr von Langermann und Erlenkamp
10th Motorized	
Infantry Division:	Generalmajor von Loeper
1st Cavalry	
Division:	Generalleutnant Feldt

Panzer Group 2 had the mission: "on X-day to cross the Bug River both sides of the fortress Brest-Litovsk, to break through the Russian front lines and reach the area Roslavl–Jelnja–Smolensk". It was important to prevent the enemy from establishing new defensive lines and to achieve a decisive operational success in the year 1941. After reaching the objective, the Panzer Group would be given new orders. The planning of the Oberkommando des Heeres (OKH) indicated that both Panzer Group 2 (Guderian) and Panzer Group 3 (Hoth) would, thereafter, be ordered to turn north to seize Leningrad.

Plan of the XXIV Panzer Corps for Operation "Barbarossa" (Extract) (see Figure 123).

In the center of gravity of the Corps the 3rd Panzer Division and the 4th Panzer Division will break through the enemy positions near the border both sides of the area of Miedna in order to reach the road between Kobry and the Muchawe River and, thereafter, proceed in the direction of Slusk.

The 4th Panzer Division shall advance on the Tank Route No 1, whilst the 3rd Panzer Division shall attack north of the route. The

239

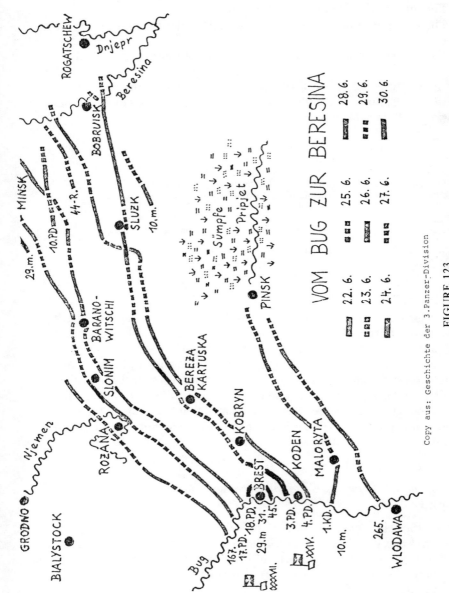

Copy aus: Geschichte der 3.Panzer-Division

FIGURE 123

XXIV PANZER CORPS OPERATIONS, 22–30 JUNE 1941

fortress Brest-Litovsk shall be passed southward and will be seized later by the following infantry.

Organization of the 3rd Panzer Division for the Attack over the Bug River (main forces only).

Group Audoersch:	Rifle Regiment 394, SS engineer battalion Das Reich, and one antitank company
Group Kleemann:	Rifle Regiment 3, engineer battalion 10, antitank battalion, two antitank platoons, and one tank company
Group Linnarz:	Tank Regiment 6, Antitank Battalion 521, 1 antiaircraft battalion, 1 heavy anti-aircraft battery (two groups had three tank battalions and one amphibious tank battalion it had received during planning or the invasion of England).
Group Corvia:	1 motorcycle battalion, Reconnaissance Battalion 1

The first and the second groups were strong in infantry, the third group was strong in armor, and the fourth group was a highly mobile group created to perform special tasks.

Crossing the Border

Before the artillery began to fire at 0315, one assault group seized the bridge and engineers crossed the Bug River in an assault boat. At the beginning of the operation at 0345, the advanced groups of infantry crossed in rubber boats, while the infantry on motorcycles and the reconnaissance troops crossed the bridge on their vehicles. Then diving (amphibious) tanks of the 3rd Battalion went across the river. All the other tanks crossed the bridge after 1000 because of crowded traffic.

Without any great resistance the attack was easily launched further to the east and the village of Stradez seized. The first difficulties arose because of ground conditions – not so much due to action of the enemy. The vehicles stuck in a swamp and a further advance could not be continued along the planned road route. After consulting with the panzer corps (General Greiherr Geyr von Schweppenburg), the commander of the 3rd Panzer Division (General Model) ordered his troops at 1500 to turn to the right and use the so called Panzerstrasse 1 (Panzer route 1) for the further advance. The 3rd Panzer Division reached this route before the 4th Panzer Division had arrived, so that both the divisions followed each other on the same route.

The 3rd Panzer Division now created a new advanced guard consisting of one rifle company on motorbikes and one tank company with engineers, and continued the attack at 1645. It was already dark when our troops reach the Muchaviec River. Since the wooden bridge had already been burned down, further advance had to be halted. We had traveled a distance of only 18 kilometers when it should have been 80 kilometers!

241

On 23 June, at noon, Kobry and the bridge over the Bug – Dnepr Canal were seized after a short attack. After a further advance of about 65 kilometers the district town of Bereza-Kartuska was also seized.

Conclusions:

–During the first two days of war the 3rd Panzer Division had destroyed 197 enemy light tanks and several hundred guns of different calibers.

– The crossing of the border and the Bug River was carried out exactly according to our current tactical doctrine. It was astonishing that the Russians in the frontline were completely surprised by our assault.
– Apart from the original plan for the assault, the 3rd Panzer Division had to make a detour because of unpassable ground conditions (swamps) and had to shift over to the sector of 4th Panzer Division. The fact that this could be carried out without any great delay or without causing confusion between the troops was the result of close control and leadership forward on the battlefield.
– Enemy tanks escaping from Brest-Litovsk to the east were captured or destroyed. Their retreat was completely uncontrolled.
– The enemy offered only light resistance in delaying actions, partly supported by ground conditions (woods and swamps).
– During the first two days of combat, unarmored troops and rear echelons suffered considerable losses inflicted by hostile enemy troops cut off from their main bodies. They hid beside the march routes, opened fire by surprise, and could only be defeated in intense hand-to-hand combat. German troops had not previously experienced this type of war.
– Enemy planes had a good chance to attack our troops because we marched on only one road, but they were unable to stop the advance.

The Continuing of the Attack

On 24 June, the third day of the Russian War, 2nd Panzer Battalion led the attack and succeeded in penetrating the enemy positions at Miloidy. The first Sczcara River defense line had been reached. Enemy counterattacks against our right flank were repulsed and 33 light tanks destroyed. The enemy now offered stronger resistance. The greatest problems, however, were experienced in crossing the rivers in mostly swampy valleys. The bridges over those rivers were generally wooden bridges which the Russians had succeeded in burning before our troops arrived.

I would like to describe a situation which might not be a typical one under normal conditions, but it is instructive and shows the type of fighting we experienced in this period. (As published in the book *Gekampft Gesiegt Verloren* by General Oskar Munzel.)

> In the evening, the 1st Tank Battalion reached the Sczcara-line but the advance had to be stopped. The bridge over the river was destroyed and still burning. The valley to a width of about 800 meters was swampy ground and could not be passed. Detours were not available. Heavy artillery fire fell in the bridge area.
>
> At sunset, the O.C. [commander] of the division arrived and he himself immediately organized an assault-group consisting of the 2nd Tank Company, parts of the 4th Tank Company, a light tank platoon and infantry in a rubber boat under command of the commander of the 2nd Tank Company.
>
> At 8 p.m. the assault group carefully approached the still burning bridge. The company commander jumped out of his tank and together with some riflemen and under the covering fire of all tanks, he succeeded in seizing the burning bridge.

This example can be regarded as a perfect combination of fire and assault delivered in surprise.

The 3rd Panzer Division continued the attack in three battle groups. I would like to show you the organization of the 1st Battle Group, just as an example:

from front to rear of the march column

- one tank company
- one mechanized company (from the reconnaissance battalion)
- one artillery battery
- one company of mechanized infantry
- one tank battalion (minus one company)
- one antitank company (self-propelled)
- H.Q. tank regiment
- H.Q. tank brigade
- one engineer company
- one battalion artillery (minus one battery)
- one mortar platoon
- one battery antiaircraft (91st Regiment)
- one battery antiaircraft (59th Regiment)

These battle groups were changed daily and new commanders constantly had to become accustomed to new troops.

The Attack against Bobruisk and Crossing the Berezina River

After a heavy exchange of fire the small town of Slusk was taken on 27 June (see Figure 124). From 24 to 27 June the division had traversed a distance of about 150 kilometers in a virtually continuous attack. On 28 June the division started the attack against Bobruisk but almost the same interruptions stopped our advance. The tanks overran the obstacles and pushed aside local enemy forces, but the following unarmored vehicles were later heavily attacked by fire from enemy troops in well camouflaged positions. Sometimes soldiers from headquarters and rear echelons had to fight like infantry. It was often even necessary to place tanks at a distance from 50 to 100 meters at heavily endangered places in order to let unarmored vehicles pass.

In the meantime, the advanced group had reached the Pritsch River, which is a tributary of Pripet River. Only three tanks were able to drive across the already burning bridge at the very last minute. Then the bridge broke down and the advance was again stopped. When the commander of the tank brigade and some soldiers of his staff advanced to the bridge, the following tank company, which had been delayed for some reasons, thought they were Russians and opened fire. The brigade commander was wounded and lost an arm. This accident could only happen when everybody expected the enemy to appear at any time, from anywhere. Nevertheless, the key problem was the lack of communications.

Finally, the small Pritsch River was crossed by means of a very difficult detour which took us the entire night, because all the wheeled vehicles had to be towed by tracked vehicles. Only at dawn were the outskirts of Bobruisk reached by two light tank platoons and one mechanized company which had formed, almost on the move, as an advanced guard. They rushed into the town, passed houses still burning from the artillery fire from the day before and raised the flag on the castle at 0500. Actually, the enemy had not offered strong resistance on the west bank of the Berezina River. The bridge, however, had been destroyed.

The enemy held strong positions on the east bank of the Berezina, making it impossible to cross the river immediately. On the contrary, the enemy launched counterattacks under cover of a heavy thunderstorm, but the attacks did not succeed. The divisional commander, who had advanced to Bobruisk on the same day, gave an order to the 2nd Battalion of Rifle Regiment 394 to build a bridgehead at all costs. Under cover of artillery fire succeeded in crossing the river by means of rubber boats, despite heavy enemy resistance. The Russians launched strong counterattacks and that single poor rifle battalion had a very hard day in defending the small bridgehead.

In the meantime, the engineers had succeeded in building a temporary

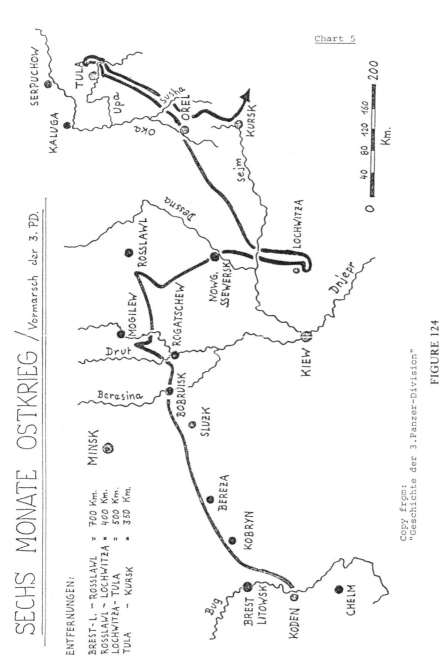

Chart 5

FIGURE 124

3RD PANZER DIVISION OPERATIONS, JUNE–DECEMBER 1941

Copy from:
"Geschichte der 3.Panzer-Division"

bridge so that both rifle regiments of the division could cross the river and enlarge the bridgehead to the north, east, and south. The Russians then withdrew to the swampy ground to the east. In the evening the bridgehead had expanded to a depth of about seven kilometers.

Conclusions

– The advance of the 3rd Panzer Division had been stopped at the Berezina River for two days. The supreme authorities of the Red Army had realized the dangerous situation and tried by all means to avoid a deep breakthrough by German offensive forces. The Soviets took other actions as well. The commander of the Soviet Western Front was dismissed. His successor was General Eremenko, who was well known as the great counterpart of General Guderian.

– Bobruisk was taken by tanks and mounted motorized infantry as a result of a surprise attack. According to accepted doctrine, mechanized infantry (mounted) and tanks fighting in forests or towns are to be regarded as an exception. It is not the normal case. When I, nevertheless, mention such an example here, I want to point out that battle has its own rules. What is important is the quick and correct estimation of the situation and, even more important, quick action.

– The infantry on foot could not maintain contact with the motorized attacking forces. The advanced combat group drove the enemy away from the road only when its own mission was endangered. The increasing distance between the advanced combat group and the infantry caused many problems, but these problems were ultimately overcome.

– The hostile air force was still very active despite its heavy losses. For example, 20 planes were shot down on 29 June and another 35 destroyed a day later by antiaircraft guns. The main role in destroying hostile aircraft, however, was played by the aviation hunter-group of Oberst Moelders. His group is reported to have shot down 100 planes in one day alone.

– Supply echelons and workshops followed the combat forces closely in short bounds. Nevertheless, shortages of ammunition, and especially of fuel, occurred as a consequence of hold-ups, road-blocks, and enemy resistance. High consumption of fuel was expected. Therefore, while in garrison two barrels of fuel were fixed on the rear of each tank for an immediate fuel supply. The crews, however, did not like these measures, and after having re-supplied once or twice, the barrels were "lost"!

This completed the first several days of action for the division. The 3rd Panzer Division had advanced a distance of from 450-500 kilometers from the Bug River to the Dnepr. Every soldier had high morale and looked hopefully to future operations. In comparison with the distance we had already passed Moscow did not seem to be very far away. But it only seemed that way.

5

The Border Battles on the Lutsk-Rovno Axis: 22 June–1 July 1941

Overview

COLONEL D. M. GLANTZ

This is the fifth and last of the major combat sectors spanning the border battles of the Eastern Front that we will examine. To the Soviets this was perhaps the most interesting sector because it was the region in which their mechanized forces were the most successful, or the least unsuccessful. Of course, part of that relative success was due to the fact that in the Special Kiev Military District Soviet mechanized forces were echeloned in strength and in depth.

Figure 125 shows the German intelligence picture of Soviet force dispositions in southern Russia (the Ukraine) before to the beginning of Barbarossa. Understandably, it reflects many of the same characteristics as the intelligence pictures we saw in other areas of the front. The Germans identified many of the Soviet rifle divisions. In general, they also correctly assessed the nature and location of the Soviet rifle forces subordinate to army and corps. They tended, however, to count more Soviet cavalry divisions than actually existed, for example, the 27th Cavalry Division incorrectly identified east of Vladimir Volynski. Some motorized forces show on the map, but there was more than a little confusion over the possible existence of tank and mechanized divisions and tank brigades. In general, there was the same German tendency to over-count Soviet rifle forces and under-count Soviet mechanized forces in the Kiev Military District.

This is the actual Soviet order of battle and the dispositions of Soviet forces (see Figure 126). The Southwestern Front, which was what the

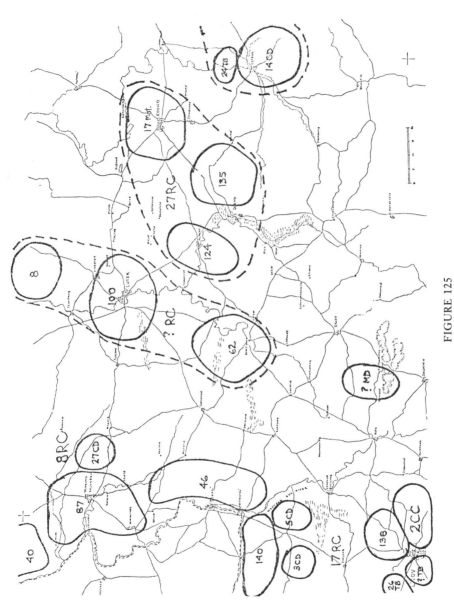

FIGURE 125

GERMAN INTELLIGENCE ASSESSMENT

Kiev Military District became after the outbreak of hostilities, was commanded by Colonel General M.P. Kirponos, a very capable officer as events would bear out. Kirponos had several armies under his command, but the two that we will be concerned with were Major General M.I. Potapov's 5th Army and Lieutenant General I.N. Muzychenko's 6th Army. Potapov's army defended along the Lutsk-Rovno axis, an axis that ultimately extended towards Kiev, and Muzychenko's Army covered the L'vov sector.

5th Army was deployed with two rifle corps forward, the 15th and 27th Rifle Corps. 15th Rifle Corps was commanded by Colonel I.I. Fedyuninsky, a man who rose to full army command (2nd Shock Army) by 1945. Notice that the corps was commanded by a Colonel, which indicates that rank often did not mean everything in the Red Army. The 27th Rifle Corps was commanded by Major General P.D. Artemenko. These two corps covered the border regions, the 15th with two rifle divisions forward and the 27th also with two rifle divisions forward and one rifle division, the 135th, displaced considerably to the rear.

Potapov's 5th Army contained one mechanized corps (the 22nd), whose disposition was very similar to the deployment of other mechanized corps that we have seen. Major General S.M. Kondrusev's 22nd Mechanized Corps had one division, the 41st Tank Division, deployed well forward. In fact, on 22 June this division was already conducting maneuvers near the front. As we will see when we look at the strength figures, this division had a considerable contingent of KV and T34 tanks. The 22nd Mechanized Corps' 19th Tank Division was located well to the rear at Rovno, and the third division of the corps, the 21st Motorized Division, was also located near Rovno.

Muzychenko's 6th Army had two rifle corps, including the 6th, deployed forward. You cannot see the second corps on this map because it was located off to the west defending along the Rava-Russkaya direction. These two corps were backed up by one of the largest of the Soviet mechanized corps, the 4th Mechanized Corps of Major General A.A. Vlasov, located at L'vov, which consisted of the 8th and 32nd Tank Divisions and the 81st Motorized Division. Also located in 5th and 6th Army sectors was an additional mechanized corps, the 15th, whose units were in fairly close proximity to the rifle corps. Major General I.I. Karpezo's 15th Mechanized Corps, stationed around Brody, contained the 10th and 37th Tank Divisions and the 212th Motorized Division.

In the depth of the defense were additional units, these generally aligned along the old fortified positions of the Stalin Line along the old Polish-Russian border. Here there was a string of fortified regions and several cavalry divisions, distributed along the length of the old border. Fortified regions were also deployed along the new border itself such as

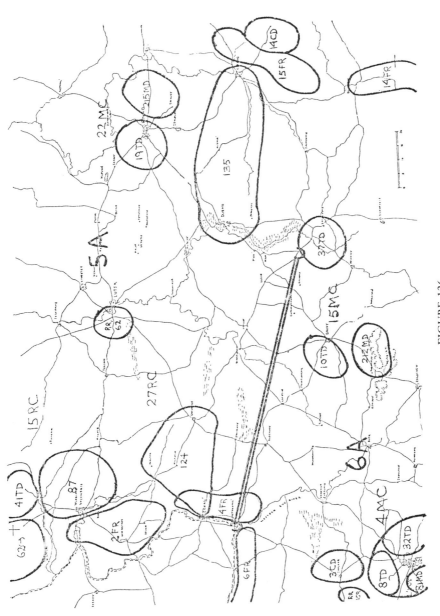

FIGURE 126
SOVIET DEPLOYMENT, 21 JUNE 1941

the 2nd and the 4th Fortified Regions. Of course, there were a series of border guards detachments defending along the border as well.

A brief look at the armor correlation of forces chart (Figure 127) shows that there were also mechanized corps located in the depths, in particular the 9th Mechanized Corps of Major General K.K. Rokossovsky and the 19th Mechanized Corps of Major-General N.V. Feklenko. These corps, which were located about 80 kilometers off the map to the west, would be directed forward once hostilities had begun. Another unit, Lieutenant General D.I. Riabyshev's 8th Mechanized Corps, was located off the map to the south. It would also be brought up into this combat sector. So there was a tremendous potential concentration of Soviet armor in the South-western Front sector, when and if the Soviets could figure out how to bring it together in coordinated fashion.

The chart also shows you the general armor correlation of forces. Basically there were many KV and T34 tanks in the Soviet force structure. The 41st Tank Division had 31 KVs and 329 older light, medium and heavy models. The 4th Mechanized Corps was also very heavy, with 460 KVs and T34s out of an overall strength of close to 1,000 tanks. The 8th Tank Division alone numbered 190 new tanks out of a total of 382. This was the most powerful of the Soviet mechanized corps in the border military districts, although we will see that conflicting orders soon dissipated the power and strength of this corps right from the start. The 15th Mechanized Corps also had some new tanks, roughly 160, and a considerable number of older models, for a total of almost 900 tanks. Its 10th Tank Division had 63 KVs and 38 T34s out of 448 tanks. The mechanized units to the rear, plus the divisions of 9th and 19th Mechanized Corps were generally equipped with only older tanks. We should bear this in mind as we watch them deploy forward to launch the attempted counterattacks.

In discussing the nature of day-by-day operation, I will focus on two sub-sectors. First, we will view the area around Vladimir Volynski to understand how the German attack progressed and how the Soviets initially committed their mechanized forces to combat. Later, we will look at the great meeting engagement and the attempted envelopment of German 11th Panzer Division by Soviet mechanized forces near Dubno. This was the situation on the eve of the attack in the Vladimir Volynski sector (see Figure 128). The 41st Tank Division was conducting field exercises in the north minus its motorized regiment which was garrisoned at Lutsk. The 124th Rifle Division had one regiment forward and two regiments back in camp. The 2nd Fortified Region had some units deployed along the border interspersed with forces of the 90th Border Guards Detachment. The 87th Rifle Division was in lager just east of Vladimir Volynski with all three of its regiments. Later we will see in detail how combat developed in the Dubno region.

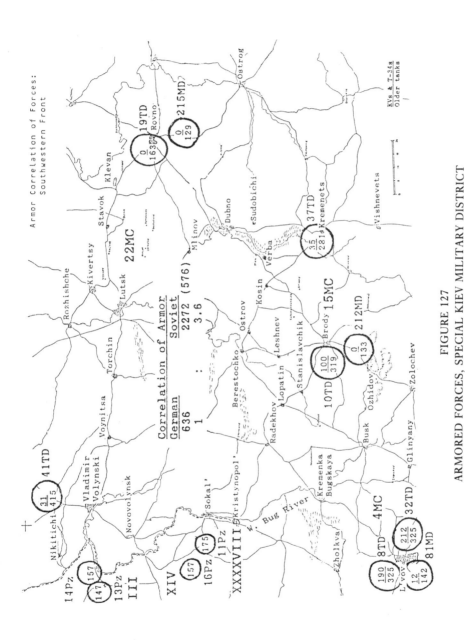

FIGURE 127

ARMORED FORCES, SPECIAL KIEV MILITARY DISTRICT

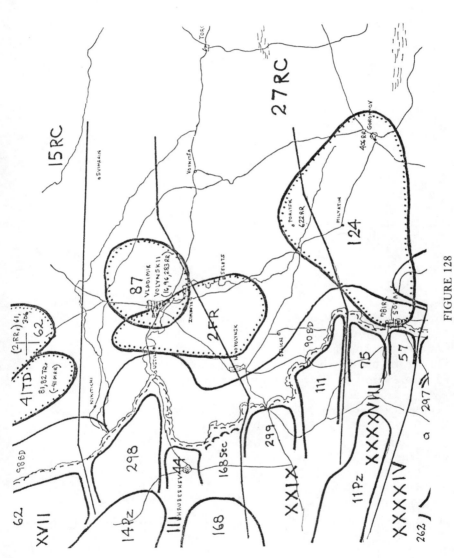

FIGURE 128

VLADIMIR-VOLYNSKI SECTOR, 0600, 22 JUNE 1941

German forces facing Soviet 5th and 6th Armies consisted basically of Sixth Army and Panzer Group 1 with XXVII, III Motorized, XXIX, XXXXVIII Motorized and XXXXIV Army Corps (see Figure 129). There were, of course, additional German divisions located off the map to the west. There was quite a stacking and concentration of German forces in this region preparatory to the main attack. German intelligence maps for the end of each day of operations show you how the intelligence picture matured as the German attack developed. The same pattern emerged here as it did in other sectors of the front. As combat progressed the German intelligence picture became ever clearer. Later, during operations at Smolensk, that process was continued. German intelligence was able to pick up Soviet reserves and those other units that they had not picked up on 22 June. Figure 130 is hard to read, but it is Sixth Army's enemy situation map. Several Soviet divisions are noted, some of them incorrectly.

On the first day of combat, 22 June, the German thrusts developed along two principal axes (see Figure 131). The first axis, in the north by way of Vladimir Volynski, initially involved operations by two German infantry divisions, the 298th and 44th. Subsequently, 13th and 14th Panzer Divisions advanced through those infantry divisions along the Lutsk-Rovno axis. In the south the initial German attack was conducted by the 75th and 57th Infantry Divisions. Very early on the infantry were overtaken by 11th Panzer Division, which then spearheaded an armored thrust along an axis running through Dubno to Ostrog. Following in the wake of 11th Panzer, but not yet on this map, was 16th Panzer Division which was, in turn, then followed by 16th Motorized Division.

During the first day of combat, the Soviet garrison troops along the border were surprised. Many of the border detachments and elements of the fortified regions were encircled, but it took the Germans two or three days to reduce those small pockets. The 87th Rifle Division reacted fairly quickly and the Soviets dispatched one of their ten antitank brigades forward. In most of the major sectors the Soviets had one, two, or even three of these antitank brigades.

The first units the Soviets dispatched forward on the expected axes of German armored advance were these antitank brigades. This one was the 1st Antitank Brigade, commanded by Major General K.S. Moskalenko, who later rose to command 40th Army. His unit was about the first to meet 14th Panzer Division as it came roaring down the road out of Vladimir Volynski. On 22 June orders went out almost immediately from Kirponos's headquarters to the mechanized corps to close forward as rapidly as possible. The first corps to do so was 22nd Mechanized Corps. Of course, that corps' 41st Tank Division was already located close to the attack sector and it was ordered to send elements southward to assist the

255

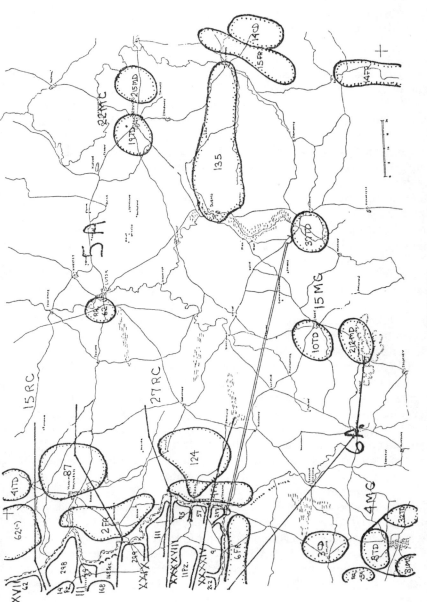

FIGURE 129
SITUATION, 0600, 22 JUNE 1941

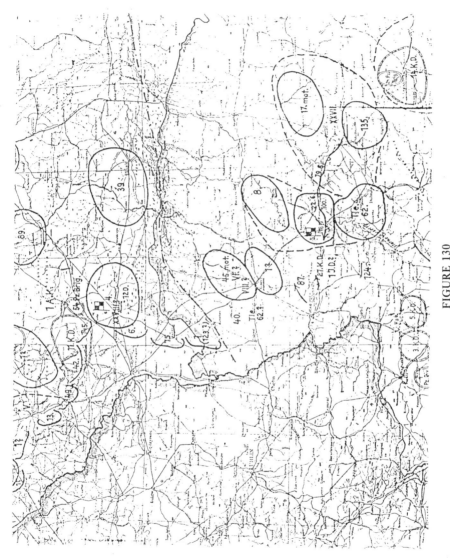

FIGURE 130
SIXTH ARMY SITUATION MAP (ORIGINAL), 22 JUNE 1941

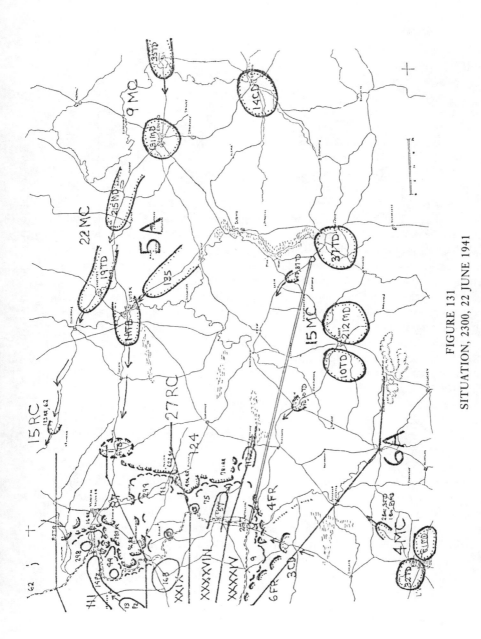

FIGURE 131
SITUATION, 2300, 22 JUNE 1941

87th Rifle Division. Meanwhile, the 19th Tank and 215th Motorized Divisions hastened forward to join in the counterattack, which was anticipated somewhere in the area east of Vladimir Volynski. Similar orders also went out to Rokossovsky's 9th Mechanized Corps and Feklenko's 19th Mechanized Corps.

Essentially from Lutsk to Rovno, and from Korosten and Berdichev further to the rear, a solid stream of Soviet armor attempted to make its way forward. In most cases this movement was severely interdicted by German air strikes. The basic lack of good roads – already mentioned – hindered the German advance, but also frustrated the redeployment of the Soviet operational and strategic reserves. In this theater that became very critical indeed. These mobile divisions arrived one after the other, and they were strung out for over 120 kilometers along the road. Hence, as they arrived counterattacks developed in piece-meal fashion.

In the south the 15th Mechanized Corps was ordered northward to strike at the German penetration forming near Radeshev. The 37th and 10th Tank Divisions sent out forward detachments of roughly 30 to 40 tanks each with some motorized infantry to intercept the German advance, engage it and, of course, hopefully to stop it. Simultaneously the 4th Mechanized Corps received the first of several conflicting orders. Being confronted with an attack from the north and other attacks off the map to the west near Rava Russkaia and Peremysl', 4th Mechanized Corps received orders to move north, west, and south. Orders came one after the other and, as a result, elements of two of the corps' divisions initially moved north. As subsequent maps show, they later moved back towards the west. The 4th Mechanized Corps' divisions moved back and forth constantly for about four days until they were finally brought back and reassembled to cover the close approaches to L'vov. This they did fairly well, thus permitting some of the Soviet units east of L'vov to escape when the situation deteriorated further.

Figure 132 is a more detailed map of action in the Vladimir Volynski region on the first day of combat. There have been many stories told about Soviet tank divisions running off the roads into swamps. John Erickson relates one such story in his book *The Road to Stalingrad*, about a commissar who led a tank division off into the muck and mire. In fact, many Soviet units ended up in swamps, partly as a result of the Germans having air superiority, and hence, it was unhealthy to travel by road. Consequently, the Soviets moved their units off the roads and the price they paid was that many Soviet mobile units ended up bogged down in the swampy parts of this region. In one instance, the 41st Tank Division ordered its 82nd Tank Regiment southward to assist the 87th Rifle Division. The regiment marched south but when it was determined that the threat was even greater to the north, the next morning 41st Tank

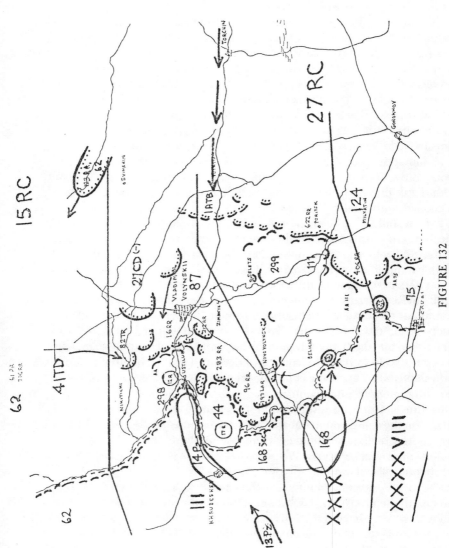

FIGURE 132

VLADIMIR-VOLYNSKI SECTOR, 2300, 22 JUNE 1941

Division received new orders to reverse course and move north toward Kovel'. By this time the Germans had cut the main road back to Kovel'. Thus, the division commander, Colonel P.P. Pavlov, decided to take a new route cross country, but he did not reconnoiter the route properly and the bulk of two tank regiments went into the mud as they headed back towards Kovel'. This was not an isolated incident. There were several others, which will be mentioned later, where Soviet units also got stuck as a result of bad terrain.

The map depicts the German advance to Vladimir Volynski and the reaction of 87th Rifle Division. All three regiments of the Soviet division deployed forward fairly quickly, and the newly arrived 1st Antitank Brigade established a defensive shield blocking the road running east to Lutsk. The German 299th Infantry Division attack split the Soviet 124th Rifle Division from the 87th Rifle Division. This was the beginning of essentially the first encirclement that would occur in the Southwestern Front sector. The German intelligence map from the evening of 23 June provided a little more mature intelligence picture as the operation went into its second day (see Figure 133).

The overall situation map for 23 June portrays the initial German commitment of 14th Panzer Division (see Figure 134). The next day both 13th and 14th Panzer Divisions launched attacks eastward along the Lutsk road. By this time 11th Panzer Division was already racing deep into Soviet defenses, engaging the forward detachment of Soviet 10th and 37th Tank Divisions and apparently doing considerable damage. They say very little about these forward detachments after this day, nor have they said much about the 37th Tank Division's fate in general. The forward detachment of 10th Tank Division fell back and joined the bulk of the 10th Division which, in the meantime, had deployed in the Stanislavchik area and established a fairly durable defense. The 10th Tank Division's 19th Tank Regiment failed to conduct reconnaissance and stuck in the mud on route, thus delaying its advance. The 10th Tank Division, of course, had a fairly sizable complement of KV and T34 tanks. Notice also the first change in direction by elements of the 32nd Tank Division, which now shifted to the west across the Western Bug River to reinforce cavalry forces fighting north of L'vov.

The most important deployment shown by this map was that the Soviets had begun the process of assembling significant reserves. The 19th Tank and 215th Motorized Divisions were ordered to join the 1st Antitank Brigade and attack the Germans' north flank. The 131st Motorized Division of 9th Mechanized Corps was ordered to establish a new defense line near Lutsk, and the two follow-on tank divisions, the 35th and 40th, were to move up and fill in that defense line south of Lutsk preparatory to launching a counterattack to the southwest. The 15th Mechanized Corps

FIGURE 133
GERMAN INTELLIGENCE MAP, 23 JUNE 1941

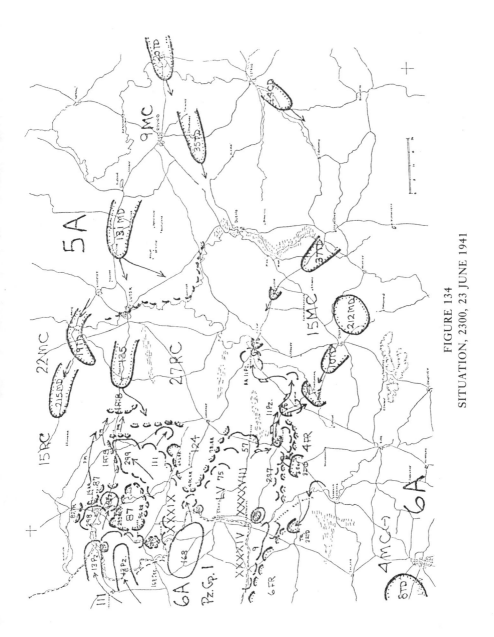

FIGURE 134
SITUATION, 2300, 23 JUNE 1941

was now concentrating north and northwest of Brody with initial orders to strike northward against the German southern armored spearhead. Very late in the day, at about 2200 hours, the 8th Mechanized Corps to the south received orders to move north and support the 15th Mechanized Corps. In essence, a large scale meeting engagement was about to begin. The issue would be settled by who could assemble and conduct the meeting engagement in more efficient fashion.

On 23 June in the Vladimir Volynski sector, the 87th Rifle Division, or at least two regiments of the division, were now encircled and isolated just south of the city (see Figure 135). 13th Panzer Division was moving forward, and by this time 14th Panzer Division had already cleared Vladimir Volynski and was preparing to race eastward down the highway toward Lutsk. German infantry had cut behind the 87th Rifle Division and severed the main road, thus rendering the 1st Antitank Brigade's positions untenable and forcing Moskalenko to move his guns back about 15 kilometers. This was the sort of development that prevented the Soviets from putting together the kind of concerted counterattacks they had hoped to conduct using the rifle divisions, the 22nd Mechanized Corps, and the 1st Antitank Brigade. Lead elements of the 135th Rifle Division were now arriving forward as well. It was literally a battle that developed before the commander's eyes. Commanders who could anticipate did better than those who could not.

The German general intelligence map of 24 June (see Figure 136) demonstrates the growing complexity of this battle as the German units penetrated deeper and as the intelligence picture became clearer and clearer. On 24 June the Germans committed 13th and 14th Panzer Division abreast down the road toward Lutsk (see Figure 137). In fact, lead elements of 13th Panzer Division managed to reach the river just north of Lutsk, basically rendering all Soviet defenses north of the city untenable. This was after the 215th Motorized and 19th Tank Divisions had launched their attacks some time after noon on the 24th. Those attacks ran into 14th Panzer Division and the Soviet infantry and tanks were driven off with very heavy losses. Consequently, on this day the first wave of Soviet attacks, conducted by 22nd Mechanized Corps in the north and by 15th Mechanized Corps in the south, totally failed.

Meanwhile additional Soviet forces continued to concentrate. The 131st Motorized Division of 9th Mechanized Corps occupied defensive positions around Lutsk, the 35th and 20th Tank Divisions moved forward through Rovno, and the lead elements of 19th Mechanized Corps now began to arrive in the region east of Rovno. A new Soviet rifle corps, the 36th, was also moving forward to fill in the gaps in the Soviet defenses of 15th Mechanized Corps, which by this time was simply occupying a defensive line along the low ground in a river valley running roughly east to

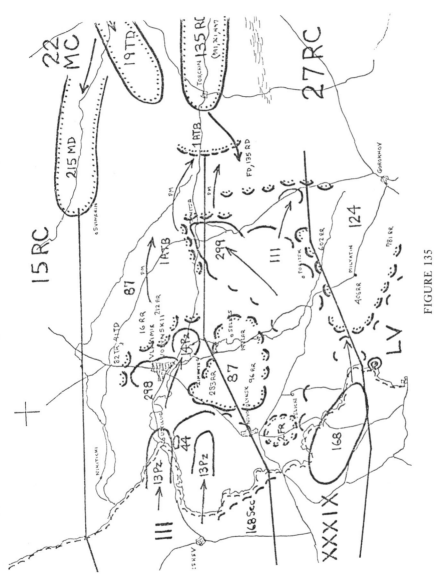

FIGURE 135

VLADIMIR-VOLYNSKI SECTOR, 2300, 23 JUNE 1941

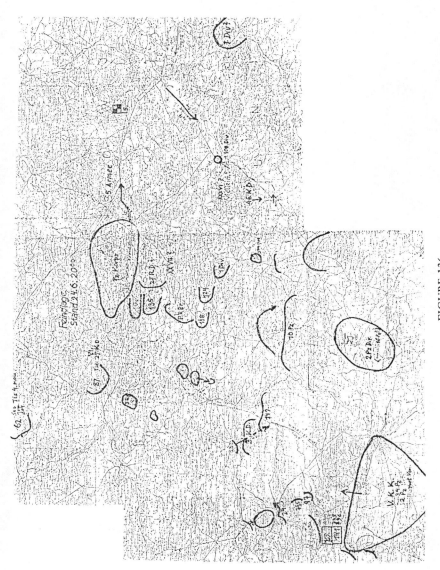

FIGURE 136

GERMAN INTELLIGENCE MAP, 24 JUNE 1941

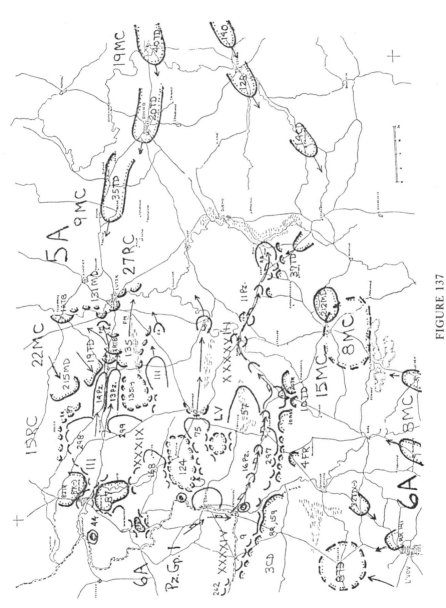

FIGURE 137
SITUATION, 2300, 24 JUNE 1941

west north of Brody. In this area more elements of the 10th and 37th Tank Divisions were also lost to swamps and bogs. More Soviet movement may be seen in the L'vov area, where 32nd Tank Division was ordered south to deploy west of L'vov and the 8th Tank Division, which had been engaging the Germans west of L'vov, was now ordered to move into positions north of L'vov.

Figure 138 is another detailed map of action in the sector between Vladimir Volynski and Lutsk. It shows the preemptive nature of the 14th and 13th Panzer Divisions' advance, which split 22nd Mechanized Corps from its supporting rifle forces. A simultaneous advance by the German 111th Infantry Division also split the 135th Rifle Division from already isolated Soviet forces further south. By this time two regiments of the Soviet 124th Rifle Division were also fully encircled south of Vladimir Volynski.

During 24 June in the Dubno sector, there occurred the first stage of what was to develop into the most severe meeting engagement in the region (see Figure 139). 11th Panzer Division was racing towards Dubno, having driven out of its path lead elements of Soviet 37th Tank Division, which had deployed in blocking positions near Ostrog. 11th Panzer then engaged 37th Tank Division's main forces near Kozin and apparently did considerable damage to the division. The Soviet 10th Tank Division, alternately defending and counterattacking further west, had been halted near Lopatin where the Germans created an infantry defensive line running east to west to contain Soviet forces while the armored units raced eastward north of that defensive line. Soviet 8th Mechanized Corps was now ordered to assemble in the vicinity of Brody by 25 June and lead elements of that corps began arriving in Brody by late evening. Many of 8th Corps' tanks fell by the wayside during the long march.

From 25 June, most of the battles just east of the border in the German rear area now became simple desperate struggles on the part of the Soviets to break out of encirclement (see Figure 140). The Germans used infantry formations to isolate the Soviet units, and the net effect was that German infantry formations were no longer available to move forward and support the deeper operating panzer divisions. That was to become a more serious problem when those panzer divisions reached even deeper positions in the Soviet rear.

On 25 June 13th and 14th Panzer Divisions secured Lutsk and sought to continue their drive towards Rovno. In so doing they ran into elements of the newly deployed Soviet 9th Mechanized Corps. Meanwhile, elements of Soviet 22nd Mechanized Corps, after being defeated north of the Vladimir Volynski–Lutsk highway, now withdrew across the river to reinforce 27th Rifle Corps' defensive positions at Lutsk. The 35th, 40th, 20th and 43rd Tank Divisions of 9th and 19th Mechanized Corps were

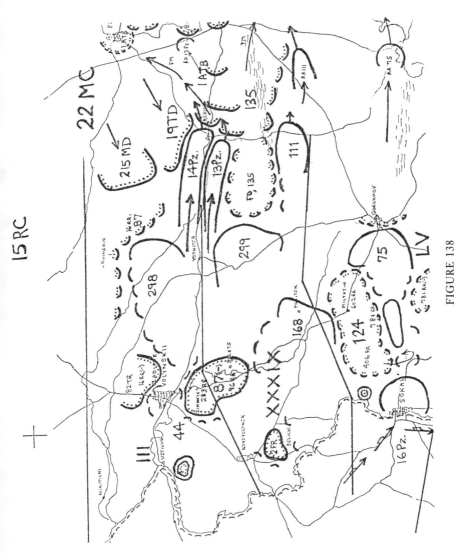

FIGURE 138
VLADIMIR-VOLYNSKI SECTOR, 2300, 24 JUNE 1941

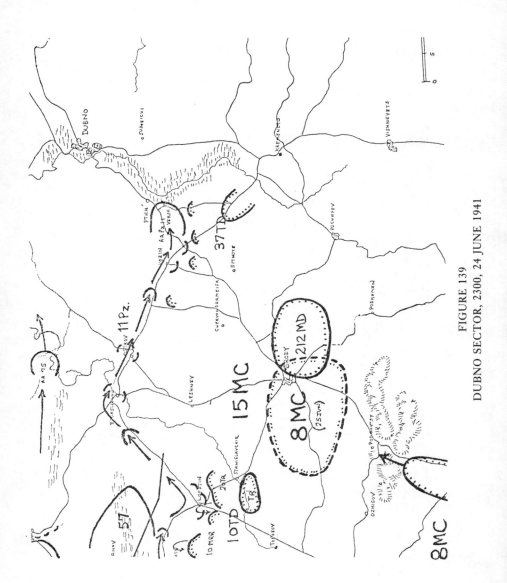

FIGURE 139
DUBNO SECTOR, 2300, 24 JUNE 1941

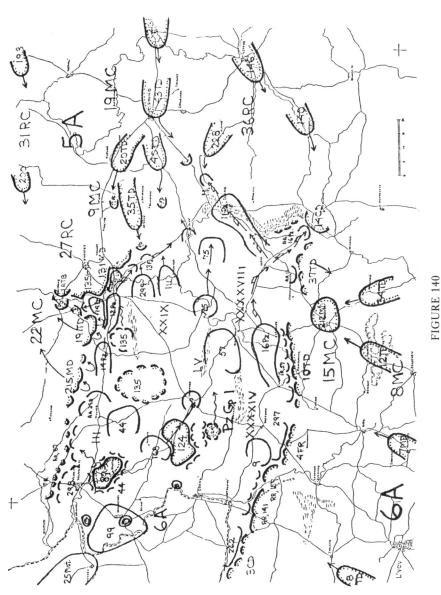

FIGURE 140
SITUATION, 2300, 25 JUNE 1941

now arriving in the area west of Rovno. This was to become the force the Soviets would attempt to concentrate for an attack to the southeast against German 11th Panzer Division. The divisions of 8th Mechanized Corps, the 12th and 34th Tank Divisions, may be seen clearing the hills south of Brody and beginning to assemble to launch a counterattack to the northeast, also against 11th Panzer Division. Meanwhile, as 11th Panzer Division moved forward, the Germans brought forward 16th Panzer Division to fill in the gap in the southern part of the main penetration (see Figure 141).

On 26 June the Soviets began their counterattack. It developed in fairly uncoordinated fashion for, in fact, all the elements of the 9th and 19th Mechanized Corps had not yet arrived on the battlefield (see Figure 142). The two corps attacked with their lead armored elements. Each of 9th and 19th Mechanized Corps' tank divisions (35th, 20th, 40th and 43rd) launched its attack with a reinforced forward detachment of roughly 30 to 40 tanks, supported by whatever motorized infantry it could assemble. These detachments moved forward and, for a time, cut the main road running between Lutsk and Dubno. Elements of 43rd Tank Division actually reached Dubno and seized it, but only after the bulk of the 11th Panzer Division had already passed through Dubno heading east. It was a very complicated series of operations with opposing forces thoroughly intermingled.

The Germans responded to this new threat by turning 13th Panzer Division southward from Lutsk. Instead of moving directly eastward as originally planned, 13th Panzer Division now turned south to strike the counterattacking Soviet forces in the flank. You will see that maneuver developing further the following day. Simultaneously, the German 75th, 111th, and 299th Infantry Divisions also veered to the southeast to drive Soviet forces away from 11th Panzer Division's line of communications.

To the southwest, the Soviet 15th Mechanized Corps began carrying out its orders to create a blocking force south of Ostrov to cover the forward deployment of 8th Mechanized Corps. The 8th Mechanized Corps' commander ordered his 34th Tank Division and a reinforced forward detachment from his 12th Tank Division to move forward and cut the main highway which served as both 11th and 16th Panzer Divisions' main supply line. Meanwhile, near L'vov, 8th Tank Division now finally moved east, in an attempt to join the Soviet counterattack force. A considerable amount of Soviet armor was on the move and all of it, of course, was moving under continuous heavy German air attacks.

Figure 143 shows a detailed view of the situation on 26 June in the Dubno area. Soviet forces of 43rd Tank Division's 85th Tank Regiment reached the outskirts of Dubno while elements of two other regiments from the 40th Tank Division deployed along the road from Dubno to the

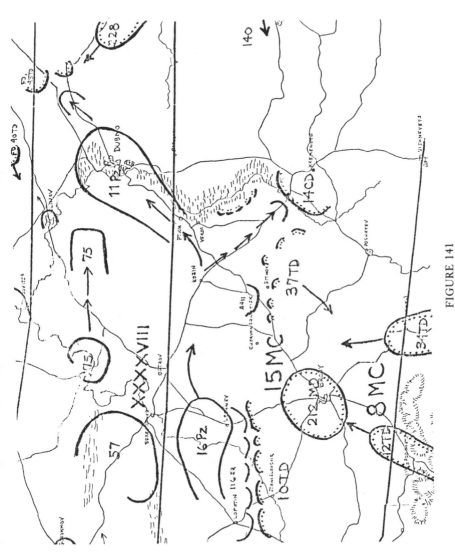

FIGURE 141
DUBNO SECTOR, 2300, 25 JUNE 1941

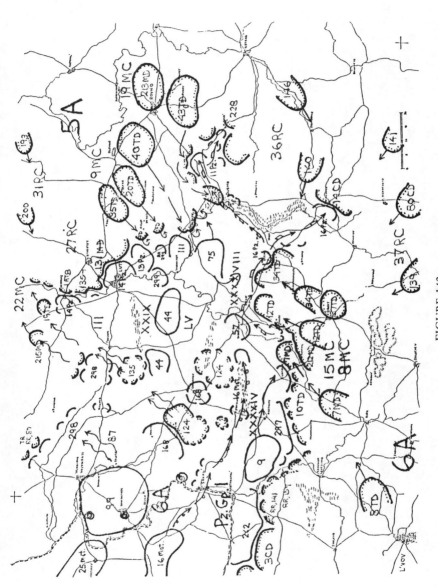

FIGURE 142
SITUATION, 2300, 26 JUNE 1941

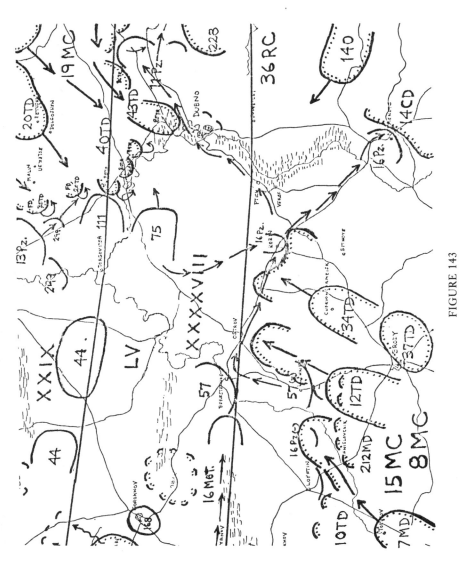

FIGURE 143
DUBNO SECTOR, 2300, 26 JUNE 1941

north. Further south, the advance of 12th and 34th Tank Divisions actually cut 11th Panzer Division's line of communications. Consequently, on the following day 16th Panzer Division was ordered to attack to the rear to clear those communications routes. The German 57th Infantry Division moved forward but also had to watch its rear area because elements of encircled Soviet divisions were there as well.

On 27 June the attack by Rokossovsky's 9th Mechanized Corps and Feklenko's 19th Mechanized Corps began to falter (see Figure 144). By placing the bulk of their combat power into the forward detachments and then, by having those forward detachments individually destroyed, the Soviet tank divisions had very little choice but to withdraw. In fact, the forward detachments, as they operated near Dubno, were separated from one another by as much as 10 kilometers. They had no communications with one another, hence they could not support one another. That became, at least according to Soviet critiques, one of the chief reasons for the failure of the counterattack – the total lack of coordination between the sub-elements of those tank divisions. In any case, on 27 June 13th Panzer Division plunged southward down the highway from Lutsk and struck the Soviet forward detachments in the flank, rolling over them one after the other. 13th Panzer then turned eastward and thrust directly toward Rovno. This movement cut across the flanks of the Soviet 35th, 20th and 40th Tank Divisions, and essentially cut off 43rd Tank Division because 13th Panzer Division ran right across its rear. Over a period of about 48 hours, while 13th Panzer Division moved eastward, Soviet forces also moved eastward behind it, trying to get out of potential encirclement. 11th Panzer Division, without batting an eye, continued its march and seized a key river crossing further east at Ostrog. This forced the Soviets to take the few reserves they had assembled at Rovno and move them south to try to block both 13th and 11th Panzer Divisions' advance.

The Soviet attack in the south, however, developed a little more successfully. The 12th and 34th Tank Divisions, a forward detachment of 12th Tank Division, 7th Motorized Division and 14th Cavalry Division all joined in the attack. 8th Tank Division finally reinforced 10th Tank Division as well. But it had less than half of its original tank strength. Basically the Soviets had committed all their remaining available armored resources from the 15th and 8th Mechanized Corps into this battle which was really nothing more than a desperate attempt to cut off German 16th and 11th Panzer Divisions and all other German forces operating east and south of Dubno.

Figure 145 is a detailed situation map of the tank battle on 27 June. As far as I can tell, the total Soviet armor strength of the combined forces of 34th and 12th Tank Divisions was about 150 tanks. These attacked northward through 16th Panzer Division's rear into the Dubno region.

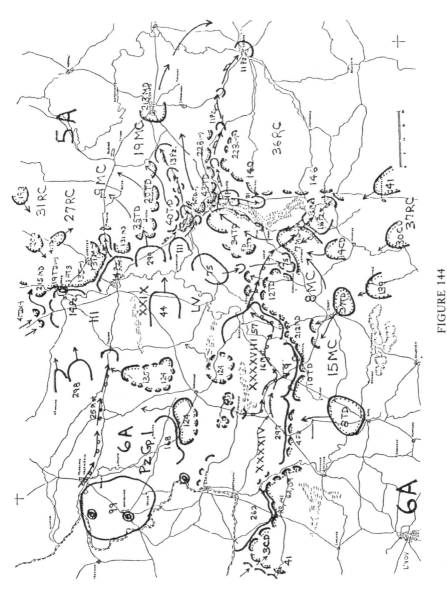

FIGURE 144
SITUATION, 2300, 27 JUNE 1941

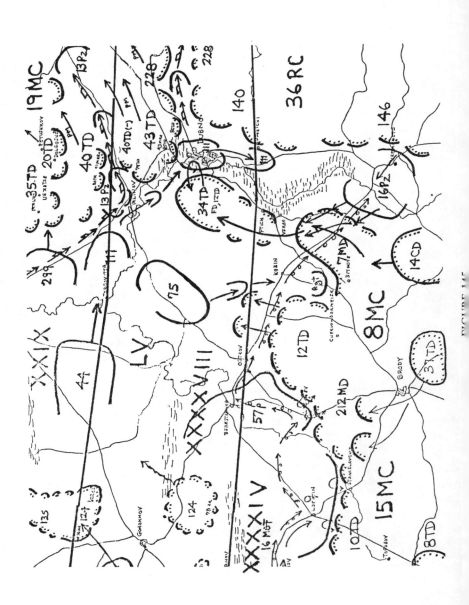

FIGURE 145

They penetrated to within four or five kilometers of Dubno, but were utterly unable to break through the 111th Infantry Division defenses. The 111th Division had been sent south in the wake of 13th Panzer, and by now it had cut a virtual corridor which separated 9th and 19th Mechanized Corps, operating north of Dubno, and 8th Mechanized Corps, attacking south of Dubno. The Soviet 7th Motorized Division also tried to thrust northward but it, in turn, was struck by 16th Panzer Division, which was attacking to the rear. Simultaneously, German 75th Infantry Division moved southward and struck Soviet 12th Tank Division, thus preventing the division's main force from linking up with its forward detachment. It was an immensely complicated battle which took place near Dubno, but one which, in the last analysis, tended to slow down the momentum of the German advance, principally by drawing forces from the north down to the south to deal with these armor counterattacks.

On 28 June the battle developed further (see Figure 146). 13th Panzer Division reached the Rovno area, but found itself without any basic infantry support since the German infantry divisions had turned south to deal with the critical situation developing around Dubno. By reinforcing their positions near Lutsk and by withdrawing elements of 9th and 22nd Mechanized Corps from the Dubno area, the Soviets were able to create a fairly firm defense line running north and southeast of Lutsk to just north of Rovno. This was the beginning of what would become a major defensive position, a virtual balcony hanging over Army Group South, which Soviet 5th Army would continue to occupy and which threatened further rapid German movement eastward toward Kiev. This strong Soviet position contributed ultimately to the German decision to move Army Group Center's main attack axis southward out of the Smolensk area and against Kiev.

On 28 June elements of Soviet 34th and 12th Tank Divisions were still struggling west of Dubno, but the bulk of Soviet armor in the area was attempting to withdraw. Reinforcements were also reaching Ostrog from newly arrived 5th Mechanized Corps, which finally blocked 11th Panzer Division's advance at that point. At the same time, new reinforcements from Soviet 37th Rifle Corps filled in the sagging defensive line south of Brody. An ominous new threat to the viability of Soviet defenses began to develop far to the west as the Germans committed 9th Panzer Division to attack the Soviet left flank near L'vov. Ultimately that maneuver would collapse the whole Soviet left flank.

Figure 147 is a more detailed look at the complex tank battle in the Dubno area on 28 June. It vividly shows the isolation of forward elements of Soviet 34th and 12th Tank Divisions and the impact of both 16th Panzer and 75th Infantry Divisions' counterattack, which split up Soviet forces and compelled the main Soviet force to withdraw southward. At this

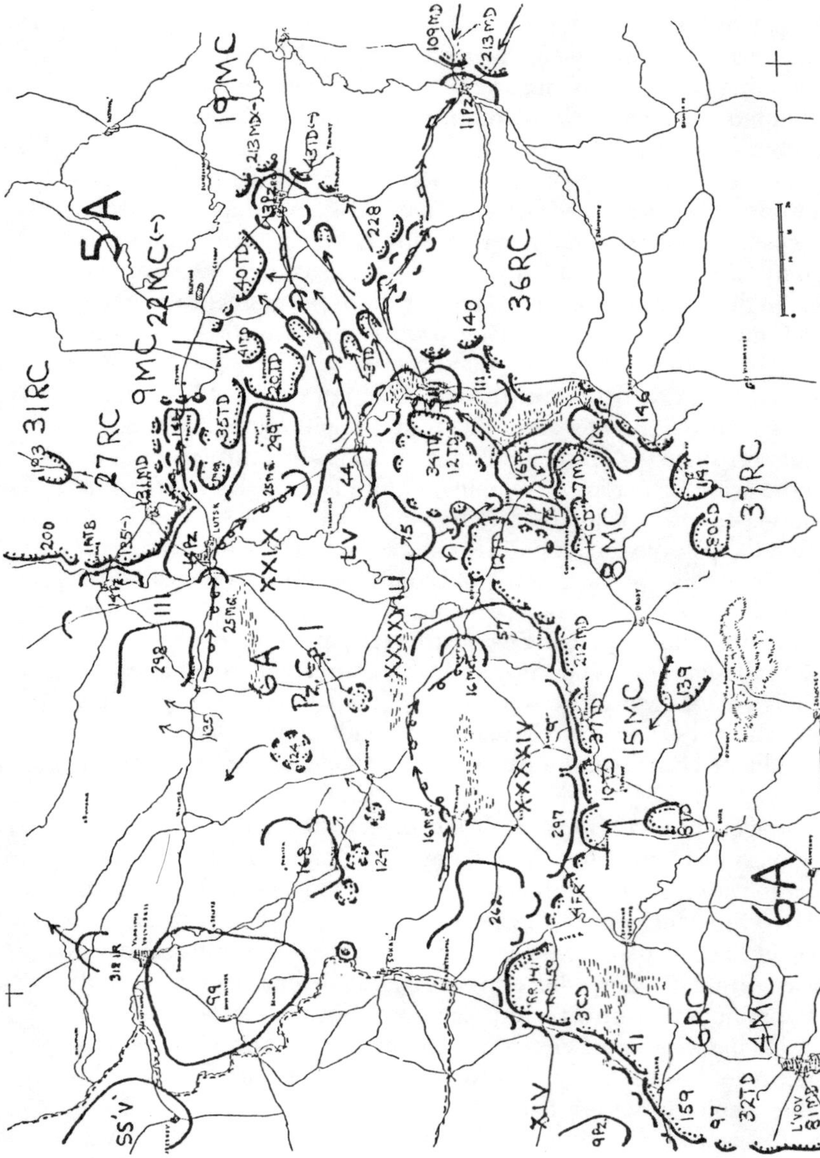

FIGURE 146
SITUATION, 2300, 28 JUNE 1941

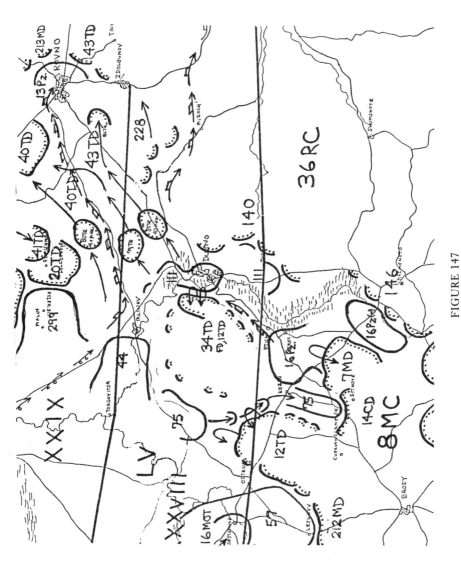

FIGURE 147
DUBNO SECTOR, 2300, 28 JUNE 1941

juncture the routine nemesis of Soviet forces again arose – renewed shortages of fuel and ammunition. Lack of fuel threatened to turn difficulty into disaster.

Disaster loomed for the Soviets on 29 June (see Figure 148). During the morning 13th Panzer Division advanced eastward out of Rovno, while Soviet forces were still withdrawing north and south of the city, literally along routes parallel to 13th Panzer's advance. By now 11th Panzer Division had been contained by Soviet forces in the Ostrog area. The battles the Soviets were still waging elsewhere were now battles more for survival than anything else, because at this point the Soviets begin running out of fuel and ammunition. Soviet tank strength dissipated, and that was why German infantry divisions were now able to deal more effectively with the remnants of 34th and 12th Tank Divisions. Because of their exertions, the 57th Infantry and 16th Panzer Divisions were able to cut off that Soviet group in the Dubno area. At the same time, 75th Infantry Division struck deep into the Soviet rear area, and you can see the resulting fragmentation of the Soviet front (see Figure 149). This critical situation was exacerbated by the attack of 9th Panzer Division, which developed north of L'vov. As will be seen on subsequent maps, 9th Panzer's attack rendered untenable the whole Soviet defense line covering L'vov and the approaches west of L'vov.

9th Panzer's attack developed on 30 June, penetrated through the remnants of Soviets' 3rd Cavalry Division, which had been defending that sector, cut behind elements of 8th and 10th Tank Divisions and, in essence, encircled the entire Soviet force (see Figure 150). Consequently, the Soviet 6th Army commander ordered his forces to conduct a general withdrawal back to the hill line east of L'vov. At the same time, remnants of 8th Mechanized Corps now reassembled in the Soviet rear, and orders were sent out to those forces encircled near Dubno to fight their way out of encirclement by whatever means necessary (see Figure 151). By this time, 14th Panzer Division had redeployed south of Lutsk to join 13th Panzer in an attempt to create a solid armored fist with which to continue the attack further east toward Zhitomir and Berdichev.

Figure 152, the 1 July situation map, shows the dwindling remnants of what had once been a fairly sizable Soviet force attempting to orchestrate a coordinated counterattack. The ensuing unsuccessful counterattack resulted in the destruction of most of the Soviet's mechanized corps in the region. The 9th and 19th Mechanized Corps emerged from combat with about 30 per cent of their original strength. The 22nd Mechanized Corps came out with about ten per cent and the 8th and 15th Mechanized Corps also survived with only about ten to 15 per cent of their original strength. The 4th Mechanized Corps probably came out in better shape than most with roughly 40 per cent of its tanks intact. The most telling effect of all

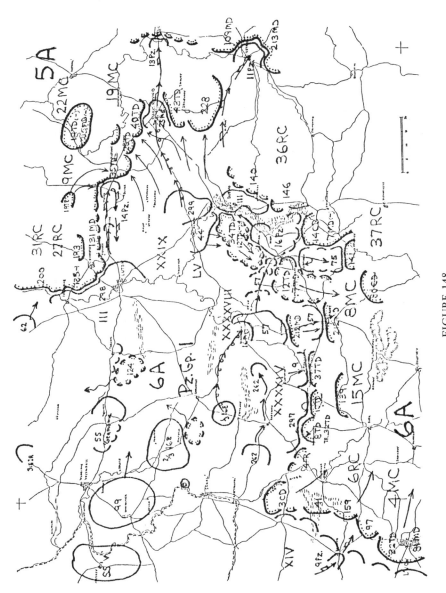

FIGURE 148
SITUATION, 2300, 29 JUNE 1941

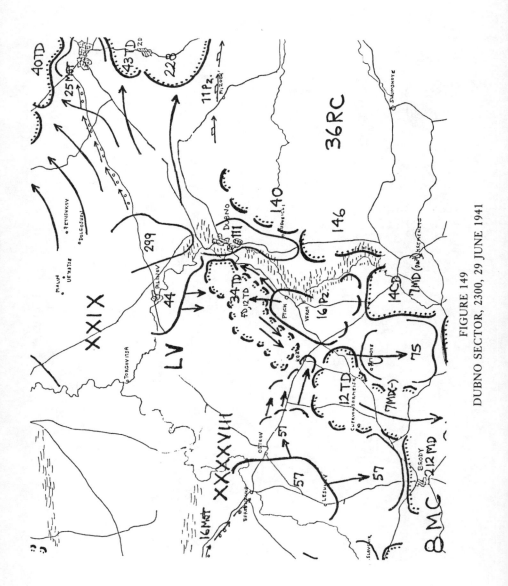

FIGURE 149
DUBNO SECTOR, 2300, 29 JUNE 1941

284

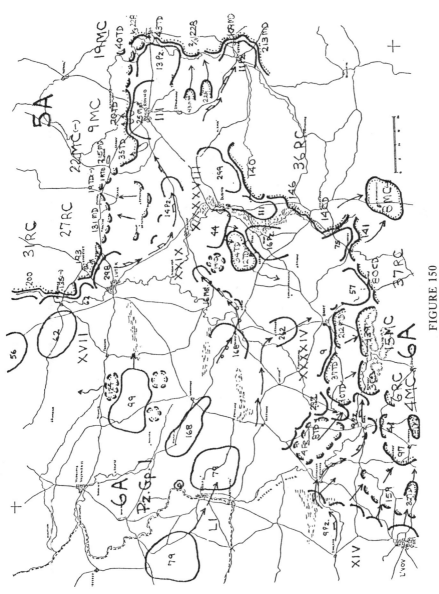

FIGURE 150
SITUATION, 2300, 30 JUNE 1941

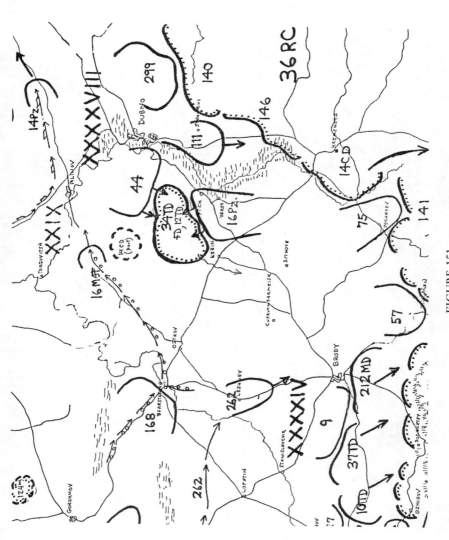

FIGURE 151

DUBNO SECTOR, 2300, 30 JUNE 1941

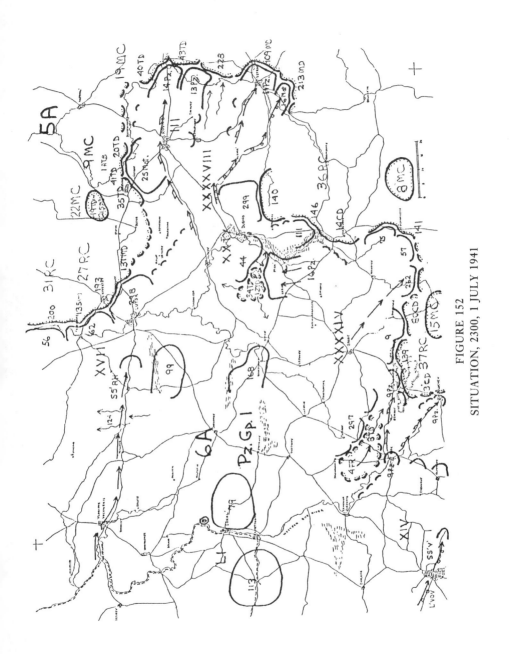

FIGURE 152

SITUATION, 2300, 1 JULY 1941

was that the Southwestern Front's sector was one of the few sectors of the Eastern Front where Soviet mechanized counterattacks actually had a big impact on German plans by causing considerable damage to advancing German forces. But it must be borne in mind from the outset that this was achieved against one of the weaker German panzer groups, in an area where the Soviets had more than the usual number of mechanized corps.

German Operations on the Lutsk-Rovno Axis

LIEUTENANT GENERAL KARL WILHELM THILO
(retired)
MAJOR GENERAL HEINZ GUDERIAN (retired)
LIEUTENANT GENERAL HANS JOACHIM VON
HOPFFGARTEN (retired)
and
BRIGADIER GENERAL E. LINGENTHAL (retired)

Introduced by Colonel Paul Adair

We are very fortunate to be able to learn about this part of the operation from the German point of view at three different levels: first, the view seen from OKH; secondly the view from III Panzer Corps, which controlled 13th and 14th Panzer Divisions; and last, from the 11th Panzer Division itself. General Thilo was at that time a group leader at the OKH responsible for operations on the southern part of the front. He served during the war partly as chief of staff of 1st Mountain Division, as troop commander in the Russian Caucasus, in the Balkan theater and in the Carpathian Mountains, and in various staff appointments in the operations branch of OKH. After the war he joined the Bundeswehr and became the commander of II German Corps at Ulm.

A Perspective from the Army High Command (OKH)

LIEUTENANT GENERAL KARL WILHELM THILO

My account is in accordance with the questions posed to me regarding the following information:

1. The organization of the unit (staff) to which I belonged in 1941.
2. My task and position.
3. The operations of Army Group South: June–July 1941.

In 1941 I served in the Operation Section ((GS) Heusinger as Chief) of the Army High Command (OKH). Along with the operations section, the Foreign Armies East Section (dealing with the enemy situation), the Organization Section, and the Quartermaster General (supply and resupply) also performed particularly important functions in the High Command. The Commander-in-Chief of the Army at that time was Field Marshal von Brauchitsch and Chief of the General Staff was General Oberst Halder.

Within the Operations Section, Group 1 (headed by Lieutenant Colonel (GS) Gehlen and later, Lieutenant Colonel Graf von Kielmansegg) had overall responsibility for the Eastern Theater of War. This section consisted of sub-groups South (Thilo), Center (Ziervogel) and North (von Rumohr) which corresponded to the three army groups. I (then a Major of the GS) was personally responsible for dealing with matters pertaining to the Southern Army Group. My task was to receive, twice a day by day telephone, the situation reports of the army groups and their armies, as well as estimates of the situation and concepts of operations. These were then put into writing and general situation maps were drawn. Figure 153 shows the area of operations of Southern Army Group. It extended about 700 kilometers from Lemberg (L'vov) to Kiev and 600 kilometers from the Black Sea to the Pripet marshes.

The main reports from the Army Group arrived during the night, in other words after the cessation of the day's hostilities. After the morning briefing with the Section Chief, there were sometimes directives or orders from the Army High Command to the army groups to be prepared and dispatched. At the same time, until around October 1941 I had to prepare

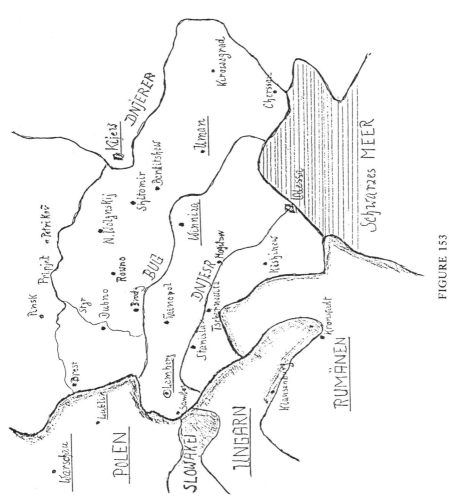

FIGURE 153

ARMY GROUP SOUTH AREA OF OPERATIONS

and maintain the Operations Section's War Diary and to submit the drafts for it daily to the Chief for his approval.

At the outbreak of war, the Southern Army Group was composed of: Eleventh Army (General Oberst von Schobert), Seventeenth Army (General Oberst von Stulpnagel), Sixth Army (Field Marshal von Reichenau), and Panzer Group 1 (General Oberst von Kleist) for a total of 36 infantry divisions, 5 panzer divisions, 3 motorized divisions (all German units), plus the Third and Fourth Romanian Armies (9 divisions and 4 brigades), later Second Hungarian Army and Slovakian units (see Figure 154). In the southern sector, the Army High Command (OKH) had at its disposal an operational reserve of five infantry divisions and one panzer division. In fulfilling its missions the Army Group had first to force the Prut and Dnester Rivers near Lvov and Odessa; and later, its main effort was to advance through Vinnitsa towards Uman and then destroy enemy forces west of the Dnepr River.

The following material is extracted from my two personal diaries which I kept in the Operations Section from 16 June 1940 to December 1942. Unfortunately, I no longer possess any maps, apart from rough hand-drawn copies. A small atlas belonging to the Operations Section with 1:1,000,000 printed copies was destroyed when my apartment in Augsburg burned down in 1944.

Let me now discuss briefly the pre-Barbarossa period. I quote the following entries from my diary:

1940

21 September – HQ, Army High Command in Fontainebleau: On the orders of the Führer (Hitler), Russia is to be photographed from the air up to 300 kilometers beyond its borders; preparations for invasion. I myself have to work on a mission for the German military attache in Moscow to reconnoiter routes and communications for three phase lines (spearheads) ...

2 October – Report by the German military attache (from Moscow) on Russian Fall maneuvers states that everyone *there* is expecting war against Germany in 1941; after England it will be Russia's turn.

10 October – Advance parties for Rumanian Military Mission (13th Panzer Division) depart: Stepping stone for subsequent offensive action against Russia.

28 October – Army High Command moves to Zossen (south of Berlin).

12 November – Molotov (Russian Foreign Minister) in Berlin.

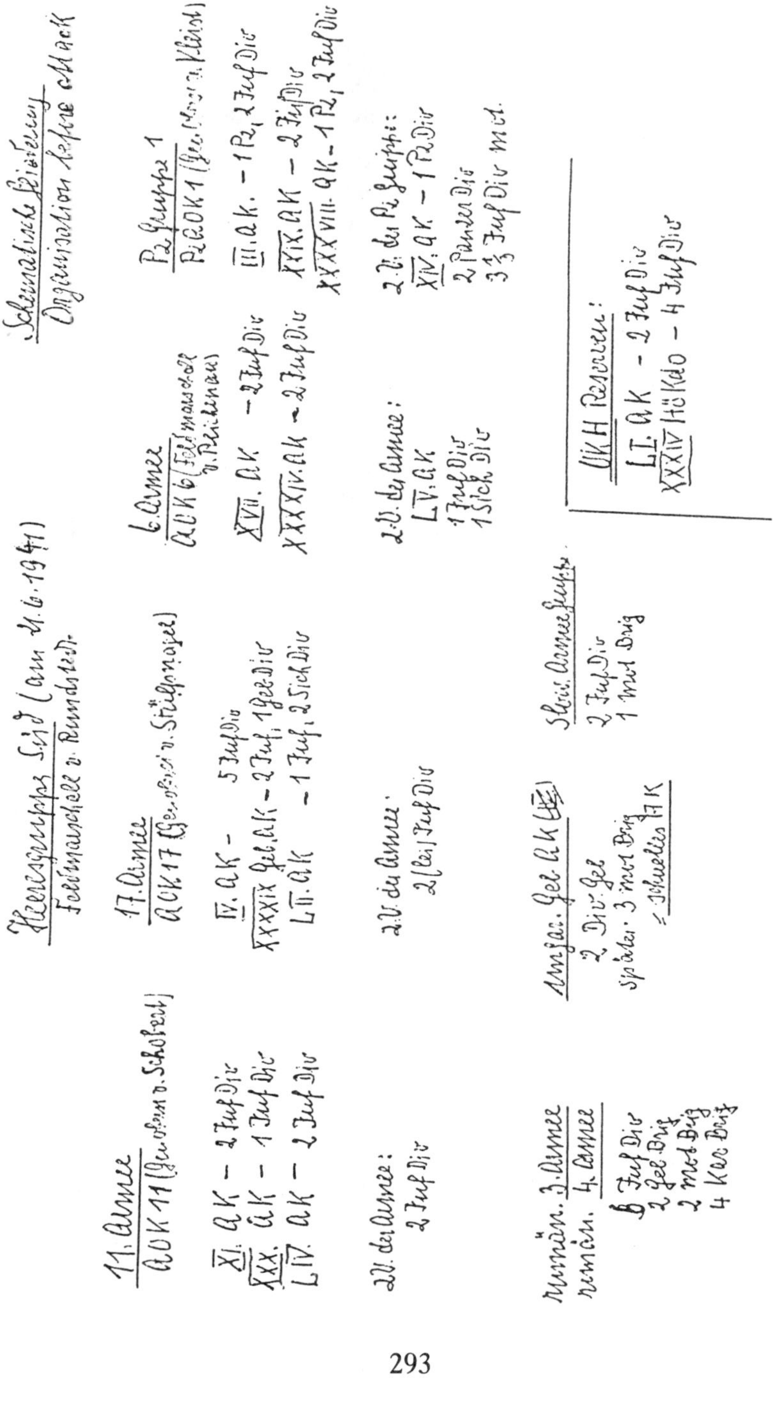

FIGURE 154
ARMY GROUP SOUTH ORGANIZATION

1941

11 January – According to the Führer's directive, preparations for Barbarossa are to continue so that offensive can be launched on May 15. [However, the Balkan campaign fatefully delayed this]

2 March – entry into Bulgaria.

6 April – attack against Serbia and Greece.

12 May – also a quote: "Incredibly, the Russians know the exact date of Barbarossa (11 June). Was it disclosed by someone in the Führer's entourage?"

That concludes the story from the Army High Command before the start of Barbarossa. And now let me quote journal entries involved with the days immediately before the operation in June 1941:

17 to 19 June – I fly as aide-de-Camp to Chief of the General Staff (Halder) via Hungary to Rumania, and to the front on the Prut River. Enemy situation in the south of Bessarabia (briefing by Chief of Army Mission, General Hauffe) – Russians are obviously withdrawing mobile forces from there to behind the Dniester River, destroying bridges and stocks in Bessarabia. Accordingly, only defensive action on southern Prut front and Danube to be expected [facing attack by German Eleventh Army].

Rumania is prepared for defensive operations, but has not yet been informed about the start of the war.

19 June – At the Hungarian General Staff in Budapest – Hungarians have no idea of the forthcoming events. Their participation in the war cannot be counted on to start with.

Operational Plans

In accordance with the Deployment Instruction Barbarossa, it was the mission of the Southern Army Group "to destroy the Soviet forces in Galicia and the Western Ukraine no further east than the Dnepr and to seize the Dnepr crossing at and downstream of Kiev as early as possible" (see Figure 155).

Originally, Halder had intended to accomplish this by means of a wide envelopment maneuver from the Polish and Romanian areas of operation. According to different instructions personally from Hitler to operate solely with a strong left wing, the Army Group's direction of main effort was determined to lie along the line Lublin–Kiev. The idea of a two-sided envelopment was maintained as a secondary solution when Winiza [Vinnitsa] was determined as an objective of attack to be launched as a combined effort by the Eleventh and Seventeenth Armies.

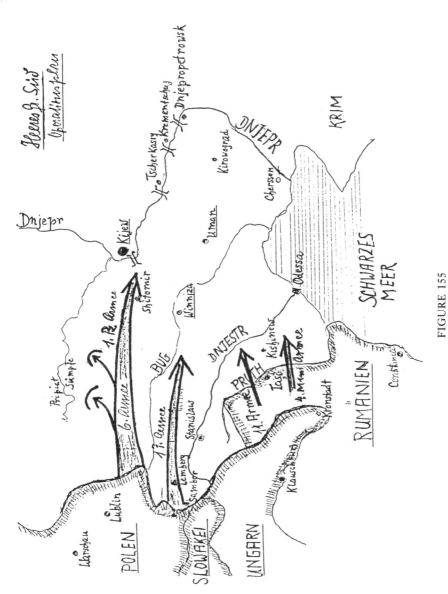

FIGURE 155

ARMY GROUP SOUTH OPERATIONAL PLAN

A line of fortifications was assumed along the Dniester River; and Kiev, Kolomyja, Lemberg, Sambor and Stanislov were assumed to be fortified. The main obstacles to the attack were the plains west of the Dniester River, rich in rivers and streams, the river itself, and its tributaries; and strong resistance was expected along the Dnepr River, especially in the Kiev area. Based on reconnaissance efforts, 38 divisions of the Army Group (without the reserves of the Supreme Command of the Army) were assumed to face 80 enemy divisions. Due to the open right flank of Seventeenth Army and because the Eleventh Army was still engaged at the Prut River and initially was not even ready for attack, the mobile forces of 1st Panzer Army were instructed to penetrate Soviet defenses in the northern deployment area at an operationally effective point in order to operate independently behind enemy lines.

This basic concept governed the overall conduct of operations. As it later turned out, and I will illustrate this, the intention of mounting a large-scale enveloping maneuver towards the Dnepr River was repeatedly jeopardized during the course of combat actions.

The Sixth Army had been instructed to penetrate enemy positions close to the border for the armored forces, to follow the armored forces closely in order to destroy the enemy in the breakthrough area, to assist and support the armored forces in river crossing operations, and at the same time to secure the northern flank of the Army Group towards the Pripet Marsh area. As will be seen later, this latter task tied up Sixth Army for a large part of the time.

The Seventeenth Army was tasked with cutting off the Lemberg area and then advancing towards Tarnopol and Winiza while the Fourth Rumanian Army was to provide security and cover along the Black Sea coast and the lower course of the Prut River.

These were the operational plans of the Supreme Command of the Army and the Southern Army Group. Now, I will stick to the entries in my diary and outline the course of events and combat action up to the battles in the Winiza and Uman area.

Conduct of Operations

22 June 0300 hours – [Wehrmacht] attack against Russia started, border fortifications and rivers not defended (except Bessarabia, Prut, Eleventh Army sector). On the whole surprise fully successful (see Figure 156).

Eleventh Army has to defend, but seizes bridgeheads across Prut River against fierce enemy resistance. Russian parachute troops dropped over Constanta.

24 June – Enemy has started fighting ahead of Southern Army Group (Sixth and Seventeenth Armies); stubborn defense. Sixth and Seven-

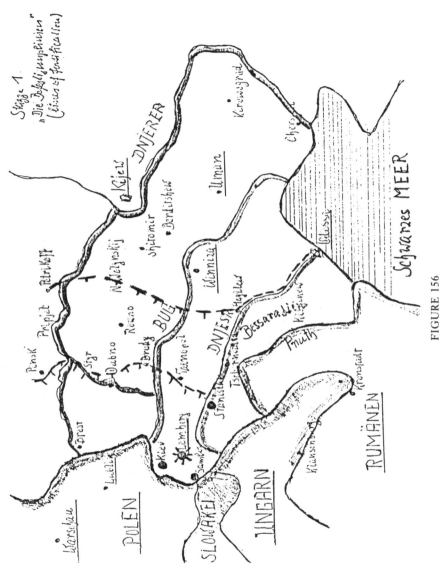

FIGURE 156
ARMY GROUP SOUTH OPERATIONS, 22–23 JUNE 1941

teenth Armies fighting for penetration (see Figure 157). Russians begin withdrawal from Lvov pocket; for cover, Russians launch counterattack against northern wing of Seventeenth Army. Panzer Group 1 in tank battle, its foremost elements (11th Panzer Division) have crossed the Styr River; Panzer Group I thus has operational freedom northward.

25 June – Enemy resistance intensified, systematic counterattacks supported by tanks. In the Central Army Group, Panzer Groups 2 and 3 advance on Minsk and start to close the Bialystok pocket (10 to 20 Russian divisions encircled).

26 June – Yesterday was the most difficult day of the battle. Seventeenth Army is fighting at Rava Ruska, where enemy is conducting numerous counterattacks employing heavy tanks. Army has gained only little ground. Heavy casualties on both sides. Sixth Army's Panzer Corps has captured Dubno and Luck, Infantry Corps have reached the Styr. Enemy has brought up reserves from the depth of the Ukraine and is attacking the flanks from the south and north. Heavy enemy forces that have come to a standstill are fighting in the intermediate area. Battle has not reached its climax by 30 June; if the Army group holds out, half the Russian Army will be destroyed. Eleventh Army is to attack (from N. Rumania) on 2 July towards Vinnitsa to close the pocket in the east. Panzer Group 1 is to close in southward via Zhitomir.

Estimate: When this battle has been fought, the Ukraine will be open. Russians are standing their ground excellently; down here there is exceptionally systematic command.

27 June – Enemy resistance broken by Seventeenth Army, Rava Ruska captured. 1200 hours – Seventeenth Army in pursuit of enemy forces retreating eastward from Lvov area. But unfortunately 2–3 days too early; Eleventh Army cannot attack until 2 July, then we would have had the enemy in a pincer. The continuous arrival and commitment of Russian reserves against the southern and northern flanks of Sixth Army forced it to employ its last reserves. Flank of Panzer Group 1 must not get deeper; therefore, fiercest enemy resistance after reaching Rovno. Closing-in of spearheads southeastward towards Stary–Konstatinov. Attack by Eleventh Army with main-attack wing on Proskurov. This inevitably means giving up the operational breakthrough to Kiev; but first certain encirclement and operational envelopment of enemy Lvov area.

After reaching the highland, Panzer Groups 2 and 3 of Central Army Group advance up to the Berezina River, where they are to repel, if necessary, forces brought up from the interior of Russia to support the encircled armies. Encirclement in several pockets is to be continued.

30 June – Lvov fallen, Seventeenth Army is continuing pursuit (see Figure 158). Sixth Army and Panzer Group 1 involved in heavy fighting in

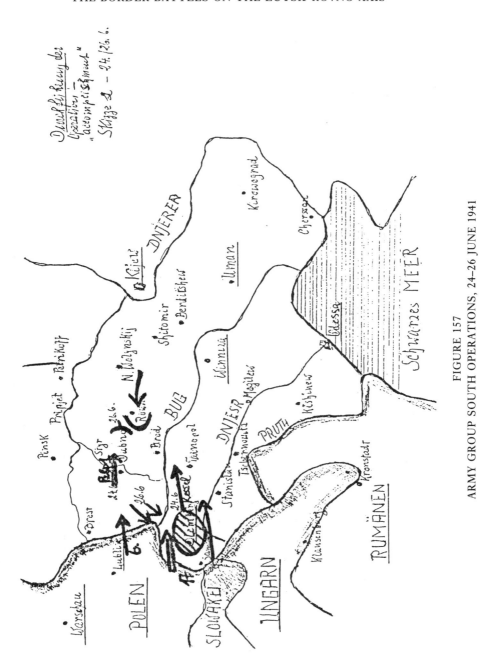

FIGURE 157

ARMY GROUP SOUTH OPERATIONS, 24–26 JUNE 1941

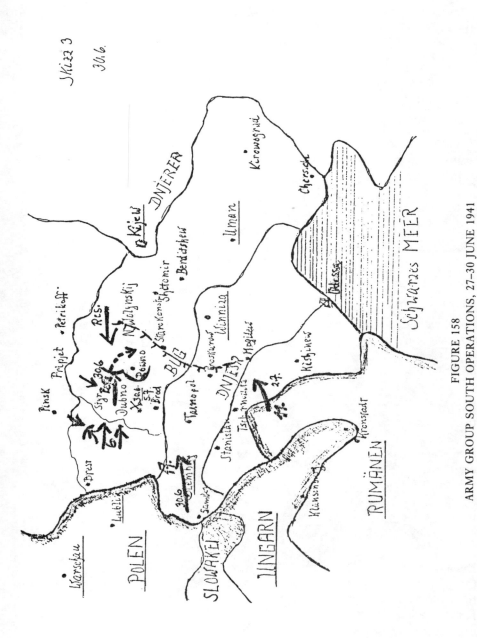

FIGURE 158
ARMY GROUP SOUTH OPERATIONS, 27–30 JUNE 1941

the Horyn sector and around Dubno (Styr), where encircled enemy forces are trying to break out. Enemy reserves brought up from the depths from the east. Slovakian Army Corps (two divisions) assembled and attached to the Seventeenth Army. In prison after occupation of Lvov found thousands of shot Ukrainians, cannot bury all the bodies, prison to be bricked up.

2 July – Attack by Eleventh Army, main effort towards Mogilev–Podolskiy–Vinnitsa.

4 July – Employment of Hungarian Mountain Corps and Mobile Corps against Dniester sector Kolomea–Horodenka–Stanislav (see Figure 159).

5 July – Enemy succeeded in blocking Panzer Group 1's advance in breakthrough attacks against flank and rear.

6 July – Battle for Dubno terminated.

Eleventh Army has advanced 30 kilometers into Bessarabia in combat with Russian rear guards.

Fourth Rumanian Army has attacked Kichinev;

Third Rumanian Army has attacked Cernovitz.

Second Hungarian Army, under good command, advanced to Dniester which it reached in three days pursuing retreating enemy forces. Seventeenth Army continuing pursuit, now no longer inhibited by enemy, but by inclement weather and muddy tracks.

7 July – Sixth Army following along the flanks of Panzer Group 1 and Panzer Group 1 has penetrated into fortification line Volynskiy – Dniesk, the so-called Stalin Line, only III Army Corps with XI Army Corps, and 11th Panzer Division penetrates to Besovichov; an operational breakthrough to the Dnepr is in the offing *if* mobile armored forces are brought up soon. But the tanks "suffocate" in the mud of the Ukrainian chermozem [black earth]. LIV Army Corps attached to Fourth Rumanian Army on Führer's orders. Was that the right thing to do? (Halder) Rumanians are using the German corps as their main-attack wing the Bug and Odessa.

8 July – *Estimate of the situation by High Command Southern Army Group:* Enemy well commanded by General Shapozhnikov (Tsarist General Staff Officer). At first, defensive operations close to the border, then withdrawal to Stalin Line with heavy counterattacks against our armored wedge. Retreat behind the Dnepr now possible. Typical Asiatic fighting technique showing no mercy for men or material.

Employment of Southern Army Group initially characterized by open southern flank. Therefore frontal attack. Operational breakthrough by

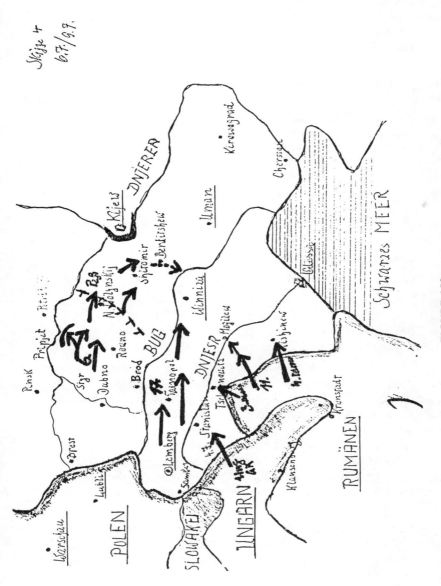

FIGURE 159

ARMY GROUP SOUTH OPERATIONS, 27 JUNE–9 JULY 1941

Panzer Group 1 *still not* achieved by 6 July; Panzer Group has destroyed five Russian armored divisions with 1,200 tanks. Envelopment of the Russian southern wing will only be possible if there are infantry divisions, while the enemy motorized units can always withdraw northeastward.

So far, 61 major units have appeared in front of the Army Group (versus 46 friendly units); at any rate, up to now we have achieved an extraordinary weakening of the enemy, especially in terms of material. Enemy elite units are fighting out of conviction; other units are fighting under "terrorist" pressure. Ukrainian population is helpful and friendly to Germans.

9 July – Panzer Group 1 continues attack across Zhitomir – Berdichev line, in the north towards Kiev to gain a bridgehead over the Dnepr. However, on 10 July Hitler intervenes as Supreme Commander and orders that the attack on Kiev be discontinued and that the Panzer Group turn from Berdichev towards Vinnitsa to form a pocket together with the Eleventh Army. 40–60 enemy divisions could be trapped in the pocket.

Up to 3 August

To summarize the events up to 31 July and 3 August: a three-day tank battle developed in the Berdichev area in which the enemy wanted to cover the withdrawal of his units to Kiev and Dnepr River (see Figure 160). On the deep northern flank of Panzer Group 1, Sixth Army was involved in a fierce defensive battle near Novograd Volynski until 18 July against enemy forces attacking from the north and northeast – from the Pripet Marshes – and threatening to thrust into the rear of Panzer Group 1. Seventeenth Army finally pierced the Stalin Line and encircled a large enemy group around Vinnista. But not until 24 July, after an advance by the Panzer Group from the north towards Pervomaisk in the Uman area, could heavy enemy forces be encircled and destroyed (3 August) (Figure 161). The elements that escaped from the pocket withdrew to the south – destination Odessa – and were engaged by Eleventh Army near Balta.

The first operational objective of Southern Army Group was not achieved until 15 August with the encirclement of Odessa, the capture of Krivoy Rog and Nikolayev and the occupation of the Black Sea coast up to the Bug. The city of Kiev and its fortifications could not be captured until early September.

Results of the two encirclement battles were:

77,000 prisoners (bloody losses at least as high),
525 tanks destroyed,
894 artillery pieces captured.

This means 20 divisions or more of the Soviet 6th, 12th, and 26th Armies were destroyed. But German casualties were also very high. For instance,

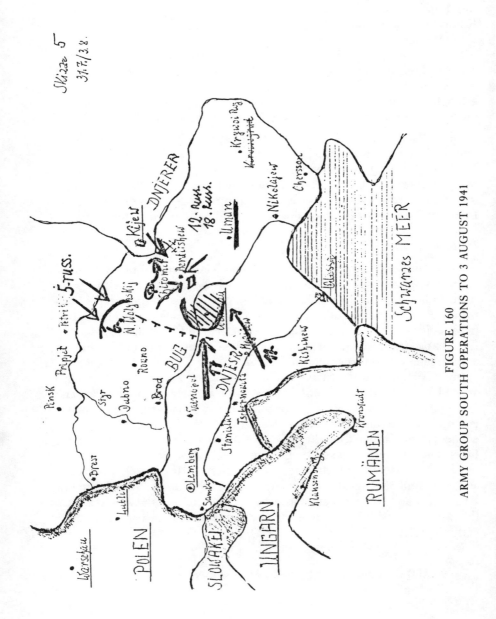

FIGURE 160

ARMY GROUP SOUTH OPERATIONS TO 3 AUGUST 1941

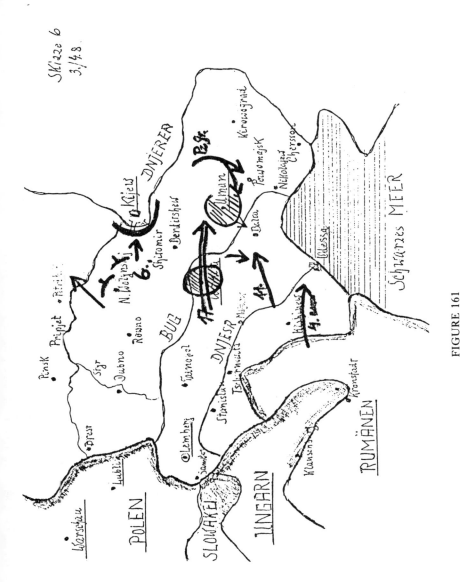

FIGURE 161
ARMY GROUP SOUTH OPERATIONS, 3-7 AUGUST 1941

HQ Eleventh Army reported some divisions had lost 25–30 per cent of their combat power.

To conclude, here is an estimate of the situation from a briefing given at the end of July by the Chief of the Operations Section to the Chief of the General Staff. It may be considered a reply to the question posed on the subject of border battles against the Soviet Union. I have taken the text from a book by Colonel (GS) Heusinger.

25 July 1941: *Daily situation briefing* to the Chief of the General Staff, General Halder.

Chief of the Operations Section:

The overall situation can be described as satisfactory, but not all hopes have been realized. In the south, the operations of Rundstedt's Army Group have been somewhat disappointing – the unexpected rainy period delayed all movements, the fierce fighting by the Russian 5th Army (Timoshenko) from the Pripet area against the northern flank of the Army Group caused more and more forces to be withdrawn in this direction, against our intentions; Hitler's order to halt the Panzer units before Kiev allowed the creation of a strong Russian center of resistance on the Dnepr and prevented rapid seizure of the bridges. It is doubtful, under these circumstances, whether the Army Group will still be able to force the strong enemy forces west of the Dnepr towards the Black Sea or to encircle them. In the central sector:

The casualties of the three army groups are tolerable. The increasing length of the supply line is beginning to show.

On the whole, we can say: we are still in the midst of fighting for a decisive success in destroying the enemy border armies. The prospects would appear to be best for Central Army Group, they correspond to expectations. In the case of Southern Army Group, the next few days will show whether the original plan will lead to success. Otherwise, army group will have to follow up as quickly as possible across the Dnepr to achieve in pursuit what it did not achieve west of the river.

Chief of the Foreign Armies East Section:

The enemy situation that we had before the start of the campaign has been confirmed in the case of Southern and Central Army Groups. The concentration of Russian troops in front of Northern Army Group appears to have been still in its initial stages.

On the basis of events so far, we can assume that in the southern sector strong enemy forces have been defeated but not destroyed. They will attempt to escape across the Dnepr and establish a new front. Here, the Russian commander under Timoshenko has proven capable, especially that of the 5th Army in the Pripet area. In the central sector, however, it has failed; it would be fair to talk of a crushing defeat. In the north ... As for an assessment of the enemy, we can say that he is very tough and brave in defense. The Russian commanders generally fail in mobile warfare; their command apparatus is not up to this task. We still do not have a clear picture of the enemy's reserve.

It should, however, be noted that this judgement was made in 1941. In 1943–44, the Russian commanders proved that they had learned to conduct mobile operations.

Russian armor is surprisingly strong, but incapable of operating in sizable formations and with long-range objective. On the whole, we have seen that the Russia Army must not be underestimated.

Were there signs that Russia intended to attack us?

We cannot draw any reliable conclusions from the grouping of forces. It may have been either intended for defensive purposes or for the start of an offensive. The latter theory is supported by the assembling of strong armored formations in Western Russia and the issuing of maps extending as far as Poland. On the other hand, we have been unable to capture any orders for preparations to attack.

III Panzer Corps Operations

MAJOR GENERAL HEINZ GUDERIAN (retired)

Introduced by Colonel Adair

General Guderian, at this time, was on the staff of the III Panzer Corps. For most of the war he was on the staff of various Panzer formations and he finished as the Ia (principal staff officer) of the 116th Panzer Division in the Ardennes campaign. After the war he became the general in charge of combat troops in the Heeresamt.

In the middle of May 1941, sadly I handed over my Panzer company and began general staff training. I became 01 (1. Ordonnanzoffizier, today comparable to S3) in the III.A.K. (Army Corps) (mot), later named III Panzer-Korps. My commanding general was General der Kavallerie von Mackensen. He wrote periodic reports about the events in 1941 for our people at home and I shall quote from his first letters later. But first I wish to answer the following questions:

1. *What was the composition of the force you fought in?*
Two infantry divisions fought with the III Corps in the first phase, the crossing of the Bug. After the build-up of forces in the initial bridgeheads, two Panzer divisions (13th and 14th) would follow and push forward. In addition, the corps had at its disposal corps artillery, corps engineers and an anti-aircraft regiment.

2. *What special training did your unit receive?*
About special training I can refer only to my tenure as a company commander. My Panzer company had been transferred in the first days of May to Rembertow near Warsaw, where it served the Fourth Army for training demonstrations in antitank combat. At this time we did not know anything about T34 or KV 1 and 2 model Soviet tanks.

3. *What was our knowledge about the enemy?*
It was very poor. In my recollection it was limited to our visual observations across the Bug River. It seemed to us that the Russians were unaware of our assembly movements.

4. *When did the first Soviet counterattacks occur?*
The first counterattacks hit us on the third day of our offensive, 24 June. They continued and increased in intensity from day to day, as von Mackensen's letters show and as Colonel Glantz's maps revealed.

308

So much for the questions. Now let me describe III Corps operations in some detail.

The headquarters of III Army Corps was stationed at Lublin. The corps fought at first under the command of the Sixth Army. When the operations of the Panzer divisions began, the corps came under the command of Panzer Group 1. The left flank was secured by the XVII Army Corps. But soon its two infantry divisions were left behind, as the Panzer divisions got under way and advanced rapidly forward. Now let me quote from the text of one of Mackensen's first letters (see Figure 162). It is interesting to hear a voice of that time, a little subjective naturally:

> When, during the morning hours of 22 June 1941, the infantry divisions of the III Army Corps stormed across the Bug near and forward of Hrubieszow, amidst the thunder of 300 guns, not even the greatest optimist dared assume that the III Army Corps might have reached its first operational objective, 450 kilometers distant, by the nineteenth day of operations, 10th July. How far away Kiev lay!
>
> It was a mission of the III Army Corps to reach the Kiev area as quickly as possible after breaking through the Russian border fortifications on the left wing of the Armored Group 1 (Panzergruppe 1) preceding the Southern Army Group, an action to form the basis for further operations. This III Army Corps had been transformed into an armored corps in Lublin only a few weeks before the outbreak of hostilities with Russia through a reorganization of its general command and its corps troops.

How was this mission accomplished in 18 days?

> The Silesians of the 298th and the Ostmark troops of the 44th Infantry Division in the first two days penetrate the tenaciously defended enemy fortifications in a bold assault. As early as the second day, first the 14th Panzer Division succeeds in advancing through the Corps' left wing, then the 13th Panzer Division succeeds in its advance through and past the Corps' right wing. Both armored divisions now compete in advancing towards their set objective, after having gained their initial operational freedom southeast and east of Wlodzimierz = Wladimir Wolynzky (Vladimir Volynskij).
>
> In their advance, the 13th Panzer Division experiences more difficulties with the terrain off the tank road, the only almost completely paved through-road between Hrubieszow – Wlodzimirz = Wladimir Wolynsky – Luck – Rowne = Rovno – Zwiahel =

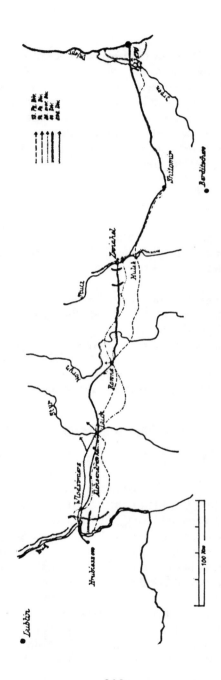

FIGURE 162

III PANZER CORPS OPERATIONS (OVERALL)

310

Novograd Wolynsky (Novograd Volynskij) – Shitomir – Kiev; whereas the 14th Panzer Division, advancing for the most part along the road, has to cope with greater enemy resistance.

While the 298th Infantry Division is still engaged to the rear of the armored divisions in holding and securing Wlodzimierz, and the 44th Infantry Division has already been placed under the command of another corps, the III Corps armored forces are fighting their first armored battle at and south of Aleksandrowka.

It ends in the destruction of 267 enemy tanks and is a roaring success. Luck is seized by 25 June and the Styr river is crossed. The 13th Panzer Division also succeeds in capturing rapidly Rowne (28 June) by advancing cross-country off the tank road southeast of Luck, some of the time against heavy enemy resistance; the 14th Panzer Division meanwhile is obliged to muster all its forces to hold Luck against repeated massive enemy attacks from the north and east. As soon as the division is relieved in its intensive battle by the untiringly advancing 298th Infantry Division, which is repeatedly engaged by the enemy, the 14th follows the 13th Division towards Rowne, avoiding the tank road. The 25th (mot) Division, which has hastened forward in the wake of the Corps, is tasked with the protection of Rowne, a task which can only be fulfilled by the division's brave men in heavy combat at the expense of many lives and loss of material.

At this point I would like to cite original reports of this division. On 30 June the I.R.119 (Infantry Regiment 119) of the 25th Infantry Division (mot) reported:

> The enemy attack could not be stopped, in spite of heavy defensive fire and serious losses. He advanced upright, firing against our positions. He also launched surprise attacks with "Hurras" at the shortest range out of the camouflage of cornfield against our flanks. He had no fear of close combat. In some cases Russians pretended to be dead (as one commissar) and began fighting again from the rear. Wounded soldiers who fell into enemy hands were shot, mutilated bestially (genitals cut off for example) and robbed ...

On the next day a whole battalion, the II/I.R. 35 (2nd Battalion, Infantry Regiment 35), was cut off from the divisions at Broniki, northwest of Rovno. The reports of escaped soldiers and the inspection of the battle-field showed the same mournful result: 153 soldiers of the battalion were dead; 132 of them were murdered, evidently in a bestial manner. You can understand, I believe, that these events formed our picture of the new enemy and of the forthcoming war (see Figure 163).

And now the report of Mackensen again:

Soon both armored divisions have reached the Horyn River, which is crossed under fire south and north of the tank road and along the road. From there they advanced towards the Slucz and thus towards the modern and massively fortified Stalin Line. Will the armored divisions be able to break through this strong defensive line on their own and so gain lasting operational freedom of movement towards Kiev, or will their capabilities turn out to be unsuitable and inadequate to the task, so that they are forced to wait for the still distant infantry divisions?

As soon as the Horyn has been crossed, the intention of leaving the tank road with the 14th Division, since the road had so far been the central target of enemy resistance, is defeated by torrential rains which turn all other roads in the black soil of the Ukraine into a quagmire and threaten to stop the operation completely. While the 14th Panzer Division is forced to return to the tank road in order to be able to advance at all, the 13th can only make its laborious way with one vehicle at a time cross-country towards Slucz.

Already 20 kilometers west of Zwiahel (Nowograd Wolynskij), the 14th Panzer Division finds itself engaged in a tenacious battle for the Stalin Line which is well distributed in depth. There the first forward bunkers must be overpowered; meanwhile the 13th Panzer Division surmounts all terrain obstacles in a surprisingly short time due to the enormous energy of leaders and men and is ready to break through the Stalin Line near Hulsk by 6 July. One day later Hulsk was seized after heavy bunker combat, while the river was crossed, a bridgehead was established, and on 8 July the tank road east of the fortifications was reached. The situation is different for the 14th Panzer Division. It is forced to take the bull by the horns: it takes the Division five days of heavy fighting to breach the fortifications, seize the town and cross the river, the armored division being well up to the task, as is the 25th (mot) Division, having joined forces with the two armored divisions, and so the Stalin Line has been breached here and just south of Zwiahel (Nowograd Wolynskij).

From then on there is no stopping the advance. With the 13th Panzer Division placed forward, the Corps storms towards Kiev via Shitomir, where light skirmishes occur, in little more than 24 hours. By the early hours of 10 July the leading tanks of the 13th Panzer Division reach the Jrpen River and are thus immediately outside the inner circle of fortifications of Kiev. Here the Corps is halted upon order from the highest authority.

The first objective of the operation has been reached. The III

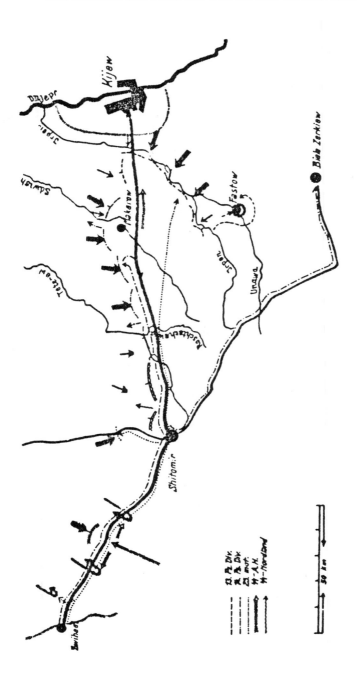

FIGURE 163
III PANZER CORPS OPERATIONS TO KIEV

Corps, thanks to the efficiency of its brave troops, is placed 120 kilometers forward of its right neighboring corps with its leading echelons, which are still engaged in heavy fighting at Berdichev, and 200 kilometers in advance of the leading edge of the infantry corps, which are at that moment engaged in relieving the rear element of the corps. Forced to rely fully on its own resources for a considerable amount of time in the foreseeable future now it is a must for the corps to hold the objective seized. The coming days promise to be difficult.

The "booty" of the first phase of the operation amounts of 14,480 prisoners taken, 868 tanks, 472 guns, 3 armored trains and a corresponding amount of other material captured. Approximately 20 enemy divisions have appeared before the corps front, 7 of which can be counted as destroyed, and 5 others as more or less weakened.

In contrast, our own casualties are 806 (65) dead, 388 (3) missing in action, 2,426 (124) wounded.

Left by itself the III Army Corps faces difficult days of battle following 10 July, when the first tanks reached the Jrpen River and the first operational objective was achieved.

Initially, only the 13th Panzer Division is on the banks of the Jrpen, and luckily at a point with a small bridgehead on the far bank. It provides protection against the inner circle of fortifications around Kiev and against attack from the southeast; the tank road is kept open by the Division in its area of responsibility, east of the Sdwish sector, through combat reconnaissance to the north.

So far the Russians have not yet recovered from the fright of our sudden and rapid appearance at the gates of Kiev. No reaction is as yet apparent. Would it have been possible for the Corps to move into Kiev without resistance if it had not been halted upon the order from a higher authority? Military history will prove the accuracy of that speculation.

On 11 July the leading element of the 14th Panzer Division arrive after having won their difficult breakthrough battle near Zwiahel and following quickly via Shitomir; the 25th (mot) Division had opened up the tank road east of Zwiahel (Nowograd Wolynskij) and the armored division itself had to surmount some moderate engagement actions west of Shitomir. This at least makes it possible to secure the rear of the 13th Panzer Division and the tank road in the entire area east of the Roshchevka sector to the north and south. As it had previously secured Rowne, the 25th (mot) Division now secured Shitomir, while the SS Leibstandarte Adolf Hitler, newly detached to the Corps from a previous commitment, is fighting its way from the southwest towards the tank road halfway between Shitomir and Zwiahel and is attempting to hold it open against heavy attacks launched from the north. However, to the right and particularly to the left of the SS Leibstandarte, the Russians repeatedly succeed in blocking the road. It becomes impossible to supply the Corps via the tank road, a situation lasting several days. The supply situation, especially with regard to ammunition, grows serious.

For the Russians have now regained their feet. Attacks against the Corps flanks, in particular the northern flank, as well as against the front along the Jrpen, are launched and continue for days without interruption; they all seem to follow a joint plan, but are fortunately not conducted under a united leadership on the battlefield: In one place it is a regiment which attacks, in another place, a battalion or a company only and yet in another place a whole regiment again. The attacks are usually conducted with the use of armor and supported by considerable artillery, but they all fail because of the calm determination, confidence and bravery of our Corps troops, certain of their superiority in all respects and steel true; the attacks are even answered by counterattacks which result in even greater gains in terrain most of the time, and thus in greater elbow room on both sides of the tank road. Numerous reconnaissance missions on the part of the 13th and 14th Panzer Divisions and the reinforced Regiment Nordland of the SS Division Wiking, recently assigned to the Corps, provide substantial information over a more and more expanding area on the task organization and organizational affiliation of the enemy troops. Gradually, the entire tank road is seized and held by the Corps.

From 13 to 18 July heavy defensive action on the part of 25th (mot) Division takes place north of Shitomir, and on 14 July the Russians thrust into the Jrpen front of the 13th Panzer Division. The combats for taking hold of the tank road, increasingly vital for supply purposes, are fought by the Leibstandarte west of Shitomir and last until 16 July. The road is then used by the 6th Army infantry for its approach; for practical reasons, the 25th (mot) Division and the Leibstandarte have temporarily been assigned to the 6th Army. From 16 to 18 July further attacks by superior Russian units, supported by armor and strong artillery forces, are launched against the 14th Panzer Division at Makarov, some of them lasting into the night. On 19 July a strong Russian attack is thrust on the Jrpen into the relief of the 13th Panzer Division by the 25th (mot) Division, which is now in position there, and another attack is launched against the 14th Panzer Division for the second time in recent days. But all these efforts by the Russian forces are in vain; a mobile and offensive conduct of operations which – in the needed pace – is only practicable by rapid formations, is the answer to all situations; the Corps' front, which is now increasingly consolidated by the approaching 25th (mot) Division and the Leibstandarte, does not give an inch of ground, although strictest economy as to the depleting ammunition stocks is required. Finally, ammunition, also, is supplied in sufficient volume.

On 20 July new orders, announced several days before, arrive and send the Corps southeast for a new operational commitment. It is now time to reap the harvest sown in the position so close to Kiev, which was seized in a swift strike and held tenaciously without fail for so long.

Here I will leave Mackensen's letters and refer to the map of the operations of III Corps to secure the rear of the other troops which fought in the battle of Uman to encircle the Russians west of the Dnepr (see Figure 164).

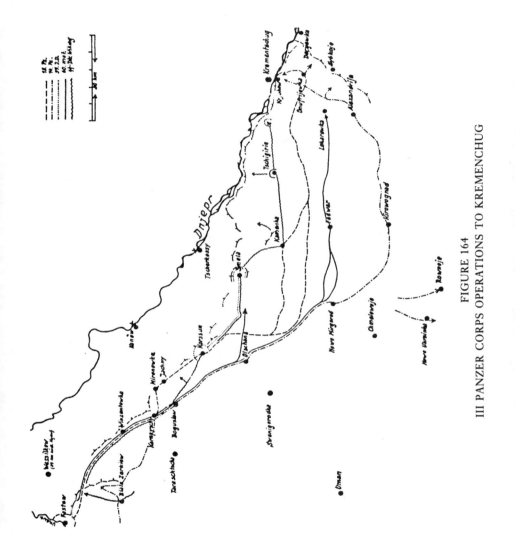

FIGURE 164

III PANZER CORPS OPERATIONS TO KREMENCHUG

11th Panzer Division Operations

LIEUTENANT GENERAL H. J. VON HOFFGARTEN
(retired)
and
BRIGADIER GENERAL EDEL LINGENTHAL (retired)

Introduced by Colonel Paul Adair

Now we come to the German point of view about the operations of 11th Panzer Division, presented by Lieutenant General von Hoffgarten, who commanded a motor-cycle company, and Brigadier General Lingenthal, who was a company commander in a tank battalion. General von Hoffgarten finished the war as the Chief of Staff of a Panzer division and in the last months as an assistant in the section of operations under the Oberkommando der Wehrmacht. After the war he was commander 5th Panzer Division and finally Deputy to COMBALTAP. General Lingenthal ended the war as the G-4 in the same Panzer division as von Hoffgarten and after the war he was concerned with weapons procurement for the Bundeswehr.

Motor-cycle Battalion 61's Operations

Lieutenant General von Hoffgarten

I shall deal with the structure and tactical use of a type of force which existed only until 1943, the motor-cycle riflemen. A brief introduction into the origins of this force will enable you to understand the philosophy and capabilities of the motor-cycle riflemen.

I. *The Origins of the Motor-cycle Riflemen (MCs)*

Motor-cycle riflemen were an arm which developed gradually following World War I. There was one company in each of the seven motorized battalions of the Reichswehr before 1935. October 1934 was an important date because on that date the 16th Cavalry Regiment of the Thuringian 3rd Cavalry Division was dismounted and reorganized into half regiments at Erfurt and Eisenach, which were motorized with side-car motor-cycles (see Figure 165). In 1935 these two half regiments became the motor-cycle Battalions 1, 2 and 3 of the first three German Panzer Divisions. Six motor-cycle battalions were quite successful in the Western offensive of

318

Establishment Motor-Cycle Battalions

16th Cavalry-Regiment

(3rd Cavalry-Division in Thuringia)

1934

1st Half-Regiment (mot) and 2nd Half-Regiment

(Erfurt)   (Eisenach)

1935

Motor-Cycle Battalion   Motor-Cycle Battalion   Motor-Cycle Battalion
No 1   No 2   No 3

1st Armoured Division   2nd Armoured Division   3rd Armoured Division

FIGURE 165

DISTRIBUTION OF MOTOR-CYCLE BATTALIONS

1940. Remember the conquest of the city of Amiens by the 1st Motor-cycle Battalion in May 1940, only ten days after the beginning of the offensive.

II. *The Structure and Equipment of Motor-cycle Battalion 61*

The battalion was set up in the fall of 1940 as a Type A Battalion (see Figure 166).

1.   Its structure was as follows:
- Staff with a signal platoon, a maintenance platoon, and a medical section;
- three motor-cycle rifle companies. Each company had 18 light machine-guns – six per platoon, one heavy machine-gun half platoon with two heavy machine-guns, and a light mortar in each of the motor-cycle platoons.
- 4th Machine-gun Company (my company) with two heavy machine-gun platoons, each with four heavy machine-guns, and a medium mortar platoon with six mortars, caliber 81mm. The company commander disposed of three light telephone-communications squads and also motorized messengers on solo and side-car motor-cycles for his command and control.
- one heavy company with an engineer platoon (light bridge equipment, large and small rubber boats); one light infantry howitzer platoon with two howitzers, caliber 75mm with an effective range up to 3,500 meters; and one antitank platoon with three antitank guns, caliber 37mm.

Each company was provided with a maintenance squad, transport for food and clothing as well as fuel, and one ammunition transporter (truck). The battalion consisted of approximately 800 soldiers.

2. *Means of Mobility*

All motor-cycle rifle companies, including the two heavy machine-gun platoons of 4th Company, were motorized on side-car motor-cycles, 750 cm, 18 horsepower, mainly BMWs. Headquarters were equipped with cross-country vehicles. The rest of the battalion, that is the heavy platoons, were equipped with Krupp cross-country vehicles. The engineers and transports were equipped with three and one a half or five ton trucks.

3. *Capabilities*

The motor-cycle riflemen were the fastest ground troops on the Continent at that time, especially where a relatively well-developed road system existed. They achieved a marching speed of 70km/per hour as a single

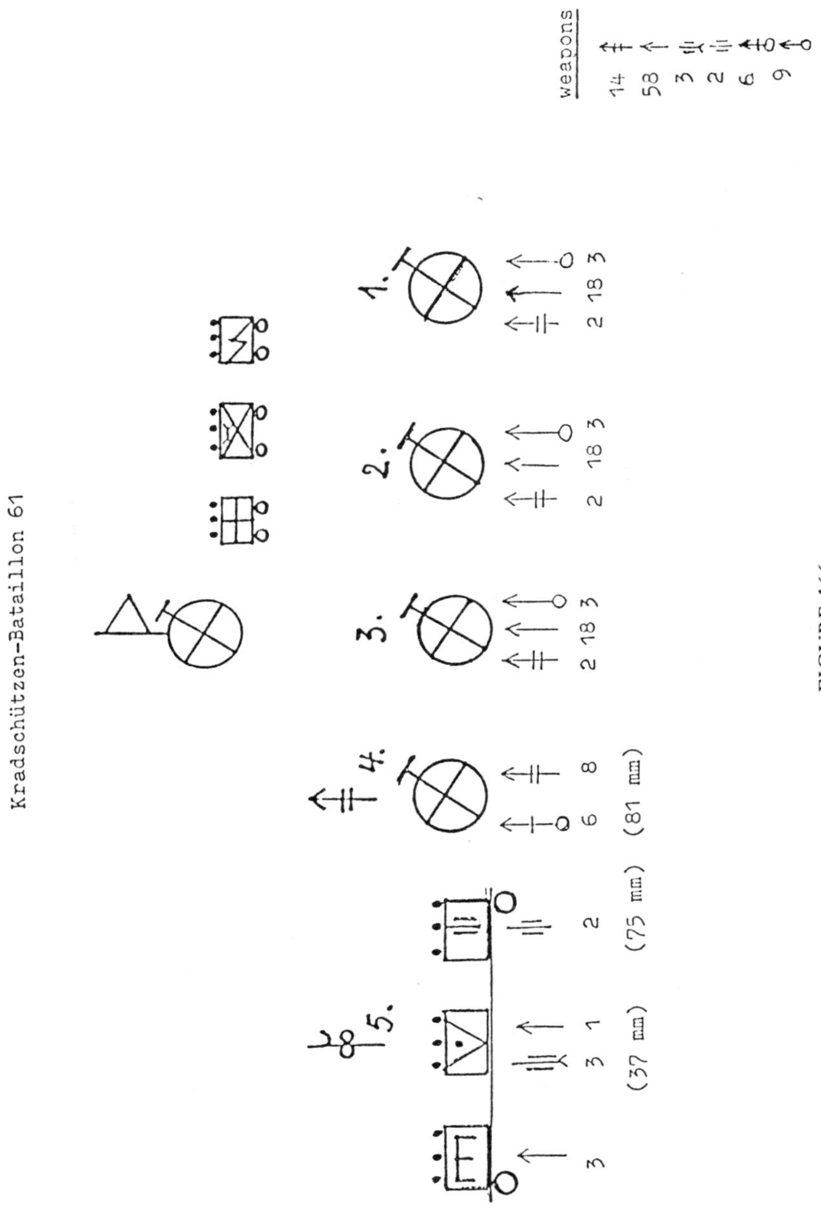

FIGURE 166

MOTOR-CYCLE BATTALION ORGANIZATION

unit, which was quite high at that time. Their cross-country mobility was good when the weather was relatively dry, and with the assistance of the two co-drivers, difficult terrain was overcome without much trouble. Motor-cycles were not affected very much by attacking enemy planes of that time and due to their maneuverability, speed and rapid dispersal capability, artillery could hardly affect them. The battalion possessed relatively good fire-power for the special tasks of extended reconnaissance, or as the advance force of the brigade or division, as well as for sudden offensive actions such as establishing bridgeheads in a raid. A motor-cycle battalion, as the division reserve, could be employed at key points in the battle within a very short time. If the terrain was dry, the co-operation of the motor-cycle battalions with the Panzer companies presented no problems whatsoever. If the worst came to the worst the motor-cycle rifle sections climbed onto the tanks!

4. Weaknesses of the Motor-cycle Riflemen

The maneuverability of motor-cycle riflemen was hindered by wet or swampy terrain and by sudden strong rain, as happened in the Ukraine on a few occasions – or by snow of depths of 30 cm and higher. In such situations only dismounted combat, like that which the mechanized rifle regiments conduct, was possible. Also, motor-cycle infantry attacking power was not always sufficient against a prepared enemy of similar strength. In the defense however, dismounted motor-cycle riflemen were fairly equal to the units of the mechanized rifle regiments.

5. Specific Characteristics of Motor-cycle Battalion 61

The battalion was established in the maneuver area of Ohrdruf in Thuringia between August and October 1940. Since I belonged to Motor-cycle Battalion 1 as a platoon leader, and then as a company commander until I was wounded during the Western campaign in 1940, and since I was then transferred to the newly created motor-cycle Battalion 61 in September 1940, I am competent enough to compare both battalions. The old battalion was more or less a unit of professionals with a full peacetime officer and non-commissioned officer corps, and was fully trained. Concerning the personnel, there were almost no reservists in the units during the Polish and Western campaigns. My new battalion did not yet possess that vital intimate cohesiveness that a good unit needs because, with the exception of one company, almost all the other soldiers had come from various units, and not even from battle experienced motor-cycle battalions. Moreover, only a third of the soldiers possessed battle experience. Therefore, we had to undertake full basic training of motor-cycle riflemen and of their tactics with them. Not until the battalion was engaged in the Balkan campaign in 1941 did they achieve their ultimate cohesiveness.

To give you an example I shall describe my newly formed 4th Machine-gun Company. It took until January 1941, when we were redeployed to Romania, for my company finally to achieve its prescribed full strength of personnel and equipment. By then our combat training had achieved a standard of good discipline. My 70 drivers, however, presented another problem. They all came from districts of Vienna and had their drivers licenses, but they had never driven their vehicles in route columns, nor had they ever experienced their baptism of fire. Nevertheless, participation in the Balkan campaign was more effective than any kind of training, and as a result, the company became a good combat unit after all.

6. *Task and Position of the Company Commander of a Machine-gun Company*

The task of a company commander of a motorized unit, like a motor-cycle rifle company, is more complex, in general, than the task of commanding an infantry company or an artillery battery. Combat control of mobile operations over spacious and constantly changing terrain requires a great deal of tactical inspiration and experience. Decisions must be made quickly and orders given immediately, just as the tank company commander has to do in his job. As it is with all units which fight in the most forward positions, exemplary personal conduct and behavior of the company commander is enormously important to his soldiers, especially in sudden critical situations.

The machine-gun company, with its mounted machine-guns and medium mortars is, along with the infantry howitzer platoon, the most important unit of the battalion commander. This applied especially to all those operations which had to be launched and executed without any support by artillery and tanks. The commander of the machine-gun company is usually in close contact with the battalion commander while the coordination of the platoons was the job of the senior platoon leader. We did not always have a combined engagement of the entire company, because the vast expanse of the combat sector often made the attachment of machine-gun platoons to the other companies necessary.

During the initial border battles, the motor-cycle rifleman battalion was very often employed as an advance force on one of the two routes of advance. For this task the battalion was organized automatically in the following manner. An advance company led with a reconnaissance section and advance platoon ahead, directly followed by the battalion commander with his tactical command echelon, where the commander of the machine-gun company with his tactical headquarters also had his place. Then the main force of the battalion followed in specified intervals: one motor-cycle company, the machine-gun company, the third motor-cycle company and the heavy company. Initially, all logistical elements stayed far behind, however, concentrated regionally. When the first enemy contact was made, the commander of the machine-gun company immediately made his proposals to the battalion commander for first preparatory orders and for employment of the heavy weapons of the battalion.

During the border battles in June 1941 several times we were confronted with the problem of the machine-gun company, second in the battalion marching column, still having to cover a distance of 20 to 25 kilometers to the front (up to half an hour) after the first employment order was given. Thus, often favorable opportunities could not be taken advantage of during the mobile combat of the border battles.

7. *Co-operation with Tanks*

While in wide open terrain tanks primarily formed the spearhead of the advance with the motor-cycles following closely behind, there were situations which required still closer cooperation between the two arms. This happened in complex terrain and when facing river obstacles, mine obstacles or enemy occupied villages. Both company commanders had to plan exactly the control of such a joint operation in advance. This was not so very easy because of the poor maps, on which usually only the main roads were drawn. Very often the motor-cycle riflemen dismounted from their motor-cycles outside the range of enemy infantry weapons and mounted the tanks, a section to one tank, a tactic which we were to experience often against the Red Army during the later war years. The commander of the motor-cycle company mounted the tank of the tank company commander. Depending on the behavior of the enemy and his efficiency of fire, the riflemen dismounted from the tanks and under the protective fire of the tanks, attacked the enemy in close combat. During such an operation all the motor-cycles and side-cars were dispersed and held under cover by the leader of the motor-cycle echelon, until the order was passed to him to bring forward all vehicles quickly.

III. *Special Training before Operation Barbarossa*

After the end of the Balkan campaign the company was redeployed westward from Vienna. This redeployment affected personnel and technical equipment alike. There were also weapon drills for all sections. During this period, from May until 20–21 June 1941, the troops had heard nothing of an impending Russian Campaign.

A rather intense full troop exercise of the 11th Panzer Division took place however, in the maneuver area Bruck/Leitha during the beginning of June. In this exercise, the motor-cycle rifle companies, which represented the enemy, had to execute a dismounted attack during which they were supposed to adjust their organization and tactics to emulate Russian infantry. As we did not possess any Russian regulations or manuals, we attacked more or less like the densely concentrated attacking groups of the Tsarist Army of World War I. I believe that our opposing infantry and tanks did not gain any knowledge from that experience with respect to combat against Russian infantry.

At the beginning of June 1941 however, the rumor arose that the Wehrmacht would practically be able to march through Southern Russia without any combat in order to attack the British either in the near East or in India.

IV. *Information about the Enemy*

After the 11th Panzer Division had been transferred to the maneuver area at Mielec, northeast of the city of Tarnow in Galicia, all the units continued their training until 19 June. Even then there was no information on the Russian Army or on the impending campaign. This was also because the distance to the Russian Border was 200 kilometers by air. The Red Army had finished deploying the mass of her troops to the Western border on 1 May 1941 and had ordered them to the highest stage of alert on 21 June at 2327 hours. That was full combat readiness!

V. *The Opening Battles from 22 June 1941 and Onward*

Motor-cycle Battalion 61 arrived at an assembly area in the close vicinity of the Bug River between Sokal and Krystynopol, that is at the USSR border, on 21 June after a two and a half day march, which covered 250 kilometers from Mielec, via Jaroslau, Tomaszow Lubelski and Rawa Ruska (see Figure 167).

After the opening of heavy artillery fire at 0315 on 22 June, the battalion had to wait until dawn to cross the river on an amphibious bridge. A small bridgehead had been created by other units. Since specifically the 15th Panzer Regiment was the spearhead from the Bug River onward, the motor-cycles were only engaged in smaller encounters between 22 and 25 June (see Figures 168–170). Enemy resistance was weak and disorganized during these days, since stronger forces had not yet appeared. It was not until 26 June that the motor-cycle battalion, as the advance force, met stronger enemy resistance in Ostrog, in the Dubno area, following a 90-kilometer march. In a surprise action the advance company succeeded in throwing the enemy infantry back to the eastern outskirts of Ostrog. Nevertheless, the situation of the advance troops became critical because the mass of the battalion could not be employed until hours later. This was

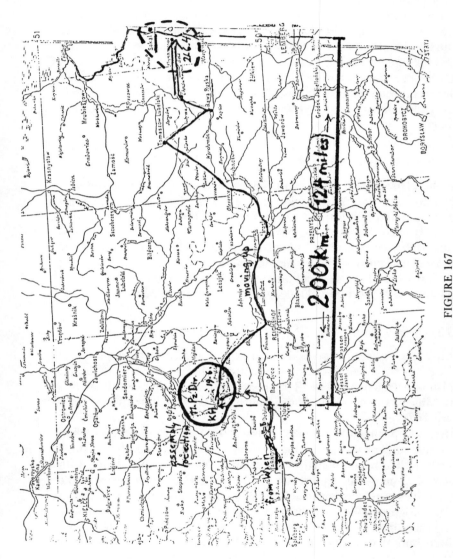

FIGURE 167

11TH PANZER DIVISION DEPLOYMENT, 19–21 JUNE 1941

due to the distance which had added up because of bad roads, having to march at night, and by the normal lapse of time between the advance unit and the mass of the battalion. After the enemy infantry had recovered from the first surprise attack, they launched several counterattacks. Our antitank guns destroyed an older Soviet tank. The attacks of one to two companies of enemy infantry were successfully thrown back by the machine-gun fire of the advance company, and because the enemy had to attack against the ascending slope in front of the eastern edge of the village. Enemy artillery was not engaged. The fire of heavy guns, however, was directed onto the city of Rowno on the left flank of the motor-cycle battalion.

VI. *The First Soviet Counterattacks*

A more powerful Russian attack, in approximately battalion strength against the eastern outskirts of Ostrog was conducted almost at the same time as the arrival of the mass of the motor-cycle battalion (see Figure 171). The attack was supported by close support aircraft, which conducted machine-gun fire and low altitude bombing. With the exception of a few vehicles damaged, casualties and losses were few because the soldiers found good cover along the walls of the houses. The situation finally stabilized when the first of our own tanks and artillery arrived around noon. The continuation of the advance however, with the objective of a breakthrough of the Stalin Line further east, was delayed until 30 June.

VII. *Breakthrough of the Stalin Line and the Capture of Berditschev*

Contrary to the expectations of our units, the Stalin Line did not prove to be the strongest obstacle against our advance. Certainly, there were some bunkers and wire obstacles, but they were far less effective than those which I experienced during the breakthrough of the Maginot Line at Sedan on 13 May 1940.

There was no organized enemy resistance. Thus, the motor-cycle battalion, as the advance unit, succeeded in capturing Schepetowka after having broken through the Stalin Line. The Russian infantry was surprised by the fast-moving attack. Our unit, however, suffered casualties through sudden air raids by close support aircraft in this open terrain of the Ukraine, where one finds only vast cornfields.

The next objective of the motor-cycle battalion was the capture of the southern section of the city of Berditschev, 340 kilometers as the crow flies from its original assembly area at the Bug River, 15 days after the beginning of operations. The battalion, functioning as the advance party of the right marching group to the right of the 15th Panzer Regiment, also

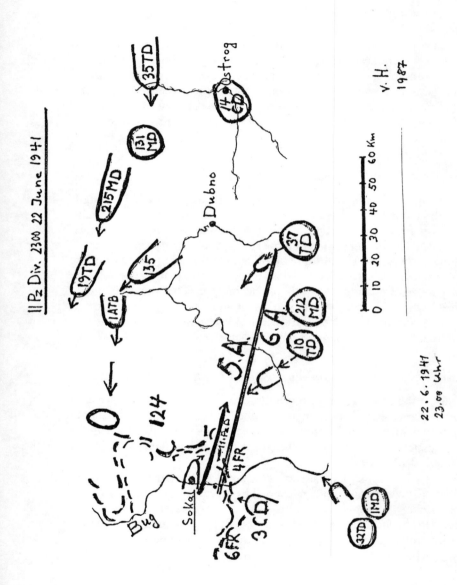

FIGURE 168

11TH PANZER DIVISION OPERATIONS, 22 JUNE 1941

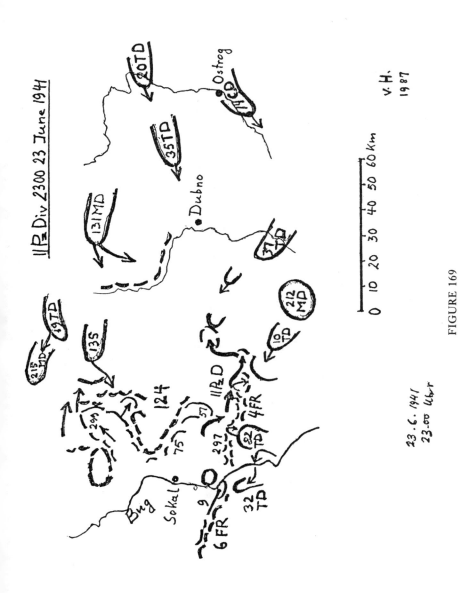

FIGURE 169
11TH PANZER DIVISION OPERATIONS, 23 JUNE 1941

329

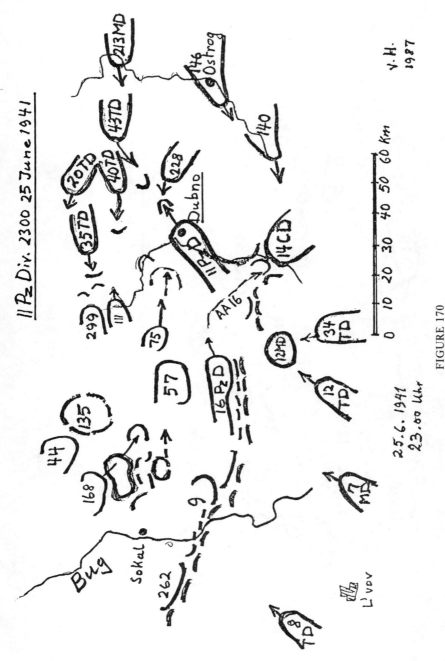

FIGURE 170

11TH PANZER DIVISION OPERATIONS, 25 JUNE 1941

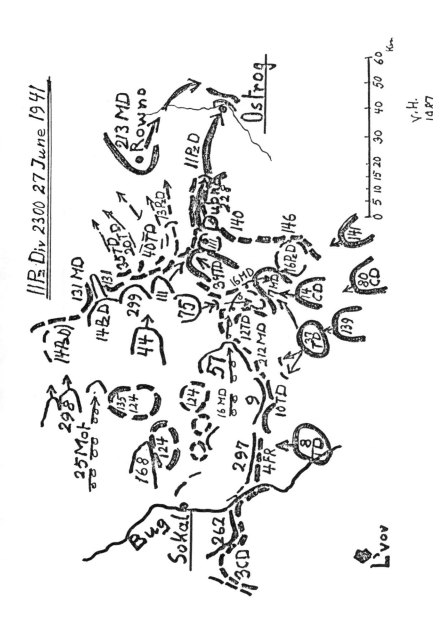

FIGURE 171
11TH PANZER DIVISION OPERATIONS, 2300, 27 JUNE 1941

331

succeeded in capturing the southern sections of Berditschev by a surprise mobile attack which threw the Russian infantry back towards the east. Since the following-on units of 11th Panzer Division were still far behind, the battalion had to organize defensive positions around the eastern outskirts of the city. My machine-gun company was now responsible for the major task of this defensive action. The two heavy machine-gun platoons with their mounted machine-guns and the medium mortars dominated the terrain up to their full effective range of approximately 3,500 meters. Our artillery had not yet arrived. The Russian infantry, however, did not make one of their usual dawn attacks, which were usually so successful and which I experienced quite often later on, or at least from the winter of 1941 onward.

It was not until 15 July that the 11th Panzer Division had fully deployed and replenished its supply of ammunition and fuel. Now the motor-cycle battalion continued on as the division advance force together with an advance unit – the size of a battalion – from the 15th Panzer Regiment. This battalion cooperated closely with the motor-cycle riflemen, who often rode on the tanks, and together they captured Kasatin and then, taking advantage of the element of surprise, raided the villages of Swira and Belaja Zerkov. The next day, during a mobile attack at dusk, the battalion, again mounted on the tanks, succeeded in breaking into the fiercely defended village of Talnoje and threw back Russian infantry counterattacks. During this night attack the most forward tank company, with their mounted motor-cycle riflemen, rushed all the way to the entrances of the village firing constantly and setting fire to the buildings, which then sufficiently illuminated the combat zone. After that the motor-cycle riflemen dismounted from the tanks and rolled up the enemy defense through numerous hand grenade salvos and the constant firing of their light weapons. It took only a few hours until the enemy, having been completely surprised, fled almost head over heels from the village. With the exception of another encounter at Taraschtscha, this battle was the final one for the motor-cycle battalion in the course of the battle of Uman and in the first part of the Russian campaign, the so-called Border Battles. All these battles had been successfully completed. Motor-cycle Battalion 61 had covered approximately 510 kilometers within four weeks of the start of Operation Barbarossa and since having crossed the Bug River, and all this movement occurred with daily enemy contact (see Figures 172–73).

This performance of the 11th Panzer Division was never accomplished again by the German Army in the later years of the Russian campaign. This success of Motor-cycle Battalion 61 can be compared with the performance of Motor-cycle Battalion 1 of the 1st Armored Division, which covered 600 kilometers within 18 days in continuous combat and

FIGURE 172
11TH PANZER DIVISION OPERATIONS, 22–27 JUNE 1941

333

FIGURE 173
11TH PANZER DIVISION OPERATIONS
22 JUNE–8 AUGUST 1941

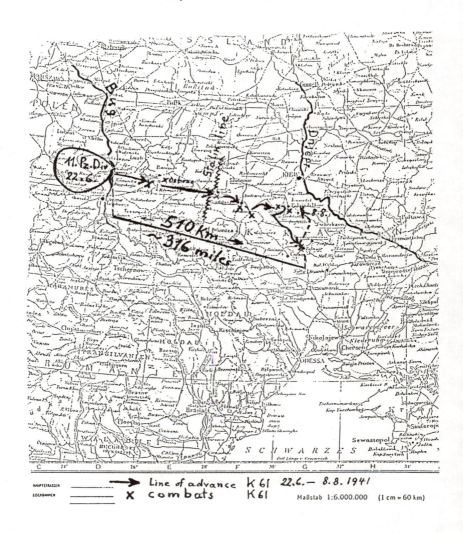

operations from the Mosel River near Cochem to the English Channel during the Western campaign of 1940.

VIII. *Reaction to the First Employment of the Russian T34 and KWI Tanks.*

Motor-cycle Battalion 61 engaged single Russian tanks only a few times in its operations. The appearance of a few older Russian tanks during the border battles did not create any particularly critical situation.

IX. *Assessment of the Soviet Soldier and of Russian Combat Tactics*

The individual Russian was well trained and a tough fighter. His infantry gunnery was excellent, a fact which was proved by many of our casualties being shot through the head. His equipment was simple but sufficient. All soldiers wore a summer uniform of earth brown, which camouflaged well. The armament of the Russian infantryman in those border battles did not differ much from our own. Their food was very Spartan and by no means comparable with ours. The Russian soldier, of course, was confronted with the completely new experience of facing the professional combat tactics of the German Panzer divisions, using all the important elements of maneuverability, surprise operations, night attacks, and close cooperation between tanks and infantry.

The Russian combat tactics in the border battles conveyed the following impression to us. Companies and platoons were left completely alone and on their own during their operations. There was practically no cooperation with the artillery or with the tanks. There was neither extended, nor combat reconnaissance. Also, radio communications from superior to lower echelons or to neighboring units probably did not really exist or work. This was probably the reason why the Russian units were surprised so very often by the fast and powerful advance of the German Panzer divisions in the Ukraine and why they were unable to conduct coherent operations during the border battles. The final battle of encirclement at Uman provided evidence of this. There were only a few independent escape operations on the Russian side. Nevertheless, the success of the German Panzer divisions in those border battles in the Ukraine caused the Russian Supreme Command (STAVKA) to imitate German operational methods. They developed these skills to a remarkable standard in later years.

Impression of the Border Battles

Brigadier General Edel Lingenthal

The advance company of Panzer Regiment 15, 11th Panzer Division, moved southward from Stojanov on the morning of 23 June. Since light Russian tanks were firing at us, the first battalion of Panzer Regiment 15 deployed with two companies in advance. When they arrived at the little hill between Sabinovka and Radziechov they recognized some 30 or more enemy tanks downhill, which immediately opened fire on them at a distance of about 800 to 1,000 meters. Five tanks – two Mark IV and three Mark III – were hit within a few minutes, with five soldiers killed and many others wounded.

The fire of the German tanks was absolutely ineffective in the beginning. Later, the Mark IV fired HE (high explosive) ammunition with delayed action fuses. This ammunition ignited the reserve fuel barrels above the Soviet tanks' engine compartments, so that some Russian tanks were destroyed. Then this encounter was broken off by both sides. I do not know why the Russians stopped the attack because they had been successful.

German armor again tried to destroy Russian tanks in the afternoon. To accomplish this they moved against the Russian's flank. But just as had occurred in the morning, the Mark III gun did not penetrate the Russian armor, not even when firing from the flank and at distances of only about 300 meters.

When the Russian units had withdrawn in the late afternoon, we took a look at the destroyed Russian tanks and reached the following conclusions:

1. We had no information or knowledge whatsoever of this new tank type, the T34.
2. This tank was superior to all German tanks fielded at that time in respect to

– armor
– armor-piercing capability of the gun, and
– mobility in rough terrain.

This was a shocking recognition to the German tank and tank-destroyer units and our knees were weak for a time. But soon the Germans took advantage of two other essential differences between the Russian and German tanks:

- In German tanks the commander and the gunner can work independently both with good vision devices, whereas the Russian gunner had to do all the tasks of the tank commander as well, so that he could only fire his gun or command his tank.
- German tanks were excellently equipped with wireless radio communications and telephones. The Russians had nothing like this on their tanks.

The T34 tanks, with which we had been engaged, were said to have belonged to a Russian tank regiment in the region for troop trials which had taken place on the Lemberg training area. That may or may not be correct. At least it was the first time that a large number of new Soviet tanks in battalion strength, engaged us.

When we reached Dubno we had to spend two nights there. We could not sleep because there was an awful smell. My regiment was close to a Russian prison and soon we detected the source of the smell. Before leaving the city the Soviet authority had killed all the people in the prison.

We had been supported tactically by reconnaissance, by fighter aircraft and by resupply flights for fuel and ammunition. Reconnaissance was done both by the air force and by army aviation. The latter disappeared in late autumn 1941. They worked in the same fashion and provided results immediately by radio to advancing armor to prevent untimely transmission through headquarters. They provided knowledge of the enemy by marking with foam. The Russians were masters of camouflage and so it was very helpful to know their location from the air. Aircraft also took air photographs and developed them at the base. While flying to their next sortie they would drop the finished photographs over the advancing tanks. That helped overcome the problem of bad maps. We could see where bridges existed and when Russian tanks had moved. Pilots often wrote down what they saw and dropped messages to us. Thus we had the intelligence information even before our division or corps headquarters.

Aircraft also provided strafing and bombing support. A special air force unit, the 8th Flieger Korps was brought up, especially trained and equipped to provide close air support. The aircraft unit sent air liaison officers to tank commanders with radios which could be installed in any tank. Thus, there were communications with higher air headquarters, with Stuka bombers, and of course with the Panzer unit company or battlegroup commander. Usually the liaison officer stayed close to the ground commander. Since he could see the same things as we could, he could react just as quickly. Sometimes the effective use of air began immediately, while in other cases it began three to five minutes later. The air liaison officer compared favorably with an artillery observer. He had the same function and effectiveness as an artillery forward observer. That was very essential for us at this time when we had no self-propelled artillery to accompany us.

The third type of air support involved resupply of fuel and ammunition but this was not as timely as support provided by the liaison officer. It was, however, very effective. Although we wished it had been constant, it was done only three or four times a month and only to support heavy fighting. As such it was inadequate.

Discussion Period

Professor von Luttichau: I would like to ask General Guderian regarding the first movement of III Panzer Corps to Kiev on 9–10 July. At that point, there is one school which believes that Kiev could have fallen, and according to Russian words I have seen the defenses were not finished, nor were they manned. The order from Hitler, however, prevented the corps from moving there to take it. I would like to know if in General Mackenson's letters there is anything that could increase our knowledge on this point.

General Guderian: The letters of Mackenson existed only in my home. We thought we could take Kiev, but even if our thinking was right, we could not prove it. So it is an open question. It is not necessary or possible to say what would have happened if we had not been stopped by Hitler. But the highest command stopped us. It's futile to discuss this.

General Thilo: Hitler had decided that the city of Kiev was not to be seized but rather simply enveloped because he was afraid the operation might delay the overall operation. The mission was to destroy the enemy forces in the Ukraine. Because of that the III Corps from the north and other units from the south were supposed to envelop the enemy and destroy him in a pocket in the area of Zhitomir and Uman.

Question: I have heard about the discourse and the independent action of battalion commanders. Could someone clarify what sort of communication was going on between the divisional and corps commanders during the action?

General Guderian: The communication between corps and divisions was mainly wire. The wire was laid very fast and effectively and it was very reliable. Only when there was no possibility of laying wire or when wire communications was disturbed did we use radio. But actually radio was slower than wire because we had to encode messages and that took a long time with the means available at that time.

Also, in this regard usually the commanders were at the decision point so there were no complicated communications necessary. With the German senior commanders it was a matter of training.

Question: We have heard that there was considerable difficulty in engaging the Soviet armor with German tanks. I have not heard how German infantry engaged Soviet tanks. Could an infantry officer address this? To place this in context it seems to me that in NATO now, while we modernize on the one hand, we seem to be decreasing the number of infantrymen on the other hand. Several German officers have remarked in their other writings that the infantryman was very important in the campaigns in the East.

General Lemm: As infantry we had a meeting with Russian heavy tanks in the area of Ilmsee, near Staraia Rusa. There we met the KVII and the first T34. We had close combat and used material from the engineers, mostly mines, and all soldiers were trained in the antitank use of these mines. Also we had in all rifle companies special troops of two or three soldiers who worked together. One man handled security and a second operated on the blind side of the tank with a mine and tried either to place the mine on the tank's rear hatch or use a hand grenade bundle (held with wire) thrown over the tank gun barrel. A third method involved using a shape charge, which was magnetic, emplaced against the tank. But the Russians then countered this by placing concrete on the armor plate so the mines would not stick. They mixed the cement with paint and simply painted it on.

General Odendahl: For those who are interested, there was a German Army training film entitled "Men Against Tanks" which was used in the second half of World War II.

Comment: This film was originally a German film but was taken by the Americans. After the war it came back to the Bundeswehr as an American training film.

Professor Macksey: Could one of the German tank officers describe the system of tank gunnery and how you engaged targets? I know how we British did it, and it was pretty primitive. I think it may answer the dilemma of not hitting targets or penetrating them.

Colonel Stoves: There was no range-finder system available as there is now in the Leopard. But the gunner was trained to use the good lenses of our tank cannons to judge a system to find the antitank range, which was a very difficult and dangerous task, and then to try to shoot and knock him out on the first shot. Now we are trained and we are able to engage targets at between 600 and 800 meters. Then the gunner was directed by the commander and we were able to do this by means of on-board telephones. The on-board telephones were expensive and given to us only in 1942, but I had a very clever fellow who invented the whole thing. I could talk to the driver and I could talk to the gunner. I could say, "800, hold on direct sight, there are two tanks", and "fire". And the next shot had to strike the objective. And it worked. On one day we knocked out 12 KV1 tanks at a distance of between 50 and 200 meters. There were also special shells which we were not to use without permission of the regimental commander. But if you are fighting with the other side, you don't ask the commander.

Question: We have heard a great deal about offensive operations. What I would like to get some feel for is what happened at night? Was it possible to maintain offensive operations by night? Did the mechanized and tank units maneuver by night and, if they did, how successful were they?

Answer: There was a Russian saying about this among the soldiers which said, "The roads and the day belong to the Germans. But the forests and the night belong to us, the Russians".

Comment: I would like to add some remarks about aiming from the tank. We had in our periscope seven scales. In the middle there was a big (wider) one, and there were three on the right and three on the left. And we aimed with the big one. First, we ourselves had to estimate the distance. Then we gave the distance to the gunner and the gunner put the correct distance in the periscope. Sometimes we used the wider one to engage targets at 1,500 meters or 1,600 to 1,800 in order to hit the tank because it was much easier to hit it at a higher distance than in the lower one. When the enemy tank was driving either to the rear or to the left, we used the first, the second, or the third of those scales on the left of our big one, so that we could compensate for the speed of the tank by aiming not with the big scale, but rather with the first, second, or third on the right side.

About night fighting, actually we did not continue fighting at night with tanks in general. There was always a struggle between the infantry and the tankers because the infantry said they had to march during the day time and lose sleep and then they had to care for the tanks' security. This happened many times, but actually at night we used our tanks only for security missions. We could, of course, provide some magnesium light and could fire at a very short distance. But generally there was no night fighting with tanks in Russia at this time.

Colonel Ritgen: The tracers for the machine-guns immediately set houses on fire and then we had illumination.

General von Kielmansegg: It must be admitted generally that the German soldier did not like to fight at night. Marching yes, but fighting not very much, and in this respect the Russians were certainly better.

General Lingenthal: There were several ways to deal with the super-heavy Russian tanks. One was, the closer the distance, the easier to aim at a certain spot on a tank. As you have heard, some of them were finished off at extremely close range. The second point was to fire at the junction where the turret moved over the hull in order to jam the turret. And when the turret was struck, of course, the tank could not fire. So at least this diminished its capabilities. This was done even with 20mm guns. Third, fire with all weapons at the enemy tank in the hope of destroying the periscope or the aiming devices. Finally, we could fire a high explosive shell at the cover of the engine because there was always a possibility that the engine, with its oil and the gasoline spilling over, would catch fire.

Question: I am interested in the relations between the army groups and the corps. How often did the army group issue orders to the corps and how often was the corps obliged to report to the army groups? How often did the army group provide information to the corps on the overall situation?

General von Kielmansegg: I think you have mixed up the relationships. Normally and usually there was never a direct connection between corps and army groups. In between, there was the army. If you replace the word corps with army then it was a normal thing. Do not forget that more and more during the war Hitler, from his headquarters, interfered down as far as battalion level. This was an impossible situation.

General Guderian: The connections between a corps and a field army were as follows: from the corps to the field army there were three regular reports required daily: the morning, noon, and evening reports. In addition to these, there was a constant exchange of information upward and downward over the telephone lines between corps and army. From army downward to corps, there was the operations order by the army, in some cases issued daily and, in other cases, every few days when the situation had changed. But generally, it can be said that over those telephone lines there was a constant flow of information.

General Thilo: I was at the OKH, the Army High Command, during the war, and the sequence of events was roughly as follows. At night starting at 1000 the reports from the army groups came in and usually it went like this. You had an earphone and there was a big map table and the general staff officer would immediately draw the situation which he got over the phone on the maps. At the same time he dictated parts of the situation to a typist. Since these reports came from several or many army groups, this usually lasted until 0200. From 0200 on, the reports were relayed to the OKW or joint staff. In the morning, Heusinger usually arrived around 0800, and he would be briefed on the situation by his general staff officers. Usually he then issued orders as warning orders to the army groups. Around 1000 he would go to Halder, and with Halder, he would go over to Hitler's headquarters. Then they would brief Hitler on the situation and obtain his decision. Usually at 1400 Heusinger would return and the operations order to the army groups would be drafted. Thus, in the afternoon or in the evening, the army groups would issue their orders. Then the whole cycle started again.

General Kielmansegg: I can confirm this since I was in OKH from 1942 to 1944. There was a small difference in timing, but I cannot resist telling you how few people this involved. The whole operations division of the Army High Command consisted, up to the end of the war, of only about 14 to 16 general staff officers and a similar number of deputies. That was all.

General von Thilo: We worked every second night for 20 hours, then we had to sleep 12 hours, and then we had to work again.

Comments: At the corps and army level there are many tens of thousands and perhaps hundreds of thousands of feet of microfilm of these records that survived. We have heard all about the details of how all this worked, but if one looks at those microfilms today and looks at, say the corps orders and what was going on back and forth, what is surprising is not the volume, but how so much operating was done with such little volume in comparison. It is absolutely astonishing how few general orders came down from on high and how much these corps and armies did, without this tremendous volume. The difference today in the types of reports and the volume, compared with what we think is necessary today and what we foresee for the future, is astonishing.

General von Kielmansegg: The secret solution to all of this is found in one word – *Aufstragstaktik.*

Comment: What worked in 1941 did not work by 1945; that is, the time cycle reflected by those very reports that you talk about being in our national archives. By the L'vov-Sandomirz Operation of 1944, and from then on essentially, the Soviets virtually continued to operate inside the German decisions-cycle, to use modern terms. From our current perspective, anybody who infers that such a time cycle could work today is medieval. The professional soldiers on active duty should not try to take a military lesson from that time sequence now. It did not work by 1945, and it will not work in 1987.

Question: I am very interested in the size and the number of command posts in the panzer group. And secondly, who in that panzer group headquarters did the movement control? Who planned the executed movements?

General Guderian: The panzer group was developed from a corps headquarters and it was about roughly the equivalent of a corps. So when we talk about the size or the personnel strength of a corps headquarters, you have roughly the idea of what the panzer group was like. There were very few officers in a corps headquarters. They consisted of the commanding general, the chief of staff, and other personnel. The personnel of Panzer Group 4 was altogether 59 officers, 20 civilian servants, 51 NCOs and 222 other ranks. Then there were standing attachments consisting of another 24 officers, seven civilian servants, 105 NCOs, and 325 enlisted men. That makes a total of 83 officers, 27 civilian servants, 156 NCOs, and 547 enlisted men. They were subdivided into the GIC (command division), the G3 division, the G2 division, and the G1 division. Then there was a special division for the so-called additional units such as the medical services, the engineers, the signalmen, and the personnel division. Then there was also the G4 division, a very strong one, and of course, also the division for all the supplies services. These are included in these numbers, all of which are from 1941. Charles de Beaulieu was the chief of staff of the army corps.

That leaves the question of movement control. In corps headquarters there was a staff officer for movement who had two assistants and that was all. All movement was done under the control of the operations officer, the Ia, and they accomplished the technical aspects of movement. The conduct of the movement was done by the military police, usually a company size at division and corps level. However, the responsibility for marking the roads was not with the military police, but rather with the units themselves. They received their marching orders, they were told which roads they were to march along, and they were responsible for marking the roads.

Comment: So this staff officer movement was only responsible for moves on a great or large scale, while usually shorter marches were controlled by the units themselves.

6

The Smolensk Operation
7 July–7 August 1941

Introduction

KENNETH MACKSEY

By the early part of July, Colonel Ritgen must have thought he had a jolly good chance of meeting the deadline of his wedding on 2 August. Things were going very well, but of course, this was reflected too at OKH where they were quite convinced the war was won and things were going marvelously well. Hitler, for once was not interfering very much. He seemed fairly happy. He was sitting back planning what to do when the peace arrived.

One factor which made it much easier for people to concentrate on the job of a fighting commander who was considering getting married was the lack of noise from enemy air power. We have rather missed out the whole question as to how on 22 June the Russian air force was almost wiped out by an incredibly well directed and powerful blow from the Luftwaffe. It knocked out a large part of the air force on its airfields and shot down a great many of the aircraft which did manage to get into the air, because the German aircraft were vastly superior to the Russian aircraft of that time.

This air blow was crucial to everything that went on. It meant that German supply lines were not being interfered with, and it also meant the Germans could use the reconnaissance aircraft, the little Heinkels, so much more easily to find out about the enemy. Therefore, they had far superior information because they were not interfered with. If we consider what is going on now we will remember that Army Group North was making its way towards Leningrad, Army Group South developing its offensive past Kiev into the bend of the Dnepr River, and Army Group Center, which was being diverted to close the pincers of Panzer Groups 3 and 2 at Minsk, was now ready to do what Hitler and Guderian had always wanted to do without stopping at Minsk: go straight for Smolensk. So they went on.

Let us look at the other vital things going on at this moment as it affected the German forces. The most important thing, of course, was the logistical situation. It was quite desperate, as we have heard on the Russian side, and though not too good on the German side, it was not at all bad. At that moment the infantry divisions, for example, were magnificent, as far as the men were concerned. They were marching at about 30 miles a day, buoyed up by success, extremely well led, and going fine.

But the infantry divisions depended very much on horses as opposed to vehicles and the horses were not so keen. They had their problems. They did not like being overworked. They did not like a seven day week, and you could not get it through to them that there were other matters which were more important. Vehicles were beginning to break down for good reasons. They were being driven down roads for which they were not designed. Maintenance facilities weren't all they could be and a shortage of spares was beginning to appear. The spares situation must have been chaotic when one considers that the German Army, besides their own vehicles, were using French and British vehicles captured at Dunkirk and elsewhere.

The roads were beginning to crumble and that did not help. It meant that petrol consumption was almost twice what it should have been in normal circumstances. There were also problems with the railways. For one thing, the conversion of the Russian railways to German gauge went forward much more slowly than had been expected. There had been insufficient rehearsal, perhaps, for the railway troops concerned, but it was a considerable problem in any case. Therefore, the railway was not moving forward fast enough. Against expectations, very little Russian railway stock had been captured, and even on the Russian gauge they couldn't be operated very well. At the transfer points between gauges, stores were held up. There were labor problems and confusion.

At this time in the German diaries, for example, that of the Chief of Staff of 2nd Panzer Group, tales about the chaotic arrival of stores begin to appear. Mud shields arrived, but not vital parts for vehicles. On occasions concrete practice mortar rounds came forward instead of the real article. This was typical of what was happening.

There was, therefore, a sort of steady decay: not total breakdown or anything like that, but things were not as good as they might have been, and this was beginning to restrict operations and make people more cautious. They looked over their shoulders, wondering whether tomorrow's supplies would arrive. Also, with the much more intense battles, ammunition expenditure was far higher than expected. For example, Army Group South was saying about now that they had only about 13 per cent of their full scale of ammunition on hand. POL resupply was often hand-to-mouth. There was little to be collected in the countryside because then, as now, there were no village petrol pumps to draw on as there had been in Western Europe. It was impossible to live off the country in Russia. The Russians had little enough petrol for themselves, let alone any for a thirsty German Army.

We were, in fact, reaching a situation which the British Army did not realize until the time of Alamein – that is, as petrol consumption goes up during pursuit, or in a high mobility situation, little ammunition is used. But when it reversed and we became more static, as we were about to do in some of these operations, petrol consumption went down and petrol supplies went up. This immutable rule was only being discovered in a big way by the Germans for the first time.

The other worrying thing, and this might come out later, was that the logistical crisis may not have been fully appreciated in OKH. That is possible.

Do not forget that Panzer Group 4 had gone up into the north toward Leningrad and found itself in an increasingly difficult logistical condition. Panzer Group 1 had fought that remarkable battle and was moving toward the Dnepr River south of Kiev. Army Group Center was now about to advance on Smolensk and people were hoping that, after that stage had been completed, then the advance would continue to Moscow, as everybody in Army Group Center wished for they wanted the glory of doing so. They really did think that this was the way to end the war.

The two panzer groups operated in tandem, with Panzer Group 3 on the left and Panzer Group 2 on the right, coordinated by Fourth Army under General von Kluge. Both panzer group commanders were showing great confidence at this time. Their casualties had not been high and morale was good. Progress was still good and everything looked fine. Indeed everything did go well, as we shall see, as they advanced towards Smolensk. Panzer Group 3 circled around Smolensk on about 15-16 July, but did not close in. At that moment it became dispersed by other orders. Panzer Group 2 of Guderian came in from the right and actually got into Smolensk on 15 July and captured it. But there was left, and would remain for some days to come, a large gap between the two panzer groups which could not be filled for various reasons. Partly, it seems, it was caused by a certain amount of error because the staff work was not that good. In addition, the Russians there were very strong and were holding the gap open.

It was well known that the gap existed, and that the Russian Army was flooding back through it. It was noted from the air by no less than Field Marshal Kesselring, the commander of Second Air Fleet, flying in his own airplane over the area. He saw it, and he did all he could do to close it by bombing and by asking others to help. Kesselring was a brilliant soldier long before he was a good airman. He knew what was going on. He did his best, but bombing could not close the gap.

One interesting point was raised about the use of airborne troops. At this point Kesselring said this was the opportunity to use the parachute and air landing division in order to fill that gap. These divisions should have been in reserve, but were not. They had been ruined in Crete and were initially out of action. A very large number of transport aircraft had been lost as well on an operation which served Marshal Goering's and General Student's ambitions. So the gap was not filled.

I will leave the subject to permit others to fill in the details. Bear in mind, we have reached the moment when six weeks is almost up. The war should be won, and Colonel Ritgen should be confidently thinking of getting married. But the war had much longer to go, and Hitler was vacillating since he had not decided whether to go north, south or forward.

Smolensk:
Reflections on a Battle

DR DIETER OSE

Introduced by Colonel Adair

Dr Dieter Ose served as an officer in the Bundeswehr and is now serving in the German Ministry of Defense and is responsible for film and print media. He is a distinguished historian, who has published a book on the Ardennes offensive of 1944.

My purpose is to acquaint you, from various angles, with the significance of the Battle of Smolensk. This operation, like others before and after it, can be examined from several levels. First, there is the tactical level, that is leading the troops into combat and in the battle area. Second, at that time the operational level played an important role, namely command and control of the forces in the battle and on the battlefield by the supreme military commanders or their subordinates. And third, strategic aspects had to be considered, namely interaction between all the supreme leadership organs and command agencies of a state or a coalition in order to ensure their existence in the event of a warlike threat.

1. *On Tactics*

I can skip this level – fighting on the front line by companies, battalions, regiments and divisions – because it will be covered by authoritative sources.

2. *On Operations*

The three German army groups attacking from 22 June 1941 encountered varying degrees of difficulty in their advance. The successes achieved by the Southern and Northern Army Groups were much smaller than those of the Central Army Group. The southern front, in particular, made very little progress, and it was not possible to capture Kiev so easily. Finally, the Central Army Group's advance also ran into great difficulties as the enemy kept reinforcing his troops in an effort to prevent an operational breakthrough towards Moscow.

This development suited Hitler's ideas, which he had already expressed during the planning phase, for Moscow did not play a very important role in his scheme. What he wanted was to reinforce the flanks and defeat the enemy around Leningrad and in the Kiev area. Hitler considered Leningrad a key position, because the seizure of this city would secure the link with the Finns and ensure the complete possession of Scandinavia. He wanted to capture the south of Russia because he required its petroleum and grain reserves. As I said, the delay caused before Smolensk by the interrupted commitment of fresh Russian troops suited Hitler perfectly.

On this subject, Heusinger once wrote, I quote:

> It is important to destroy the enemy. This must be accomplished through a series of partial actions. There are opportunities for such partial actions at the boundary of the Southern and Central Army Groups against the Russian 5th Army and the Gomel Group, and further on against the units that have escaped to the eastern bank of the Dnepr river in the face of the Southern Army Group. To this end, the right wing of the Central Army Group with the 2nd Army and Panzer Group 2 had to turn southeastward. A further opportunity was to employ Panzer Group 3 in a northeasterly direction to the Valdai Hills into the rear of the enemy facing the 16th Army. The Northern Army Group could also only destroy the enemy front piece by piece.

And now comes the decisive sentence which characterized an already hesitant Hitler: "The Russians simply do not recognize great operational successes and are not at all influenced by them."

The fact that the Army High Command was of the opinion that Moscow was in all respects a decisive factor – militarily, politically, and from a movement point of view – cut no ice with Hitler. Nor could Hitler be convinced by the fear that the "halt" in the center could herald the start of a transformation of the sweeping operation into only fragmented actions. The High Command of the Armed Forces had the impression that tactics, rather than operations, were now being conducted, especially since Hitler intervened in the command of individual divisions.

The struggle for a joint course of action lasted over three weeks. The protagonists were the Commander-in-Chief of the Army, Field Marshal von Brauchitsch, the Chief of the Army General Staff, Colonel General Halder, and Chief of the Operations Division, the then Major-General Adolf Heusinger on the one side, and Hitler on the other side. Heusinger was of the opinion that operations should not be conducted for the sake of economic and political goals, but with the sole objective of defeating the enemy. As I have already stressed, the Army High Command considered that this could be achieved by attacking Moscow.

These considerations concerning an attack on Moscow were gradually necessitated, not the least, by the deployment of forces. There were 50 enemy formations facing the Southern Army Group with around 50 divisions of its own and around 23 enemy formations facing the Northern Army Group with its 26 divisions, while around 70 enemy divisions had assembled in front of the Central Army Group's 60 divisions. This, therefore, was where the enemy was at his strongest and it was, in fact, irresponsible that subsequently forces were withdrawn from this front sector only.

Here, as Heusinger wrote, "the decisive blow (was) thus possible and it had to be dealt first."

Nevertheless, the struggle that lasted several weeks did not lead to success. Finally, Hitler issued his famous directive of 21 August 1941, from which I would like to quote briefly:

> I am not in agreement with proposals submitted by the Army on 18 August. The primary objective is not the capture of Moscow, but rather the occupation of the Crimea, of the industrial area of the Donets basin, the cutting of the Russian supply routes from the Caucasian oil fields, the isolation of Leningrad and linking up with the Finns.
>
> The situation presents an opportunity for a concentric operation with the wings of the Southern and Central Army Groups against the Russian 5th Army to prevent the latter from withdrawing. To this end, the Central Army Group must employ all the forces necessary, regardless of later operations. Only this will enable the Southern Army Group to continue its operations towards Rostov-Kharkov.
>
> Capture of the Crimea is of the utmost importance to secure our supplies from Rumania.
>
> Not until we have isolated Leningrad, linked up with the Finns and destroyed the Russian 5th Army will we be able to create a basis and release the forces needed for a fresh attack by the Central Army Group.

Almost with an air of resignation, but in the adept and polished language of the grand operator, the chief of the operations division, Adolph Heusinger, describes this development:

> The Army High Command's opposition to this decision had been in vain. Hitler had brushed all their arguments aside. He left the ground of purely operational command following basic military principles in favor of other aspects. This was the decisive turning point in the Eastern campaign.
>
> In a personal verbal report by commander in chief of Panzer Group 2 to Hitler, a final attempt was made to convince Hitler of the

difficulty of having the armored group turn southeast. It failed: Then the orders had to be issued.

Heusinger, on whom I have written a volume in the "Innere Fuehrung" series of publications of the Bundeswehr was after all, one of *the* great German soldiers of the twentieth century - a superior operator.

3. *On the Strategic Level*

At the strategic level, or, in other words, for strategic reasons, Hitler had taken this decision against which the operations staff had advised him. As we shall see, this decision also had great disadvantages from the point of view of overall strategy. These disadvantages were based on the simple fact that at this time Japan did not yet know or was not yet quite sure whether or how it should enter the war against the Soviet Union. Influential circles were in favor of further expansion of the Greater East Asia Co-Prosperity Sphere eastward, while others advocated an expansion southward. We must not forget that it was precisely at this time that the Americans had imposed a total oil and scrap embargo against Japan, and it was vital for Japan to decide in which direction its sphere of influence was to be extended in order to obtain vital raw materials. The standstill before Moscow, the apparently temporary success of the Soviets, caused not least by the turning away of sizeable forces of the Central Army Group southward and northward, gave prevalence again to those in Japan who favored a greater spreading of Japanese influence into South-East Asia rather than East Asia.

The intervention of the Japanese against the Soviet Union promised to the German Foreign Minister by the Japanese Ambassador at the beginning of August did not materialize. The German allies were not informed of Japan's revised assessment of the situation, so that they continued for several weeks to expect that Japan would still enter the German-Soviet war.

4. *Concluding Assessment*

A general strategic and operational framework to the significance of Smolensk now follows. In the final analysis Hitler's decision not to capture the most obvious, politically and militarily important objective of Moscow resulted in considerable disadvantages in the operational field, namely overextension of the front in general, weakening of the area of main effort, scattering of forces towards the flanks, and in the process, the actual objective of Operation Barbarossa – to bring the campaign to a victorious conclusion before the onset of winter, including the capture of Moscow – was lost sight of.

352

However, from the point of view of overall strategy, it also had fatal consequences because Japan did not enter the war against the Soviet Union, which meant that Soviet formations were released from the eastern frontier and could be employed for the counterattack before Moscow at the beginning of December. This marked the start of the final failure of Operation Barbarossa.

Overview
Phase 1: to 20 July 1941

DR JACOB KIPP

Introduced by Colonel Adair

Dr Kipp is a senior researcher at the Soviet Army Studies Office. He has taught Russian history at university level for about 20 years, so he is most conversant with his subject. He has published widely on Soviet military affairs and, in particular, on Soviet naval history, on the nature of the initial period of war, and on the difficult subject of the Soviet approach to future war.

I propose to look at the battle of Smolensk. My approach will be the Soviet perspective.

My point of departure will be the Soviet conception of the battle of Smolensk as they have presented it in their military historiography. Figure 174 lays out what they perceive to be the phases in the engagements around Smolensk [*srazhenie pod Smolenskom*]. There were four periods, run roughly from 10 to 20 July, from 20 July to 7 August, from 7 to 21 August, and from 22 August to 11 September. There are reasons why the Soviets have created this periodization, and it will become evident as we look at the operation.

First let us look at some of the Soviet perspectives about the nature of this operation which delineates it or sets its parameters:

Distinctive Features of Operations

A. Large scale in terms of area of actions and forces involved.

B. Continuous combat with constant changes in situation.

C. Strategic operation involving main groupings of forces for both German and Soviet sides.

D. Major combat involving an entire complex of offensive and defensive operations by *fronts*/army groups and armies of both sides.

E. Operational-tactical situation dominated by open flanks and efforts to protect one's own and to exploit the enemy's.

F. First operation on the Eastern Front where the "tyranny" of logistics began to be felt by German panzer and motorized formations.

G. Major influence on the course and outcome of the summer-fall

354

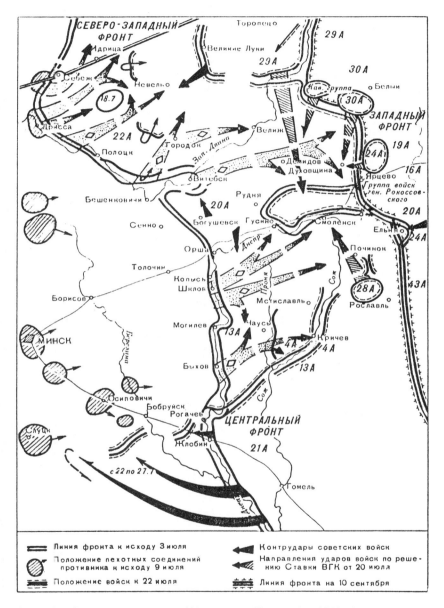

Схема 24. Смоленское сражение (10 июля — 10 сентября 1941 г.)

FIGURE 174
THE BATTLE OF SMOLENSK (SOVIET VIEW)

campaign, leading to improvisation of further plan for campaign because of failure to achieve anticipated outcome of Smolensk Battle, i.e. destruction of Western Front and opening of path to Moscow.

The first feature, and it may be self-evident, is its scale. In terms of area, we are talking about a front of roughly 600 to 650 kilometers in length, and a depth of 200 to 250 kilometers. We are also talking about the scale of forces committed. On both sides, this was by far the largest concentration of troops at this particular time of the campaign. Second, it was noteworthy for its continuous character, that is to say, the duration of on-going combat in one sector or another. While there were short pauses, in general, one side or the other was always struggling for the initiative.

Third, this was a strategic operation, and this is a rather important notion on the Soviet side. What is meant by this is that the main forces of both sides were engaged head on. The Soviet perception of the battles of the frontier is that the main German concentration had hit a sector where the main Soviet forces were not located. That is, the covering armies in the Bialystok salient of the Special Western Military District were not the primary Soviet concentration, and, therefore, the correlation of forces was quite unfavorable to the Soviet side. Here, the Soviet perception is that both sides were striving for the initiative, both sides were concentrating their combat power, and therefore, this was, indeed, a strategic operation.

The next point is that the operational-tactical situation was dominated by open flanks. Obviously, we have been talking about open flanks in a tactical sense and the ability of the Germans using *auftragstaktik* to deal effectively with situations at the tactical level. The Soviet perspective here is that quintessentially, with the advance of German forces beyond the barrier of the Pripiat Marshes and with the continued existence of Soviet forces in the north, in the Polotsk, Nevel, Velikie Luki areas and in the foothills of the Valdai Hills, there was a situation where all three German army groups had a perception of the problems of open flanks, and parenthetically from the Soviet side, the same problem was emerging.

We can speak, early in this phase of the campaign, about essentially two clearly separated axes of advance north and south of the Pripiat. Now, once Army Group Center had advanced beyond the Berezina River between Rogachev and Zhlobin, one is talking of an integration of those northern and southern efforts. This figured prominently, at least from the Soviet perspective, in the developing character of the operation.

Next, in the historiography of this campaign one of the most controversial issues is the crisis in command on the German side and the intervention of the political leadership into operational matters. Soviet scholars emphasize the fact that by its very nature, a political military crisis had evolved and that both sides' command systems were tested. There had to be adjustments, they say, because of the nature of the operational–strategic situation. We will see the Soviet system adjusting and we can judge for ourselves, in a comparative way, which command system adjusted more effectively.

Finally, the battle around Smolensk had a major influence on the course and outcome of the summer–fall campaign, and by implication, on the outcome of the war. That is to say, the battles led to shifts in planning for the conduct of successive operations. Soviet military literature concerning the prewar period emphasized that topic. Last, but not least, the Soviets realized that in this set of operations the "tyranny of logistic" became self-evident and began to influence the freedom of action of both sides in the conduct of this operation.

This operation divides into four separate phases:

1. 10–20 July – Period of the German panzer group breakthroughs on the right wing and center of Western Front, culminating in the encirclement of the 16th and 20th Armies in the Smolensk sector.

2. 21 July–7 August – Western Front's counter offensive and the battle of encirclement of the 20th and 16th Armies in the Smolensk pocket.

3. 8–21 August – Army Group Center attempts to liquidate the threat of Soviet forces to its right flank. Defensive operations by Central and Briansk Fronts. Beginning of Western Front's second offensive along with units of Reserve Front.

4. 22 August–10 September – Right flank forces of Army Group Center mount an offensive against Central Front to aid Army Group South and develop encirclement of Southwest Front forces in Kiev pocket. Reduction of El'nia salient by Soviet forces. Defensive battles by Western, Briansk and Reserve Fronts. We will examine the first two phases in detail, but first we will look at the nature of the area of operations using German maps from 1942 (see Figures 175–176).

The Smolensk Theater of Military Actions

A. *Area:* 600–650 kilometers north to south (Sebezh and Velikia Luki in the north) to Loev and Novograd–Severskii in the south) and 200–250 kilometers from west to east (Polotsk, Vitebsk and Zhlobin in the west to Toropets, Iartsevo, El'nia, and Trubchevsk in the east).

B. *Major terrain features:* This is the area of the land-bridge between the Western Dvina and Dnepr Rivers with the city of Smolensk in the north-central part of the region. This region divides into two distinct parts on the east-west axis. The northern third, south to Vitebsk is dominated by swamps, lakes, and woods over to Demidov where the land begins to rise in gentle hills. The hills themselves protrude south, ringing the northern suburbs of Smolensk and follow the Dnepr around in a semi-circle through Iarstevo to Dorogobuzh. This terrain was not particularly auspicious for mechanized warfare and tended to confine Hoth's 3rd Panzer Group to a shallow envelopment of Smolensk from the north. South of Vitebsk down to Gomel' the ground is more open and flatter and less wooded; it is cut by many small streams and several secondary rivers running north–south. This is much more favorable country for mechanized warfare, making for a more fluid battlefield with greater opportunities for envelopment and counter envelopment. Heavy woods and hills protrude between El'nia and Roslavl' limiting maneuver in that sector. The problem of open flanks would plague both Guderian's 2nd Panzer Group and the opposing Soviet army commanders.

The two major rivers define the land-bridge. The Western Dvina flows in a southeast to northwest direction down to the town of Vitebsk where it shifts to a northwest–southeast flow. The Dnepr flows in a north to south direction from Orsha to Zholbin. In this region on the west bank of the Dnepr stood the city of Mogilev, a regional capital and major road and rail center. Beyond Orsha the river flow is west to east until just east of Smolensk where it forms an ox bow to the south and then turns north toward the ford at Solov'ev and the town of Iartsevo. The oxbow itself is dominated by many small streams flowing into the Dnepr from the north and was cut by gullies and marsh.

Along the east–west course of the Dnepr stands the town of Smolensk which is located on both the north and south banks of the river. An industrial town and rail center, Smolensk had a population of 147,000 on the eve of the war. The heart of the old city was on the south side of Dnepr, but the rail yards and main highways were located in the Petersburg suburbs on the north side of the river.

A belt of low hills (200+ meters) extending from Rzhev through Viaz'ma to Briansk formed the northeast and eastern borders of the theater. The southern edge of the theater is framed by the tributaries of the Dnepr–Seim and Desna which flow northeast to southwest and the Pripiat which flows west to east out of the Pripiat Marshes into open country at Mozyr and then southeast to the Dnepr. The Berezina River, which also flows into the Dnepr at Loev, is just beyond the theater for most of its course. Across the middle of the theater flows the Sozh River from Smolensk through Krichev to Gomel' where it joins the Dnepr. The Vop' flows from north to south joining the Dnepr at Yartsevo, east of Smolensk.

C. *Railroad and highway system:* The Minsk–Smolensk–Moscow axis was served by rail line running through Orsha and a highway passing north of Orsha, both running on the north side of the Dnepr. This was the shortest and most direct railroad axis connecting Moscow and the western border. Another highway ran from Orsha through Liady and Krasnyi to Smolensk on the south side of the Dnepr. A third line through Smolensk connected

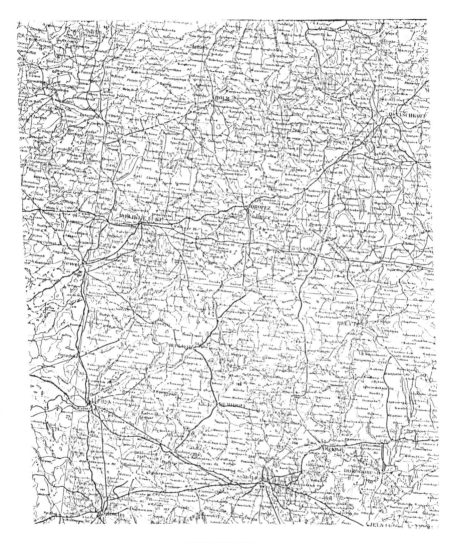

FIGURE 175
THE SMOLENSK REGION

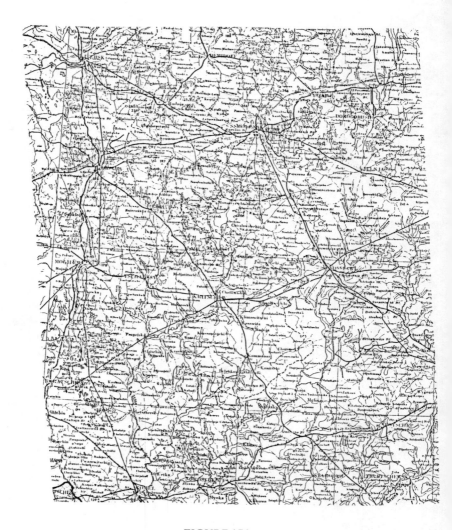

FIGURE 176
THE SMOLENSK REGION

Polotsk–Vitebsk–Smolensk–El'nia and then to Tula. A rail line also ran Smolensk–Roslavl'–Briansk. Smolensk was thus a major transportation hub. Control and use of this hub was critical to both sides in the defense of Moscow or in launching an attack upon it. Other north–south lines and a road net ran along the Vitebsk–Orsha–Mogilev–Gomel' line. Another line linked Viaz'ma–Briansk in the east.

East–west lines ran north and south of the main Minsk–Smolensk–Moscow line. (Northern ran Riga–Velikie Luki–Moscow. Southern ran Zholbin–Krichev–Roslavl'–Moscow). All of these lines made it possible for the Soviet High Command to deploy fresh armies and *Stavka* reserve and the Southwestern Front into the battle in a timely fashion. Given the shortage of motorized units and tank forces, such rail mobility figured prominently in Soviet operational deployments.

D. *Geographical-Historical Significance:* Smolensk region has always been the gate to Moscow. Invaders from the West have had to take the city: successful 20-month siege of 1609–11 by Polish troops; site of heavy fighting during the Russo-Polish War of 1632–34, and Russo-Polish War of 1654–67 (retaken by Russian troops in 1657), site of first major battle of Fatherland War of 1812 in August, when Napoleon tried to cut Russian 1st and 2nd Army off from Moscow. The symbol of the old Duchy of Smolensk was the Kremlin fortress and a cannon. In the 1920s and 1930s the Soviet General Staff had expected the Smolensk region to be the site of major fighting in any future Soviet–Polish or Soviet–German–Polish War. Down to the annexation of eastern Poland in 1939, Western Front's operational rear had embraced the Smolensk region.

E. *Field Fortifications in Theater:* Major fortified regions were created at Polotsk and Mozyr in the 1930s but work stopped after movement of the border west and many positions were stripped of materiel (machine-guns). These formed a powerful barrier to the German advance in July 1941. Such fortified regions were designed as economy of force measures and were not analogous to the massive fortifications along the Franco-German border existing during the same period.

Opposing Forces

Let us look first at the German situation. If we look at Halder's diary we can appreciate why Colonel Ritgen expected to be able to get married in early August. As yet it had not been perceived as a difficult campaign back at OKH. Things were going reasonably well.

Figure 177 shows the German High Command structure, most of whose major characters have been mentioned before. The only adjustment was in Fourth Army where von Kluge now commanded both 2nd

361

3rd Panzer Group. These are the German forces available, first infantry and then mechanized forces (see Figures 178–179). Note the weight of the mechanized forces and where the power was. 2nd Panzer Group was far stronger than 3rd in the north. Then there is the composition of German forces on 4 July (see Figure 180). We should note, however – and this was a crucial problem – that the nature of fighting in the initial two weeks had created a substantial gap between the infantry formations and the armored/mechanized forces. This meant that the initial blows in this part of the summer campaign would be fought by the mechanized formations, and the infantry would only be closing on the battlefield as combat developed.

FIGURE 177
ORGANIZATION OF ARMY GROUP CENTER
As of 4 July 1941

Commander:	Field Marshal Fedor von Bock
Ninth Army Commander:	Generaloberst Adolph Strauss
Second Army Commander:	Generalarmee Maximillan Reichsfreiherr von Weichs zur Glon
Fourth Panzer Army Commander:	Field Marshal Gunther von Kluge
2nd Panzer Group:	Generaloberst Heinz Guderian
3rd Panzer Group:	Generaloberst Hermann Hoth
Supported by 1st Luftflotte:	Commander: Field Marshal Albert Kesselring

FIGURE 178
STRUCTURE OF ARMY GROUP CENTER (INFANTRY), 4 JULY 1941

Army Group Center
102 Inf. Div.
Mot. Brig. 900
XXXXIII Army Corps
131 Inf. Div.
134 Inf. Div.
252 Inf. Div.

Divs. recalled to Army Group
162 Inf. Div.
87 Inf. Div.
403 Inf. Div.
221 Inf. Div.
286 Inf. Div.

Ninth Army
XXIII Army Corps
206 Inf. Div.
86 Inf. Div.

Second Army

VI Army Corps
26 Inf. Div.
6 Inf. Div.
V Army Corps
35 Inf. Div.
5 Inf. Div.
161 Inf. Div.
VIII Army Corps
28 Inf. Div.
8 Inf. Div.
XX Army Corps
256 Inf. Div.
129 Inf. Div.
LIII Army Corps
267 Inf. Div.
255 Inf. Div.
52 Inf. Div.
167 Inf. Div.

OKH Reserves
197 Inf. Div.
15 Inf. Div.
260 Inf. Div.
112 Inf. Div.

XXXXII Army Corps
110 Inf. Div.
106 Inf. Div.
96 Inf. Div.

Army Com. XXXV
45 Inf. Div.
293 Inf. Div.
XIII Army Corps
78 Inf. Div.
VII Army Corps
258 Inf. Div.
23 Inf. Div.
7 Inf. Div.
268 Inf. Div.
IX Army Corps
263 Inf. Div.
137 Inf. Div.
292 Inf. Div.
XII Army Corps
31 Inf. Div.
34 Inf. Div.

FIGURE 179
STRUCTURE OF ARMY GROUP CENTER (MECHANIZED FORCES),
4 JULY 1941

PzGr.3
12 Pz. Div.
114 Mot. Div.

XXXIX Mot. Corps
20 Mot. Div.
20 Pz. Div.
7 Pz. Div.
LVII Mot. Corps
18 Mot. Corps
19 Pz. Div.

Fourth Pz. Army
Inf. Reg. GD

PzGr. 2
1 Cav. Div.

XXXXVI Mot. Corps
10 Pz. Div.
SS Reich
XXXXVI Mot. Corps
29 Mot. Div.
17 Pz. Div.
18 Pz. Div.
XXIV Mot. Corps
10 Mot. Div.
3 Pz. Div.
4 Pz. Div.

FIGURE 180
COMPOSITION OF ARMY GROUP CENTER, 4 JULY 1941

Infantry Divisions:	44
Motorized Divisions:	7
Panzer Regiment:	9
Cavalry Divisions:	1
Motorized Brigades:	1
Motorized Regiments:	1
Total:	61 + Divisions

363

Figures 181 and 182 show the Soviet command structure. Two things are important to note. First, Timoshenko had taken over from Pavlov, and on 10 July he took on another title. He was now both commander of Western Front and commander of Western Strategic Direction. This latter organization was a new entity created by the Soviets. There were three of them: one for the northwest, one for the southwest, and one for the western axes. Timoshenko, in fact, left a great deal of the management of the first echelon struggle along the Berezina River in the hands of his deputy *front* commander, Eremenko, who became a fireman for the Western Front staff.

FIGURE 181

SOVIET COMMAND STRUCTURE, 10 JULY 1941

Western Front Commander:	Marshal S.M. Timoshenko
Deputy Front Commander:	General-Lieutenant A.I. Eremenko
22nd Army Commander:	General-Lieutenant F.A. Ershakov
19th Army Commander:	General-Lieutenant I.S. Konev
20th Army Commander:	General-Lieutenant P.A. Kurochkin
13th Army Commander:	General-Lieutenant F.N. Remezov
21st Army Commander:	General Colonel F.I. Kuznetsov
4th Army Commander:	Colonel L.M. Sandalov
16th Army Commander:	General-Lieutenant M.F. Lukin
Air Forces of Western Front Commander:	Colonel N.F. Naumenko

FIGURE 182

FRONT OF RESERVE ARMIES, 10 JULY 1941

Front of Reserve Armies Commander:	S.M. Budennyi
30th Army Commander:	General-Lieutenant V.A. Khomenko
29th Army Commander:	General-Lieutenant I.I. Maslennikov
24th Army Commander:	General-Lieutenant S.A. Kalinin
28th Army Commander:	General-Lieutenant V.Ia. Kachalov
31st Army Commander:	General-Major K.I. Rakutin
32nd Army Commander:	General-Lieutenant N.K. Klykov

There had been other command changes as well. Kurochkin had just taken over 20th Army. One of the problems the Soviets had during the early stages of the Smolensk operation was the radical changes in personnel which had occurred at *front* and army levels and the need to conduct operations in an attempt to preempt German movement. That created an almost impossible situation in trying to manage the attacks. We can get an idea of the air situation when we note that there was a colonel running the Soviet air force of Western Front. He had only patched-up aircraft. The Soviets would struggle to get aircraft up at night and they would try to carry out aerial resupply into Mogilev, but the assets were very limited. The common refrain of Soviet commanders in this phase was, "We are under constant air attack and air reconnaissance. We do not know where the enemy is but he knows where we are. His combination air-ground action is devastating".

Figure 183 shows the composition and structure of the Soviet second strategic echelon, which was actually the first echelon in the battle of Smolensk. Note that just in simple order of battle terms, the mechanized corps had disappeared. There were still a few, such as the 5th, 7th and 25th. Two of these were destroyed very early on during the counterattacks at Lepel. Subsequently, armor would be in very short supply for the Soviets.

There was however, another asset, the one Eremenko was immediately charged with. These were Soviet forces which had some combat organization and which were deployed out in front of the Dnepr River (see Figure 184). These were assets which were asked in late June and early July to provide a delaying action. They were to provide enough time for a new defensive line to be created on the Dvina River, the land-bridge, and the Dnepr. The hope was they would hold out until 10 July. As we will see that was a very thin hope.

FIGURE 183

SOVIET FORCE STRUCTURE, FIRST ECHELON, 7 JULY 1941

(Defending Western Dvina–Dnepr Line)

		51st Rifle Corps
		170 R. Div.
		112 R. Div.
	22nd Army	98 R. Div.
		62nd Rifle Corps
		174 R. Div.
		Polotsk FR
		176 R. Div.
FRONT RESERVE		
16th Army		
32 Rif. Corps		20th Rifle Corps
46 Inf. Div.		128 R. Div.
152 Inf. Div.		23 R. Div.
		7th Mech Corps
57 Tank Div.	19th Army	147 T. Div.
	25th Rifle Corps	187 T. Div.
20th Army	no divs. arrived	153 M. Div.
34th Rifle Corps		69th Rifle Corps
no divs. arrived		244 R. Div.
		233 R. Div.
		73 R. Div.
		5th Mech Corps
		177 T. Div.
		13 T. Div.
		109 M. Div.
		1 MR Div.

365

61st Rifle Corps
137 R. Div.
53 R. Div.
110 R. Div.
13th Army   172 R. Div.
   132 R. Div.   45th Rifle Corps
   148 R. Div.   187 R. Div.
20th Mech Corps

67th Rifle Corps
102 R. Div.
63rd Rifle Corps
21st Army   61 R. Div.
   47th Rifle Corps   167 R. Div.
   121 R. Div.   117 R. Div.
   143 R. Div.   154 R. Div.
   184 R. Div.

FIGURE 184
SOVIET UNITS OPERATING BEFORE THE WESTERN
DVINA–DNEPR LINE, 7 JULY 1941

2nd Rifle Corps
100 R. Div.
1 MR Div.
44th Rifle Corps
161 R. Div.
47th Rifle Corps
121 R. Div.
28th Rifle Corps
4th Army 4th Abn. Corps   143 R. Div.
   8 Abn. Div.   155 R. Div.
   121 Abn. Div.
   55 R. Div.

(2nd and 44th Rifle Corps falling back from Borisov toward Orsha. 47th and 28th Rifle Corps and 4th Airborne Corps were falling back on the Berezina and toward the Dnepr crossing at the seam between 13th and 21st Army and were being withdrawn from combat for reconstitution.)

Situation 7–20 July

Figure 185 shows the situation on 7 July. What we can note in this situation, and what will have an impact on the conduct of the battle, are those Soviet forces that have been identified, which were out in front of the Dnepr River. Some units, indeed, were still in front of the Berezina River and were struggling desperately to get back. Attempts were made to stabilize the situation, but German armor had already penetrated them and reached the Rogachev area south of Mogilev. When we look at this

366

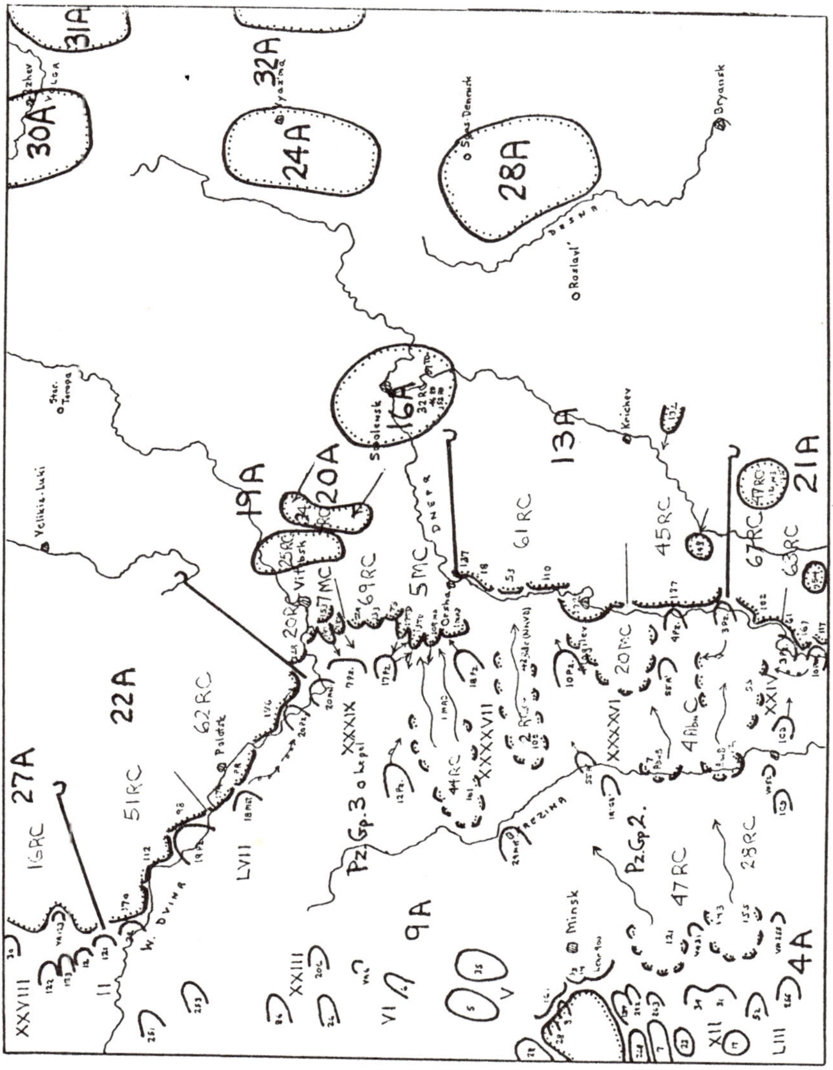

FIGURE 185
SITUATION, 2300, 7 JULY 1941

map we should note a particular problem for the Germans which would have an impact on later stages of the operation. In the north was the boundary between Army Group North and Center, and Soviet 22nd Army sat there in a rather prominent position. The German Army Group North commander had to deal with the situation in Courland and towards Leningrad, and he also had to deal with that exposed right flank facing Soviet 22nd Army. Therefore he was concerned about an operation to eliminate 22nd Army. He proposed such an operation based on captured Soviet documents and he believed the operation was feasible. His dilemma was that Army Group Center had to cooperate by using elements of 3rd Panzer Group.

On 7 July the German LVII Corps had already reached the Western Dvina River. In that area the Soviet defense was extremely thin, partly because the Soviets were relying on the troops and fortifications of the Polotsk Fortified Region (as an economy of force measure). There was a possibility to develop an attack toward Velikie Luki both north and south of Polotsk. 18th Motorized and 20th Panzer Divisions were in position to attack south of Polotsk. Simultaneously Army Group North forces were poised to attack further north.

At this time a Soviet counterattack was under way, which began on 6 July. Two mechanized corps (5th and 7th) were attacking southwest from Vitebsk under 20th Army control. Kurochkin, the 20th Army commander, had just taken over from General Remezov. The two corps attempted to advance to Lepel and the operation was an absolute disaster as Soviet tanks ran into prepared German antitank defenses without adequate reconnaissance. There was no armor-infantry coordination and, as the attack developed, Vinogradov, commander of 7th Mechanized Corps, insisted over the objections of his staff that the attack be continued despite losses. German aircraft added to Soviet problems and essentially the corps was destroyed.

The situation map of 10 July shows how the attack developed (see Figure 186). Note the three separate axes of combat. What happened for the Soviets, and it was quite crucial, was that the German attack was now preempting the full-deployment of the Soviet second strategic echelon along the Western Dvina–Smolensk–Dnepr River line. The Soviets said they had 39 divisions in the area, 24 of which were available along the front. The average defensive frontage of a Soviet rifle division along this front was 25 kilometers. Prewar notions of an adequate and stable defense was 8–12 kilometers per division. Most of these divisions were in a single echelon configuration, there were no units behind them to use in counter-attacks, and few mechanized units were available to counter deep break-throughs. It was a very thin defensive shell at this stage.

In the north the situation had become very critical. Army Group North's

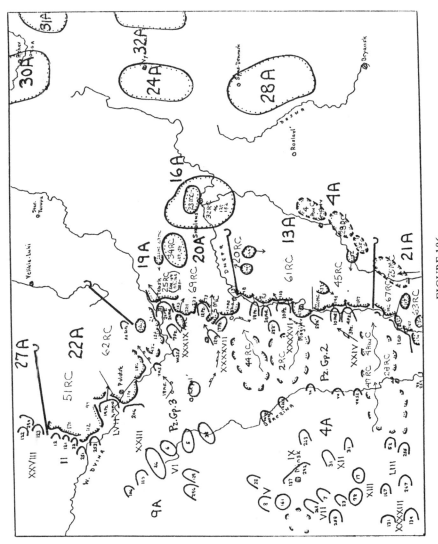

FIGURE 186
SITUATION, 2300, 10 JULY 1941

infantry corps were exerting pressure and the attack north of Polotsk by 19th Panzer Division and half of 14th Motorized Division was progressing. South of Polotsk 20th Panzer elements were attacking across the river. For all practical purposes the Polotsk Fortified Region had been bypassed and no uncommitted Soviet reserves in the Velikie Luki and Nevel areas existed to deal with the threat. 22nd Army faced the prospect of rapid encirclement.

Probably more serious from the perspective of the entire defensive position was the situation at Vitebsk. The Soviets hoped to convert Vitebsk into a strongpoint but the Germans seized it from the march. Soviet units in the counterattack were literally coming from the trains into combat. 19th Army was in the process of deploying and as the attack developed Konev, its commander, desperately tried to take what he had, about one and a half divisions, and launched a counterattack. That was the last coherent action by 19th Army as a combat formation. They were overwhelmed, and in fact when Eremenko came to visit Konev on 13 July, they were both almost captured by German motorized infantry. The line had been broken.

A look at the development of the rest of the land-bridge attack shows probes by 12th Panzer Division, pressure in the direction of Orsha, and the withdrawal of the remnants of 5th Mechanized Corps from the Lepel area. Around Orsha itself, the situation was relatively stable. 2nd Rifle Corps was attempting to get back to Orsha, while further south most of the other Soviet units were streaming toward Rogachev in the south or Mogilev in the center. Mogilev was a particularly critical point on the Dnepr River for forces trying to get back across the river.

I should say something about Lukin's 16th Army near Smolensk. Note the 23rd Mechanized Corps was in place. This unit was not the original mechanized corps attached to 16th Army. That was the 5th Corps which had been pulled off for the Lepel attack. In general, Lukin had been promised that his army would be rebuilt by newly arriving reserves. Timoshenko charged Lukin with being a strategic reserve of the *front* in this sector and the hope was that more combat power would become available to stabilize the situation around Smolensk. As will be seen, 16th Army was actually the size of a corps with a few attached units. At one point Timoshenko promised Lukin anything he could gather himself. Lukin sent out dispatch riders and either the roads were cut or new units had been designated for use elsewhere. Lukin received some formations from withdrawing units, for example, fragments of defeated 19th Army. Some of 19th Army units withdrew north and northwest, while others headed back to join 16th Army at Smolensk.

Further south will be seen the expansion of 2nd Panzer Group's operations as it forced its way across the Dnepr River both north and south of Mogilev. Mogilev was a city of 99,000 people at that time and it was a major rail center. It was also one of the first Soviet cities where what the Soviets called mass heroism occurred. That meant the mobilization of its civilian population to create irregulars, militia, and labor forces. At Mogilev party, state and military institutions created field defenses and raised about one division of militia. These troops were armed with English rifles, supplied with limited quantities of ammunition, and issued with gasoline, bottles and rags. It was not a pretty formation but it was raised to stabilize the position in this area. In addition, units were also withdrawing from the Berezina River line into Mogilev to reinforce its defenses. The model for this was a place called Kokovka out of the Russian Civil War, a position on the Dnepr where the Soviets organized a city area as an antitank barrier. It was the first antitank defense erected by the Soviets.

German penetrations developed in the south at Staryi Bykov and in the north at Kopys and Shkov. There were very few Soviet reserves to deal with the situation in the north, while in the south one division was moving up to try to pinch off the developing penetration. Note also what happened to 4th Army. Those units which had just escaped encirclement were being placed in new defensive positions for reconstitution. They were not supposed to be engaged in combat for a while but as the battle developed they were drawn into combat.

By 13 July the German northern attack had developed, and pincers were closing around 22nd Army despite attempts by 51st and 61st Rifle Corps to prevent it (see Figure 187). South of Polotsk 18th Motorized Division was advancing deep and threatening 22nd Army with encirclement. The rest of 3rd Panzer Group had broken through at Vitebsk and XXXIX Panzer Corps was swinging to the northeast with 20th and 7th Panzer Divisions, driving 19th Army elements before them. Shortly after, the panzer corps struck southeast through Demidov and Dukhovshchina. 12th Panzer Division broke through south of Vitebsk, compromised 7th Mechanized Corps' position, and advanced along the road toward Rudnia.

Meanwhile 17th Panzer Division secured Orsha. Its action plus that of 12th Panzer, created a crisis in 20th Army. The Soviets feared the German drive would envelop all of 20th Army in front of Smolensk. At this point the *front* commander received authorization to commit an experimental unit – the first BM–13 Katyusha battery which was used to counterattack at the Orsha railroad station. They delivered 320 132mm rockets in a ten second barrage. The battery itself did not survive but the Soviets were satisfied with its impact. Soviet troops were just as surprised as the Germans over the firing of this "stun" weapon, as the Soviets referred to it. The General Staff made a decision to put the weapon into full development. After being used on several occasions the first battery, then in encirclement, was destroyed by its commanders.

371

Figure 188 shows a map from General Guderian's famous memoirs, and it provides the impression that General Guderian had of the next development, what he called the Timoshenko counterattack, which occurred in the south from the Rogachev area. The number which Guderian cites is 20 Soviet divisions. There probably were 20 divisions but it was much worse than Guderian suggested. It was not twenty divisions in front of him, but 20 divisions all around him. The main striking power was coming out of Rogachev in the form of 25th Mechanized Corps (just arriving), 67th Rifle Corps, cavalry forces attacking from the south, and units which had come out of the Mogilev pocket or had been part of 4th Army's bedraggled forces moving back to regroup. It was an extremely confused situation, all the more so because of the attack by 28th Rifle Corps, which struck the flank of German units. 4th Panzer Division was in a difficult situation and, consequently, 3rd Panzer Division would soon be moved south from Mogilev to help out.

In the north, on 14 July Soviet units of Lukin's 16th Army were scattered all along the Dnepr River; flying detachments sent out by Lukin when he realized the Germans had broken through, had reached Gorki, and were advancing to Liuda and Krasnoe. He put together combat teams made up of antitank guns, artillery, and reconnaissance elements from rifle divisions and pushed them down those roads to occupy blocking positions. In some cases they did well and stabilized the situation. In other cases they were overrun by the Germans. Many of them were pushed back toward the Dnepr and exfiltrated across the river through the village of Ustinov.

In the city of Smolensk itself, Lukin tried to emulate the garrison commander at Mogilev by transforming the city into a bastion. However, he did not succeed very well. Smolensk, with a population of 147,000, raised a brigade rather than a division. Very little was done on mining or preparing positions and tank traps because the Germans had pre-empted those actions. There was, however, from the Soviet perspective, one saving grace. The 129th Rifle Division arrived and the garrison commander blew the bridges. Lukin, in his memoirs said he cursed the fellow out saying "How dare you do that on your own authority?" But it was done and Lukin recognized that "Thank God, it was done".

Before the 129th Rifle Division arrived, German units could probably have penetrated the northern part of the city fairly easily. As it was, the 129th Division took up positions, particularly in the cemetery and Vodka manufacturing establishment, one of those objectives which would naturally be strongly defended. In general, extremely intense, very violent and very costly hand to hand combat ensued. This was urban combat in the Soviet variant. Note, however, that Eremenko said that the city was not prepared for it. Smolensk did not receive a designation of "hero city" for

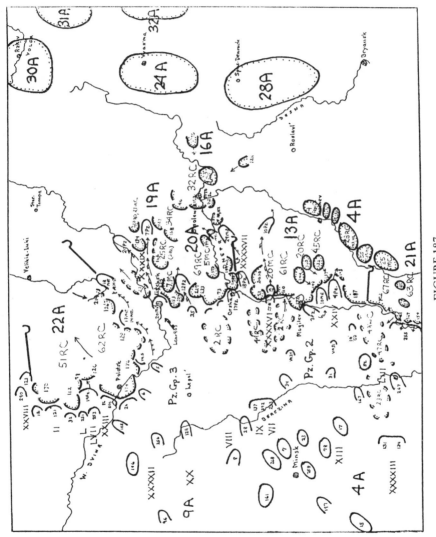

FIGURE 187

SITUATION, 2300, 13 JULY 1941

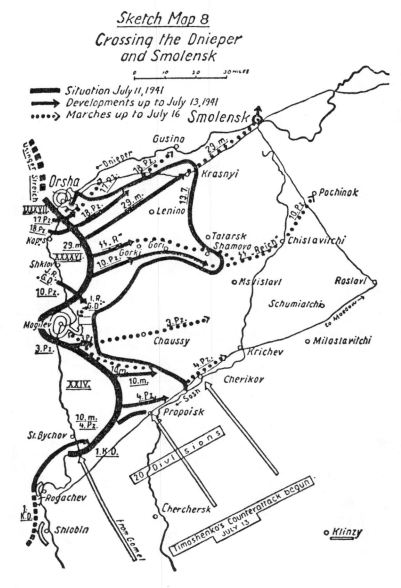

FIGURE 188
GUDERIAN MAP OF TIMOSHENKO COUNTERATTACK

this action, as Mogilev did. The Soviet propaganda machine turned Mogilev into the Soviet Madrid. Parenthetically, there is an interesting iteration of the name here. Mogilev's Russian root comes from *Mogiles* or "grave", and the question is, Whose graves? As we shall see, in the garrison's case this was a bad omen.

Meanwhile, in the south the German attack continued with the breakthrough developing in 13th Army's sector. The Soviets attempted to stabilize the perimeter around Mogilev, and a new Soviet defense line gradually emerged along the Sozh River and the Dnepr near Rogachev. This was partly a result of the unavailability of additional German mechanized formations and, in particular, the lack of German infantry to fill in the gaps. There was a period here when German mechanized forces desperately needed but did not have the infantry support. It was to change the situation and permit more operational flexibility when it did arrive, but for now, it was not there.

The penetration of German 7th Panzer Division north of Smolensk was an absolute disaster in the offing since there were few Soviet troops along the Dnepr River or defending the Minsk–Smolensk–Moscow highway. It was a desperate situation for the Soviets. Timoshenko said they had a disaster with no tanks to deal with German mechanized formations which had broken through. The Soviets resorted to improvisations at this point. One of the things the General Staff has taught at its academy was that a battle is going badly when the number of detachments multiply. That means creating *ad hoc* units to deal with immediate situations and creating detachments which are extraordinarily unwieldy. For example, at Khalkhin–Gol in the July fighting, it was noted by General Staff officers who came out to see Zhukov, that he had created so many detachments that his field orders for the reinforced corps fighting there were like a book with multiple cross-attachments. The staff officers with Shtern got things back into some order, but here the Soviets responded with detachments. The Soviets created headquarters without staffs and they created operational groups without subordinate formations. If time permitted, they hoped these *ad hoc* units would grow into something else.

From a German perspective, the one feature which developed on 16 July which was not particularly pleasing was the situation in the north (see Figure 189). Note that 19th Panzer Division of XXXIX Panzer Corps could swing in one of two directions and create pockets. It could swing north and threaten Soviet 51st Rifle Corps or it could swing south to encircle 62nd Rifle Corps. In either case, what would result was what von Leeb of Army Group North thought this operation was about – namely the encirclement and destruction of major elements of Soviet 22nd Army. There were disputes regarding what might be accomplished by this move. Von Leeb's estimate looked forward to destroying five or six Russian divisions. Others thought it would be higher, but all expected something to come out of it. To make a long story short, there were two army groups operating here with a panzer group, a panzer corps and a division. In the process of communication, 19th Panzer Division, while dealing with a tactical situation, decided that motorized forces could deal with its flank problems. The commander decided to race ahead and seize Velikie Luki. There were good reasons to seize Velikie Luki. It was a main rail line from Riga to Moscow. But in so doing, if the pockets were not closed off, Soviet forces could come back and join a new Soviet army, the 29th, forming behind Velikie Luki.

I want to point out that German intelligence during this period was quite good. Fourth Panzer Army's map for 19 July (see Figure 190) shows quite clearly the amount of information the Germans had about Soviet unit locations. It was a pretty good assessment throughout the entire front and also of the confused nature of the battle and Soviet counterattacks.

By 20 July the situation can be summed up quite clearly (see Figure 191). The trap did not close in the north nor did the pocket close around Smolensk. As von Leeb said, "There is only one pocket and it has a hole in it". Although 3rd Panzer Group developed the attack it had not been able to link up with XXXXVI Panzer Corps. German units had reached El'nia but note the gap between those units and those following behind. The Soviets had been able to stabilize the situation along the Sozh River, but also note the arrival of German infantry, which would provide 2nd Panzer Group with a great deal more latitude to maneuver.

To sum up, the Germans had broken through and smashed the Dnepr River line and on 11 July, when Halder heard about the crossing of the Dnepr, he said the war was over for all intents and purposes because the enemy had no strategic reserves. As can be seen on the map they may not have been very well organized or had the staff, and they may not have been full armies, but there were Soviet formations appearing. Soon the Soviets would attempt to restabilize the situation and create an uninterrupted defense line.

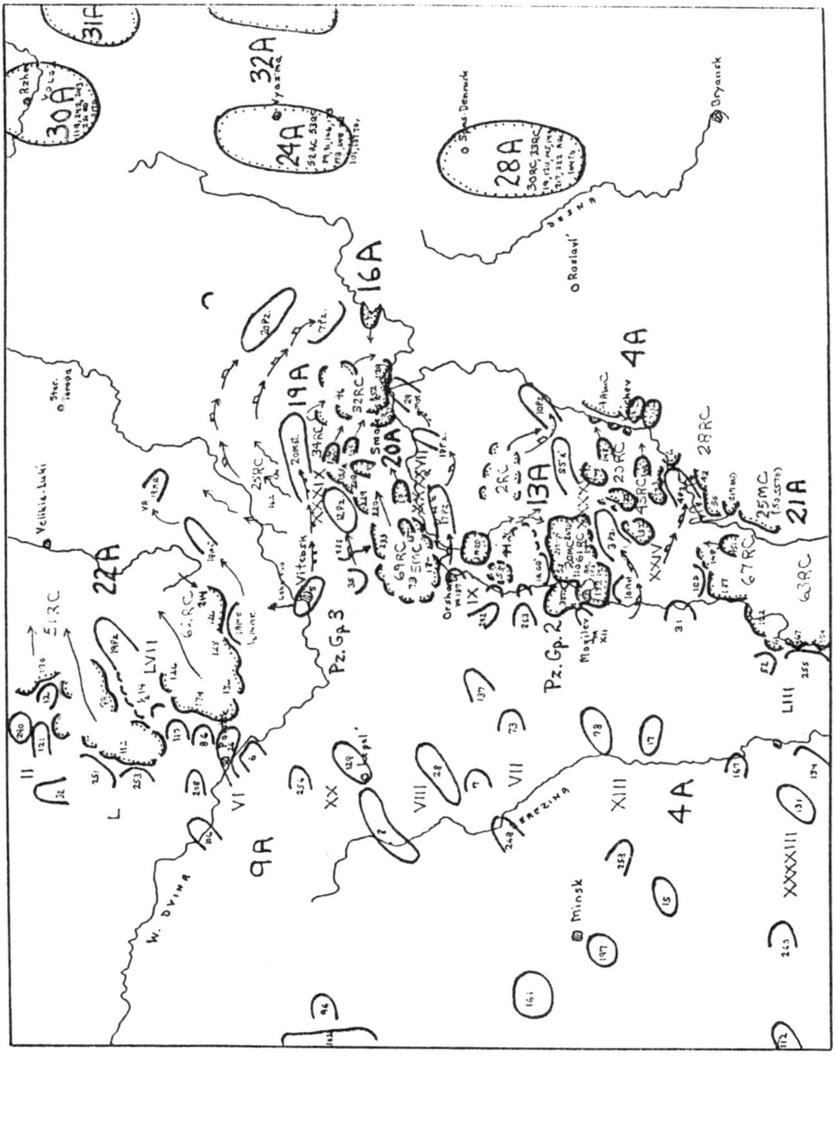

FIGURE 189
SITUATION, 2300, 16 JULY 1941

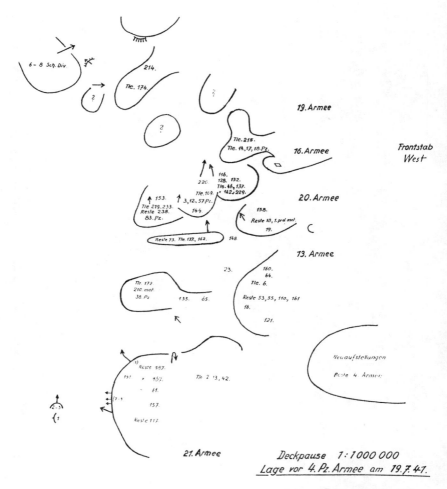

FIGURE 190
FOURTH ARMY SITUATION MAP, 19 JULY 1941

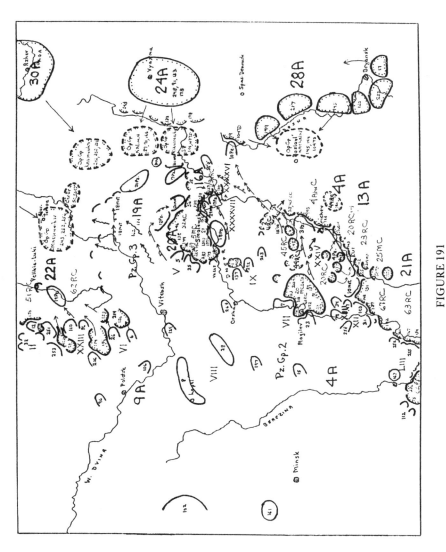

FIGURE 191
SITUATION, 2300, 20 JULY 1941

7th Panzer Division Operations

COLONEL HERMANN ROTHE (retired)
and
MAJOR GENERAL H. OHRLOFF (retired)

Colonel Rothe:

In June 1941 I was battalion signal officer in the 3rd Battalion, Panzer Regiment 25, responsible for radio communication of that unit. For that purpose I had available three command tanks with radios and two telephone sections. Every tank had a radio set, so that the platoon, company and battalion commanders could communicate with each tank under their command. Hard communications training with all users during the year before the Eastern campaign was carried out as a result of good radio discipline on the part of all grades. It was one of the principal requirements to be successful as a commander of tanks.

My task is to tell you about 7th Panzer Division operations beginning on 1 July 1941. On that date my division was located west of Borissov on the Berezina River (see Figure 192). Our task was to cross the Berezina River as soon as possible. On 1 July the Division attacked along the autobahn near Borissov, but without success because of strong Soviet defense lines. Consequently, the division commander changed the plan to advance via Zembin to the north. But on 2 July heavy rains prevented rapid movement. Finally, at midnight on 2–3 July Rifle Regiment 7 and Panzer Regiment 25 attacked out of the Zembin area and succeeded in taking the bridge west of Lepel. The bridgehead there was important for success in the subsequent action.

The 7th Panzer Division had to tolerate excessive heat and dust. Since 1 July however, the routes became an impenetrable morass. Instead of taking Vitebsk in a quick attack, 7th Panzer Division, as advance-party of the XXXIX Panzer Corps, took two days to reach Lepel, which was only 90 kilometers away. At 2215 on 3 July, the units of the division arrived at their ordered areas as follows:

– Panzer Regiment 25 – 7.5 kilometers west of Lepel,
– Rifle Regiment 6 – east of Bieolin,
– Rifle Regiment 7 and Panzer Reconnaissance Battalion (*Panzer Aufklarungs Abteilung* PzAA) 37 – Swjada
– Motorcycle Battalion (*Kradschutzenbattalion*) 7 – in Kosciuki,

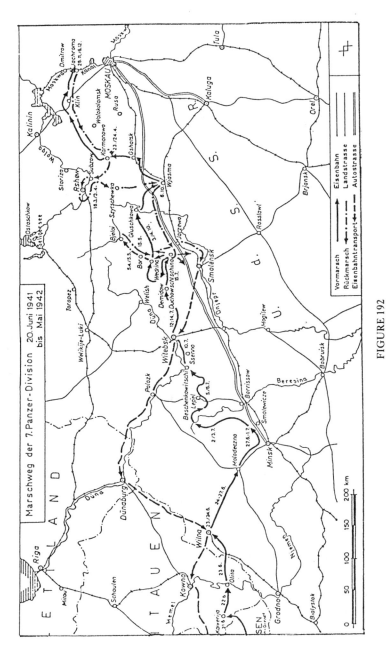

FIGURE 192

7TH PANZER DIVISION OPERATIONS, 20 JUNE 1941–MAY 1942

– Division assembly area (*gefechtsstand*) – 3 kilometers west of Lepel.

The company commander of 6th Company, Rifle Regiment 7 reported at 2200 that the airfield eight kilometers southwest of Lepel was in our hands along with 30 airplanes, three POL stores, and much other material.

On the morning of 4 July the commander of Artillery Regiment 78 received an order as commander of the advance party to attack through Tschanschniki, secure river crossings for the division near Tschanschniki and Olschanka, and to advance further toward Vitebsk. At 1520 the advance party reported capture of the bridge near Tschanschniki. At 1900 Panzer Regiment 25 was ordered to create a new bridgehead south and southeast of Tschanschniki.

On 5 July at 1220 division headquarters was told that 20th Panzer Division was to attack Ulla. By 1400 headquarters 7th Panzer Division had reached Beschenkovitschi. That evening at 2100, the G2 of XXXIX Panzer Corps gave the following information to division headquarters: "2–3 divisions around Vitebsk. The corps wants to cross the Duna near Ulla and to attack Vitebsk from the north."

On the morning of 6 July, strong enemy counterattacks occurred near Dubki and Schoteni. A combat group of the 3rd Battalion, Panzer Regiment 25 with PzAA. 37, one company of Rifle Regiment 6, and one battery of the artillery regiment was ordered to attack the enemy and advance forward. The battle report of the 7th Panzer–Division read: "6th to 10th July, Breakthrough of the Duna position, Duna – crossing near Ulla and Beschenkovitschi, taking of Vitebsk". From 7 to 9 July heavy fighting raged in the division's sector between Lischatschi and Ostrowo with tanks and artillery supporting both sides.

Major General Ohrloff:

Attack by Reinforced 11th Company of Panzer Regiment 25 on Senno 7 and 8 July 1941

3rd Battalion of Panzer-Regiment 25 had prepared defenses on the right flank of 7th Panzer Division on the approaches of the Stalin Line west of Vitebsk (see Figure 193). However, the lines of defense of 7th Panzer Division were fiercely attacked by the Russians who obviously wanted to eliminate this threat to one of their major fortified lines. Senno, which was situated at the southern flank of the division in a slightly forward position, represented an important bridgehead for German forces. The roads leading through Senno were as important to the Germans as they were to the Russians.

On 6 July the Russians had managed to regain Senno with tank support, and in the evening they were still pressing onward. First Lieutenant Ohrloff, commander of 11th Company of Regiment 25, was ordered to carry out a probing attack against the enemy's flank from the north. This was to be done early on 7 July with his company which, at that time, was held as a reserve for the Panzer battalion defending Schoteni. The purpose of this order was to relieve *Kradschutzen* (motorcycle infantry) Battalion 7 which was fighting very hard. In case of massive enemy resistance, the commander was free to bypass Senno to the westand to establish contact with the *Kradschutzen* battalion from there. An infantry gun platoon, an antitank gun platoon and one Type IV tank were attached to the company.

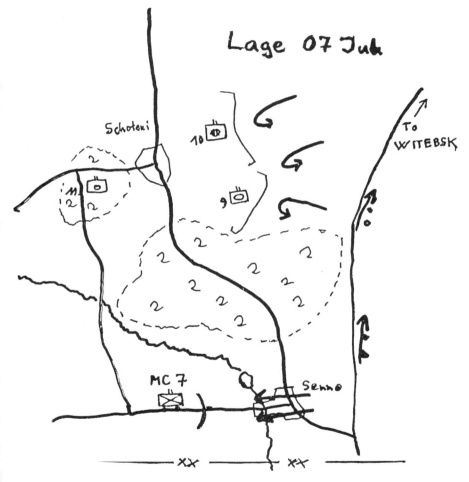

FIGURE 193
7TH PANZER DIVISION SITUATION, 7 JULY 1941

At first light on 7 July, the assembled tank crews received the order from the company commander himself to break through the enemy positions in a surprise attack in order to establish contact with the motorcycle infantry [*Kradschutzen*] battalion as soon as possible. For this reason firing was not permitted until they had passed the forest just north of Senno to avoid waking the enemy. Afterwards the tanks were deployed line abreast, the infantry guns took up their firing positions, and the antitank guns started fighting the Russian tanks under cover of their own tanks.

At about 0300 the company moved southward through the thick forest until they had a clear view of Senno (see Figure 194). On the fringe of the village about 30 Russians were receiving their morning coffee and much

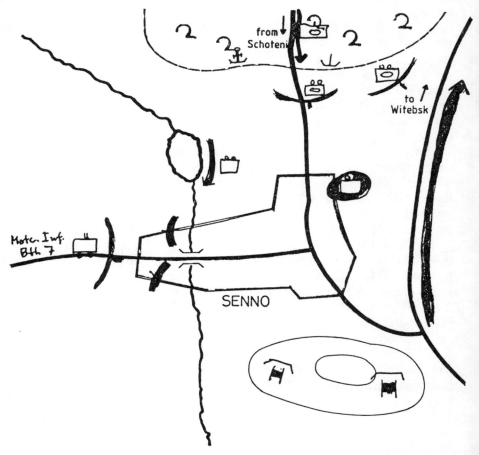

FIGURE 194
7TH PANZER DIVISION SITUATION, 0300, 7 JULY 1941

traffic occupied the road eastward – tanks, trucks and reconnaissance vehicles. A rapid decision was made: one platoon equipped with a Type IV tank was to attack and destroy the vehicles. Initially during the attack, the Russians collapsed and almost no one escaped. Their vehicles burned out and houses burst into flames. However, their resistance soon revived, and from a distance of 25 to 30 meters they fired at our soft-skinned vehicles, of which there were only a few, and some of our soldiers were hit.

The German tanks advanced further while firing at Russians trying to defend themselves from within the houses. A Russian unit marching along a lake-front 300 meters away from the Germans was hit by machine-gun fire from the commander's tank. Individual Russian tanks trying to interfere with the battle were destroyed. The company then reached a creek with a demolished crossing and after reconnoitering, a tank was ordered to ford the creek (see Figure 195). It reached the other side and the company followed.

The company was fighting its way through heaps of rubble from previous battles until finally white flares went up indicating that contact with our own forces would soon be established. One of the German tanks broke down in the village because it lost a track. The commander returned to the village with some tanks to recover the disabled tank. An enemy tank trying to interfere with the recovery action was destroyed.

Despite the motorcycle infantry battalion being relieved and the Russians suffering heavy casualties, Senno remained under Russian control. The panzer company received an order to return to Schoteni and rejoin the battalion. On the march to the north, west of Senno, the company was attacked by Russian aircraft. However, they did not suffer any casualties and rejoined the battalion in the afternoon.

The next day, 8 July, Senno was finally seized. To accomplish this objective, one battalion of Panzer Regiment 25 was to envelop Senno from the east, and 11th Company, which knew the place from the day before, was to engage the enemy from the north to destroy resisting enemy forces. To carry out this operation the company was reinforced by an armored platoon and three Type IV tanks.

The priority mission of that day was to break the remaining resistance rather than to attack the enemy by surprise (see Figure 196). The company had just passed the forest when Senno was attacked by a German fighter bomber. The company capitalized on this well-timed weakening of the enemy, and tanks and armored infantry soldiers started an all-out attack. Every single house was fired at, some houses burned out, and enemy tanks were destroyed in an almost classical manner. Posting a panzer platoon to secure the area, the commander, together with another platoon, fought his way through to the motorcycle infantry battalion to establish contact with it. The commander ordered the tanks and motorcycle infantrymen to drive the Russians out of the village from the west. Soon afterwards violent battles for every single house and every position ensued – a combat in built-up areas. The Russians put up a brave but unsuccessful defense.

The platoon that was to secure Senno from the east reported attacks by enemy tanks and infantry during which several German soldiers were wounded. The commander ordered the securing action to be continued until contact had been established between his platoon and the platoon

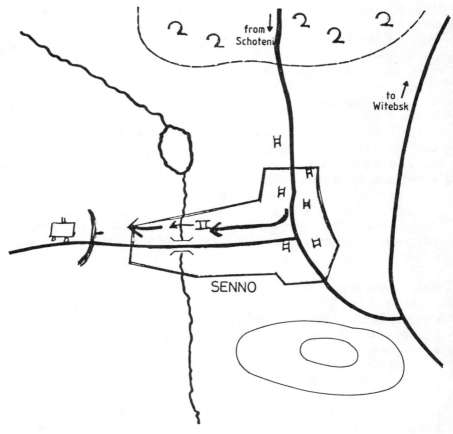

FIGURE 195
7TH PANZER DIVISION SITUATION, 7 JULY 1941 (PM)

fighting its way through from the west with the motorcycle infantry. It did not take long to succeed and overcome the crisis. Meanwhile, 3rd Battalion of Panzer Regiment 25 reported: "Hostile resistance too strong, battalion is returning to its initial position".

The situation finally stabilized, and Senno came under German control. Many Russians soldiers were killed there, and an almost intolerable cadaverous smell soon spread. Twenty-two tanks, two armored reconnaissance vehicles, six guns and several trucks were destroyed and 50 Russian soldiers were captured. German losses were eight soldiers killed and two tracked vehicles damaged.

Experience gained from this operation was as follows:

1. Without infantry support, tanks can be used in built-up areas only if these areas can be passed through quickly and if the tanks succeed in surprising the enemy.

2. If tanks and gunners cooperate in built-up areas or in close terrain, the latter have to protect the tanks against armor-piercing weapons. For this reason the gunners usually have to attack in advance, whereas the tanks effectively support the combat of the gunners.

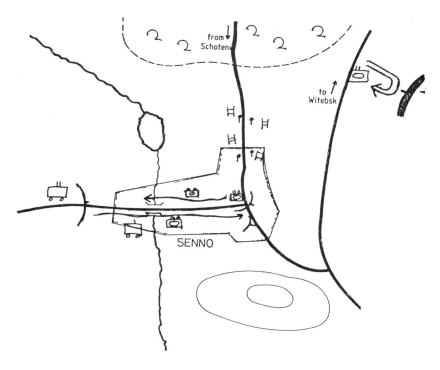

FIGURE 196
7TH PANZER DIVISION SITUATION, 8 JULY 1941

3. Soft-skinned vehicles have to be protected by armored vehicles, but they have to take cover and be detached from their march column in good time.

4. It is important to make immediate contact with other units which have to be coordinated with your own action.

All these are basic problems which must be fulfilled.

Colonel Rothe:

On the afternoon of 7 July, the 10th Company was attacked east of Tylizy by enemy tanks, including for the first time three KVII tanks with 150mm guns. Two tanks were destroyed and one sank into the swampy ground. I remember very well in the battalion headquarters we heard artillery firing at various intervals and the company commander reported heavy Soviet tanks of an unknown type before our positions. From what I can remember the order was given to fire with our 37mm guns at the turret base of the tanks in order to jam the turrets. Because we were successful and suffered no losses, our tank crews were not excited about the KVII tanks. It was no question that this KVII was a surprise. Fortunately, the Soviets did not use it effectively.

On 8 July headquarters 7th Panzer Division received a report from Panzer Reconnaissance Battalion 37 that written orders had been found on a captured Soviet officer. They were important and told us that railway transports were on the way north from the Ukraine and from Orel to be unloaded at Vitebsk. Consequently, the commander of Panzer Group 3 ordered the 20th Panzer and the 20th Infantry Divisions to attack these Soviet formations which were under the command of Generals Konjew and Kurotschkin.

7th Panzer Division was prepared on 9 July to attack Vitebsk, but the Panzer Group 3 commander wanted to postpone the attack until 10 July. At 1415, 2nd Battalion, Rifle Regiment 7 reported the capture of Dubrova. At 2100 10 July Panzer Regiment 25 arrived at Dubrova as well. Both regiments had reached the area southeast of Vitebsk but they were not able to take the town.

Meanwhile, an improvised crossing over the river was found for the infantry and another for the tanks. After clearance of mines it was possible to capture a bridgehead east of the Duna River on the morning of 11 July. In the afternoon a renewed attack was successful near Semschina and Panzer Regiment 25 arrived just east of Vitebsk. The enemy tried to stop them with powerful counterattacks. In addition, a deep system of trenches with artillery and dug-in tanks had been built by the Soviets. Our 3rd Battalion of the Panzer Regiment was deeply depressed by the heavy losses. Five lieutenants died after being shot through the head. Soviet sharpshooters were able to do this because our tanks had no escorting infantry. Air reconnaissance soon reported that the enemy seemed to be withdrawing back to Smolensk.

Let me add a few words about the division's own air reconnaissance. Three aircraft, Focke-Wulf 189s, were under command of the division commander. These aircraft had FM radios and were very helpful for reconnaissance in the divisional sector. So far as I remember the 7th Panzer Division lost these aircraft in late summer 1941.

On 11 July the commander of Panzer Group 3 issued the following appreciation of the situation:

> The Duna crossing by 3 Divisions of the XXXIX Panzerkorps between Beschenkowitschi and Ulla and the taking of Vitebsk is an important change in our own situation. In the Dnepr – Duna front of the enemy there is a wide gap. Therefore it is necessary to take an operational risk in the next few days.

On 12 July the day's objective, the railway station at Smeleva (50 km southeast of Vitebsk on the railway line Vitebsk–Smolensk), was taken and with its capture the attack on Demidov was resumed. We reached Demidov on the night of 14 July. Panzer Pioneer Battalion 58 rebuilt the bridge into the town by 1330. Shortly after, an advance party with 1st Battalion, Panzer Regiment 25, 1st Battalion Artillery Regiment, one company of Rifle Regiment 6, one company of Engineer Battalion 58, and one platoon of Antitank Battalion 42 broke through the enemy defense lines and took the area 20 kilometers east–southeast of Demidov at 2055.

On 15 July the VIII Air Corps (Flieger-Korps) informed the division that it could provide extra support that day. Meanwhile a combat group of Rifle Brigade 7 captured the autobahn near Jarzevo and became involved in hard fighting against enemy tanks and infantry. On 16 July the division sector was hardly attacked at all by the enemy and the lines of defense were moved forward to the Vop River near Novosselov. There was no combat on 17 July with the exception of activities of Soviet bombers and much Soviet air reconnaissance.

On 18 and 19 July, heavy attacks were conducted by Soviet tanks and infantry during which more than 50 enemy tanks were destroyed. The division asked for support by Stukas which helped the situation on 20 July. Panzer Regiment 25 reported on 21 July the following tank situation:

	Beginning Strength	Losses	Repairs
Pz I	17	7	3
Pz II		55	24
Pz 38 (t)	167	112	78
Pz IV	30	15	10
PzBefehlswg. (command tanks)	15	8	5
	284	166	96

That meant a total loss of 70 tanks within one month.

The war diary of the commander, 7th Panzer Division, Major General von Funk provided the following entry for 21 July:

> In these critical days of heavy defensive battles, HQ PzKorps ordered the Division to destroy the bridge over the Vop. The enemy shouldn't have a chance to penetrate in this sector. But I take the risk only to prepare the demolition as a guard against enemy action: After the time of crisis [has passed] the Corps HQ is happy to learn that the bridge is still intact.

Between 21 and 26 July the enemy attacked again and again. Counter-attacks against enemy penetrations by the Panzer Regiment and Panzer Reconnaissance Battalion were successful.

On the morning of 26 July, the enemy broke through defense lines of a battalion and at 0200 reached the battalion headquarters (see Figure 197). Reserves counterattacked at 0600 and retook the old positions. To stabilize the situation a new combat group attacked in the area where the Vop River flows into the Dnepr. XXXIX Panzer Corps informed us later in the morning that enemy mechanized convoys were traveling in an west–east direction along the autobahn Smolensk–Jarzevo. Corps ordered the Division to seize the Dnepr River crossing near Ssolovjeva. The VIII Fliegerkorps announced it would support us in defensive battles around Jarzevo.

At 1000 Panzer Reconnaissance Battalion 37 captured the railway bridge in front of Jarzevo. In the early morning Soviet planes controlled the airspace, but later, German fighters were able to predominate. Panzer Regiment 25 took Gorki in the late afternoon and then arrived in Ssolovjeva. Two infantry battalions successfully advanced to the Dnepr and destroyed the bridge. But the enemy attacked again and again, and critical situations often resulted.

On 27 July divisional defenses were organized as follows:

– Combat group Rifle Brigade 7 with Infantry Regiment 30 and Rifle Regiment 7 and three artillery battalions on the left flank.
– Combat group Rifle Regiment 6 with Rifle Regiment 6 and Panzer Reconnaissance Battalion 37 and two artillery battalions on the right flank.
– Panzer Regiment 25 in defensive positions around Borissovschtschina.

On 30 July at 0300 the Soviets attacked in strength against the positions of the 7th Panzer Division with infantry and heavy artillery support. Defense and counterattacks were successful and at 1600 the front was again intact. On the early morning of 31 July, the enemy attacked again with infantry and some tanks. From statements of prisoners we learned that it was the Soviet 64th Division. Heavy artillery fire occurred in all sectors of the defense lines. At 0230 the enemy broke through the lines of Infantry Regiment 30 which was under the command of Rifle Brigade 7. A counterattack by one company of our own tanks together with two companies of engineers was successful, and we regained our old lines at 0615. This combat group remained under brigade command. In the afternoon the enemy again attacked with infantry and more tanks. In late

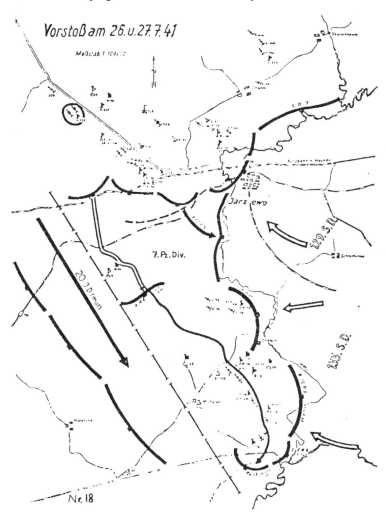

FIGURE 197
7TH PANZER DIVISION SITUATION, 26–27 JULY 1941

391

evening Rifle Regiment 7 received the order to attack against the enemy bridgehead near Jarzewo and the attack began at 0245 on 1 August. By 0730 the attack had secured the western part of the town, the railway station, and the autobahn bridge at Jarzevo.

Soon the division received the first orders to hand over the division sector to an infantry division. XXXIX Panzer Corps gave the information that on the night of 2 August one regiment of the 161st Infantry Division would arrive in trucks with two batteries of Assault Gun Detachment (*Sturmgeschutz-Abteilung*) 184, which would come under the command of 7th Panzer Division.

At 0225 all sectors of the defense line reported heavy enemy attacks, and at 0600 Soviet fighters attacked the sector of Rifle Regiment 6, when the bridge near Pischtschano was destroyed. After repeated counter-attacks, by 0830 the situation in all sectors of the division was restored. In the fighting four enemy tanks were destroyed. Infantry Regiment 364 finally arrived by rail in Gluchova and prepared to be handed over to 7th Panzer Division on the night of 3 August. Attacks by the enemy during the night were halted and 22 more enemy tanks were destroyed.

In the morning the commander of 7th Panzer Division reported to the Chief of Staff XXXIX Panzer Corps about the situation. After three long weeks of heavy defensive battles units were low in strength. In the afternoon the division again asked for Stuka support and in the evening another Soviet attack near Pischtschano achieved no success. At 1000 on 4 August XXXIX Panzer Corps reported to us that a large enemy motorized convoy with bridging material was moving from Dorogobusch to Ssolovjova escorted by Soviet fighters.

On that day it was generally quiet in the division area. At 2130 the Corps order for the relief of 7th Panzer Division by the infantry division was implemented. Subsequently, on the night of 5–6 August, the sector of 7th Panzer Division was taken over by the 161st and 8th Infantry Divisions. The rest area for the 7th Panzer Division after 7 August was along both sides of the autobahn near Kamenka, 20 kilometers southwest of Jarzevo and to the north of Smolensk.

3rd Panzer Division's Advance to Mogilev

COLONEL HORST ZOBEL (retired)

Continuation of 3rd Panzer Division's Attack

Before resuming, let me remind you that an advance group of 3rd Panzer had seized Bobruisk in a surprise attack early in the morning. A small bridgehead was created and one battalion of riflemen resisted strong enemy attacks. The engineers built two more bridges across the river.

Now there was a complete change of the general situation. Early in the morning of 1 July, the main portion of 3rd Panzer Division crossed the Berezina River on a pontoon bridge. On 3 July Rogatschev was taken by a strong combat group reinforced by amphibious tanks. The next day 3rd Panzer Division started the attack to seize crossings over the Dnepr River. While the attack of the 2nd Battalion of Rifle Regiment 3 failed, the 2nd Battalion of Rifle Regiment 294, supported by diving tanks, succeeded in crossing the river and building a bridgehead on the east bank.

To exploit the success of 4th Panzer Division, the XXIV Panzer Corps decided to regroup its panzer divisions. While the rifle regiments of 3rd Panzer Division remained in their positions on the Dnepr River, the 6th Panzer Regiment was subordinated to the 4th Panzer Division which was to lead the forthcoming attack beyond the Dnepr River. But this plan was suddenly aborted since the enemy started a surprise counterattack.

The Battle of Slobin

The 10th Motorized Infantry Division, which was advancing on the right flank of the 3rd Panzer Division, met strong enemy forces at Slobin on the night of 6 July, despite the fact that its own reconnaissance elements had reported the area clear only 1 hours before. The Soviet 117th Infantry Division had crossed the Dnepr River in the darkness. Their intention was obviously to cut off our forces from their communications routes near the Dubysna River in the rear, which was generally crossed by more than 250 vehicles a day. During the Soviet attack the 10th Motorized Infantry Division suffered serious losses. Some of the infantrymen were massacred and mutilated.

The 6th Panzer Regiment of 3rd Panzer Division was alerted and rather than joining 4th Panzer was subordinated to the 10th Infantry Division. It received the mission to attack the enemy forces and to secure our positions at Slobin. Since the 2nd Panzer Battalion had to advance through difficult ground, the 10th Division ordered the 1st Panzer Battalion not to wait for the 2nd Battalion but rather to attack immediately because the situation was very critical. This battalion met a strong enemy force in a closely confined and partly swampy area. The tanks had to engage the hostile tanks and antitank guns at very short distances. The battalion succeeded in destroying 19 enemy tanks, 21 guns, three antitank guns and two anti-aircraft guns, but 31 of its own soldiers were killed and 21 of its own tanks destroyed, i.e. half the total number of tanks which went into battle.

The 2nd Battalion arrived on the battlefield somewhat later. In an immediate attack the advance tank company destroyed, 23 enemy tanks, three antitank guns and one armored train. I mention the number of enemy weapons destroyed only to demonstrate the strength of the enemy and the danger of the situation caused by the strong surprise river crossing of an entire enemy division. By noon the enemy had been completely defeated, but we had suffered very heavy losses in the process.

Conclusions

– In a general sense, the advance up to the Dnepr River can be regarded as one of the openings of the Russian war. Despite having the advantage of good defensive ground (forests, swamps and rivers) the Russians could only fight delaying actions against the rapid advance of our troops. But when the Russian soldiers fought, they did so with bravery, letting our troops pass-by their positions, and fighting again against the follow-on troops.

– Along the Dnepr River the enemy had built up a strong defensive line, the so-called "Stalin Line".

– In the sector of the XXIV Panzer Corps along the Dnepr river, the Russians started a night attack in divisional strength with an operational aim for the first time. Thus, we had entered a phase of the war which was quite different from what had happened before.

– For our tankers, as well as for other experts and for higher headquarters, it was a great surprise when the Russian appeared with their new T34 tanks, which had stronger firepower and better armor protection than our tanks.

– The collision of the 10th Infantry Division with the Soviet 117th Infantry Division was a typical encounter battle. Obviously, the 10th Division had, at least, partly neglected to carry out continuous reconnaissance. Only the immediate and unconditional attack by our tanks, even across unfavorable ground, made it possible to restore the situation before the Russians could reinforce their troops and then cut the route.

– It was terrible to see how the Soviet soldiers had massacred our infantry people.

The following summary shows the tank strength of Panzer Regiment 6.

Summary of the Tanks Ready for Action in Panzer Regiment 6

On 22 June the regiment started action with the following number of tanks in its three battalions:

58 tanks Mark II (20mm machine-gun)
109 tanks Mark III (50mm short barrel gun)
32 tanks Mark IV (75mm short barrel gun)
Total – 199 tanks

During the period from 22 June to 9 July the following tanks were totally lost:

13 tanks Mark II
24 tanks Mark III
8 tanks Mark IV
Total – 45 tanks

On 9 July the following tanks were sent to workshops for repair:

2 tanks Mark II
7 tanks Mark III
Total – 9 tanks

On 9 July the following tanks were ready for action in the regiment:

43 tanks Mark II
78 tanks Mark III
24 tanks Mark IV
Total – 145 tanks

*3rd Panzer Division in the
Breakthrough of the Stalin Line*

Now I will describe 3rd Panzer Division's actions in breaking through the Stalin Line. The XXIV Panzer Corps now had the mission to cross the Dnepr River by any means. The 3rd Panzer Division had left its positions at Rogatschev and was now in a lager south of Mogilev. While the 4th Panzer Division received the mission to attack Staryi–Bychov, the 3rd Panzer Division had the double mission of securing the flank of the corps by taking the town of Mogilev in a quick attack and securing a crossing of the Dnepr River for tanks.

Soviet forces at Mogilev were very strong, brave and well supplied. The

3rd Panzer Division started the attack against Mogilev with two combat groups. The right group proceeded for some distance, but then the attack had to be stopped because of very strong enemy resistance. The left group immediately ran into a disaster. The infantry on motorcycles, who were to accompany the tanks, stuck in deep sand and could not reach the line of departure on time. The commander of the tank company started the attack without being supported by infantry. The area of attack, however, was the training ground of the Mogilev garrison, in which mines had been laid and trenches dug. The tanks ran into a minefield, and at the same time artillery and antitank guns opened heavy fire on them. Consequently the attack failed. The company commander of 5th Panzer Company was killed and 11 out of 13 tanks were lost. Leading the advance platoon, I remember quite well that when we encountered mines we were immediately engaged by antitank guns. We had to dismount and stay behind the tanks all day until we could be evacuated.

By order of the division this attack on Mogilev was stopped. There is no doubt that this attack on Mogilev was based on a risky plan. The enemy was much stronger than had been expected. Mogilev had already been attacked before by an infantry division and that attack had been repelled. That meant that the enemy had been forewarned and had improved his defensive positions. Much later the town was taken by a complete infantry corps after several days' fighting. The existence of Mogilev in our rear had an adverse impact on subsequent operations.

The 4th Panzer Division, however, had succeeded in crossing the Dnepr River and had formed a bridgehead. Somewhat later the division built a pontoon bridge over the river. The 3rd Panzer Division then received the mission to follow the 4th Panzer Division.

It might be of some interest to know that before the attack on the Dnepr River, a dispute arose between Field Marshal von Kluge and General Guderian about the continuation of the operations. Field Marshal von Kluge intended to wait for the infantry before attacking the Soviet defensive positions at the river. On the other hand, General Guderian wanted to continue the attack immediately. Finally, Field Marshal von Kluge agreed with General Guderian's plan after the latter had argued that the preparations for the attack had already gone so far that they could not be halted. The success of the attack of the 4th Panzer Division proved that the plan of General Guderian was correct.

In 12 days our panzer corps had traversed about 600 kilometers between the Bug and Dnepr Rivers (almost 50 kilometers a day). Apart from the normal problems of combat, special questions arose which our soldiers had to address while continuously fighting, marching, and resupplying. These might be of interest.

Sometimes we fought continuously in tanks for 24 hours. This was usually while we were on the march or detailed to a security mission. That does not mean continuous 24 hour fighting. Of course, there were always places where the crew could rest or nap. They slept either in the tank or on the rear of the tank, which was pretty warm from the engine. Sometimes they dug holes underneath the tank which provided them secure rest uninterrupted by night bombers often flying over.

The first man of the crew who required a rest during a stop was the driver. We had to care about him and he was seldom used on a security or outpost mission. Therefore the tank commander, regardless of rank (unless company or battalion commander) had to share in those tasks.

Let me also say something about medical treatment in battle. Our doctors followed the attack in positions near the battalion commander. The doctor had a tank with a red cross on it. I am sorry to say this is no longer done in our army, which we should rethink.

Regarding command and control, a topic others will address, let me add that, against attacking tanks, the enemy is always the first to open fire. He fires the first shot and the crew must react. This is an important factor of crew drilling.

4th Panzer Division's Crossing of the Berezina River

BRIGADIER GENERAL R. KOCH-ERPACH (retired)

Introduced by Colonel Adair

General Koch-Erpach finished the war as first staff officer of Panzer Lehr Division. After the war he joined the Bundeswehr and finished as Defense Attaché in Paris.

First, let me summarize 4th Panzer's activities up to the Berezina River. My briefing covers the activities of the 1st Company, Rifle Regiment 12 (S.R.12) during the period from 22 June 1941 until 3 August 1941. On that day the 4th Panzer Division and other forces occupied the important crossroad at Rosslavl, some 400 kilometers west of Moscow and some 650 kilometers east of Brest Litovsk, where we had crossed the Bug River.

Rifle Regiment (*Schutzenregiment* 12-S.R.12) was one of two motorized infantry regiments which belonged to 4th Panzer Division. The division was at that time under the command of the XXIV Panzer Corps, part of Panzer Group 2 led by General Heinz Guderian. Figure 198 shows the organization and main equipment of 4th Panzer Division and the 1st Company, S.R.12 at the beginning of its operations in Russia. All panzer divisions were similar in equipment, but different in task organization.

4th Panzer Division was much weaker than 3rd Panzer Division and my company with its 16 APCs was the only armored rifle company in the whole division. During the coming operations it was usually assigned to Panzer Regiment 35 or stayed with its own regiment (S.R.12). Shortly before 22 June 1941 the company received, in addition to its normal equipment, three antitank guns (3.7cm) which were mounted on the APCs of the three platoon commanders. This made the vehicles somewhat nose-heavy but it was a very welcome addition to our fire power. With the half-track and light armored APCs the company was better off than the other companies of the regiment, especially in view of the bad road conditions. This resulted in a lower rate of losses, even though the company had more combat days than the other companies.

The company had already been employed during the campaign in Poland (at that time it had not yet been equipped with APCs) and had

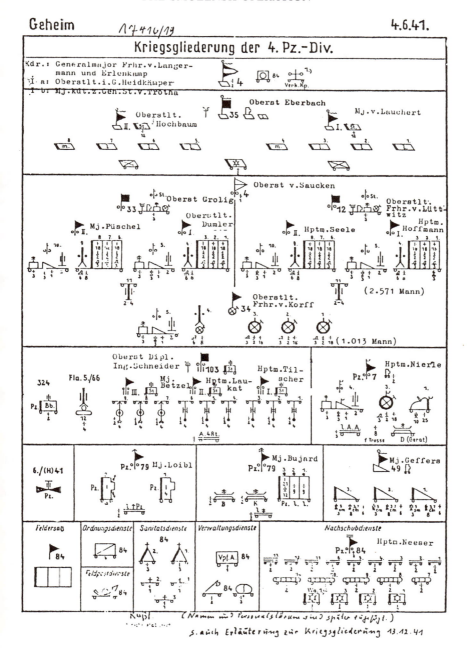

FIGURE 198
4TH PANZER DIVISION ORGANIZATION, 4 JUNE 1941

taken part with distinction in the battle in France. So the men of the company were experienced soldiers, especially the NCOs. Fifty per cent of them came from the Austrian *Bundesheer* and their training and experience were excellent. During the early months of 1941 4th Panzer Division remained in the area of Bordeaux, where all units had to undergo rather tough training involving, in part, long foot marches for days with full equipment, etc. This turned out to be very fruitful for us given the conditions we would encounter in Russia. But at this time none of us let our imagination wander so far east.

I had taken over command of this unit in early 1941 after the French campaign. As a great help I had an excellent first lieutenant and a remarkable and competent sergeant major. All APCs were fully manned and the company was a compact unit, well equipped and well trained. We were all convinced that we could carry out any reasonable mission successfully.

As far as this mission was concerned, in the summer of 1941, we did not fully realize the kind of warfare we would have to cope with and the roughness and vastness of the country we were to attack. I remember General Guderian warning us of a different mission we would presumably face after a major exercise on the Warthelager training area in May or June 1941. But in view of the rather poor performance of the Russian Army in Finland and without any knowledge of the Soviet equipment (especially tanks, antitank weapons and artillery, which were superior to ours) we did not doubt that we could break any resistance. On the other hand we were fully aware that we would meet a tough fighting soldier who would defend stubbornly when we crossed the Bug River.

On 22 June 1941 we crossed the river south of Brest–Litovsk. My company was relatively late, since we had to wait with the APCs until the engineers had built the bridge. Evidently the German attack in this sector was a tactical surprise as enemy resistance was rather weak in the beginning. So on this day, just as on the two or three following days, the main obstacle to rapid forward movement were the sandy roads, heat, dust and swampy ground, all of which especially hindered the wheeled vehicles. One thing we noticed with surprise was that all the bridges, even those across small streams, had evidently been reinforced not long before.

Figure 199 shows the route of our advance up to Roslavl. Major natural obstacles were the rivers Berezina, Dnepr and Szosch. On our right flank were the Pripet swamps, which we hoped would give us some protection. I will not explain our activities day by day along the road to Roslavl, but rather I will give you some highlights.

The whole distance was divided in four major periods. The first period included the battle between the Bug River and the Berezina River. The second encompassed the crossing of the Dnepr River and the breakthrough of the so-called Stalin Line. The third included the battle around Propoisk, and the fourth involved the seizure of Roslavl.

During the first period the main event was the capture on 27 June of the town and airfield of Baranovice in the face of heavy Soviet resistance. In the continuous hand-to-hand fighting for the town we faced soldiers on the Soviet side who would rather blow themselves up with a hand grenade than surrender. This period ended with the successful raid against the bridges across the Berezina River at Swislotsch. There were three bridges: one railway bridge, a wooden bridge and a wooden footbridge. Marching on the night of 29 June through a rather dense mist we managed to overrun the guards, take the bridges and build a small bridgehead on the eastern side of the river. In the morning an armored train approached from the eastern side of the bridge. We (the reinforced battalion including my company) soon had to ask for further reinforcements and air support. Together with the newly arrived tanks and the air force (Stuka) support we managed to destroy the armored trains and throw back the enemy infantry pouring out in large numbers from the transport train. The fighting had fluctuated very much and we had to leave some of our wounded men in the hands of the Russians. After the battle we found them killed and cruelly mutilated. This was a shocking experience for our men. The enemy air force had attacked several times but without great effect. On our continued advance, blown-up or burnt bridges would more effectively slow our movements.

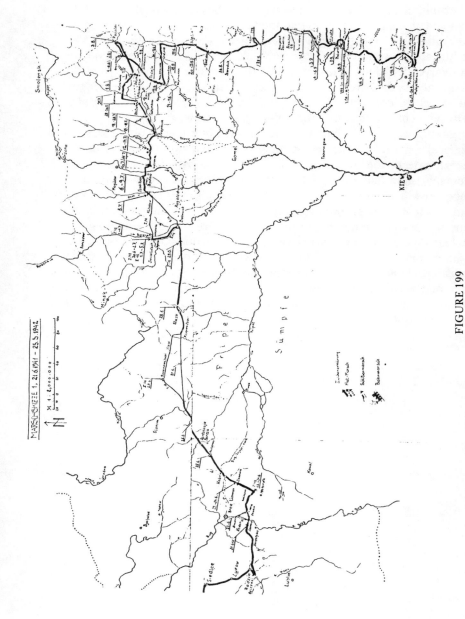

FIGURE 199
4TH PANZER DIVISION ADVANCE TO ROSLAVL, 21 JUNE– 3 AUGUST 1941

4th Panzer Division's Crossing of the Dnepr River and the Advance to Roslavl

BRIGADIER GENERAL R. KOCH-ERPACH (retired)

After we had crossed the Berezina River in a swift action we attacked to the east to reach the Dnepr River. The most important event during the second period was the crossing of the Dnepr River. This could not be accomplished by a surprise attack as had been carried out on the Berezina. It required regular artillery deployment and full air support. While looking for a suitable crossing site we were, fortunately in this case, misled by our very poor maps. Later, when capturing an enemy headquarters we found very good maps. So we attacked instead in a sector where the enemy had not yet dug out too many bunkers or other fortifications. Ferrying over in the first wave in rubber boats, the company drifted against a steep embankment on the enemy side where we landed out of sight in the dead space and could not be reached by their infantry weapons. So we reached our objective without loss. The terrain however, was so swampy that the division had to find another site on which to build a bridge.

If enemy resistance up to that time had been stiff in places but not so well organized, in the area south of Mogilev, we now had to defend against well-led counterattacks in division strength. Between 10 and 14 July several times we were forced to change over to a defense with open flanks and in all directions.

The third period consisted of a continuous forward advance and sudden defensive actions along the so-called "Rollbahn", when we asked ourselves from time to time who was encircling whom? In the days up to 31 July the company was again assigned to Panzer Regiment 35. The tasks mostly involved mopping-up enemy antitank positions in woodland and small villages with which the enemy tried to stop our advance. In those instances, the company had to disembark and fight on foot. Later, when embarked again, we had to follow the tanks. We learned how to protect ourselves against Molotov cocktails and mines, which the Russians laid very cunningly. But I cannot remember that my company ran into T34 tanks before we had reached Roslavl.

For the attack against Roslavl, which was the most important activity during the fourth period, the company returned to Rifle Regiment 12. There we had two days for rehabilitation and repair of our vehicles. Fifty per cent of the APCs required thorough overhauling. It was a miracle that the wheeled vehicles had continued operating up to that time.

So we prepared for the attack on Roslavl, which took place on 3 July. With support from our heavy machine guns and mortars, my company managed to overrun some enemy anti-aircraft positions. Heavy hand-to-hand fighting developed and for the first time we had to fight against women with weapons, a rather shocking experience for our soldiers. The occupation of Roslavl finished with the encirclement of four Soviet divisions.

The performance of the soldiers of the company in these six weeks was outstanding. Beside the riflemen the drivers repaired their vehicles while their comrades were taking short naps. The sergeant major and his men, truckdriver, mechanics, medical personnel, cooks, were equally ready. There was a strong will, with all the exhausting days behind us, to carry on, so that we would still reach Moscow in 1941. There was also still unbroken confidence in higher headquarters' decisions.

The division as a whole and especially the fighting units had suffered heavy losses. The equipment, which had proved efficient in the previous campaigns, was not robust enough for battle under the conditions prevailing in Russia. Russian equipment seemed to be more robust and less sensitive. Therefore, whoever got hold of a Russian tommy-gun kept it. From time to time logistical problems (gasoline, spare parts, ammunition) would limit our advance.

The simple Russian soldier was as tough as we had expected him to be. His ability to dig in and to camouflage was better than in our units. In difficult situations he defended himself stubbornly. We found his flexibility limited especially when he was left without clear orders. During our advance we took a lot of prisoners. We sent them back, but had not too much control over whether they arrived at the collecting point. (You could not detach a full APC with six men to guard three or four prisoners.)

This certainly contributed very much to the amazingly quick establishment of partisan units. We were embarrassed later to find official rules and regulations for the organization of partisan units and partisan warfare, a kind of warfare we had not been prepared for, but which we could have expected after a study of Russian history.

Overview, Phase 2: 20 July–7 August 1941

DR JACOB KIPP

The Soviets see 20 July as the beginning of the second phase of the battle of Smolensk. To understand those events we need to step back just slightly and mention a Soviet mobile detachment from the 46th Rifle Division involved in the fighting around Demidov, north of Smolensk. That particular detachment, made up of light BT tanks, some antitank guns, one company of sappers, and an infantry reconnaissance battalion of the division was involved in the fighting around Demidov. In a night attack on 14 July it was able to reach the village itself and in the process captured German staff documents. These were passed to General Lukin of 16th Army and then to the STAVKA in Moscow. These documents provided the Soviets with enough information to develop a broad picture of the battle around Smolensk, and particularly the situation on the northern flank where 7th Panzer Division was involved.

This situation, combined with the stabilization in the south, brought to a head the Soviet perception within STAVKA and supported by Stalin, that the time was right for a concerted counterattack. From the Soviet perspective, the vehicle for this was the five operational groups that had been created for the purpose (see Figure 200). The Soviets developed an operational plan for these groups.

Central to the Soviet conception of the next phase of this battle and to their plan for a counteroffensive was the perception that General Lukin's 16th Army could fight encircled and survive. Before the war Soviet General Staff writings had addressed the problems of battle in encirclement; not just of encirclement and how to encircle someone, but rather what to do with forces when they are encircled. Timoshenko was fairly confident that Lukin could carry out his assigned task. As he told Rokossovsky when he was being sent up to the front to head an operational group, "Lukin is in a sack, but he has no intention of getting out of it". That was not quite true, but there was a good deal of dependence in the Soviet operational concept on the stability of that pocket. The Soviets believed that while the pocket moved east it could maintain its combat integrity.

Figure 201 shows the situation on 20 July in greater detail and we can see the Soviet operational groups in the process of formation. The

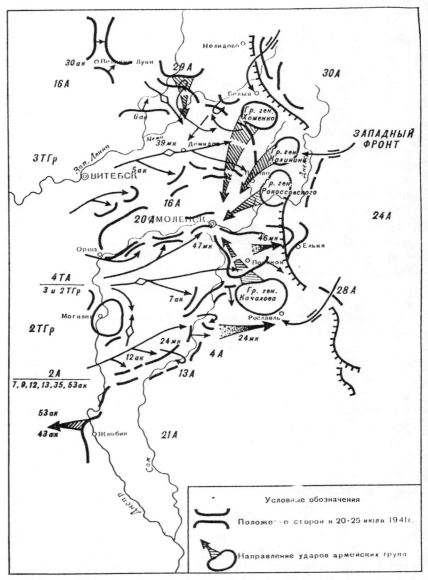

Схема 1. Обстановка на Западном стратегическом направлении к 20—25 июля
и формы оперативного прорыва и первом наступлении в районе Смоленска

FIGURE 200

SITUATION, 2300, 20 JULY 1941, AND SOVIET OPERATIONAL GROUPS
FOR THE SMOLENSK COUNTERATTACK

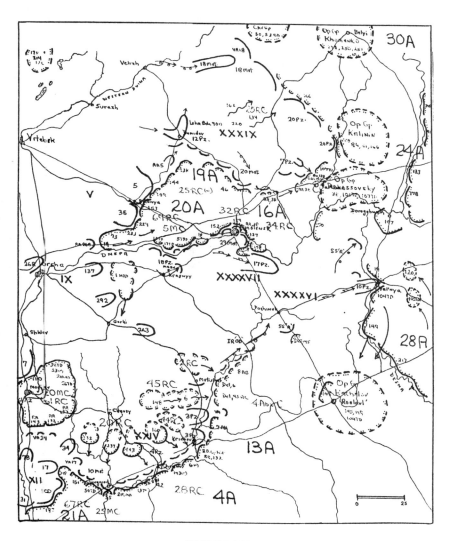

FIGURE 201
SITUATION, 2300, 20 JULY 1941

most important from our perspective were the Cavalry Group in the north composed of two divisions; Khomenko's Group forming at Belyi, which the Germans had a good idea of thanks to signals intelligence; the Kalinin Group, north of Iartsevo; Rokossovsky's group battling in front of Iartsevo; the pocket itself; and the gaps east of Smolensk. This was extremely difficult terrain on both sides of the Dnepr River. It was marshy, boggy, and bisected by numerous small streams. Maneuver was difficult especially between Iartsevo and the Dnepr crossing at Solov'ev.

In the south the Soviet situation was stabilizing with Soviet units attempting to get behind the Sozh River. Most important from the perspective of the developing Soviet operational concept was the appearance of Operational Group Kachalov around Roslavl. Note the problems the Germans had regarding units to cover the area between the spearhead of 10th Panzer Division, which had reached Elnia, and the fighting east of Krichev.

Let us not forget the situation in the north with 19th Panzer Division beyond the map to the north. It was not now in a position to contribute in any way to the developing situation in the eastern end of the Smolensk bulge in support of the remainder of 3rd Panzer Group. That division would be pulled pack and arrive in time to deal with the counterattack. It was not available, however, at this stage, when the Soviets could possibly have been preempted. In the south, near Mogilev, German infantry divisions were beginning to appear and Soviet units continued to flow out of the pocket and back toward the Sozh. Also substantial instability still existed along the axis between Mogilev and Rogachev.

STAVKA was still developing its plan when Timoshenko went to Stalin. Stalin said that up to this time he had been feeding Timoshenko bits and pieces of forces. Now Stalin declared "We will form fists": assemble divisions together and try to regain the initiative. The fists, as they developed, and the ensuing counterattacks essentially involved a three-pronged drive, would, they hoped, be simultaneous (see Figure 202). In the north Group Khomenko was to strike south out of Belyi towards Smolensk, supported on its left by Group Kalinin, the 91st Division of which was already in position across the Vop River. Rokossovsky's Group was to launch a fixing attack near Iartsevo.

At this stage Rokossovsky was hardly in a position to do anything. In his memoirs he described this period as the most difficult fighting he had ever experienced. His staff was literally on wheels. Half his staff officers were dead after six days of fighting and he was in a horrendous situation. At that juncture STAVKA released to him the staff from 7th Mechanized Corps. For all intents and purposes Rokossovsky set about creating a command team there which would, in fact, last him for a very long time. Rokossovsky merged in this period as a highly charismatic and effective commander with a great deal of loyalty from his staff and personnel. General Kazakov, commander of his artillery made that clear. We talked about *Aufstragtaktik* and Rokossovsky's style was much the same. He expected his junior officers to take the initiative with the general concept of operations as they developed. Indeed, he suggested that without a formal staff it was the only way they could function.

The character of this man mattered here, for while units were coming through the pipeline from Viaz'ma, he was also able to rally formations coming out and gathered substantially more combat power than one would expect. Rokossovsky's task, however, was to do nothing more than pin down German forces.

The instructions to Lukin's 16th Army were to stabilize the situation around Smolensk and then move back. On the other side, to the south, Kachalov's Group was to strike northward along the Roslavl–Smolensk road and cut off the German formations to the east. It was essentially an attempt to turn a German envelopment into a Soviet double envelopment. Furthermore, south of Rogachev the Soviets created a Cavalry Group which was to strike out in the German rear toward Bobruisk to break up German logistics. The cavalry group consisted of cavalry divisions. Obviously the terrain adjacent to the Pripiat Marshes provided advantages for use of such a force.

Thus, as you can see, the situation was one of ongoing development. What is noteworthy to us is what German intelligence picked up on 22 July (see Figure 203). As you can see the gap still existed. SS Das Reich still had not reached the north, but 7th Panzer Division had taken Iartsevo after very heavy fighting, but the pocket still had a hole in it. The pressure of 20th and 29th Motorized Divisions created a danger for the Soviets of closing the pocket. The Soviets would attempt by counterattacks to retake the southern portion of the city and relieve that pressure.

The situation on 22 July is shown by Figure 204. The supposedly simultaneous Soviet attack did not develop that way at all. Partly, this was because of German air attacks and also because of staff breakdown. The forces did not come onto line together to provide simultaneity and the attacks occurred independently. At Roslavl, Group Kachalov had already attacked while Khomenko was poised to attack and Group Kalinin was not yet ready to strike.

The most important development on 23 July from the Soviet perspective was Kachalov's advance along the Roslavl road and his attempt to envelop German Infantry Regiment Grossdeutschland which was not receiving support from 18th Panzer Division (see Figure 205). The situation had German infantry divisions now moving up from the rear and 17th Panzer attempting to refit. The outcome would depend largely on who could get forces to the area more rapidly. The dilemma for Group

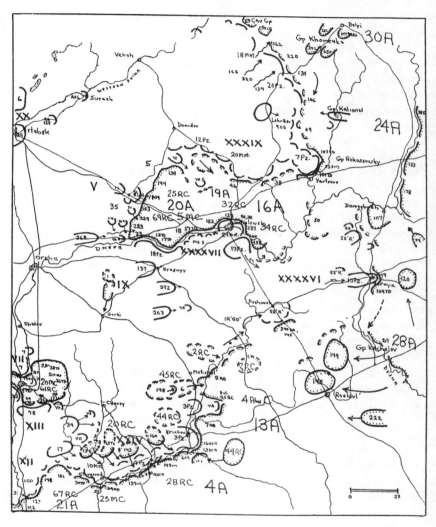

FIGURE 202
SITUATION, 2300, 21 JULY 1941

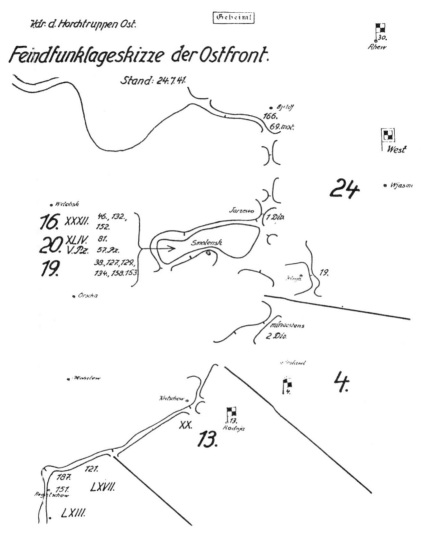

FIGURE 203
GERMAN INTELLIGENCE MAP, 24 JULY 1941

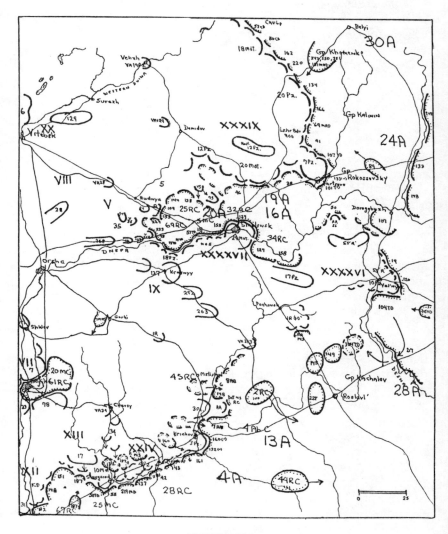

FIGURE 204
SITUATION, 2300, 22 JULY 1941

Kachalov was that he had no reserves available to him. Note also 19th Panzer Division attempting to reach the Smolensk area.

While Kachalov attacked, Khomenko joined battle from the north. German intelligence kept up with event fairly well and also noted the beginning of Group Kalinin's attack. The Germans detected movement of Soviet forces out of the Smolensk area and the continued painful attacks of Rokossovsky near Iartsevo.

By 24 July it again looked as if the Soviet pocket west of Smolensk was threatened with encirclement and cut off, as the Soviet forces of Groups Khomenko and Kalinin continued their pressure on German defenses (see Figure 206). That day the Germans halted Group Khomenko's attack and drove back Group Kalinin to bridgeheads on the Vop River. Rokossovsky's force maintained stability around Iartsevo and reserves were gathering to his rear. Das Reich reinforced German positions at Elnia elements of 17th Panzer Division were beginning to regroup, and 29th Motorized Division was being relieved at Smolensk by the 137th Infantry Division.

Kachalov's attempted envelopments continued to develop but ominously, German infantry divisions were arriving forward. They would make a major difference in the battle by threatening Kachalov. Further south Mogilev remained isolated and the front along the Sozh River continued to stabilize.

On 25 July the Germans continued regrouping south of Smolensk, while on the Soviet side Lukin fed forces out of the pocket and Rokossovsky strove to hold the narrow corridor open (see Figure 207). Additional Soviet divisions reinforced Rokossovsky while others formed a new defensive line west of Viaz'ma. A grave situation from a Soviet perspective developed in the Roslavl sector where Kachalov had done about as much as his force could do without additional reserves. German units were now concentrating on Kachalov's left flank. The Soviets mounted a breakout from Mogilev, where some Soviet forces went partisan initially, while other units came out intact but in small groups.

Also appearing on the map is the STAVKA decision to split the Western Front and create the Central Front under General Kuznetsov. The Soviets also reorganized their army structure. 21st Army remained defending north of Rogachev but 13th Army absorbed the remnants of 4th Army plus 4th Airborne Corps. Zhukov, Chief of the General Staff in this period, said this was clearly the weakest Soviet *front*, it was an invitation for a German attack against it, and something had to be done to reinforce it. In fact, Zhukov's removal as chief of staff concerned the issue of the Central Front. To get assets to deal with this problem, Zhukov proposed pulling forces back beyond the Dniepr and giving up Kiev. Zhukov made an official report to that effect, and Stalin called him up, with Mekhlis, Chief

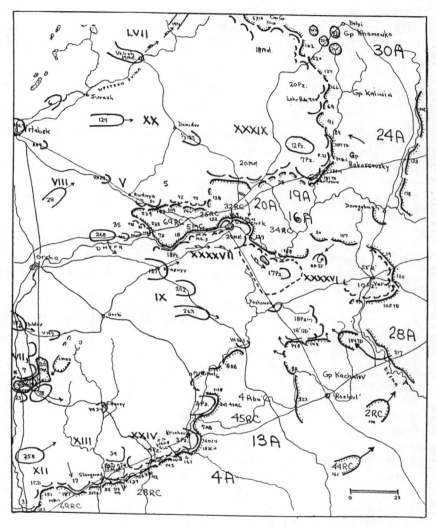

FIGURE 205
SITUATION, 2300, 23 JULY 1941

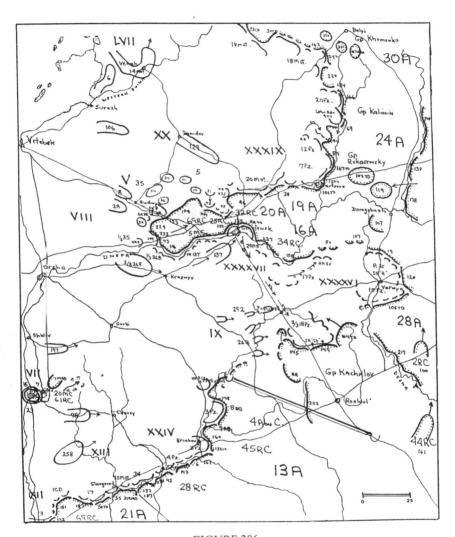

FIGURE 206
SITUATION, 2300, 24 JULY 1941

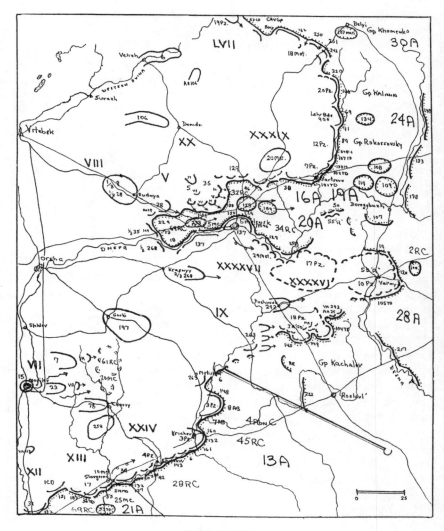

FIGURE 207
SITUATION, 2300, 25 JULY 1941

of the Main Political Administration, also present at the meeting. In the first edition of Zhukov's memoirs he said he felt inhibited at this meeting. The new edition of his memoirs relate a different story. First, Zhukov did not get the meeting he had asked for. Instead he was summoned, and a fourth member of the group was present, Lavrenti Beria. The presence of Beria at such a meeting did not mean it was a Georgian social group. As head of the secret police, this was a confrontation. And Stalin was rude. He used the expression "What is this *chepukha* [nonsense] about giving up Kiev. What do you know about it." Mekhlis chimed in that you could not give up Kiev because of the Ukrainians. Zhukov said they had to give it up to strengthen the Central Front and, more importantly, they had to mount a counteroffensive to seize back Elnia, which Zhukov viewed as the most appropriate axis for an attack on Moscow. Zhukov realized that while the immediate vulnerability of Soviet forces was in the south vis-à-vis Central Front, the likely axis of a German attack, the center of gravity, was on the Moscow axis. Therefore, he was willing to give up territory and shorten his line in the south at Kiev in order to create reserves to strengthen the southern wing and stabilize forces for the defense of Moscow.

Zhukov was relieved as Chief of the General Staff. While a great deal of historiography on the western side hinges on the crisis between Hitler and his generals, one should not ignore the fact that a crisis was also on the other side. The question was which side could manage its way through it. In the case of the Soviets, quite clearly the removal of Zhukov was on the one hand a reassertion of Stalin's authority, but on the other hand the replacement of Zhukov was a voice coming directly out of the Soviet General Staff. Shaposhnikov was brought in to become its head. This is important because one of the persistent complaints, not only by Stalin, but by the General Staff team in STAVKA, was that Zhukov really did not have the details of staff work down at this stage. There were too many detachments, too many *ad hoc* decisions, and too many things slipping through fingers. Shaposhnikov was considered a man with whom junior general staff officers like Shtemenko, Vasilevsky and Vatutin could work and cooperate. The change here was not someone brought in from the outside but rather someone inside the General Staff, who everyone understood had a very special relationship with Stalin.

Let us now return to the combat situation. By late on 26 July 19th Panzer Division had returned from the north and the situation there had stabilized (see Figure 208). Group Khomenko, with few reserves available, could make only limited progress. The weight of Soviet forces shifted south in support of Rokossovsky and there was another crisis as German 20th Motorized Division and SS Das Reich Panzer Division again threatened to cut off the Smolensk pocket.

Soviet units streamed out of the Smolensk pocket as best they could while further south Kachalov made one last lunge for Smolensk. In the Krichev sector German motorized forces were pulling out of line and would be followed by panzer units, who could in the future threaten Central Front's thinly held lines with penetration and envelopment.

On 27 July in the south 4th Panzer began regrouping while 3rd Panzer created bridgeheads east of the Sozh River from which future attacks could be launched (see Figure 209). German infantry continued to flow forward to free the mobile units. Threats to the narrow Soviet corridor east of Smolensk grew as the pocket was practically closed while German troops west of Smolensk continued to compress the Soviet pocket. That pressure would continue in the following days and attempts at relief by Groups Khomenko and Kalinin were easily repulsed. Throughout the period German forces continued to regroup south of Smolensk as the infantry arrived forward. Again these moves can be followed on Fourth Panzer Army's intelligence map which reflects reality well (see Figure 210).

By this stage the German High Command, based on information available to it concerning the condition of the armored forces, now concluded that a pause was necessary. The pause was dictated by crisis in matériel and manpower, and it would last ten days. The mobile divisions pulled out of line were a part of that process. Meanwhile heavy fighting took place within and adjacent to the Smolensk pocket (see Figure 211). In the south German regrouping continued as the 197th Infantry Division's lead elements engaged Kachalov's left flank. Notice 4th Airborne Corps, the German objective. This unit, or in reality remnants of the corps, had been in continuous contact with the Germans since Minsk. After heavy fighting along the Berezina River, they were brought back to refit and now held the critical hinge of Central Front's 13th Army and Western Front. It was an extremely vulnerable position, as Zhukov had anticipated.

By 30 July the pocket had been virtually closed off although it would periodically reopen in the future (see Figure 212). Soviet units inside the pocket regrouped to force the corridor open. The divisions in the pocket were bare remnants of their former selves and they number hundreds of men. They had not received replacements, food, fuel, or ammunition since 15 July and had been involved in intensive fighting. Their combat power was limited. Nonetheless, Lukin pulled units out of line to attack back toward Iartsevo. In the south XXIV Panzer corps was poised to renew the attack on Group Kachalov. The correlation of forces in this region was particularly bad for the Soviets who had both flanks weakly held. German armor was about to strike at the weakest point along that front.

Guderian's memoirs provide a German representation of the development of this new attack (see Figure 213). Second Army and 2nd Panzer Group were to launch the attack, spearheaded by 3rd Panzer Division

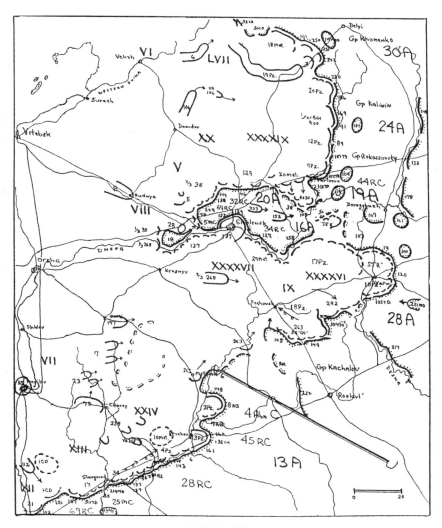

FIGURE 208
SITUATION 2300, 26 JULY 1941

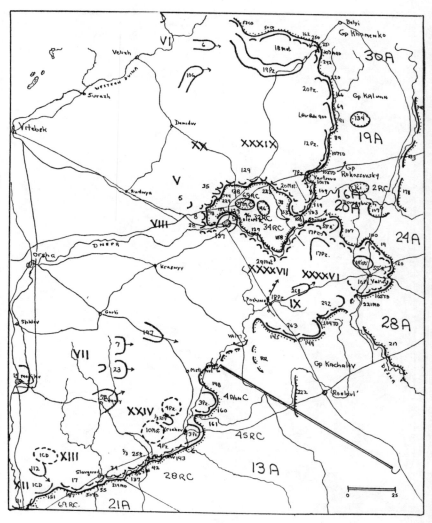

FIGURE 209
SITUATION, 2300, 27 JULY 1941

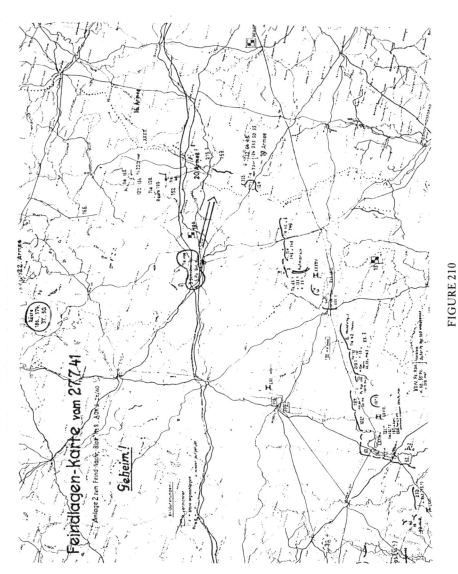

FIGURE 210

FOURTH PANZER ARMY INTELLIGENCE MAP, 27 JULY 1941

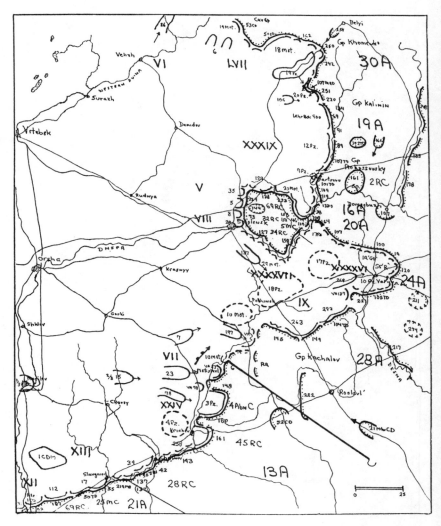

FIGURE 211
SITUATION, 2300, 29 JULY 1941

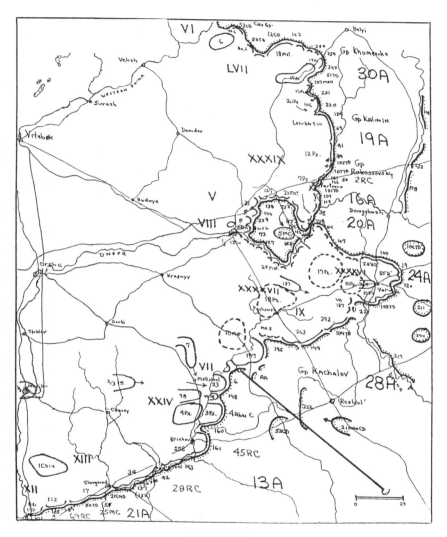

FIGURE 212
SITUATION, 2300, 30 JULY 1941

followed by 4th Panzer Division. The attack met virtually no opposition in its initial stages. German forces soon assembled for an attack from the north as well. The map of 31 July shows the initial German progress (see Figure 214). As the attack developed over the next several days the entire Soviet position was rolled up towards Roslavl. Notice also the small corridor east of Smolensk, which the Soviets were able to pry open near Solov'ev crossing in very difficult fighting. Meanwhile heavy attacks and counterattacks occurred to the north, only in local sectors, and Soviet forces began concentrating in the Elnia area.

By 1 August 4th Airborne Corps had been shattered and Group Kachalov's left flank was crumbling (see Figure 215). Soon Kachalov shifted forces from his right to his left flank to try to restore the situation. At the same time 28th Rifle Corps shifted its reserves to the east to assist the beleaguered Kachalov. The German intelligence assessment of 1 August clearly revealed the situation (see Figure 216). Air intelligence picked up Soviet movements including rail movements from Viaz'ma. The picture in the north, however, was less clear. Moreover the Germans had not picked up Soviet strategic reserves forming in the Viaz'ma area.

On 2 August the Soviets continued evacuating forces through the Solov'ev corridor while the front north and south of Iartsevo stabilized. German panzer and motorized units continued to reassemble in the rear while infantry replaced them. The Elnia salient became a much harder nut to crack than Zhukov had originally thought. Kachalov's forces were nearing the point of crisis. His left flank was destroyed and now German infantry struck his right flank, threatening to encircle his group at Roslavl. Other Soviet units attempted in vain to retake the Krichev–Roslavl road which was a critical reinforcement artery of 13th Army. Now all reinforcements had to come in from the south, from Gomel.

The map of 3 August shows the final collapse of the Smolensk pocket (see Figure 217). Soviet units streamed eastward in chaotic heavy fighting and with heavy losses. Divisions were hardly recognizable but most of the forces did get out. At Roslavl the Soviets faced disaster as Kachalov's forces collapsed and were encircled. Roslavl was by now in German hands. In terms of Soviet vulnerability, the battle of Roslavl clearly made it evident that the Soviets were extraordinarily vulnerable along that axis. What had concerned Zhukov was now also clearly evident to the German command. The situation was so bad for the Soviets that, as that situation developed Eremenko was pulled out of the Western Front and told to organize a new *front* at Briansk to try to support Central Front in its battle. He was given that task because according to Soviet propaganda he was the man who had stopped Guderian. Vasilesky suggested that Eremenko had read too much of his own propaganda and had too high an assessment of his own capabilities with the forces available.

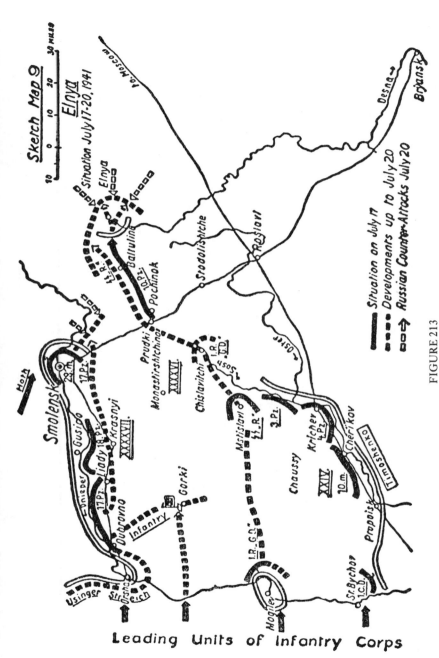

FIGURE 213

GUDERIAN MAP OF GERMAN ATTACKS, JULY 1941

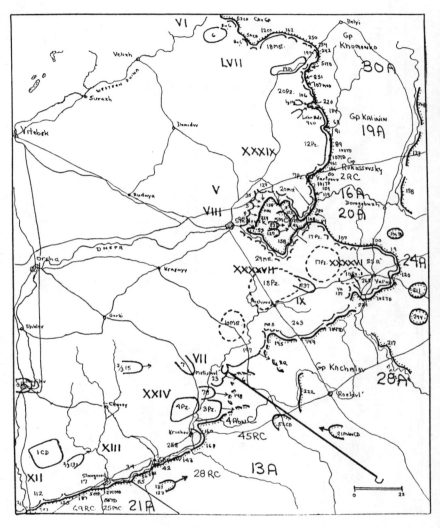

FIGURE 214
SITUATION, 2300, 31 JULY 1941

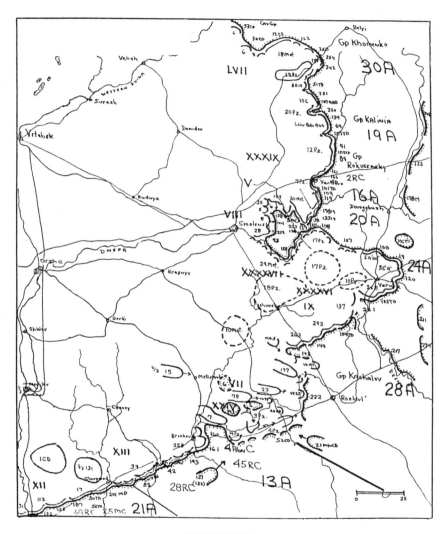

FIGURE 215
SITUATION, 2300, 1 AUGUST 1941

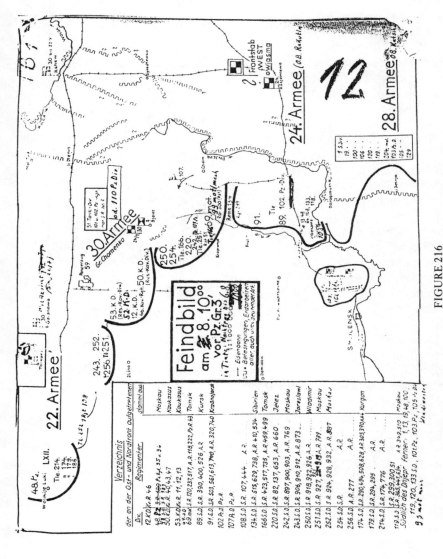

FIGURE 216

GERMAN INTELLIGENCE ASSESSMENT, 1 AUGUST 1941

What we can see evolving in this situation is a stabilization. The German mechanized units had been pulled out of the line not by whim but rather by necessity. There had to be a pause to refit those units. At the end of the ten day pause there were fundamental questions to be answered. One can argue forever about the nature of the answer to those questions.

Figure 218 is a chart from Halder's diary similar to the one mentioned earlier, which shows the German losses. They may not have been large but they were a far cry from those in the first ten days of war. Casualties were mounting with 150,000 wounded at this stage of the campaign, compared with 44,000 after the first ten days. What was probably more serious was the beginning of a crisis on manpower losses. Manpower problems would begin to affect how subsequent campaigns.

Halder put this rough correlation of forces into his diary on 1 August. Much of it was favorable but look at the figure for GHQ reserves – 0:28. That entered into calculations made at the higher levels. This table gives you a picture from the other side of the hill (see Figure 219). It shows Soviet formations raised from 22 June to 1 December 1941. The combat power of those formations may have been minimal, for some were *opolchenie* (militia) with *butylki* (bottles) of gasoline and old rifles, and this may not have looked like great combat power. The Soviet state however, has a remarkable ability to raise and sustain forces. The picture was a finely honed finite instrument, and the German Army was fighting in an environment which was testing that instrument in ways never envisaged. Here was a duel between a man with a fine rapier, great fencing skills and wonderful talent, and a large fellow with a large meat axe. Granted the fencer would strike telling blows, but ultimately that man with the meat axe was going to impose his war, a *voina unichtozheniia* [war of annihilation], on his enemy. It will test that fine instrument. Partly this is a function of the fact that in the Soviet way of war, despite all the mechanization, two things went hand in hand. One designed one's forces as far as one could for initial operations involving mechanized forces to gain back the initiative, but one also prudently planned for a long war in which those resources would finally make themselves felt.

In 1929 when Triandafillov wrote about the nature of contemporary armies he divided Europe into two realms: Western Europe, where the mechanized operations were not only possible but likely; and Eastern Europe, where the nature of terrain, society, and levels of technology (what he called the peasant rear) would tax the logistical system and force a reversion to another, more elemental kind of warfare. When mechanization and modernization took place in the 1930s, many said it was no longer a problem. In fact, the combat formations which fought the second half of this campaign; the cavalry divisions, tank brigades and rifle divisions, are that army. It was an instrument of bludgeon and not a fine tool. But if it

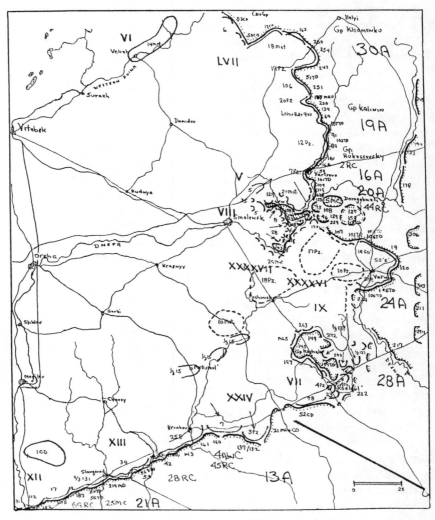

FIGURE 217
SITUATION, 2300, 3 AUGUST 1941

survived and Soviet industry produced, that bludgeon could be turned into another instrument. It was a horribly bloody, horribly costly, and not very neat process, but it suggests a great deal about the Russian way of war, certainly under Soviet power.

```
                    CORRELATION OF FORCES
                    GENERALOBERST HALDER
                      (AUGUST 1, 1941)
```

	German	Soviet	Ratio
Finnish Front (Karelian)	5 Div.	5 Div.	1:1
Army Group North	20 Inf. Div 3 Pz. Div. 3 Mot. Div.	13 Rif. Div. 2 Tank Div.	3:2
Army Group Center	42 Inf. Div. 9 Pz. Div. 7 Mot. Div. 1 Cav. Div.	26.5 R. Div. 7 Tank Div. 1 Cav. Div.	5:2.7 9:7 1:1
Army Group South	41 Inf. Div. 6 Pz. Div. 4.5 Div.**	29 Rif. Div. 8 Tank Div.* 2 Cav. Div.	5:3 1:1

```
* two tank divisions without tanks
** 4.5 Hungarian, Rumnian, Italian and Slowak units

OKH Reserves:   0              Russian Reserves 28 Divs.

Halder, KTB, III, 141.
```

FIGURE 218

HALDER DIARY ENTRY ON COALITION OF FORCES, 1 AUGUST 1941

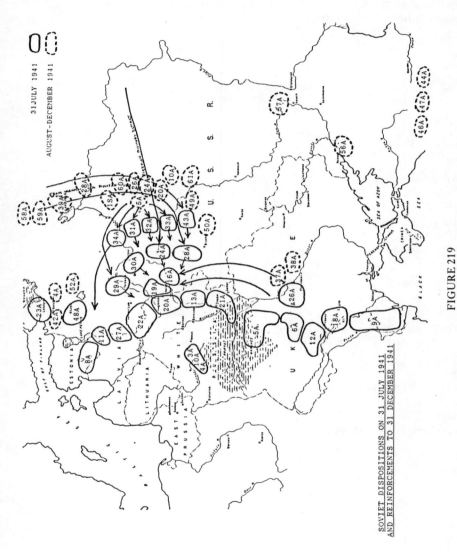

FIGURE 219

SOVIET MOBILIZATION, 22 JUNE–1 DECEMBER 1941

SOVIET DISPOSITIONS ON 31 JULY 1941
AND REINFORCEMENTS TO 31 DECEMBER 1941

31 JULY 1941

AUGUST–DECEMBER 1941

3rd Panzer Division Battles in the Smolensk Area

COLONEL HORST ZOBEL (retired)

Let me now describe the second phase, that is the engagement of the panzer division east of the Dnepr River. Panzer Group 2 gave the following missions to its corps after crossing the Dnepr River:

XXIV Panzer Corps to advance into the direction of Propoisk – Roslawl and secure the right flank against enemy attacks from Slobin – Rogatschew and the left flank against Mogilew:

XXXVI Panzer Corps to advance into the direction of Jelnja and secure the right flank against Mogilew;

XXXVII Panzer Corps to attack Smolensk and secure the left flank against the Dnepr line between Orscha and Smolensk and against the town of Orscha itself.

On 13 July the main forces of the 3rd Panzer Division crossed the Dnepr River (See Figure 220). Enemy forces around Mogilew actively endangered the flanks of the Panzer Group 2 for several days. Difficult detours for by-passing Mogilew also caused problems for the attacking troops. Tschaussy was the next objective for 3rd Panzer Division. But first a partly swampy and partly sandy piece of terrain had to be crossed in the area where the enemy soon launched counterattacks out of Mogilew and from the east. Only at sunset did the 3rd Panzer Division reach the western outskirts of Tschaussy.

Early on 15 July the division started the attack against Tschaussy with two combat groups. The attack was successful and the town taken on the same day. It was, however, not possible to continue the attack because of the destroyed bridge over the Bassja River and the flank attacks by the enemy out of the Mogilew area. Instead, the division regrouped and started to attack the railway bridge south of Tschaussy. Before sunset, the bridge was taken.

In the meantime, the situation in front of the division had changed. Our reconnaissance elements became aware that the enemy had started to withdraw from the Bassja River. The division immediately gave the order to build a footbridge over the river. Armored vehicles forded through the low water and a bridgehead was soon built east of Tschaussy. On 19 July the advance guard of the 3rd Panzer Division built a bridgehead over the Ssosh River near Kritschev.

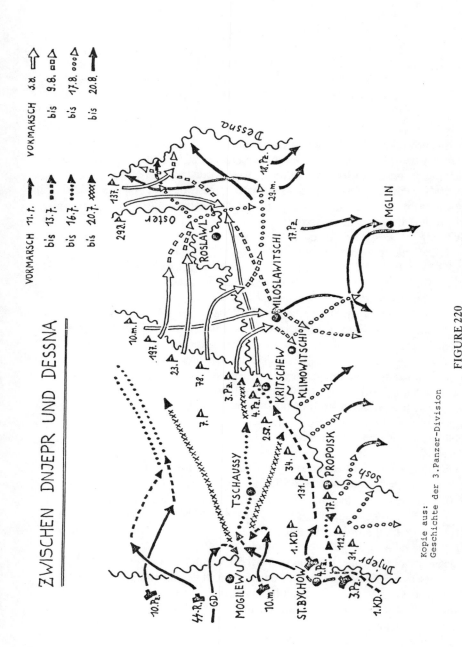

FIGURE 220

3RD PANZER DIVISION OPERATIONS, 11 JULY–20 AUGUST 1941

Kopie aus:
Geschichte der 3.Panzer-Division

The next day, Smolensk was captured by 17th and 18th Panzer Divisions and the 29th Infantry Division (motorized). At the same time Jelnja was taken by the 10th Panzer Division, the Division Das Reich, and the Infantry Regiment Grossdeutschland. Remaining follow-on foot-bound infantry stayed in the Gorki area. Finally, on 1 August Roslawl was taken by the XXIV Panzer Corps, and enemy forces were surrounded in the area of Smolensk–Jelnja and Roslawl. Heavy and continuous counterattacks were repulsed.

At the end of July, discussions arose at the highest level about the next operational objectives. Finally, Hitler decided not to give priority to a further attack against Moscow but instead to surround enemy forces in the Ukraine. The 3rd Panzer Division also received an order to attack southward and to help to complete encircling the great Kiev pocket. These figures sum up the armored status of our division at this stage of the operation.

Summary of the Tanks Ready for Action in Tank Regiment 6
On 10 July the regiment again began action
with the following number of tanks:
43 tanks Mark II
78 tanks Mark III
24 tanks Mark IV

Total – 145 tanks

During the period from 10 July to 30 July
the following tanks were totally lost:

4 tanks Mark III

During the period from 10 July until 30 July
the regiment had to give up to the tank brigade:

5 tanks Mark II

On 30 July the following tanks were given
to workshops for repair:

3 tanks Mark II
39 tanks Mark III
8 tanks Mark IV

Total – 50 tanks

435

On 30 July the following tanks were ready for action
in the regiment:
35 tanks Mark II
35 tanks Mark III
16 tanks Mark IV

Total – 86 tanks

I would like to explain the situation which, while not typical, was certainly instructive, regarding the nature of fighting at that time. This is described in the book by General Munzel. In the evening the 1st Panzer Battalion reached the Schara River line but the advance had to be stopped because the bridge over the river had been destroyed and was still burning. We met the same situation we confronted several times. The valley which was about 800 meters wide, was swampy ground and could not be traveled by tanks. Detours were not available and heavy artillery fire rained down upon the bridge. At sunset the division commander arrived and immediately formed an assault group consisting of the 2nd Panzer and parts of 4th Panzer Company, an antitank platoon, and riflemen with a rubber boat. The commander of the assault group was the commander of the 2nd Panzer Squadron of our regiment.

At 2000 the assault group carefully approached the still burning bridge. The company commander jumped out of his tank, and with grenades and under cover of tank fire, succeeded in seizing the burning bridge. The reason I cite this example is that in my opinion it was a perfect combination of fire, assault, and surprise. Even in a very difficult situation the man who leads the assault must be the best one, in this case the commander of a tank company.

Let me re-emphasize the point I made earlier. I said that the defensive enemy generally is in the favored position to open fire when he wants to. This fact is generally not recognized in troop training and in crew drill. As an inspector of armored troops, I often found misleading situations given to trainees by instructors. To spot and recognize the enemy before he fires his first shot is not in accordance with war experience. As a consequence training against war experiences is not a mistake, it is an offense.

We like to speak about tactical maneuver, and fighting and killing the enemy. This is not very fair to those who keep the tanks running, the supply echelons and even more the maintenance people. It is important to consider where to employ them. On the defense, workshops can be located far to the rear. In an attack, however, maintenance units should be placed close to the fighter elements. Support soldiers must be well rewarded for performing their difficult job. The repair of damaged and often bloody tanks is a very hard job.

Four principles of motorized troops were applicable to operations in former times and to operations today as well:

– Motorized, and especially armored troops have to be led from a position well forward. Everyone speaks about this but few practice it.

– Leading on the battlefield must be done by short orders, mostly orally or by wireless. From battalion down they should be oral in so far as possible. The following short story is true; if it is not true, it could be true.

The commander of a division rushed on a motorbike to the leader of the advance general, handed him a map saying "Here is the connection map, go ahead and break through". This is not what I mean by "leading by oral order". Sometimes, however, orders have to be given in an improvised way.

– The next point was that German motorized troops were used to fighting in combat groups with permanently changing organization – sometimes even daily.

– Finally, during an attack logistical echelons should be integrated into fighting echelons. These include ammunition, fuel and food, as well as the doctor and his assistants.

28th Infantry Division Operations

COLONEL DR ALFRED DURRWANGER (retired)

Following our tank divisions to Smolensk, my 28th Infantry Division reached that area about 25 July. It now began the task of squeezing more and more Soviet units that had been encircled in the pocket of Smolensk by our tank divisions. This combat offered no new ideas, so I would like to provide you with some hints, from our experiences, concerning the special characteristics of Soviet warfare. First let me repeat: the Soviets were surprised, but not at all unprepared.

It was interesting to observe on the part of the Soviets a considerable lack of tactics knowledge of know-how to guide a unit and how to coordinate operations at all levels. Individually the Soviets were very brave and obstinate soldiers, but their units were badly organized and often ineffective.

There may have been different reasons for this including:

– first, the assassination of hundreds of higher ranking officers by Stalin three years before the war began (1938);
– second, the lack of training in coordinated operations and how to combine operations; and
– third, the immense confusion after the first defeats during the border battles and thereafter.

Thus we perceived, for example, that to our great surprise a whole Soviet company passed us, marching on our right flank, just as if it were peace time, without any protection or any reconnaissance. It was just as if there was no war. In another instance, an artillery unit tried to occupy a position in a big valley directly in front of us. We were hidden in a little forest. Consequently, they lost all their equipment after we fired a few shots from our guns.

The lack of good maps on our side sometimes led to certain confusion. At first, we received only maps on a scale of 1:100,000 which were much too old and almost of no use. Therefore, in some areas German units collided, whereas in other areas all went smoothly. Sometimes the Soviets exchanged local signs of towns and villages, if they had any at all, just to confuse us. Therefore, it was always good to know at least some words in Russian, for example: *kak nazywajetsa eto mesto* (what is the name of that place)?

438

To demonstrate the nature of Soviet warfare, I would like to point out additional examples. Several times my comrades found among the many corpses Soviet soldiers who simulated death. Evidently they breathed with their eyes closed. When unobserved, some tried to escape while others murdered a German soldier maliciously. Sometimes Soviet soldiers, after being encircled by our units, would commit suicide.

Once, while marching with my company along a narrow, but otherwise open piece of terrain far away from combat, we were suddenly fired upon, although nobody was to be seen. We wondered what had happened. Finally we realized that a Soviet soldier had hidden his loaded Sten gun in a tree and tied the trigger by a long cord to the foot of a cow. When the cow moved the gun fired. We asked ourselves: Had he read Karl May?* It cannot be denied that the Soviets were very experienced in combat within forests and in camouflage technique. They had much more contact with nature and knew how to make use of it much better than German soldiers.

While for some days the regiment remained in defensive positions, my people in the frontlines, that is, the observation post of one of my platoons, observed that a Soviet commissar, standing behind a thick tree, trained his soldiers in an open area in front of our observation post about 100–150 meters away from it. We guessed this was probably intended to accustom his soldiers to war conditions. It was one of the most cruel methods we ever experienced. Our observation post could hear the orders the commissar gave to his people. Is this the way to establish military discipline?

During a halt at a little river near a small bridge where we were watering our thirsty horses, an explosion was suddenly heard. The reason was that the Soviets had hidden a mine where they supposed German troops would halt. A German soldier and his horse were killed on this occasion.

The rapid organization of the partisan movement that was very effective behind our lines was another surprise for us in the Soviet war. Therefore considerable forces were necessary to protect important routes or points or stores of ammunition, food and so on.

Another consequence of combat was to make the battalions of German infantry regiments more independent by providing them with more artillery (that is one of my platoons). In the Soviet war the lowest-level combined arms unit gradually became the battalion, and no longer the regiment, as it had been in Poland and in France. The lowest autonomous tactical unit was now the battalion. Will this development go on in the future?

---

* A German writer who excelled in imagination.

Discussion

CHAIRED BY GENERAL HOSTER

Question: Where was the artillery when you advanced so rapidly in this campaign?

Colonel Zobel: Our 3rd Panzer Division had Artillery Regiment 75. This artillery was towed by halftrack vehicles. When we were attacking, the forward observer always followed the 1st Company and had one battery in position and one battery moving. I cannot remember an occasion when we attacked without artillery support. They fired one control (registration) shot and after this the entire battery fired. This was during an advance. During a halt or a prepared attack, the entire battery was prepared to fire. We were well supported by our towed artillery, even in a mobile advance.

General Guderian: Also in the Western campaigns, the armored forces had a 20cm mortar. If there was a halt during the attack, the mortar was available immediately to provide fire support.

Colonel Rothe: From 1942 onwards we had the same system in our artillery regiment and in other panzer divisions. The 1st Artillery Battalion was self-propelled. That meant the 1st Battalion belonged to the panzer regiment. Wherever we were, the artillery commander was in a command tank together with the regimental commander. Thus, this artillery battalion provided direct support for the panzer regiment wherever we were.

Colonel Stoves: The artillery battalion was attached to the commander of the armored or motorized combat group. The recce teams of each battalion or battery were mounted on light APCs with the same radio equipment as the panzer units. They were able to listen to all radio communications. They received orders in 1st Panzer Division from the mixed combat groups, and they were able from tanks or light APCs to direct the fire of two battalions of unattached artillery as well as one attached to the assault group.

Professor Macksey: Regarding fire support coordination, did the German Army at that time have what the British had developed in 1941–42? That is, a capability to bring down in one concentration, at about 20 minutes' notice a complete divisional fire plan or concentrated fire.

General Lemm: Of course, without any doubt we had the capability. The problem was not the system, but rather communications. Especially at night, all the radios did not function.

General Ohrloff: In 7th Panzer Division, our lead element did not have artillery. The artillery required many hours to get into position. The distance from forward elements (motorcycle battalion) to the mass of the division was one to four hours or 20–30 kilometers in the Ukraine.

Question: Could someone comment on the use of artillery in the direct fire role, for example against tanks?

General Lemm: Of course in the normal situation the artillery was not used in direct fire. Only in an exceptional case, in breakthrough operations, when tanks approached the gun positions, were they used in this role. During the campaign, the infantry took some howitzers or guns to forward positions to use in this way. If a howitzer was able to destroy a tank it received a white ring around the barrel to show what it had done. In the course of the war, there was a customary relationship between one artillery battery and one infantry battalion.

The normal division had an artillery regiment with three light detachments from three battalions. Thus, every infantry regiment had the support of one light battalion. The forward observers were always assigned to the same regiment and even to the same companies. In addition, there was a heavy artillery regiment which was only employed at the point of main effect of the division.

Comment: In the dual situation of tank and howitzer, normally the tank was the winner because the tank is built to do exactly this – to fire at points. Normally we did not use the artillery in this role because we needed the artillery urgently in their normal indirect fire role.

Question: Someone mentioned operations by the Brandenburgers in the north. Can you comment on their use throughout the front? Could Dr. Kipp and Colonel Glantz comment on the lessons the Soviets were drawing out of these experiences and how these experiences are regarded today?

General Lemm: There has always been too much fuss about the Brandenburgers. They were not as important as some believed. It was a small unit, deployed on only a very few occasions (for example to seize a bridge). They never had an operational importance. I would add that from the regiment a division was organized, and this was a normal type division.

Question: In a modern context, both in defense and in offense, there are certain distances from the left flank to the right flank which must be covered. They are greater on the defense than on the offense. When you were attacking what was the width of your battalion, brigade or division? What were your defensive frontages as well?

441

General von Hoffgarten: On the attack we never had limitations in the widths of a battalion or a regiment. We only had objectives. The width depended on the enemy resistance. Sometimes the width of the advance guard was the width of the attack. Generally speaking however, a company had 200 meters and a battalion 1,000m in attack.

General Niepold: When we were forced to change from attack to defense, of course it depended on the enemy and on our diminishing forces. So sometimes a panzer division had to cover 20 kilometers with four infantry battalions and one panzer battalion. Infantry Divisions had to cover even greater widths of up to 30 kilometers.

Question: Based upon your experience in the 1941 campaign, how was the engineer force (battalion) structured later in the war? I refer, in particular, to engineer work necessary to maintain roads in difficult terrain.

General Guderian: There were basically no changes in the organization of a pioneer engineer battalion throughout the war. The engineer battalion of a panzer division consisted of two motorized companies, one armored engineer company, and one bridge company. There was some doubt on bridging capacity, but in 1940 we crossed the Maas River in the west with this company. I suggest the capacity must have been 100 meters plus. As far as repair of roads was concerned, this battalion had no capacity whatsoever. So we had to draw construction machines either from the country or from a special German organization called Organization Todt. This was a civil construction organization also used in the war. Before the war they built the autobahns.

General Lemm: Besides the engineer battalions of a division, which were only used in defense or in the advance to lay mines or to detect mines, they had rubber boats to cross rivers. or recce parties, or they were used with the infantry to form bridgeheads. Aside from divisional engineers there were also army group engineers. Their specialty was building bridges, and they were brought forward in time to support attacking divisions. They could also build roads, for example in the Pripet swamp region.

Question: Can you comment on the quality of the German officer corps in the war? We have heard of the high quality at the beginning. What changes occurred due to losses during the war? And could you compare that with the Soviet side? Did Soviet quality improve?

Colonel Ritgen: Certainly the quality of the German officer diminished during the war. The duration of officer training was reduced at the beginning of the war and it was not possible to train an officer in one year or 18 months like a peacetime officer, who needed at least two years. Furthermore, the Wehrmacht had expanded considerably. There were the three forces: Air force, army and navy; and Goering took the best men into the air force until Himmler came and demanded the best material for his SS. Finally, the army was the last organization to get replacement material for officers. They tried to comb everyone who was suitable as an officer replacement, and in 1942 I knew the figures of one of the nine officer replacement corps. There were 10,000 officers in the entire Wehrmacht and 1,100 in armor. These officers came to the front green, and since they lacked experience their casualty rate was much higher than that of the older officers.

I was in Panzer Lehr Division at the end of the war, and I can only state that in this unit the general quality of our officers was quite high. Of course, the panzer troops had better conditions than the infantry. I think it was a miracle that we could maintain a certain standard for officers up to the end of the war.

May I add that many of the replacements were men who had been wounded and returned. They did have great experience. The rate of wounded was, of course, much higher than the death rate.

Dr Kipp: If we look very closely at the commander in many of the border engagements, and if we look at the command personnel of Soviet *fronts* and armies at the end of the war, we will see that many of those men leading tank armies and corps at the end were survivors of these first combats. In a sense, one could say these men, like Peter the Great, could have done an apocryphal thing in 1945, of toasting their teachers in the most difficult way of learning. These men learned by combat, and gradually they mastered their skill as survivors and rose up the chain. One could see the process of Soviet lesson learned among those who survived.

Secondly,. the Soviet officer education system, although reduced in length of time, remained functioning even throughout the most difficult periods. The schools were withdrawn and protected (unlike World War I when the Russian General Staff closed the General Staff Academy). No such decision was made in this war.

In the specialized arms, particularly in aviation, there was a continued investment and a husbandry of resources, even in crisis periods. School classes were not disrupted just to meet immediate combat situations. At lower levels there were extraordinary losses during the initial period of war. The level of leadership however, would improve as the war continued. The focus here is on the very low level of experience when the war began, partly as a result of the purges, and on the rapid recovery that followed.

Question: The difficult terrain and the lack of maps must have created a command and control nightmare trying to move over 70 divisions eastward. How often did units get lost, and how did you prevent that and or regain control of your units?

General Lingenthal: Nobody was lost during the campaign. For the region close to the border we had 1:100,000 maps, which were printed in different colors and were rather bad. Up to Moscow we had maps with only brown print. Only the Smolensk–Moscow autobahn was colored violet and they originated from the year 1870. Those maps were of no great use for panzer divisions. Panzer divisions were well trained in reading maps, nevertheless, sometimes they missed their objective by eight or more kilometers. Only from August onward, when we captured Russian 1:50,000 maps, did the situation improve. Those maps were the same quality as German 1:100,000 maps. They were used by the artillery as well. We reprinted those maps in each of our corps' sectors and the situation was much improved.

General Lemm: Returning to the infantry, the infantry was in a very bad position because of those poor maps. One problem was that Russian maps were in Cyrillic, and we had to overprint them with German names. The readability of the map was not improved by the overprints. Although nobody was lost, many battalions made big detours in order to finally reach their objectives. On one square kilometer you could find three villages with the same name, or at least that sounded the same. This was an additional problem in the context of readability.

Question: Was a major logistical plan developed for Barbarossa which allocated resources to the panzer groups based on certain time factors? Second, if the Americans could not have supported the Soviets with material, could the Soviets have won the war on their own?

General Niepold: There was someone who looked after overall logistics before the campaign. This was General Wagener, a quartermaster general. Many map exercises and calculations had been conducted to determine what was needed in the campaign. All these logistical goods were stored close to the border. Thus, the logistical organization was there. They also created civilian transportation regiments, and used the railways to organize logistical transport. A member of the OKH who did this was the so-called general for transport.

General von Plato: There was a practical problem on the ground, particularly in looking after the panzer groups, since they had just been created, and they lacked their own logistical troops. They had to draw their supplies from neighboring armies. Of course, it was planned they would have their own supplies organized after the first eight days. But this was a bad solution and it did not function optimally.

Comment: Of course, there was logistical as well as operational planning. Nevertheless, both planning parts were on thin ice. Nobody had calculated the bad weather and bad road conditions. The consumption rates for fuel, for example, were double what had been predicted. Therefore, the older calculations were wrong. There were no construction machines with the engineer battalions, so our soldiers had to build the roads themselves by cutting down trees and laying them across the roads (corduroy roads). Above all, we did not calculate for "General Winter". Everyone planned to finish the war before winter. This was a political rather than a military consideration (by Hitler). No one knew beforehand that the winter of 1941–42 would turn out to be a very severe one. In February 1942, the panzer formations, having lost most of their tanks, fought over the white snow in their black uniforms. This, of course, added very much to the overall logistical problem.

General Ohrloff: Today it is very difficult to find in Germany a map of the Soviet Union under a scale of 1:1,000,000. Can you find smaller-scale maps?

Dr Kipp: What is available in terms of maps in Soviet stores for the population is indeed extraordinarily limited. One could not find smaller-scale maps in stores. Obviously, they produce them for other consumers. The appropriate section of the General Staff probably has more than adequate maps.

There was a second part of the question regarding US assistance to the Soviets, but it is a dangerous question because it requires a judgement. Let me begin with two separate approaches. First, you posit the question of Allied support in matériel – its impact, and what if it were absent.

One must note that while Lend Lease was agreed to early regarding provision of goods and services, the pipeline did not flow all that rapidly immediately. There was a digestion problem even with what arrived in 1941 and 1942. By 1943–45 certainly in terms of the mechanization of the Red Army, it is inconceivable to talk about it without considering the availability of American trucks and combat matériel.

There is a more fundamental side of that question. If we look at Soviet impressions of the impact of Lend Lease, there were four important areas. First, there was the psychological impact, which preceded the appearance of goods themselves. It was a commitment that the Soviet Union was not alone. Therefore, whatever sacrifices were being made, others were carrying on the fighting. We have all heard the complaints that the Second Front was not coming, but one should look at Soviet propaganda in 1941 and 1942, when the emphasis was on the Allied coalition and "we do not stand alone".

Second, in terms of combat matériel, do not dismiss the Soviets' own production. In most of the important indices of military goods the Soviet Union produced and sustained its own war effort (in armor, artillery tubes, and aircraft). Allied contributions were an addition.

The third area which is often overlooked is the economic impact of Lend Lease. With the tremendous areas which were lost to German forces in 1941 and 1942, the Soviet Union had lost a sizeable portion of its raw materials and a sizeable portion of its industrial base. Lend Lease played a very crucial role here with such items as cracking agents for oil to enable the production of high-octane gasoline, which was a requirement of Soviet aviation. One should also look at the impact of non-military but vital consumer goods.

My wife's grandfather, Viktor Nikolaevich Kornilovich was a naval engineer who before the war commanded the naval yards at Murmansk and, during the war, the naval yards at Astrakhan. The Astrakhan yards produced motor torpedo boats, and there was a constant problem with providing for worker morale. The workers would say to Viktor Nikolaevich, "The difference between you and the Reds is that you Baron, push and push while giving us something, while they push and push and never give us anything". The context of the story was a sit-down strike inside the wharf, in which its workers said they were not going to work any more. The choice was to compromise or shoot people. As the workers said, "What can you do to us, you have taken everything?" In this case, the technical director managed to get his hands on American canned goods. He gave the workers Spam and other canned goods, and gave them 48 hours outside the yard. Before this, they had been kept inside. Of course, they did not eat the Spam but used it on the black market. But morale was restored. We do not appreciate the effect of those things on the Soviet economy.

The appearance of trucks also made it possible to make the linkage inside Soviet factories and industrial complexes between rail and road. That was a multiplier outside the frontline. So, if you ask whether Allied support made a difference, quite obviously it did. The ability of the Soviets to wage war was greatly increased.

Could they have won by themselves? If you mean by that the total disappearance of Allied powers, obviously not. But Britain and America were not going to disappear. If you mean less Lend Lease getting through, but Allied combat power still being applied, it was only a question of time. The Soviet Union would provide for itself and, if not a victory on the Eastern Front in 1945, then it would be later. The Soviet Union was close to its last gasp in 1945 in terms of manpower and production, yet within 90 days the Soviets were able to move substantial combat power from the European theater to the Pacific and mount a vigorous and decisive campaign against the Japanese.

Question: Would Dr Kipp comment on the role of commissars at this stage of the war and, in particular, the political police?

446

Dr Kipp: There are two aspects of this question. First, the reintroduction of the commissars was quite clearly aimed at the command nexus, the distrust of officers, and also however, aimed at the political restabilization of units. Professional soldiers tend to see it as only affecting officer–soldier command relationship. On the Soviet side it was a function of general ideological and political preparation. That clearly did affect junior command, but from the Soviet perspective it was an absolutely critical device for indoctrination and control.

Please note that unlike Western military institutions, the party was not separate from the military. Officers were expected to be party members under political discipline. Therefore, that relationship with the commissar was not so alien. It had existed before, during the Civil War.

Second, the political police were used extensively. Terror did not end. It continued, and it was used throughout the war. It was aimed at officers and any dissidents inside the Soviet Union, and special units were used to restore discipline behind the front lines. I have talked with one man who was 17 years old in 1941 and in such a unit. The unit's instructions were to shoot anyone coming back, with no questions asked. That was certainly a feature of the system. Russians fought for the motherland (*za rodinu*), but the political system did not disappear. *Time* magazine may have changed Uncle Joe into a Democrat, but Uncle Joe never changed into a Democrat.

Question: One question in connection with the campaign has not yet been addressed, but is pertinent. At the tactical level how good was Soviet intelligence and how did the German counter these intelligence and reconnaissance efforts?

Colonel Stoves: I served as an S-2 under the G-2 of 1st Panzer Division in 1942. We were not afraid of the G-2 work on the other side. In our opinion they had much to learn. We improved our own tactical recce results by creating an interception-recce team in each of our signal battalions. A special trooper came from signals command in Berlin. He brought special equipment which enabled us to tap into the main Russian wire line from Moscow to Leningrad, which was 45 miles away. We listened to command communications on that line. We noted all tactical intercepts, and when we took prisoners later, the numbers of the divisions on the other side matched. This was during the Moscow operation.

General Guderian: In 1941, when German forces were advancing rapidly, the Soviets had a poor picture of the German formations. After this period however, when the fronts became stable, they had excellent opportunities to find out what was occurring on the German side, especially when they used partisans behind German lines. Many partisans were equipped with radios. I would say from 1942 onwards the Soviets had a very good picture indeed.

General Niepold: Colonel Glantz provided an excellent example of the effectiveness of the German G-2. As you could see the picture was not always very clear. The Germans were even worse in discovering where the Russian industries were. Since the early 1930s, many German technicians worked in Russia. When they came back in 1938, we obtained only a little information about Russian industrial capacity. Very likely the Germans, as a whole, disregarded the importance of the entire G-2 business.

Second, let me relate the story of the G-2 division of the German High Command (OKH) at the beginning of the war (the so-called *Fremde Heere Ost*). Colonel Kinzel was in charge of this division, and he reported to the Chief of the General Staff, General Halder. During those first months of the war, the reports and assumptions were rather bad. At the beginning of 1941, LTC Gehlen took over, and after a few weeks the improvement was dramatic. Gehlen, however, had to suffer from the fact that Hitler did not believe his reports and analyses.

Question: Between the end of the French campaign in 1940 and the beginning of Barbarossa, ten German panzer divisions became 21 new panzer divisions. Were the new ones as good as the old? Was there a change in attitude and staff procedures in the new divisions?

Comment: The reorganization was done only by a trick. The old divisions were cut in half regarding tanks and in this way we had double the number of divisions. The number of tanks was not doubled.

Colonel Stoves: In the Polish and French campaigns, I served in the oldest panzer division (the 1st). After the campaign, the 33rd Infantry Division was reorganized into the 15th Panzer Division, which was done by motorizing those two infantry regiments which had fought on foot in France with vehicles only for antitank and engineer companies. They now received an old panzer regiment (No. 7) to form the new 15th Panzer Regiment of Rommel. I fought six months in this division until being wounded. If you ask me honestly, I can say I saw no difference between those old, very famous panzer divisions, and the new one which fought in North Africa. It depended on the men, the commander, and the situation you fought in. Some were lucky, some were not.

Professor Macksey: I have had some experience with this on the British side. We did this sort of nonsense of trying to turn infantrymen into tankers. With all due respect to infantry, it was not a great success in many cases. We had to throw out half of them for starters. Everything had to do with the commander. We got around it by putting the Royal Tank Regiment in charge at the higher and key levels, such as the commander and technical quartermaster. We converted many infantry battalions into tank regiments, and I served in no fewer then three of them myself. It took about 15 months in the British Army, under less pressure than the German Army, to make this conversion. After a bit, they were quite good, but there was always the tendency to think in an infantry way instead of in a tank division way.

The other thing that went wrong was that we decided in about 1942 to change the infantry division into a mixed infantry division. We took one infantry brigade out of the division and replaced it with an armored brigade. This was a crashing failure because the balance and mentalities were all wrong. It is a difficult thing to do, and all I can say is that it really did not matter which German panzer unit you faced, it was all hard!

General Guderian: As one who came out of the oldest panzer division, I would like to support the younger a little and assure them that I regard them as of a similar quality. The 13th and 14th Panzer Divisions of III Panzer Corps were newly organized. 13th Panzer skimmed from the Magdeburg Motorized Infantry Division, and the 14th Panzer came from the 14th Saxon Infantry Division. After reorganization, they were as good as the older panzer divisions. The problem in this context was that they had to learn at first to cooperate with the other arms within the division. They coped with this very quickly. It was also highly dependent upon the quality of the commander to get this process going.

As a member of the armored corps, I am moved that we were able throughout the war to put elements of very difficult formations together and produce armored formations, including infantry, cavalry, and truck formations.

Dr Kipp: There were three questions asked between sessions that are worthy of answers.

(1) What appears to be the reason behind the Soviets emphasizing infantry strength and minimizing armor strength in the pre-22 June period? What is the evidence and what is only opinion?

Colonel Glantz: That question is in the form of a hot potato. I came upon the phenomenon, which I described to you, in the midst of my research. Previously, I had spent over two years researching Soviet deception planning during Soviet offensive operations throughout the war. This research produced first, an initial study of selected cases and, ultimately, forced me to conclude that you cannot look at individual cases only. Rather, you must examine everything if you are to assess whether strategic, operational, and tactical deception were being used. That larger study is now complete, and to make a long story short, from detailed study of over 90 operations, it is clear to me that the Soviets were masters of deception. They were, of course, much better at it after the initial period of war. Their first major successes occurred in late 1942, and their first strategic successes came in 1943. Thereafter, they experienced even greater success in 1944 and 1945. It was however, not a new phenomenon, because they devoted considerable time to the study of deception before the Second World War. They devoted much attention to the planning and conduct of orderly and comprehensive *maskirovka*.

When I began research on June 1941, I noticed the same features that would characterize Soviet deceptive practices in some 90 subsequent wartime operations. Essentially, the principal indicator of deception was the gap between what German intelligence saw and assessed and reality, in the form of what was actually there in terms of Soviet forces. What results is essentially a measuring stick regarding the degree of deception and hence, the degree of surprise. The intelligence gap was clearly present in June 1941, although I have not fully answered the question of why that gap existed. I do however, have some ideas as to why. First, the deception seems to have served two purposes. It multiplied German perceptions of Soviet rifle force strength through a variety of means including perhaps signals. At the same time, the Soviets hid the bulk of their mechanized forces.

When addressing the question why, the first tentative conclusion I have reached is that by displaying increased rifle force strength, the Soviets could hope to prevent or delay the attack. But if deterrence failed, by hiding their mechanized strength they were in a better position to implement defensive and counterattack plans. Those are just tentative conclusions.

The reverse aspect of this question concerns intelligence or that which is necessary to validate or verify the results of deception. In this case, Soviet strategic intelligence failures, probably politically motivated, negated the effects of successful deception. In fact, through 1942 Soviet intelligence was weak, hence their deception was also weak. After late 1942, as Soviet intelligence immeasurably improved, so also did Soviet deception improve. It is not inconceivable that from the summer of 1943 on, the Soviets possessed a capability analogous to Ultra. After all, the machines that began this Ultra process were, in the first instance, Polish. And during the first two years of war the Germans on several occasions, lost Enigma machines to the Soviets. These are suppositions, but the intelligence tale, when it emerges, will be an interesting one.

Dr Kipp: The second question is for the German officers. In view of the points made in question number one and the apparent complete surprise appearance of the T34 and KV tanks, to what extent did *maskirovka* and technical resources have on your operations? Could you describe what you consider to have been significant successes or failures of Soviet *maskirovka*?

Colonel Ritgen: It was extraordinary that we knew nothing about the KVI and T34, although the first KVs were apparently lost in the Finnish War. It is even more extraordinary that in the memoirs of the German generals, for example, the book of General Munzel and the diary of General Lemelson, commander of XXXXVII Panzer Corps, they never mention that the heavy tanks were there. I think that we had such confidence in ourselves that it did not matter what tanks we faced. The only panzer group which mentioned the heavy tanks was Army Group North, and this resulted in a commission of German experts being sent immediately from Berlin to the battlefield. I myself had no idea that other panzer groups faced the same situation, at least until two years ago. It was never mentioned in literature, and I think the impact of those new tanks was felt only after August and September 1941, after our own tanks had become victims of attrition. Then suddenly the superiority of the Russian tanks became obvious.

General Guderian: There is an interesting comment from General Guderian, senior. When Hitler was with Army Group Center in Russia, he mentioned to General Guderian that if he had known that the Russians had such a number of tanks he would not have started the war. Second, Guderian wrote a book in 1938 entitled *Achtung Panzer*, in which he mentioned that the Russians would have more then 10,000 tanks. He was criticized very much by the General Staff, who said the figure was far too high.

Professor von Luttichau: Hitler also made this same remark to Mussolini. It is in the German diplomatic papers.

Colonel Stoves: May I supplement my battalion commander, General Guderian? I was doing some of the chart work for Paul Carrell's work *Operation Barbarossa* and heard of a discussion between two generals – a Colonel General and a Lieutenant General. One was Chief of Staff of Rommel's Afrika Korps in 1941, and when they asked this question of the G-2 service people, they said they did not know about the KVI or KVII. I said "Sorry, gentlemen, the first T34 we ran into was near Ostrog". If you study all the literature, it is extraordinary to learn that those people in our own embassy at Moscow, who informed the other side about the D-day of Barbarossa, did not inform us about KVI and KVII. There is no question that I was informed the T34 was developed at Kazan, in a training installation, and was offered to the German Army. The German General Staff said no because it was too expensive. Then later the Russians built and produced them, and they appeared as a surprise.

Dr Kipp: Writing in the 1920s, Colonel A. A. Svechin, author of the first Soviet book on strategy, laid out the problem of technological surprise vis-à-vis technological initiative. Looking at the surprise element, he said that fundamentally it would have only tactical impact, because anyone who tried to obtain operational and strategic surprise would find the process of carrying it out too complex and difficult in terms of preparing the units and concealing them. He did, however, say that there was a good prospect of seizing the technological initiative – that is, confronting one's opponent with the unexpected. He suggested that there were two parts of that process. First, there was an ongoing, massive, systematic, sustained effort to gather intelligence about the opponent, both in his military areas and in his civilian economy; and second, the intent was to conceal all information of any technical or military significance from the adversary. I believe the Soviet model is well outlined there.

A small side comment. In my work in the German military archives I came across some papers from an *Abwehr* summary of intelligence, picked up from the Polish General Staff intelligence section. In it the Poles identified a T34 and gave its main armament, weight and characteristics. The German officer who wrote the summary, noted "Oh no, this must be the T35". Anyone who compared those two weapons systems would know the difference.

Steven Zaloga: I have done two histories of the T34 in English and much research in Russian of German language sources. I do not think the German Army was totally unaware of the T34. Documents in the archives in Washington identify it by the prototype number T32. So German intelligence did know the Soviets had a new medium tank T32, but they did not know the significance of it. The numbers mean nothing, if you do not know the armor thickness, its type of gun, how many will be produced, etc. The mere fact of a new medium tank was not significant. I doubt the Poles knew of a T34, because in 1939 it was called A20. So it was probably a mistake, a misidentification of T35.

There was a German study on Soviet war industry in 1941 immediately before the outbreak of war with Russia. The study went down factory by factory and indicated what each factory produced. It listed in the factory at Khar'kov, which did produce the T34, the designation T32, medium tank – new tank in production. They obviously had a source. T32 was the early prototype designation for T34. When in testing it was T32. When it went into production it was T34. Thus a German source knew it was produced at Khar'kov, which was correct. There is a great difference between knowing the number and knowing its capabilities.

Concerning KVs, there were two sent for testing in Finland. Those were never seen by the Finns. What was seen was a prototype of KV with two turrets called SMK. One was knocked out and photos of it are in the German archives. But it was a different tank and not a KVI. So the Germans had very little information about KVI.

General Guderian: Before 1941, a Russian delegation came to see the production of MkII and MkIV tanks. They were astonished that those two tanks were the most modern in the German Army. The industry managers reported this to higher echelons, and they argued that the Russian officers would have been very inquisitive. The managers concluded the Russians had something better than those two tanks. But there was no reaction.

7

Conclusions

Conclusions from the Soviet Perspective

COLONEL D. M. GLANTZ

We now undertake perhaps the most important task of all; the task of reviewing all that has gone before, and reflecting on what it means in a contemporary sense. Consideration of these events in isolation really has no meaning. Meaning can only be derived from how we synthesize what we have learned, and how we use the information in the future. I will first briefly set out what I call tentative conclusions derived from analysis of operations in 1941 from the Soviet standpoint. Then there will be a short analysis from the German standpoint, followed by perhaps the most important section from the standpoint of contemporary war, a section on the topic of the initial period of war (*nachal'nyi period voiny*). This topic has dominated Soviet thought since 1958 and certainly dominates Soviet military thought today.

During the initial stages of Operation Barbarossa, clear advantage went to German forces. First and foremost, the strategic offensive was a surprise, although, of course, it should not have been. The more highly developed German industrial base accorded to the German Army a technological advantage clearly evident in the high quality of German weaponry. Even after Soviet production had increased, this technological advantage remained. We must, however, note several clear exceptions to this rule, in terms of the T34 and the various KV model tanks, which certainly provided the Russians with a degree of technological surprise. However, that does not really accord advantage if these new weapons do not reach the battlefield. This new weaponry, although strong in firepower and armor, in the first two years of war often could not reach the battlefield. We are talking here principally about the realm of maintenance and logistics and the ability to field new technology.

Thorough German planning and offensive preparations for at least the

454

initial stages of the operation contrasted sharply with Soviet indecisiveness when attempting to implement effective countermeasures. While German panzer groups thrust deep into the Soviet Union along separate axes, Soviet forces often conducted hasty and uncoordinated counterattacks which were doomed in advance to failure. German war experience, derived from operations in Poland and France, combined with crisper command and control and more efficient training at all levels to accord a marked advantage to the Germans over the often poorly trained and ineffectively led Soviet forces.

Soviet failures and problems only accentuated these German advantages. Obviously, the highest Soviet political authorities had mis-assessed German intentions and thus deprived the armed forces of the opportunity to undertake prudent defensive measures. This is a lesson for all time. Soviet forces were in a poor state of readiness, particularly along the border. Rifle units were at 60 to 80 per cent strength, armies were not fully organized, and major items of equipment, in particular modern tanks and radios, were lacking.

Soviet forces were also poorly deployed. Although their strategic echelonment of forces reflected defensive planning, within those echelons the forces' military posture was suited neither for the offense nor for the defense. Armies deployed in linear fashion, often with one rifle corps forward and one mechanized corps to the rear. Rifle divisions had one of their regiments forward and the bulk of their forces were in camps to the rear. Mechanized corps' units were scattered and out of mutual support-ing range. The antitank brigades, the heart of Soviet antitank defenses, were usually not co-located with the mechanized forces. All of these conditions subjected the Soviet covering armies to early penetration and rapid defeat. They did not inflict on German forces the damage that the Soviet command expected. They were, in effect, preempted. This, in turn, paved the way for German preemption of subsequent Soviet defense lines along the Berezina and Dnepr Rivers.

Barbarossa has provided one of the first major modern examples of how forces can perform in the initial period of a theater war. Unfortunately for the Soviets, the Germans provided the favorable example, at least initially. Barbarossa demonstrated the strategic importance of a strong initial blow, delivered by surprise, by a major force organized essentially in single echelon. The ultimate failure of that attack, however, reflected the German failure to mobilize the entire nation for war in support of a coherent strategy.

There were a few marked characteristics of the summer fighting which stood out vividly. First, there was the great breadth, depth, and tempo of operations which so characterized *blitzkrieg*. German armored advances averaged 40–50 kilometers a day and, in some cases, as many as 70 kilometers. Operations developed along deep axes or directions. This proved particularly effective against Soviet defenses which were linear in nature with divisions defending wide sectors of from 25 to 45 kilometers. Once these linear defenses had been pierced, they became irrelevant, and subsequent combat became essentially a series of meeting engagements between German deep operating forces and the forward deploying Soviet reserves, which were often attempting to create new defense lines.

Soviet *frontal* forces were committed to combat in piecemeal fashion as they were mobilized. Only in late July were these forces sufficiently numerous to slow the pace of the German advance. The only exception to these words, of course, were the operations in the south. The dominance of the meeting engagement as the principle form of combat gave rise to complex operations where a premium was placed on rapidity, agility and flexibility on the part of commanders and command and control systems. This accorded a marked advantage to the better trained German forces as well. The net result of this fighting was that the Germans seized the initiative and forced Soviet forces to undertake an extensive strategic defense.

Figure 221 shows all Soviet armies as they mobilized and deployed forward roughly from 7–30 June. The principal message that emerges from this map is the deeply echeloned nature of that strategic defense. The Soviet strategic defense plan sought to halt the German advance, weaken German forces by basic attrition, secure time for further mobilization and deployments, and create conditions conducive to successful counterattacks and a regaining of the initiative. The STAVKA of the Soviet Supreme High Command, created in July, formed strategic defensive groupings to defend along threatened strategic directions and conducted strategic maneuver of reserves, perhaps one of the most important aspects of the summer operations.

Initially, Soviet strategic reserves were concentrated in the south where the Soviets expected the main German thrusts to occur. Subsequently, however, these reserves, in particular the 16th and 19th Armies and the 25th and 5th Mechanized Corps, redeployed for defense on the western direction. By June 1941, strategic defence occurred along all three strategic directions. On the western direction, the defense ultimately consisted of three strategic echelons deployed to a depth of almost 400 kilometers. *Front* and army forces defended along strategic and operational directions under STAVKA control, essentially in single echelon with only small reserves. *Front* defenses usually consisted of a series of armies deployed side by side. Fortunate *front* commanders had perhaps one or two rifle divisions in reserve (see Figure 222). There was virtually no depth to any of these individual defense lines. Army defenses reflected those of *fronts* (see Figure 223). Usually they consisted of a single echelon

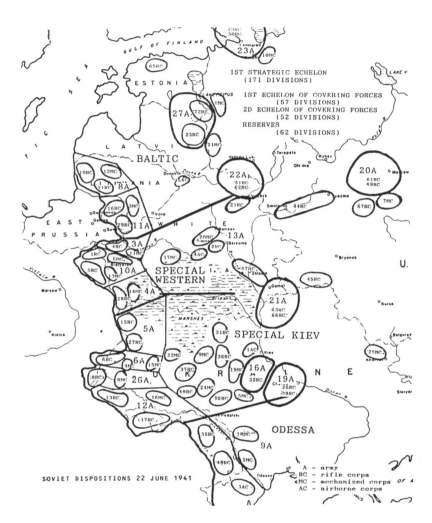

FIGURE 221
SOVIET STRATEGIC DEFENSE, JUNE 1941

of rifle divisions, perhaps a small tank reserve (often the remnants of the mechanized corps). By July the Soviets had, in fact, abolished the surviving mechanized corps and created in their place separate tank divisions which were themselves only a short-lived experiment. One of the marked deficiencies of this defensive structure was the lack of antitank defense, signified by the paucity of antitank regions in the defense. Rifle divisions on the defense, as we shall see, suffered from the same negative characteristics.

These strategic defenses were easily penetrated by concentrated German forces. However, and this is a very important however which begins to emerge at Smolensk, and will be seen again at Moscow, it was questionable whether German forces had the logistic sustainability and the resilience to conduct successive operations necessary to overcome these deeply echeloned strategic defenses.

Now let us focus on a few operational characteristics and problems confronted by the Soviets in the summer of 1941. The principal Soviet operational problem was defending against the German panzer groups whose mobility, firepower and flexibility vastly exceeded that of the Russian forces. In particular, lack of antitank and antiair defenses severely hindered Soviet defensive efforts, as well as Soviet attempts to launch coordinated counterstrokes or counterattacks. Antitank defenses of an organized nature were non-existent except where antitank brigades operated, and that was in only a very few sectors. By late July, the first Soviet antitank strongpoints had been formed to strengthen tactical defenses. The best example of the first use of antitank strongpoints occurred at Iartsevo, where Rokossovsky assembled a fairly decent defense after much difficulty.

Poor command and control at the operational level hindered Soviet efforts, partly as a result of the paralysing effect of surprise, partly because of the inexperience of Soviet commanders, and in part because of poor Soviet staff training. Faulty communications procedures and a lack of radios forced reliance on land lines, which were very quickly cut and of no use in mobile operations. In general, Soviet communications security was non-existent, allowing German intelligence to establish a good picture of the Soviet order of battle by mid-July. But as we march into the war as a whole, the Soviets turned this problem around. They deliberately used poor communications security to convey to the Germans false images. And that poor security later in the war would basically be used in support of deception planning.

Engineer preparation of the defense was very weak during the initial period of war. The Soviets prepared only the main defensive belt, which was essentially formed by grouping battalion defensive regions together to form, in essence, a non-continuous strongpoint defense.

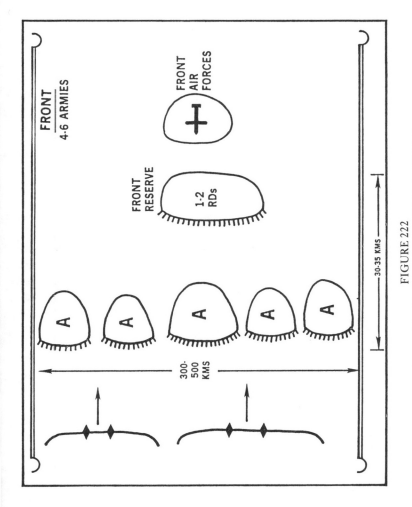

FIGURE 222
FRONT OPERATIONAL FORMATION (DEFENSE),
SUMMER 1941

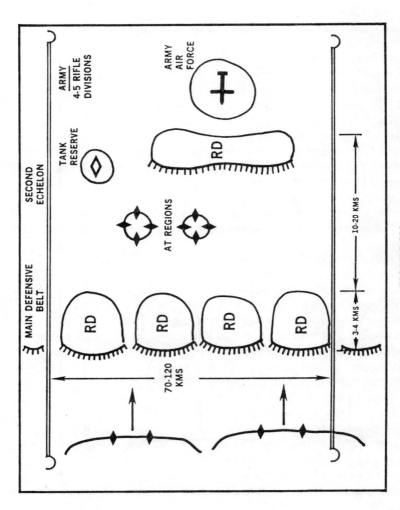

FIGURE 223
ARMY OPERATIONAL FORMATION (DEFENSE),
SUMMER 1941

Tactical defenses were characterized by their shallowness and weakness in terms of armor, engineer and artillery support. Figure 224 illustrates graphically the way in which rifle divisions operated in 1941. Essentially divisions defended in single echelon configuration of rifle regiments. Each of those regiments also had their battalions aligned in single echelon. Perhaps a battalion or two would be retained in reserve. The division had weak artillery support and the evolution of special groupings for artillery support which would evolve later in the war had not yet occurred. In general, antitank and antiair support was also weak.

Divisional defenses were broad and weak with low tactical densities of forces. The low number of artillery weapons which, by Soviet calculation, reached roughly two to three guns per kilometer, provided inadequate densities of defensive fires, in particular, defensive fires against enemy tanks and mechanized infantry. We shall see those densities steadily rise throughout the war to the neighborhood of 150 to 200 guns per kilometer of front in 1943, a far cry from the situation in 1941. Planned artillery preparations and supporting fires for counterattacks were weak and ineffective as well. All this tended to produce higher than normal infantry losses. Those very high losses would continue for at least another 18 months.

The Soviets generally used the available armor to simply strengthen infantry defenses, to repel German counterattacks where possible, and to provide support, although relatively poor, to those few Soviet counterattacks. Armor operated in small groups to provide infantry support. Attacks were also made by small groups of tanks, often without proper reconnaissance and without thorough integration into a combined arms configuration with accompanying infantry and artillery. The poor artillery and inadequate antiaircraft support led to very high armored losses and less effective tactical defense in general.

All Soviet offensive problems tended to reflect the defensive problems already mentioned. If we analyse how the Soviets organized counterattacks and counterstrokes, *fronts* generally operated on the offense in single echelon (see Figure 225). But more importantly, the armies or groups conducting the counteroffenses were normally organized in linear fashion with a total lack of concentration. In other words, the force was dispersed over a broad front, and this situation would persist through 1941 and well into 1942. The very small reserves with very weak tank forces made it almost impossible to sustain offensive success. At the army level, again there was a tendency to organize in single echelon (see Figure 226). Most of the armor was integrated in support of rifle divisions, and virtually no armor was used for the exploitation of offensive success. What would emerge as the sole Soviet force capable of any sort of deep operations in 1941 was the cavalry corps, which we first saw operating near

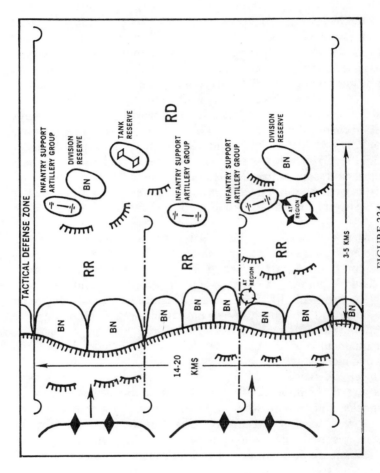

FIGURE 224

DIVISION COMBAT FORMATION (DEFENSE), 1941

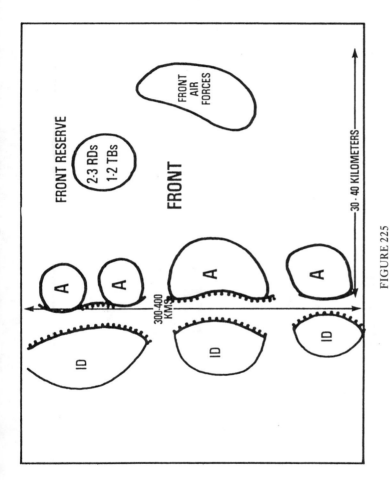

FIGURE 225
FRONT OPERATIONAL FORMATION (OFFENSE), 1941

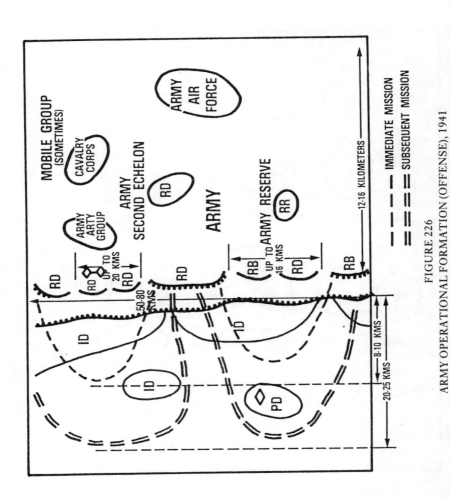

FIGURE 226

ARMY OPERATIONAL FORMATION (OFFENSE), 1941

Smolensk and Rogachev. Later these corps would operate more success-fully around Moscow.

Soviet rifle division combat formations did accord with the 1936 and 1941 Regulations. Divisions tended to organize for combat in double echelon with two regiments forward and one back. However, given the deployment of *fronts* and armies on a broad front, what this did was to bring into battle only a small portion, roughly one-half to two-thirds of the Soviet combat power. The Soviets would solve this problem in late 1942 by mandating the single echelon use of all forces to bring all scarce combat power well forward to bear against the German defense.

In conclusion, looking at strategic, operational, and tactical problems, the crisis faced by the Red Army emanated from several distinct sources. These included the surprise nature of the attack, poor leadership, uneven training, inadequate logistics, and an over-ambitious force structure which looked good on paper, but did not function very well in practice.

Hence, Soviet initial expectations of how their forces would perform in war were not met. The covering force in the Northwestern and Western Front areas failed to inflict requisite damage on German forces. This in turn caused preemption of subsequent defenses and Soviet resort to a strategic defense in depth principally organized along the western direc-tion toward Moscow. That strategic defense, however, began taking its toll on over-extended German forces at Smolensk and ultimately, that over-extension and resulting attrition of German forces would force the Germans to alter their strategic plans.

The Soviets, by late July and early August, had defined the problems facing them fairly well and had begun to propose solutions to those problems. As early as late July, the Soviets began truncating their force structure in an attempt to create a force which their inexperienced commanders could actually operate with more effectively on the battlefield (see Figure 227). Basically, force structure truncation involved the aboli-tion of a level of command in both rifle and armored forces. The abolition of the rifle corps and the mechanized corps, or at least those that had not already been destroyed, ensued. Hence, by October 1941, rifle armies were made up of only rifle divisions, which themselves had shrunk in size, and of rifle brigades, which were, in essence, light divisions without a regimental link – a simple grouping of artillery and rifle battalions. Tank brigades, which replaced mechanized corps, were small armored outfits with an initial strength of 65 tanks. This became the largest armored unit in the Soviet force structure by the late fall of 1941. Cavalry corps continued to be made up of cavalry divisions, but even here the Soviets lightened their structure by creating light cavalry divisions, whose strength was roughly half that of the regular divisions.

This restructuring was a temporary expedient. The Soviets had no

RED ARMY FORCE STRUCTURE

JUNE 1941

o RIFLE ARMIES

  o RIFLE CORPS

    o RIFLE DIVISIONS (14,500-16)

o MECHANIZED CORPS (36,000-1,031)

  o TANK DIVISIONS (11,000-375)

  o MECHANIZED DIVISION (11,600-275)

o CAVALRY CORPS

  o CAVALRY DIVISIONS (9,000-64)

o AIRBORNE CORPS (10,400-50)

  o AIRBORNE BRIGADES (3,000)

DECEMBER 1941

o RIFLE ARMIES

  o RIFLE DIVISIONS (11,600)

  o RIFLE BRIGADES (4,400)

o TANK BRIGADES (1,470-46)

o CAVALRY CORPS

  o CAVALRY DIVISIONS (6,000)

  o LIGHT CAVALRY DIVISIONS (3,400)

o AIRBORNE CORPS (12,000)

  o AIRBORNE BRIGADES (3,300)

FIGURE 227

SOVIET ARMY FORCE STRUCTURE, JUNE-DECEMBER 1941

desire for it, and they realized that one of its implications would probably be very high losses. However, this was a structure the Soviets had to have in order to train their commanders and allow them to grow in scope and capacity so that they could take command of larger units in the future. The tank brigade commanders of October 1941 would become the tank corps commanders of May 1942 and, in turn, the tank army commanders of 1943. As soon as they could, the Soviets would reform the light forces and again make them heavy. That process would begin in May 1942.

At the highest level, the Soviets centralized control of planning by creating a STAVKA to coordinate operations and three distinct strategic direction headquarters. These headquarters controlled operations along the Leningrad, Moscow and Kiev approaches.

The summer operations also began the long process of educating the Soviet officer corps. Although the Western Front commander, Pavlov, and his air force chief were summoned back to Moscow and summarily executed, other commanders were treated more leniently. There was a remarkable tolerance for error within the Red Army evidenced by the ultimate rise to senior command of many of those who had survived the disastrous summer operations of 1941. The STAVKA, at the same time, began the practice of selecting its most brilliant and capable officers and dispatching them on missions to control distinct operations. Zhukov, Timoshenko, and Eremenko were the first of these representatives of the *Stavka*.

In the summer of 1941 the Soviets began the total mobilization of all state resources. From 22 June onwards, it was to be a total effort ruthlessly enforced and aimed at the achievement of only one goal – the defeat of Germany. This, I would maintain, was a markedly different approach from that the Germans took, at least initially in the Russian war. By the end of the summer, the Soviets had also begun the process of harnessing war experience in the service of the war effort. At first this was admittedly haphazard, but eventually the Soviets did this in a systematic and effective fashion. This process is still under way today and was evident in Soviet analysis of the conflict in Afghanistan.

As the Soviets implemented short-term solutions to their many problems, they also pondered those major reforms necessary to produce an army capable of achieving operational success. That meant the ultimate rebuilding of the army force structure and the creation within it of mobile forces capable of conducting sustained deep operations. That mobile force would require tested operational and tactical techniques to function properly and a command and control system to guarantee its efficient operation. The process of meeting these needs began in the summer of 1941.

All of this was but a hope, and a dim one at that, in June and July 1941.

The survivors of those disastrous summer months, the commanders and staff officers of shattered mechanized and rifle units, would begin to learn to compete with German forces. Necessity drove them on as they undertook to achieve what no other European army had yet achieved, to meet and defeat *blitzkrieg* before it crushed the Soviet Union. The first major round of that match occurred around Smolensk in July. The second round would occur at Moscow in December.

Conclusions from the German
Perspective

LIEUTENANT GENERAL GERD NIEPOLD (retired)

Dr Kipp appropriately compared the struggle of the two armies to one between a man fighting with a rapier and a man using a butcher's hatchet. You could also describe it as a fight of a bullfighter against a bull. Two facts have impressed me most. The infantry divisions of the German Army fought a different kind of war from the war fought by panzer divisions. In spite of that, the German High Command was able to conduct one coordinated operation with both types of divisions.

As far as German operations were concerned, it could be said that they were conducted in an elegant manner, if the word elegant is appropriate at all in war. In contrast, on the Soviet side there was a completely unsatisfactory way of coordinating operations in which the Russians were not able to concentrate forces into one major counter-operation. As an example, Figure 228 shows an excellent map drawn by Colonel Glantz. This map indicates that the Germans always succeeded in tearing enemy lines apart in their operations.

We did not mention much about German close air support, which actually only functioned properly and effectively in 1941. In today's or tomorrow's warfare it is highly doubtful if we can expect effective close air support at all, because the air force will have very different missions in future wars.

What will Soviet leadership look like today? They learned their lessons in the second half of World War II very well. I think that the higher level of command in the Soviet Army will be well qualified in major operations, but I would expect the lower levels of command still to be relatively inflexible based upon their ideological background and mainly on their political system.

About the quality of the soldier, we have heard and we have experienced the fact that the Russian soldier was enormously tough and brave. Comparing the two types of soldiers, the German soldier was extremely well-trained, while the Russian soldier was closer to nature in his way of fighting. In the West the number of men who are close to nature and know how to use nature has not increased since then. Because of that, it is very important to conduct tactical training and not indulge too much in

469

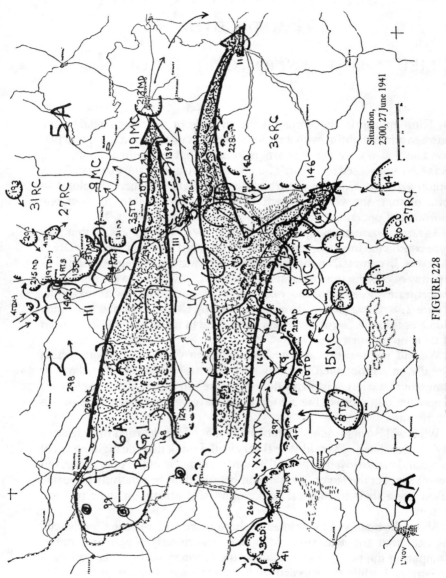

FIGURE 228

GERMAN OFFENSIVE SUCCESS (AN EXAMPLE)

Situation, 2300, 27 June 1941

theory. I can speak only for the German Army, but it will not be much different in other armies.

We must keep evaluating these battles, and in the context of the ability of soldiers, we must think about the role of deception and camouflage in war. We must also not forget that even in mechanized forces the infantryman must maintain his capability for fighting dismounted.

In war nothing happens as it has been planned. You cannot issue an order on the Rhine that is supposed to be valid all the way to Moscow. Orders have to be issued for the near future, for the first hours and intentions for the next day's battle. It is the role of leadership to conduct the battle phase by phase and adjust to changing conditions. In my long experience with staffs, I have always found that the best piece of paper is that which has not yet been written on.

Regarding *aufstragtaktik*, or mission-type orders, I cannot stress how important orders like these are. The tragedy of the German Army was that after 1943 Hitler virtually forbade all kinds of operations, and insisted on employing large units down to regimental level personally, as commander-in-chief of joint forces. From the Obersalzburg, he personally conducted operations in the Minsk region. That was impossible.

As you have seen, we were surprised by the Russians very often, and equally often we surprised the Russians. The most important factors of command are reconnaissance, liaison, communications and information. When I was a commander in the Bundeswehr, I insisted that every command vehicle have those four words written on the windshield to remind the leader of their importance. In situations such as we have seen, it was very difficult for commanders to locate their units. That is why I insisted on regular reports at short intervals regarding where my left flank was, where my right flank was and in which direction I was fighting or advancing. The commanders and leaders of all ranks had to make sure of this personally by going forward to verify the reports.

I think our staff of today is too large. In 1944 the staff of a panzer division had 28 officers in all. In the command post there were only eight officers. There were only two general staff officers per division, and after 1944 I was the only general staff officer in my division headquarters. The G-2 and G-4, however, were very good reserve officers. I also feel we are bringing too many electronics into lower-level command posts. I do not think electronics have any business in brigade command posts and lower, but maybe I am a little old-fashioned.

Our major field exercises involve too much preplanning. We should make sure there is freedom of action among units, and the sequence of events should not be too rigidly prescribed. When I can read in the newspaper two weeks before an exercise on what day and in what area a certain brigade will launch an attack, I think then we are overdoing it. In those exercises the free decisions of the commander should be made possible and be stressed. We should not be afraid of making mistakes in those exercises. The whole of war is generally mistakes and we should have the courage to accept those mistakes in peacetime. That, of course, means that whenever a commander makes a mistake, the superior commander must protect him.

It is important to educate our soldiers and, in particular, our commanders to a feeling of superiority and a belief that we can win. We must educate them into intellectual flexibility and we must educate them to be willing and eager to accept responsibility. They must act according to their mission and not wait for orders from higher commands.

To conclude, we must maintain the characteristics of a fencer with a rapier, but we must become as strong and as determined as a bull.

The Lessons of 1941 and Implications for the Future

DR JACOB KIPP

It would be interesting if we could say that, indeed, there are profound lessons in what we have heard which would give us formulas for dealing with the complexities of tomorrow. The historian must say to you, "that I cannot do". By definition, the future must in many ways be unknown to us. There are no formulas to deal with it. There is, however, a sense of mental agility and a willingness to look at the past, if not to find the answer, at least to formulate the question about future problems, and to hone those skills which one associates with the act of foresight. Soviet military literature says that the most important characteristic of a military commander is foresight (*predvidenie*). Soviet military officers are told that the essence of military science is future war.

The concept of the initial period of war did not emerge with the Soviets in 1941 as a consequence of the war that was inflicted upon them. Quite the contrary. The concept of the initial period of war as an element of military science emerged in the late 1920s, when on reflection, and looking at the experience of armies as they went to war in 1914, the Russian General Staff said it would not happen that way again. This is a very important phenomenon. It will not happen that way again. Having said that, one loses a great and fundamental element of confidence because the dearest thing we want is that what we know is what will be. The Soviets said "No, it will not be like that". If we look at Soviet military literature between 1929 and 1931, there was an intriguing linkage made between *nachal'nyi period voiny* (the initial period of war) and *operativnaia iskusstva* (operational art). In essence, in the Soviet perspective the two were inter-linked and joined. For the Soviets, the operational level of war was a new and emerging phenomenon. It was one which would clearly have a fundamental impact on the conduct of war. No longer could one talk about the operational line or simple mobilization and concentration, but rather one needed to think in operational terms. Indeed, in this period emerged the Soviet concern about successive operations.

Soviet military officers understood, however, that fundamentally, in peacetime, the only operation for which one could plan was the initial one. At that time, with reasonable certainty, one had some idea of what would

473

transpire. There was however, no certainty about anything beyond that initial phase. Thus, on the Soviet side there was a high premium placed on attempting to achieve initial success. But prudence suggested that if it did not come one must anticipate a long and sustained struggle.

There was a profound debate in the Soviet Union about Delbrouck's categories, in which Delbrouck was addressed, but that does not concern us here. What does concern us is that debate was followed by an intensive period of examination of how wars began after that. That is to say, from 1931 to 1941 the Soviet military elite, the General Staff, was trying to grasp what the next war would be like in terms of its initial period from what they were seeing. One can say that a major consideration in Soviet thought in 1941 was this problem of creeping up to war. Indeed, the Soviet approach, which created many of the problems in 1941, was precisely an element of that.

If the origins of this problem can be related to Soviet dissatisfaction with the experience of the First World War, we might ask ourselves what was the conditioning phenomenon. The conditioning phenomenon that brought the initial period of war to the foreground was the industrialization and mechanization of warfare, its assumption of grand scale, and the emergence of time *(vremia)* as an absolutely vital element in military calculation – time not only in a tactical sense, time not only in a strategic sense, but the fusing of the two. As we know, the old definition of tactics was what one dealt with on the battlefield, and strategy was what one did to get forces to the field. The time scales were totally different in pre-industrial armies. Now there was a recognition that time itself and the conduct of operations, in particular the movements of large forces and the planning of operations, were an absolutely critical element. Indeed, in the 1920s the very notion of Soviet norms and staff processes was addressing the problem of time under an intriguing topic called the scientific organization of labor. Many people look at this and ask why the Soviet General Staff was studying something called Taylorism. They were studying it because it addressed particularly this time problem.

The concept of the initial period of war disappeared from Soviet military literature between 1942 and the late 1950s. It is not used as an intellectual category, either in military thought or in the other available publications. It declines as a phenomenon which is not particularly significant. The interesting thing concerning that is that first there was a political impact. There was a legacy of Stalin's Five "permanently operating factors", there was a downgrading of the importance of surprise to a purely tactical-operational consideration, and there was a political culture playing a role in it.

What we should note, however, is that since the late 1950s there have been four occasions during which major discussions appeared in Soviet military periodicals about the initial period of war. The first occasion, from 1958 to roughly 1961, coincided with what the Soviets had identified as the nuclear rocket or first-generation scientific-technical revolution. In that period Soviet authors tried to draw on the experience of the Great Patriotic War to deal with what was indeed the concept of future war. It was a rather unsatisfying experience because the weapons themselves loomed so large that they seemed to negate the very categories of military discourse. Soviet authors, for instance naval officers, had a very difficult time talking about naval tactics in such a situation.

However, after this initial look the one thing that was emphasized in that first period was outcome. Looking at the initial period of war in the 1930s, the Soviets said it could influence the next stage of the war. One could argue objectively that the very nature of initial period of war influences the course and outcome of war because we have seen the impact on the structure of Soviet forces, and we have seen the nature of struggle which emerged on the Eastern Front. But Soviet literature before the war had said no: it would only influence that succeeding period. It would give the initiative to one side and certain advantages, but it could not influence the full course and outcome of war. The nuclear revolution clearly suggested that, indeed, the course and outcome of war would be simultaneous with, and would involve, the initial period of war. Certain categories which earlier had significance in Soviet military thinking, such as concentration and maneuver, were dismissed by some contributors to the so-called Sokolovsky volume on military strategy. Deep operations became deep nuclear operations. What is interesting is that that period was an essential anomaly in Soviet military thought.

If we look at what followed it, and there were at least three other intensive periods of examination of the initial period of war since the period from 1958 to 1961, we can see a re-emergence of the concerns that sparked Soviet military thought in the inter-war period and concentrated on the categories of 1941 and the events surrounding it. The first period, 1965–66, coincided, interestingly enough, with the emergence of flexible response on the US and NATO side and involved the recognition of the possibility of a conventional first phase to what was granted to be a nuclear war. The conventional first phase however, was given various weights by various authors – what could be achieved in it and what its purposes and function would be. The content of that period was the re-emergence of a consideration for deep operations. Indeed, the very use of the term by Marshal Zakharov, who was then Chief of the Soviet General Staff, was to emphasize the problems of time, speed and depth with both conventional and nuclear forces and a military posture which could go in both directions.

The second phase of interest coincided with the publication of General

Ivanov's book *The Initial Period of War*, which has been translated in the US Air Force series and which looks at the experience of the Second World War, not just the Soviet experience. It also included the Pacific campaigns, the general events in the first period of the war, and the nature of that period. It stressed the relevance and the increased importance of conventional operations, the role and impact of surprise, and a trend towards the increased decisiveness of the initial period of war with modern means of combat.

The period 1974–75 also coincided with another phenomenon – and they cannot be separated in the Soviet context – which involved a new and very profound look at local wars. Some people thought this was clearly an indication of Soviet interests in and commitment to military activities outside the "bloc". That may have increased, but I do not think this literature was addressed to that. What the Soviets observed was that while the first period of the initial period of war, in the Second World War, offered increased scale of combat and the nature of force-structure which they perceived a general war between the social systems would take on, they recognized increasingly that new technology and new elements in the military system had to be taken into the picture. What happened in the Middle East, for instance in 1973, and earlier in Vietnam, had to be part of the military equation, and therefore it was a joining of interests in the historical topic of initial period of war as defined by both the Second World War and the Great Patriotic War, and the new demands of local war. It is important to note that the Soviets stressed the themes of surprise, deception, gaining and maintaining the initiative, and seeking to influence the course and outcome of the conflict. Not just to change the correlation of forces, but to reach a decision, emerged as a characteristic.

The third and last period in the post-nuclear debates of 1961 has emerged since 1984. We have had a series of articles on the initial period of war. Generals Matsulenko and Evseev have written on this topic, both looking at the experience, not only of the Great Patriotic War, but generally the initial period of war in the twentieth century. Given their ideology, what Soviet authors are attempting to find are law-governed patterns for change in trying to understand this phenomenon of the initial period of war. This does not mean that they are trying to get a canned answer. Rather they are trying to look at trend lines and places where leaps can transpire.

They have identified, I think, a number of phenomena which make the initial period of war now seem to be even more decisive. Soviet authors have commented upon the impact of new weapons systems and weapon systems based on new physical principles, and on the problem of simultaneity throughout the depth. Obviously, in the nuclear period we had simultaneity throughout the depth by the use of fire. Now, however, in a combined arms way, the Soviets are talking about a wide spectrum of conventional military instruments. It is a very difficult thing. We use the term conventional to describe non-nuclear. These are non-conventional weapons in the historical sense. They are new ways of putting together combat power to achieve synergistic effects which will tear apart an enemy's defense.

As the situation now stands regarding the initial period of war from the Soviet perspective, first, the length of the initial period of war is shortening, and becoming shorter and shorter. Evseev's article says the initial period of war in World War I was about a month and a half, during which initial armies moved to contact in the theaters. Generals Kir'ian and Evseev ask "How long was the initial period of war in the Great Patriotic War?" The definition now is mid-July, essentially what we have covered. It consisted of the first few weeks to mid-July. As a result, we have moved from a situation where engagement of covering forces influences further developments to one where the Soviets expect initial operations to influence the course and outcome of war. That is, they emphasize the decisive influence of the initial period of war.

Not surprisingly, the Soviets emphasize the absolute necessity of combat readiness. The higher the level of combat readiness of the troops available, the more successful will be that side in the initial period of war. Surprise has absolute utility in the initial period of war. It is the vehicle for seizing and gaining the initiative, but it involves not just time, but also the nature of the attack, the structuring of forces, and the objectives to be achieved. Peter Vigor has argued on the basis of Ivanov's book that the Soviets have a *blitzkrieg* theory. No Soviet author would accept that at all. The reason they would not accept it is that *blitzkrieg* is understood very differently in the East from the way it is understood in the popular nomenclature of the West. We associate *blitzkrieg* with a combination of combined arms in the initial operations of the Second World War. On the Soviet side *blitzkrieg* is also applied to German military leadership in the First World War. It is the notion of attempting to achieve an initial quick decision by the military instrument alone without taking into account political preparation, economic mobilization, the creation of coalition against the target, and the political isolation of the target.

The Soviets like the term "lightning operations" which they have used to refer to their attack against Sixth German Army at Iassy Kishinev, which, at first glance, did not seem to have been during an initial period of war. It was not. But it brought about an immediate and radical political transformation as a consequence of a military outcome, the dismemberment of the German coalition in the Balkans and the opening of that region to Soviet political and military penetration. The Soviets also used the term to refer to their operations in the Far East in 1945. While that was certainly a single-operation run continuously from end to end, and the combination of arms that we have seen were there, let us note the political preparation preceding it. The Soviets had isolated completely and totally the target of the attack and had politically legitimized the gains they would make at the end of it.

This brings me to a central element in the Soviet approach to the initial period of war. It is the political context of war. For the Soviets, peace is not the absence of conflict. Conflict goes on in peacetime. Ideological, class and social struggle are means to be used to achieve the ends of the Soviet Union. War, however, is a different matter. Very often we hear the Soviets called Clausewitzians. That is to say that war is a continuation of politics by other means. That is so. But one must understand the fundamental redefinition of politics involved in that formula – Lenin is a transformation of it. The politics are not the politics of state to state. The concept of Chancellery war, or the concept of the neat, clean struggle in which one is talking to like-minded statesmen on the other side, is alien to the Soviet concept. The preceding political struggle will find its manifestation in armed struggles. The armed forces may be the most important *Schwerpunkt*, the destruction of which will bring about the changes that one wants. But ultimately the target is the other society and its transformation.

On the Soviet side this manifests itself in examining the problem of the transition from peace to war. Mobilization and management of resources, a planned and centralized economy, military standardization, and, in general, a constant emphasis of the nature of the external threat, make it possible for the Soviets to achieve in peacetime high correlations of what we would call economic, scientific-technical potential, and military potential – far higher rates of economic, social, and technological transformation. Trotsky in his debates with Frunze said, "Our opponents are technological wizards, they transform the world. But they are as children in politics", and the politics he had in mind were politics of the society. There is an emphasis on psychological transformation.

I have mentioned the concept of mass heroism, which is a function of love of fatherland, but it is also politically prepared. In 1930 the Soviets did their analytical history of the Civil War. One of the important outcomes of that study was the need to look at partisan warfare and to examine the relationship between partisan war and regular war. Because, as the Soviets said, partisan war will have a major role to play in European conflicts, but also, and even more important, a role to play in the wars of the colonial peoples against their masters. The Soviets were publishing articles in the 1930s on the conduct of partisan operations by the Chinese communists and analysing them. From 1931 on, a section of their General Staff was engaged in the study of partisan warfare and the preparation for it. Many of these officers, in fact, served in Spain.

478

The Soviets would emphasize the importance of the initial battles of the war and, indeed, the need to preempt, not militarily but psychologically, one's opponents in order to disarm them in the process of struggle itself. Earlier studies of the initial period of war emphasized the problem of pauses and regrouping of forces. Soviet contemporary literature on the initial period of war emphasizes the need to avoid pauses and maintain the pace of combat operations right up to decision. Deep operations remain a hallmark of how the Soviet General Staff would like to conduct war. There is an emphasis upon simultaneity and the use of a wide range of military capabilities including airborne and airmobile, mechanized forces, raids, forward detachments, and the infamous or famous operational maneuver, which I will call a mobile group. All of these fit together as part of a concept, emphasizing simultaneity throughout the depth and integrating the elements of air and land combat.

Last, but not least, we should understand that from the Soviet perspective the core of Clausewitz remains correct. War is a continuation of politics by other means. There is a calculus involved with the decision whether war will be a rational or irrational instrument of policy. One means of dealing with Soviet military power and the ideological and political competition between East and West, is to maintain a credible deterrent so that on the Soviet side it is quite clear that should the political contest degenerate into a military one the Western alliance has the means, the resolve and the capabilities to answer the Soviet attack. On the other side of that equation, it is also fundamental to note that the Soviets, as rational actors in the conduct of that political and ideological struggle, also understand the nature of total war. They have good reasons not to come to warfare lightly. The initial period of war in 1940 and 1941 must be, within the Soviet General Staff which understands all of the problems which the Soviet Union faced, a restraint on military adventurism.

We are, however, entering a time and a generation where those experiences of 1941 are becoming more distant. The Soviets have decided that they will do another ten-volume history of The Great Patriotic War. For the first time in a Soviet publication the authors have acknowledged – and this is from the preliminary blurb of the publication – the individual bravery of German soldiers. That is a small profit of *glasnost*. As a historian I would argue that there are fundamental reasons why Western military analysts and historians and Soviet military analysts should examine the initial period of war together, as we have done here, and in that examination attempt to draw the appropriate lessons regarding the applicability, or more importantly, the inapplicability of war as an instrument of foreign policy, when used in a most reckless and short-sighted fashion. Both sides would be served by such a situation. It would not end political struggle and it would not end ideological hostility. But it would create a situation in

479

which both sides would be talking with one another, about what are pressing problems not only for our profession, but also for both societies.

Discussion

CHAIRED BY GENERAL ODENDAHL

Question: I would like a clarification on the ratio of air forces in the beginning of the campaign in 1941 and at the end of the year. I think thereafter the German air force slowly disappeared?

Colonel Glantz: I did not show the correlation of forces for air power primarily because I did not calculate it. It is clear that, as was the case with armor, the Soviets possessed a large air force and overall numerical superiority. Many of the aircraft were older models, but they had newer ones as well. The Soviets have provided figures for aircraft in the western military districts and these figures undoubtedly exceeded German air strength [Ed. Soviet acknowledged strength in modern aircraft was 1,540. Total aircraft probably numbered between 8,000 and 10,000]. The bulk of these forces in the border regions were destroyed in the first few days of war, many of them on the ground. The Soviets have provided figures for losses which amounted to 80 per cent of their air force in the Special Western Military District. This accorded the Germans air superiority, a condition which endured throughout 1941. In late 1941 and early 1942 the Soviets began restructuring and rebuilding their air force. The imbalance would slowly be redressed in late 1942 and early 1943, and by mid-1943 it had shifted in the Soviets' favor.

General Farndale: Can the German veterans relate the time it took to mount a divisional or corps counterattack or operation?

General Niepold: It differed greatly. But I will try to be more concrete. Of course, the preparation of the initial offensive took a long time. If we had enough time it took two weeks. During the operation it was possible for the corps to give a completely new mission to a division within 24 hours and to turn a division with two combat groups around could be done in only a few hours. I can provide an example. Even in 1944 it was possible to withdraw a combat group from battle at 2000 and launch a new attack that same night at 0200, with a short replenishment and rest period for the soldiers. These are times which we must also be able to achieve today.

Question: Can you comment on the German decision to delay the attack on Moscow? Could the attack on Moscow have been delayed until 1942?

General Guderian: The decision had to be made in 1941. I must state that according to my judgement there were valid reasons for both decisions.

They both had some logic behind them. I say this in spite of the fact that my father was a strong defender of the Moscow version. What was irresponsible in this problem was the delay that was encountered. It was not the decision of whether Moscow, central or south, but rather the delay. It took three weeks for the army headquarters to reach a decision. Maybe it was because the OKH was not behind Hitler's decision and approached the subject in a half-hearted way. But then there was a shifting around of corps from one army group to another, and then there was another nine weeks' delay with Army Group Center and Army Group North. That may have been the decisive factor, not the question of whether the decision was right or wrong. When we add this waste of time to the delay that was caused by the Balkan campaign, then we might have the real reasons why the campaign failed in 1941 in front of Moscow.

Dr Ose stated that the Japanese decision not to enter the war against Russia was influenced by the result of the campaign in front of Moscow. According to my knowledge, the Japanese–Russian pact of Nonaggression was signed in April 1941, when the Japanese Minister of Foreign Affairs traveled from Berlin to Japan via Russia. So according to my judgement this decision had been made much earlier than Moscow and because of that, I do not think that the German failure to capture Moscow influenced the Japanese political decision.

Question: Dr Kipp noted that two of the fundamental principles the Soviets look at when viewing the initial period of war were first, a need for absolute readiness; and second, a reliance on surprise. In terms of time these two things seem to conflict. It takes time to mobilize and train. All of these detract from the element of surprise. How do the Soviets deal with the contradiction?

Colonel Glantz: The answer to that question lies in the definition of what surprise is and how it is achieved. We often assume surprise to be associated only with the factor of time or offensive intention. In fact, *vnezapnost'* (surprise), in the Soviet definition, is achieved not only by concealing intention and time (and, in fact, time may be the least important ingredient for success) but also by concealing the form, location, size and scale of attack. As the Soviets look at their experiences in the Second World War and elsewhere (and there had been experiences elsewhere, including Hungary in 1956 for example), they tend to admit that achieving absolute surprise in terms of attacking timing is difficult and can be best achieved in only hazy fashion. In other words, if you can muddy the enemy's perception as to when an attack will occur you have probably achieved about as much as you can. In essence, it may be enough to achieve through deception a marked advantage in preparation time, so that the enemy defense is weaker than it otherwise might be.

Now obviously there is a difference between the initial period of war and war while it is under way. In the initial period, you should attempt to conceal intent as well as timing. But you should also focus on deception regarding the form, size, scale, and location of the attack. Now, of course, we are also considering surprise in a global context. We are considering simulations, diversions and various activities conducted somewhere which can assist in the achievement of surprise regarding where the Soviets have determined the main effort will occur, be it in central Europe or elsewhere. The point is that the new Soviet definition of concentration and the term surprise are not mutually exclusive. It is difficult to bring the two together, but the Soviet definitions of concentration and mass have also changed with time. They are now time dependent. Traditionally, we tend to look at concentration as involving a huge mass of prepositioned manpower and material, all sitting for an extended period opposite from where it is going to be employed. It is difficult to conceal that today. The Soviets look at concentration and mass as much more of a maneuver concept with rapid concentration at the very last minute before the attack and attack from the depths into the depths and attack from the march. Only when you look at the refined definitions of concentration and mass and the more refined definition of surprise can you begin to actually articulate where it might be, when it might be, and how it might actually develop.

Question: One of the element of surprise is deception. Can you say something about Soviet deceptive measures at the operational level during the campaign?

Colonel Glantz: By the time of its full development, and this dates from late 1942 and early 1943, the Soviets had determined that for deception to be effective at any level it had to be centralized at the highest level. It had to be under secure and tight strategic control by the STAVKA. It was no coincidence that Soviet deception began to be effective when its most successful practitioners at the *front* and army level rose to higher staff positions. General Antonov, for example, as Chief of Staff of the Southern Front, had run several successful deception operations at Rostov in 1941 and Barvenkovo–Lozovaia in 1942. He was brought into the General Staff in 1942, and he brought with him the proper techniques.

In the summer of 1942 the Soviets made the first tentative, well coordinated attempts to implement strategic deception. These really did not achieve success on a strategic scale until mid-1943. But from that point on they were coordinated from the very top and strictly implemented down through *front* and army. There were written plans at STAVKA level, *front* level, and army level. These plans delineated the objective of deception, the means of deception, the timing of deception, and the responsibilities for carrying out each precise measure. We do have from

Soviet open sources today examples of deception plans at *front* and army level. If one questions the validity of those examples, we also have one of the classified Soviet War Experience volumes, No. 2 issued in late 1942, which has in it a deception plan used in one of the Demiansk operations.

What is even more surprising is that this was not new. If you go back into the 1930s, you will find an article published in 1937 in the General Staff journal *Voennaia Mysl'* (Military Thought), which stipulated precisely what should be in a deception plan and how deception should be carried out. There was a tremendous continuity. Deception was based on written plans and involved precise responsibilities. There were forces allocated to carry out elements of the deception plan, and I mean specific *maskirovka* companies and *maskirovka* battalions, as well as designated line units that were detached specifically to perform *maskirovka* duties. I am now talking about massive simulations, diversions, as well as attacks launched with deliberate avoidance of any sort of *maskirovka* measures designed to draw enemy reserves away from other sectors of the front. A good example was the Mius River operation in July 1943 when German intelligence knew precisely where every single Soviet unit (rifle and mechanized) was located before the Soviet attack. Yet that attack, when it occurred, even though it was a failure, persisted for something like two weeks, right up to the precise date (3 August) that the main attack was occurring elsewhere, the attack from which the German operational reserves (in this case, SS Panzer Corps) had been drawn. [Ed. the Belgorod–Khar'kov offensive.]

So the Soviets employed a combination of diversions, deceptions, very active communications deception, the establishment of dummy radio-nets, and the bogus use of code books associated with units in simulation areas. If you look closely at German records, you can track precisely the degree of success the Soviets achieved in these simulation efforts. Then, of course, there was the other aspect, which was perhaps most important: the passive measures, the hiding of large forces, which by 1944–45, in some cases, amounted to upwards of 50 per cent of the attacking force successfully hidden from German intelligence prior to operations.

Question: I presume it would not be as easy today as it was then? Is that a valid question?

Colonel Glantz: It is certainly a valid question. The Soviets, I think, firmly believe that developing technological means on one side can be countered by similar developments on the other side. In addition, they point out that intelligence collection has outstripped analytical capabilities. Intelligence agencies may be inundated and paralysed by too much information, which can be as damaging as too little information. So I would not place too much confidence in our technical collection means.

Question: Could you respond to a comment on Soviet deception in a successful period like 1944 and 1945? A few conceptual things are often missed when we write similar plans today. First of all, the plan must make military sense. Secondly, and most critical, a fact we Americans often forget is that the deception plan must threaten somewhere or something that the enemy is nervous about. For instance, if you create a deception plan showing you are going south while you are really going north, if the opponent does not care whether or not you are going south, the plan is irrelevant. The splendor of successful deception plans of the Soviets in 1944 was that the Soviets knew where the German psychological center of gravity was, and they threatened it. Thus, the Germans responded. We must do the same today and get inside the enemy's mind. We must ask what threat makes them nervous and forces them to overreact.

Colonel Glantz: There are two comments I would make in that regard, if you were to distill everything that I have looked at regarding deception. Two things emerge, both a bit frightening. First, Soviet deception has played upon the enemy's misconceptions and misperceptions. In virtually every Soviet strategic deception plan, in particular those in 1943 and, perhaps the best example, those in the summer of 1944, the Soviets played upon German misperceptions regarding where the main strategic thrusts would occur. The Soviets reinforced German misperceptions and attacked elsewhere. Take the often cited case of Targul Frumas, for example, in Romania, where an excellent German tactical example of victory occurred. Here was a small portion of a larger Soviet deception plan, an order to 2nd Tank Army to conduct operations to show *aktivnost* (activity) on the Romanian border by launching a violent attack, which turned out unsuccessful. As a result of that attack, in German intelligence reports, 2nd Tank Army remained riveted to German intelligence reports along the Romanian border long past the time it had moved some 800 kilometers to the north to the Kovel' area. At the time when 2nd Tank Army was participating in a new offensive (15 July 1944) and at the time when 2nd Guards Tank Army was 100 kilometers behind German lines and marching toward Warsaw, only at the point did it disappear from the German order of battle maps in Romania. That was successful deception.

The other point is that the psychological issue which you have pointed out is very valid. There was a tendency on the part of the German command during the Second World War to overestimate the size of the Soviet Army and to treat it as a gray, faceless, overwhelming mass. At the same time the Germans underestimated the individual capabilities of Soviet soldiers and officers. That was a deadly mixture, because it conditioned successful deception. Over and over again, major attacks occurred and German intelligence, very frankly, did not know until days into the attack what forces had actually participated in it. Their gut reaction was to say "we are outnumbered ten to one, or eight to one, and therefore they can attack wherever they wish". Yet, in reality the Soviet superiority on that axis was not only because the correlation of forces was so great in the Soviets' favor. Often it was because they had stripped large forces from elsewhere along the front and had concentrated these forces operationally and tactically along that particular axis.

I worry about stereotypes, because I have seen on the Eastern Front and in the case of Japan in 1945, nations victimized by their stereotypes and misconceptions, which have come back to haunt them. That also relates very closely to the issue of deception.

Question: I was most impressed by the comparison of the German perception of the enemy situation and then, in contrast to that, the reality of the enemy organization. Could you answer two questions? What value did the different means of reconnaissance have, such as electronic, questioning of prisoners, air-reconnaissance, etc? What was their value in compiling this picture? And secondly, what will the future reconnaissance means be? Where do you think the most importance will be in the future?

Colonel Glantz: When you talk of reconnaissance and intelligence collection, you are talking essentially about the means of receiving intelligence and the means of collecting and processing intelligence. That is to be the subject of my next volume. I have concentrated in this deception volume on the degree of deception, the relative success of deception, and to a lesser extent, on what means the Soviets employed to verify the results of that deception, which was in essence intelligence. It is clear, however, from looking at all those matters that the Soviets used a wide variety of intelligence sources, much of it developed after 1941. Perhaps the most important means was human intelligence (Humint) provided by a variety of agents and special operation forces which were routinely and extensively inserted into the German rear. An excellent map illustrates this point. It shows German intelligence plotting of the activity of Soviet special operations or reconnaissance and diversionary forces before the Vistula–Oder operation in January 1945. It also shows where the various special operations (SPETSNAZ) teams operated. Between East Prussia and the Carpathian Mountains there were perhaps 50 teams detected by German intelligence. It is interesting to note that these teams were used not only for reconnaissance, but also to deceive the Germans. In fact, the heaviest density of those diversionary forces were operating along the axis where the Soviets wished to pretend they were going to attack. So you could also employ those collection means for two or three purposes and use them to deceive as well.

Communications intelligence played a considerable role, and the Soviets have written quite a bit about that. If you look at the Hungarian operations of October to December 1944 you will notice, but only from a day to day study, that within 24 hours of a German unit leaving its position in one part of the front to move elsewhere, a Soviet attack of some scale would occur shortly thereafter against the position the unit had vacated. Over and over again, for a period of roughly 2½ months, that was the pattern, and it was a pattern that enabled to Soviets to gnaw away steadily at German defenses. And yet suddenly in December 1944, German IV SS Panzer Corps arrived in the Budapest area from central Poland. That corps deployed forward and conducted a series of counterattacks in January and February 1945. Each time those counterattacks caught the Soviets by surprise. The Soviets apparently could not keep track of the movements of the SS unit. I do not know what the answer to that question is, but it seemed to indicate that the Soviets were well attuned to regular German Army communications, although they may not have been well attuned to the communications of the SS panzer corps. No firm answer is available on that issue, but it is one point illustrative of communications intelligence.

Aerial reconnaissance was certainly important from 1943 on, as the Soviets gained dominance in the air. They have written considerably about aerial reconnaissance as well. Human, communications, ground and aerial reconnaissance were all principal sources of intelligence, but to give you absolute answers based on archival materials will have to await more research.

General Odendahl: Let me try to answer part two of your question, what the future of reconnaissance and intelligence is going to be.

First, like all aspects of modern life, collection of intelligence is characterized by a growing complexity and by the amount of means available. Our present intelligence-gathering effort is a combination of a great number and variety of technical and other military means. We can divide them into *strategic, operational* and *tactical* intelligence.

We are now trying, in peacetime, to collect information on what is going on in Russia, in the center of the country; so let me call that strategic intelligence. We are using not only espionage as we did in the past, but also satellite information. The latter has probably become our primary means of strategic intelligence.

The second effort we are making is to gather operational intelligence. That means intelligence in the depth of the enemy; what is going to happen in the first days of war or in the preparation for war. This field is mostly covered by electronic intelligence. Electronic intelligence has become more complex. It is important not only to find out enemy communications, the nets, and the information that comes through these nets, but also to discover what type of radars are employed. Through the wavelengths we can identify the type of radar, and from that we can deduce what kind of unit is opposing us; and this, in turn can give indications on enemy intentions.

Now for tactical intelligence. Air reconnaissance is another means of reconnaissance that has become more efficient and more complex, but at the same time more difficult to handle. We now have drones in the German Army that cover the area of interest of the corps and have the capability for aerial photography. Long-range patrol companies are also in that area, and, finally, there is reconnaissance by cavalry units and the constant reconnoitering by units in combat.

Our problem is not how to collect that information, but rather how to digest it. There is so much intelligence that we cannot always handle it. That is why we have formed so-called intelligence collection cells in all command posts. They are composed of all the different branches of arms and representatives from the reconnaissance units. It is the job of the G2 to evaluate this information.

So we have become much more efficient and thorough in intelligence; but there are two problems to be overcome. One is the amount of information. We are overwhelmed by the mass of information, and we have to find somebody who makes the right conclusions and, in that enormous quantity of intelligence information, find out what is right and what is misleading. That is a management problem.

The second problem is the time factor. In the old days, it was only important to find out the destination of a second echelon army. Until it arrived at the front line, we had enough time to prepare our counter-measures. But today we try to hit that second echelon with air forces while it is still on the move. Therefore, we must discover the answer at once, and we must make up our mind immediately when and where to send the air force for their interdiction efforts. Thus, there are two great problems: the quantity of information that has to be digested; and the short time left to react under present conditions.

Colonel Glantz: The Soviets issue one warning to nations who over-emphasize collection and under-emphasize analysis. That is that too much material paralyses, it adds to the fog of war, and it can be exploited.

Closing Remarks I

GENERAL SIR MARTIN FARNDALE

These discussions have been so valuable to those of us still following the profession of arms. Our job, after all, as serving soldiers today, is to prevent a war at any price. To do this we must be seen to be credible. If we are to be seen to be credible we must be capable of fighting, and be seen to be capable of fighting. But where do we get our experience from as the years go by? We can study at our staff colleges and at our academic institutions. They certainly have a role to play. We can do exercises, we can do CPXs, we can do FTXs, and I note General Niepold's advice to us on this type of training. Nevertheless we do have some problems with our exercises. I suspect the German Army in Russia did not have to organize a joint visitors' bureau, an exercise damage control office, or an allied press information center. Nevertheless, the points you make are of critical importance to us.

Then we can learn from a study of military history. I believe in this most strongly, but it has to be used correctly. We should not get too involved with the details of tactics, but rather we should study principles, because they do not change, although the execution of them will change. Nevertheless, we also need to know the flavor of war, and that is where the experience of what actually happened is so valuable. So you veterans have left us with a job to do. How are we going to apply your experience to the defense of the Central Region in the 1990s and onwards? That is our problem.

But you have proved a good many things to us. One thing that I have always believed, and you have illustrated, is that the only thing we can be sure about in a war in the future is that it will be quite different from what we expect. Therefore, we must be ready for the unexpected. We must be prepared to move from total peace to total war in a matter of hours. Clever analysts in peacetime cannot predict the nature of war in the future. Forecasting battles is like forecasting the weather, which is usually wrong. We must fall back on the principles. We have heard that no plan survives first contact. But, of course, plans are necessary because a good plan will get you to the start line with the right stuff at the right place, and at the right time. Then it is up to the commander to pull out the appropriate golf club and use it correctly.

I will not go through all of Clausewitz's ten principles of war now, as I know that every one of you could recite them. But one of the key ones, "Surprise and Deception", clearly needs our attention. Planning for deception is an important component of our work now. Next, "Offensive Action" – seizing and maintaining the initiative and then maintaining momentum – we try to develop this on all our exercises. I remember at the end of one of my corps exercises when I had 400 tanks locked in battle on the Hannover plain, and to use all the bridges and engineer devices I had to get those tanks over relatively small obstacles, it was not easy to keep them going. Next comes "Concentration of Force", mainly the ability to bring firepower in the right place at the right time, achieved as Colonel Glantz said by rapid maneuver. That is what we try to do, but it is not easy, particularly when an enemy is trying to prevent you doing it. And then there is "Flexibility".

So how then do we apply this to what we do today? We look first to achieve cohesion in our defensive layout. But we must remember not to put too much emphasis on achieving cohesion, because only achieving cohesion will not win the war for us. We must also achieve depth, but depth is difficult because it also has a political content which we have to realize and take into account. Nevertheless, we can achieve quite a lot. Depth is necessary to give us time in which to work out what is going on, then we need space to connect powerful and effective reserves at the operational level of command.

So what is our situation in Northern Army Group today? Our problem, in the Central Region from Hamburg to the Harz Mountains and on down to the Austrian border, is to meet attacks right across the front. First, we nominate reserve divisions and use them concentrated. It looks easy, but as many of you know, the move of such a force over 30 or 40 kilometers, probably crossing a main river, is not the easiest thing to achieve. But if we *can* do it, we have a chance to win. We have to fight a battle like this while external reinforcements are arriving from the United States. Then, if all goes well, we have an even more difficult task to carry out, which is this one (the counterattack by a reserve corps). That is why what you have been saying has been of such value to us. Because you have been describing to us the reality of achieving these actions.

I was interested also in Dr Kipp's description of the initial phase of battle because it equates to the conventional phase of the war as we see it. It is *our* initial phase of battle. We have to fight it in the way I have described because by the time we get to that big final arrow (the corps counterattack) our sustainability will be causing us problems. We then have to consider the whole process of the horror of nuclear war. This brings me back to where I started: we must ensure that we never do it at all.

So, it seems that your advice to us for the future includes the following points. *Aufstragtaktik* is critical in conducting the kind of operation we

490

contemplate. The creation of effective reserves, and the use of those reserves, is also critical. We can use our reserves in counter-penetration, but that does not win battles: such action merely postpones the main battle. We can counterattack to seize an objective and hold it against an enemy attack. This is much better, but still we are not going to win the war because such an attack must lead to something else. Then there is the counterstroke. This is much more difficult to achieve. It is an attack whose aim is to destroy the enemy and is not so concerned about seizing ground. The counterstroke is much more difficult, but of course, it gives a real chance of winning the battle.

As far as our nations are concerned there is much to do if we are to conduct such operations properly. Our divisions must be as interoperable as possible. They must fire the same shells and bullets, and their radios must be able to speak to each other. We have a long way to go, but we are beginning to improve. We must also improve our speed of reaction. Our staff colleges tend to teach us a rather pedantic way of carrying out operations. We must look at the size of our headquarters which have grown too big. Today, they have to be bigger than the ones you had, for the very reasons that General Odendahl gave earlier. But perhaps we are now too big, and perhaps as a result our reaction is too slow. Our communications and intelligence processing machinery must be improved. So these are the problems you have highlighted.

As we go into the future, there is one problem that is facing us all. NATO force levels in the Central Region have not changed since NATO was established in 1956. We have the same number of divisions and brigades, if anything marginally less. Of course we have improved our quality. But we have watched the Warsaw Pact forces increase out of all proportion, in both quantity and quality. Today we ask those same forces once designed to operate in support of nuclear weapons ("massive retaliation"), to fight a conventional phase alone. And now we see our politicians debating the reduction of the one weapon which would virtually guarantee peace in future. In addition, we also watch our nations spending less on defense. To me the only way through this is even more integration between our forces to wring out the last ounce of value from them.

We have also covered a whole range of other points. The vital importance of air power, the problems of moving reserves across country, the importance of logistics, and the effect of the right leader being at the right place at the right time, and how he personally can change an event and alter the course of history. Many of you stressed the importance of maintaining the momentum no matter what happened, even when divisions were down to a handful of tanks. Others stressed the effect of terrain on battle. One thing that you perhaps did not stress too much, but I know you were referring to, was the importance of getting inside your

491

opponent's decision-making cycle. If we can achieve this we have a big advantage. We should attack at such a speed that, although he spots us, and finds out what we are doing, he cannot react in time because we move so quickly.

Closing Remarks II

GENERAL ODENDAHL

No war plan survives initial contact as Moltke has stated already. My contribution was originally conceived to be the lead-in to the climax of the battle, to COMNORTHAG'S summary. But now it has turned out to be a rear guard action. But this is a very small price to pay for flexibility in command and organization which we have stressed as an important lesson from the Second World War. General Farndale and I were asked to make a few closing remarks on behalf of the postwar military leaders presently in command. The two of us, being used to playing doubles in international matches like this, have agreed on de-conflicting our contributions – another example of NATO interoperability, you might say. General Farndale, as COMNORTHAG, has addressed the operational aspects. I, as *Amtchef, Heeresamt* (COMTRADOC), responsible for training, for doctrine of the branches of arms, and for the development of equipment in the German Army, so I will deal with the lessons for military training, armament and tactical concepts on the unit level.

What lessons can be learned from the Second World War, after we have had the Falklands War, the Israeli War, and the Vietnam War, which are much more recent? There are lessons to be learned. There is the same potential enemy with his historical, ethnological and political background. The Second World War was the last war which was fought with large armor formations. The later wars were on a much smaller scale. But there are also limitations on the lessons to be learned from the Second World War. First, it *is* the same enemy, but on the other hand, it is not *quite* the same enemy. We have heard about poor leadership because of decimation of the Soviet officer corps by Stalin. We have heard of their lack of capability to coordinate combined arms operations. Today they are intensively trained on just that subject.

Secondly, the use of radios provided a tremendous advantage to the German leadership in those days. Today, with the possibility of jamming everything that goes through the air, we have to reconsider whether we can use the radio for our command and control in the way the Germans did it in the Second World War.

To me, the most important limitation on the lessons to be learned from the Second World War is the following. In those days the vast majority of forces were straight-leg, foot-slogging infantry. Only 20 per cent were motorized or armored divisions. That meant that these few armored and motorized divisions outclassed the bulk of the forces by a ratio of between 5 and 8 to 1 in mobility. That is a big difference, because nowadays every infantry division is motorized. There is no advantage of tactical and operational mobility in favor of the armored forces any more. That is a lesson we should not forget. It makes a big difference to what we can learn from the Second World War.

Let me turn now to the lessons learned,. I am in complete agreement with General Niepold's résumé on initiative, size of staff, practical vs. theoretical training, and the importance of leadership. I will make four additional points.

The first point deals with commanding from the front. There are now two schools of thought in the German Army. One says that the commander must lead from where he has the best overview of the situation, and he has the best communications. That is from the division CP, about 12 kilometers behind the forward lines. The second school of thought teaches leading from the front. I am a proponent of the second, because to me leadership in battle is not only a question of issuing good orders based on all the information you have or, especially, based on *waiting* for all the information you can have, but instead, there is a psychological factor to consider. Soldiers who can see their commander feel strengthened by the fact that "the old man" is there. I am in agreement with General Patton who said that leading in combat is like moving spaghetti across the table. You can pull it from the front, but you cannot push it from the rear.

Second, regarding decision-making and flexibility. We have stressed flexibility very much here and I am in complete agreement with that, but with one reservation. You can also overdo flexibility. The worst example of this was that of the Soviet 4th Mechanized Corps. It was the most formidable armored unit that existed in the area and it moved around for three days in four directions. The French have a very apt description for that, *ordre, contre-ordre, désordre*. You must be courageous enough to make a bold decision when it is required, but you must also be courageous enough to stick to that decision until you have no other choice but to change it. Because counter-orders lead to confusion of the troops and the psychological impact is considerable. That is another lesson that we should not forget in always stressing flexibility. There are limitations.

My third point regards the development of equipment. We have heard that the German troops were surprised by the appearance of the T34, a tank that was virtually impregnable to German antitank weapons. In those days that psychological shock was overcome by well-trained cocky veterans of three victorious campaigns. But what is going to occur when something like this happens to our inexperienced soldiers on the first day of the war? A surprise like that may never happen again! We may never again force our infantrymen into a situation where they have to jump at enemy tanks and destroy them with mines virtually in hand-to-hand combat, with the staggering losses that resulted. So, as military leaders responsible for armament and development of modern equipment, we must make every effort not to lose the race between firepower and protective armor.

My fourth point concerns the importance of replacement of losses. It was very vividly demonstrated by the fact that the Russians had 28 reserve divisions and German personnel reserves were zero. Are we sure that this could not happen again? The conclusion is that we have to be very concerned about the training of our reservists, whether we have a professional army or whether we have a conscript army. Yet we think about what is going to happen on day seven of the war and on day 14 or day 20. I feel uneasy with the NATO doctrine that a war will be over in a few days. Remember the experiences of our forefathers. In every war in the past, everyone was optimistic of being back home in a few days. All these wars lasted for years. We should not make the same mistake again.

Regarding replacement of personnel and materiel losses, I recall that Panzer Regiment 25 lost 166 tanks, repaired 96, and because of that, had 214 back in operation. If these repairs had not been successful, they would have had only 118 tanks instead of 214, which is a big difference. I think in the past we have overlooked the requirements of doing battlefield repair. That is something we have started to do now, together with the Americans and the British, with very interesting and important results. It is a little late, but we are learning.

The Germans eagerly research the Falklands, Vietnam and Israeli Wars, while completely disregarding their own Second World War experiences. And on the other hand, it is of the greatest concern to the American and British soldiers to learn from their former enemies how they did it in the Second World War. To me that shows that we have grown together as an alliance and that we are friends now, trying to complement each other and learn from each other. This is a result that to me is even more important than all the lessons on war-fighting that we have learned.

The symposium was concluded with acknowledgements from Dr Bruce Menning, General von Plato, Dr Dieter Ose and Colonel David Glantz.

Index

CASS SERIES ON SOVIET MILITARY THEORY AND PRACTICE
Series Editor: David M. Glantz

This series examined in detail the evolution of Soviet military science and the way the Soviets translated theoretical concepts for the conduct of war into concrete military practice.

1. David M. Glantz, *Soviet Military Deception in the Second World War* (ISBN 0 7146 3347 X cloth, 0 7146 4063 8 paper)

2. David M. Glantz, *Soviet Military Operational Art: In Pursuit of Deep Battle* (ISBN 0 7146 3362 3 cloth, 0 7146 4077 8 paper)

3. David M. Glantz, *Soviet Military Intelligence in War* (ISBN 0 7146 3374 7 cloth, 0 7146 4076 X paper)

4. David M. Glantz, *The Soviet Conduct of Tactical Maneuver: Spearhead of the Offensive* (ISBN 0 7146 3373 9 cloth, 0 7146 4079 4 paper)

5. David M. Glantz, *The Military Strategy of the Soviet Union: A History* (ISBN 0 7146 3435 2 cloth)

6. David M. Glantz, *The History of Soviet Airborne Forces* (ISBN 0 7146 3483 2 cloth, 0 7146 4120 0 paper)